THE
COLD
WAR

BRIDGET KENDALL

THE COLD WAR

A New Oral History

In collaboration with series producers

Phil Tinline and Martin Williams

BBC
BOOKS

3 5 7 9 10 8 6 4 2

BBC Books, an imprint of Ebury Publishing
20 Vauxhall Bridge Road,
London SW1V 2SA

BBC Books is part of the Penguin Random House group of companies whose
addresses can be found at global.penguinrandomhouse.com

Penguin
Random House
UK

This book is published to accompany the radio series entitled *The Cold War:
Stories from the Big Freeze* first broadcast on BBC Radio 4 in 2016.

Series producers: Phil Tinline and Martin Williams

First published by BBC Books in 2017

This paperback edition published by BBC Books in 2018

www.penguin.co.uk

A CIP catalogue record for this book is available from the British Library

ISBN 9781785942600

Commissioning editor: Albert DePetrillo
Project editor: Bethany Wright
Inset design: O'Leary & Cooper
Production: Alex Merrett

Typeset in India by Integra Software Services Pvt. Ltd, Pondicherry

Printed and bound in Great Britain by Clays Ltd, St Ives PLC

Penguin Random House is committed to a sustainable future for our business,
our readers and our planet. This book is made from Forest Stewardship
Council® certified paper.

Contents

CONTENTS

CONTENTS

Introduction

I shall never forget the August morning in 1991, when I was stationed in the Soviet Union as BBC Moscow correspondent, and was woken early by the BBC news desk to check out a statement that had just turned up on TASS, the Soviet state news agency. It declared that the Soviet President, Mikhail Gorbachev, had been taken ill and a state of emergency imposed. By mid-morning there were tanks rumbling through the city's main thoroughfares, taking up positions on bridges and around the Kremlin walls, and it was clear that an attempt to seize power was under way by Soviet hard-liners who feared that Gorbachev's reforms had given too much power away.

What I remember is the extraordinary reaction of local people. Many of them were incredulous, both nervous and yet remarkably unafraid. Our elderly cleaning lady, Masha, made her way out on to the street outside the office, still in her apron and headscarf, and began to scold the soldiers who emerged from the turrets of the tanks, which they had parked on the verge.

'What are you doing here?' she rebuked them. 'You should be ashamed of yourself! Go home to your mothers where you belong!'

Within three days the coup plotters lost their nerve and their attempt to seize power collapsed.

It was one of the most vividly memorable episodes of my life. So much hung in the balance. If this coup by the old guard had succeeded, it would have reinstated Soviet power, reasserted the primacy of the Communist Party and returned the world to a new freeze. Some people find worrying echoes of Cold War antagonism in the more recent mistrustful stand-off between Russia and the West. But if those coup plotters had managed to turn back the clock in August 1991, Cold War tensions would never have abated at all, and we might now be living in a very different world.

I was fortunate to be there at that theatrical turning point. It was a privilege to be a BBC news correspondent reporting from Moscow at that time, a moment of global history in the making. But the events of late 1991 represented only one final scene in a geopolitical drama that spanned the globe and endured for nearly half a century.

Everyone who can count themselves as one of the Cold War generation probably has some searing experience associated with that strange, strained era, which veered from clandestine conspiracies and political brinkmanship to vicious blood-letting and agonising, cataclysmic wars. For those untouched by the devastating proxy clashes and spasms of brutal repression, the Cold War was often a backdrop, neither war nor peace but something running dimly in the background, hidden in twilight hues, in between. But for everyone who lived through those years there were some moments when the magnitude of the conflict loomed out of the shadows and its dramas took centre stage.

Beginning in 1944, even before the Second World War had ended, and continuing until the Soviet Union collapsed at the end of 1991, the Cold War lasted for well over four decades. The initial spotlight was on Europe, but within a few years it had spread to Asia. In time, countries as far apart as Vietnam, Chile and Angola were all caught up in its web.

The tensions that developed into the Cold War grew out of the Second World War and the question of what to do with the war-wrecked lands vacated by the retreating German armed forces. Once the menace of Hitler had been overcome, the wartime alliance between the United States and Britain on the one hand and the Soviet Union on the other began to unravel. Attempts by the Allied powers to agree on a post-war division dominated several summits, starting with the Tehran conference in 1943, Winston Churchill's private meeting with Joseph Stalin in Moscow in October 1944 and the so-called Percentages Agreement it produced, the Yalta conference of February 1945 and, five months later, another three-way summit in Potsdam. But the diplomacy only went so far.

Across Eastern Europe, Soviet troops were moving in and Communist takeovers were swiftly following. The Soviets were keen to take advantage of this opportunity to spread their Communist ideology westwards. They also wanted to make Eastern Europe a buffer zone to protect themselves against any future incursions from Germany or any other part of Europe.

Western powers, alarmed by the speed with which the Soviets were occupying territory, began to coalesce around a series of policies to contain the advance. The Truman Doctrine of 1947 sought to counter the expansion of Soviet geopolitical influence. The Marshall Plan poured billions of dollars of American aid into Western Europe to rebuild it after the war. The NATO military alliance followed in 1949, a collective defence pact to act as a counterweight to the threat posed by Soviet armies stationed in Eastern Europe. Within a few short years of the end of the Second World War, Europe once again found itself to be a conflict zone, not this time for a fighting war, but as the central focus of an ideological and political split, with the divided city of Berlin at its heart. And instead of Britain, France and Germany dominating the continent's diplomatic chessboard, now the leading powers facing each other across the divide were the United States and the Soviet Union.

From 1949, the Cold War spread further round the globe with the emergence of another Communist giant – Mao Zedong's 'Red' China. The disclosure, that same year, that the Soviet Union had acquired atomic weapons, and the start of the Korean War in 1950, brought tensions to a new peak. Revelations of Soviet espionage and fears of infiltration whipped up an anti-Communist crusade in the United States. Strident anti-capitalist rhetoric and paranoia about all things Western accompanied a new wave of Stalinist repression inside the Soviet Union, while in Eastern Europe new Communist regimes set about murdering and jailing their enemies. And even though the death of the Soviet leader Joseph Stalin in 1953 brought hopes of a thaw and better East–West relations, that did not last. The violent suppression of an uprising in Hungary in 1956 and a crisis over the stationing of Soviet missiles in Cuba in 1962 served as reminders that the world was staring into an abyss, caught between two global systems that viewed each other as mortal enemies and which could all too easily slip into nuclear war.

The 1960s brought new dramas in Europe with another uprising brutally suppressed by Moscow – in Czechoslovakia in 1968 – but the global ramifications of the Cold War continued. The two major Communist powers, China and the Soviet Union, fell out, and the United States found itself embroiled in an unwinnable war against Communists in Vietnam.

By the 1970s, the division of Europe had become a fact of life, codified into a 'new normal' by the process of détente and an 'Eastern Policy' – 'Ostpolitik' – to foster better links between the two sides of a divided Germany. But if the old battleground of Europe adjusted to a 'cold peace' and both superpowers agreed that any conflict involving nuclear weapons had to be off limits, this did not mean that the era of confrontation was over. Far from it. In Europe, the Cold War remained a conflict of nerves, but in Asia, Africa and Latin America it erupted into bloodstained battles, as the big powers fuelled and engineered a series of coups and civil wars, acting out their rivalry in distant proxy conflicts.

The denouement of this four-decade-long drama came unexpectedly in the mid-1980s, largely as the result of a change of leadership in the Soviet Union. Few people anticipated that the challenge that would overturn Soviet Communism and destroy its empire would come from within. But within six short years, the reformist Kremlin leader Mikhail Gorbachev overturned preconceptions and overhauled the Soviet Union's internal and global relations, leading to the abrupt collapse of Soviet rule, first in Eastern Europe and client states elsewhere, and then also inside the Soviet Union in December 1991.

The story of the Cold War did not end there. For many Soviet citizens, especially those in Russia, the overnight erasure of their country from the map was a terrifying cataclysm and a source of trauma from which it would take years to recover. Many of them agreed with their subsequent President, Vladimir Putin, that the end of the Soviet Union was a great tragedy and a terrible loss. And geopolitical tensions between East and West did not entirely disappear. In later years, they would re-emerge in disagreements and even conflicts, like the long-lasting, simmering war in eastern Ukraine, caused in part by unfinished business left over from the Cold War years and the Soviet Union's hasty disintegration.

But what happened in December 1991 did at least confirm that the confrontation that had dominated the globe since the end of the Second World War was over. And the extraordinary ideological battle between two very different philosophies, Communism and capitalism, which split Europe and the world in two for most of the second half of the twentieth century, was finally at an end.

As for those who were participants, on one level the story of the Cold War must be seen as a strategic fight for territory and power, the responsibility of those involved in warfare and diplomacy, the preoccupations of soldiers, spies, diplomats and members of political elites. But in almost every country its impact was also felt by ordinary citizens. This was a battle between two opposing systems, waged on a global stage, disrupting the lives of millions of people. Many of them found themselves with ringside seats and pivotal roles as key episodes unfolded, and sometimes with heart-rending personal experiences to relate.

In this book, it is their stories that we want to bring you: the personal perspectives of people who happened to be present at key events, sometimes as spectators, sometimes as actors, sometimes as unwitting chroniclers. These are the unsung foot soldiers of the Cold War. And their powerful accounts of what they saw with their own eyes offer a vivid taste of what this multifaceted and long-lasting conflict really felt like when experienced close up.

Some of our testimonies come from people who were small children at the time: the eight-year-old Greek boy, sent out on the streets by his father to experience what was happening as the Battle of Athens unfolded in December 1944; the six-year-old girl in East Berlin whose main worry during the East German uprising of 1953 was whether her birthday party would go ahead as planned.

Some of our eyewitnesses were young adults whose experiences scarred them for life: the young North Korean researcher who fled south during the Korean War but then found himself unable to go back, and never saw his mother again; the young Japanese fisherman who happened to be on the edge of the blast zone when the first hydrogen bomb was detonated on a Pacific atoll; the two brothers who were forced to stand helplessly by while their father was hounded to his death by their classmates during China's Cultural Revolution; and the young US soldier who discovered to his horror that what he thought would be America's fight for South Vietnamese freedom had degenerated into the indiscriminate murder of Vietnamese civilians.

Some of our stories come from people who happened to find themselves at the heart of events: a British soldier who saw a sniper's bullet whistle past him and nearly kill Winston Churchill; the young son of the Soviet leader Nikita Khrushchev, watching his father react to the fact that the volatile tyrant Joseph Stalin was dead; the student standing next to Chile's first ever Socialist President, Salvador Allende, as he made his final speech before being bombed by his own armed forces, under the direction of his chief of staff, General Pinochet; and the Russian tank commander who resolved to ignore orders to use violence against protestors during that fateful attempted coup in Moscow in August 1991.

And some of the testimony comes from people who had no intention of being caught up in the heat of the action but who found the Cold War drew them in anyway: the Hungarian student who joined a peaceful demonstration and within 24 hours found himself armed and amid a revolution; the Gdańsk shipyard worker who described how Lech Wałęsa's late arrival for a strike protest lit the spark that ignited the Polish Solidarity movement; and the young British mother, appalled at the thought of nuclear armed cruise missiles being installed at an American airbase near her village, who scaled the perimeter fence in protest.

Through this book and the BBC Radio 4 series, *Cold War: Stories from the Big Freeze*, which it accompanies, many of these stories are being shared with a wider public for the first time, and we give those who spoke to us our heartfelt thanks for agreeing to take part. It is a kaleidoscope of richly varied reports, wide-reaching, sometimes distressing, sometimes even joyful, and always intensely personal. In gathering and processing the material, we were all profoundly affected by these accounts. We hope you will be too.

'Then all hell broke loose'

The Greek Civil War
(1944–9)

It is often said that the Cold War emerged out of the power vacuum left by the Second World War, following the Nazi retreat from a devastated Europe. Yet in Greece the fault line between East and West, between Communist and anti-Communist, was already opening up well before the formal German surrender in the early summer of 1945.

The main Greek Civil War ran from 1946 to 1949, pitting Communist-backed fighters of the Democratic Army of Greece against Western-backed government forces. But our story begins earlier, with the so-called December Events, or *Dekemvriana*: the Battle of Athens at the end of 1944. This was the prelude to the Greek Civil War, erupting a full six months before the Second World War in Europe came to a close. It marked the first salvo in the Cold War, the opening scene in a drama of global rivalry and antagonism that would last nearly half a century.

The Greek Civil War grew out of a longstanding left–right split in Greek society and an ideological struggle to decide which side would fill the post-war void. The Nazi occupation had been brutal, and the country was in ruins.

By 1944, friction between rival resistance groups had already led to armed clashes. But for many Greeks, the country's real heroes in driving out the Nazis were not the members of Greece's internationally recognised government-in-exile, but the resistance fighters of the National Liberation Front (EAM – Ethnikó Apeleftherotikó Métopo) and its military wing, the Greek People's Liberation Army (ELAS – Ellinikós Laïkós Apeleftherotikós Stratós), which was mainly controlled by the Communist Party of Greece (KKE – Kommounistikó Kómma Elládas).

EAM supporters saw the end of Nazi occupation as a chance to start afresh. Their goal was to rid Greece of all foreign occupiers and transform the country into a republic – an anathema to other right-wing groups, including monarchists, who wanted to bring back the King of Greece from his wartime exile in Cairo and London.

The trouble began in the autumn of 1944. In early October, the Germans retreated from Athens, the last part of Greece still under occupation. Concerned at the extent of Communist support in the countryside, the British Prime Minister, Winston Churchill, despatched British troops to Athens to secure the city and prepare for the safe return of members of the government-in-exile. They were also there to bolster the authority of the British officer, General Ronald Scobie, who had been put in temporary command of all resistance forces.

When the British soldiers landed in Athens, several days after the Nazi retreat, they were given an enthusiastic welcome. As their military columns marched through streets festooned with celebratory banners, crowds met them with delighted shouts of 'Inglese!' and rushed forward to greet them as wartime allies and liberators. But the welcome did not last. By December the mood had soured.

EAM and ELAS partisans considered themselves the main liberators, but now they felt that they were being sidelined by the new provisional government, which the British helped to put in place. What was worse, Greek officers who had collaborated with the Nazis were being rehabilitated. The former resistance fighters accused the British, and particularly Churchill, of trying to reinstate the King against the people's wishes. In their eyes, the Greek monarchy was tarnished for having cooperated with Greece's pre-war military dictatorship. Then, on 2 December 1944, General Scobie and the provisional government decided that, rather than integrate the resistance fighters into the Greek army, they would order the disarmament of all guerrilla forces.

The simmering tensions exploded on 3 December, when left-wing demonstrators marched on Constitution Square in central Athens. Trying to control the crowd, Greek police opened fire. British troops were also present and found themselves embroiled in clashes. By the evening at least 28 people were dead and dozens more had been injured.

It was the start of four weeks of mayhem, with British soldiers, backed by tanks and air power, fighting alongside Greek government troops against the same left-wing partisans who only months before, in the fight against the Nazis, had been British allies. Now these ELAS fighters were above all regarded as Communists, in league with Stalin's Moscow, and a potential danger to Europe's fragile cohesion. In a pattern that would repeat itself in the Cold War decades to come, the British troops in Athens found themselves in league with strange bedfellows: Nazi sympathisers and collaborators who were also fighting to save Greece from the Communists. It was an even more bizarre marriage of convenience given that the war against the Nazis in Europe was not yet quite over.

Throughout December the battle raged. The Greek capital, having survived the horrors of wartime occupation, was once more engulfed in violence. The city was subjected to constant aerial bombardments by RAF aircraft targeting EAM and ELAS strongholds. The street fighting was vicious and even extended to the temple of the Acropolis, where British paratroopers dodged between the ancient columns to avoid partisan sniper fire. The explosive drama was captured on newsreels, broadcast worldwide by the BBC and other news outlets. World leaders had good reason to follow events closely. Elsewhere in Europe, the last major Nazi counter offensive of the Second World War was catching Allied forces by surprise in the Ardennes Campaign (also known as the Battle of the Bulge). But the Battle of Athens was also a cause for concern, the centre of what now appeared to be a new struggle to determine which forces would shape post-war Europe.

The renewed fighting in Athens caused consternation in London, especially as it pitted British forces against a resistance movement that had only months before been Britain's ally. Objections were raised both in the press and in Parliament. In a bid to end the bloodshed, the British Prime Minister decided to intervene personally. Winston Churchill arrived in Athens to preside over an international conference on 25 December 1944, Christmas Day, with the hope of reaching a peace settlement.

The conference at the Hotel Grande Bretagne in Athens was a high-level gathering, which included Soviet, American and French representatives, as well as the British Foreign Secretary, Anthony Eden, accompanying the Prime Minister; the Archbishop of Athens, who was the Regent of Greece; and representatives of both the Greek provisional government and the resistance fighters. But from the start it was beset with problems. Hours before it began, nearly a ton of explosives, primed for detonation, was discovered hidden in sewers beneath the hotel and had to be hurriedly removed. Winston Churchill travelled about the city in a heavily plated armoured car, but all the extra security precautions could not prevent one partisan sniper from taking a potshot at him. The conference was abandoned, having failed to achieve a breakthrough.

In early January 1945, the Battle of Athens ended with the defeat of EAM and ELAS forces, who had been heavily outgunned by the British. But atrocities and recriminations continued on all sides, and in 1946 the civil war restarted in earnest, lasting until 1949. At first, it involved British support, until a war-weary British government announced it could no longer afford to shoulder the burden and abruptly withdrew its troops. Then came American economic and military backing for the Greek government, as Allied fears grew that Greece might be taken over by Communists and give the Soviet leader Joseph Stalin a strategic foothold on the Mediterranean.

In fact, for all the Western concern about Soviet expansionism, when it come to Greece Stalin showed himself remarkably ambivalent, about coming to the aid of local Communists. Possibly he viewed the civil war as an insurrection that was unlikely to succeed. Possibly his detachment was part of a broader calculation not to provoke Western ire over Greece and thereby risk upsetting his plans to extend the Soviet hold over other Eastern parts of Europe.

There was also the informal 'Percentages Agreement', which he reached with Churchill during a private late-night discussion in Moscow in October 1944. Churchill apparently showed him a handwritten note sketching out a possible plan to divide post-war Eastern Europe and the Balkans into British and Soviet spheres of influence.

Yugoslavia and Hungary would be shared 50–50; Romania would be 90 per cent in the Soviet camp and 10 per cent in the British; Greece would be the other way round: 90 per cent British-American and only 10 per cent Soviet. And indeed, several months later in February 1945, when the British and Soviet leaders met again – this time with the American President, Franklin D. Roosevelt – for their landmark Yalta conference to shape a new security and political order for liberated Europe, it was agreed that Greece should remain firmly in the Western sphere of influence.

The Greek Civil War was also important for another twist in the emerging alignment of post-war political forces: its contribution to the split between Stalin and the new Communist leader of Yugoslavia, Marshal Josip Tito, who headed the only Communist government in Eastern Europe to have come to power in the wake of the Second World War without outside help.

A highly charismatic former resistance fighter, Tito had forged close ties with left-wing Greek partisans during the Nazi occupation and was determined to continue supporting them during the civil war, regardless of what Moscow thought. This characteristically independent streak irritated Stalin. In 1948 Moscow expelled Tito's Yugoslavia from the so-called Cominform, an international organisation of Communist parties designed to consolidate Soviet control over its satellite states in Eastern Europe. The rift moved Yugoslavia out of Moscow's orbit and left it throughout the Cold War the only independent Communist state in Europe, a thorn in the Soviet Union's side for years to come. It also prompted Tito to become a founding member of the Non Aligned Movement, made up of countries around the world that stated they were not to be aligned with any major bloc.

As for Greece, American concern at the possibility that it might join the Communist camp was an important factor in the emergence of the policy proclaimed by President Harry Truman known as the Truman Doctrine. The aim of President Truman's speech to Congress in March 1947 was to explain why the United States had to keep Communist influence at bay in the Eastern Mediterranean by providing economic and military aid to Greece and Turkey. He presented it as an ideological struggle between freedom and oppression, and thus his Truman Doctrine articulated a principle that would underpin American policy towards the Communist bloc throughout the Cold War – that America was the 'leader of the free world', whereas Communism represented tyranny and subjugation.

Eventually American support facilitated the Greek government's victory over the Communists in 1949, placing the country resolutely in the Western camp. In 1952 Greece, along with Turkey, joined the recently established North Atlantic Treaty Organization or NATO military alliance, defining the ideological balance of power in the Aegean Sea for decades to come.

Western fears of Soviet meddling in the Greek Civil War may have proved unfounded, but the conflict did mark an important shift: the moment when the wartime Allies' united front against Nazi fascism fractured and Western powers turned to a new battle, to stop a Communist takeover in Europe.

My name is **Zozo Petropoulou-Kritzilaki**. I was born in 1925 in Patras. We came to Athens when I was seven-and-a-half months old. We were so exposed to danger; we were children, very young. The fact that my generation survived after the Second World War is just luck. Because of the conditions we were living under, we could have been killed 100 times.

When the war started, some British soldiers came to Athens, but I have read that they were little help. The Germans arrested most of them, and they were kept in the Archaeological Museum. We used to save our pocket money to buy biscuits and chocolates, and after school we would go and throw them to the prisoners.

I started being more political when I was 16 years old. First, I became a member of *Lefteri Nea* ['Free Young'], which was a branch of EAM. Later on, EAM and all the youth organisations decided to become one, and that's how EPON [Ethnikí Pánellenios Orgánosis Neoléas/National Panhellenic Organisation of Youth] was created. I was a fifth-year student at the 3rd Gymnasium of Athens and, one day, the school yard was full of flyers, handwritten on torn notebook pages: 'Young girls, come join *Lefteri Nea* to drive Nazism from our country.' We ran and we took them, and we joined *Lefteri Nea*. You could be in contact with only three people, and just one, the team leader, was in contact with the leading team. I was part of a team with two of my co-students and the leading member, a teacher. She would bring us short texts to write on pages torn from notebooks then throw them around the school and the National Gardens.

At the time, we were listening to whatever news we could. We tried to listen to the BBC because this was what we considered to be a legitimate source of news. So we'd listen to the BBC, then we would write the news on our flyers and throw them around.

*The day that **Nicholas Rizopoulos** woke up and discovered that the German troops had left Athens was 12 October 1944.*

I remember that very distinctly, even though I was only eight-and-a-half years old, because there was this general feeling of exultation and relief. Never before in my life had I experienced this feeling of freedom. And then to go out into the streets and watch all the Greek and British and French and Russian flags and American flags flying from all the various balconies and windows of people's houses – people in the streets just jumping and shouting and having a marvellous, marvellous time – this is something I will never forget.

I had never heard 'It's a Long Way to Tipperary' before, obviously; that's not a tune one heard during the occupation. But it was explained to me that this was a very famous tune, going back to the First World War, a favourite with the British public and British troops, and it was a very catchy tune. There were these spontaneous little parades taking place in central Athens in which the bands of the police force and the fire department were going through the boulevards playing 'It's a Long Way to Tipperary'. People were singing the lyrics as well, but – as was explained to me later – mangling the English words. People were so happy to be able to sing certain songs that had simply not been allowed during the occupation. This was 12 October 1944. The Germans had left Athens, but the Allied troops had not yet arrived.

We were an upper-middle-class Greek family, but we were basically impoverished. My father was a criminal lawyer, 45 years old. He had married my mother in the early 1930s, and I was an only child, born in 1936. We lived in Thessaly until the Italian invasion of Greece in 1940, when we were forced to leave everything behind and move to Athens, where we stayed throughout the occupation. We rented a small apartment two blocks from the British embassy. My parents divorced in the first year of the war, and my mother moved to the same part of Athens, about a 20-minute walk away. I stayed with my father, who introduced me, among other things, to the forbidden fruit of listening late at night on short-wave radio to the BBC Greek Hour. This was completely prohibited, so you took your life in your hands by having an illegal radio transmitter so that you could hear real news instead of what Athens Radio was broadcasting under the direction of the Germans. So I became progressively aware of what was happening in the war.

During the occupation, my father, who was fluent in German, worked for the International Red Cross as an interpreter, which gave him an opportunity to travel all over Greece and thus to have first-hand knowledge and experience of what the various resistance movements were doing and what they were preparing for come liberation. By travelling and talking to the locals, he became absolutely convinced that the KKE and ELAS were up to no good. He was apprehensive and worried and, at heart, very much an anti-Communist. He was one of a small minority of Greek intellectuals who had never bought into the siren song of the 'Workers' Paradise' that the Soviet Union was putting together. He was absolutely terrified at the thought of Greece falling under Communist control, and his anxiety grew and grew throughout 1943 and 1944. He was very well connected and he knew what was already happening in Bulgaria, where the Red Army was in place, and in Yugoslavia and Albania. He was convinced that, unless we put up a fight, Greece too would join the Soviet paradise.

Once the Germans had gone, for a period of five or six days, we had no idea who was in charge. We had barely survived the occupation years. As a young boy, I had this constant feeling of anxiety and insecurity: where was the next meal going to come from? But my father was very kind and reassuring, and he took it upon himself to instruct me. Essentially, the message was this: 'There are Communists who are going to try to establish themselves as the superior political and military power in Athens, and this would be a terrible thing – we as middle-class people would be in danger if they succeeded in taking over Athens. The fact that the Germans have left does not solve all our problems.' And so I began to feel much, much better when, beginning on 18 October, the first Allied troops arrived in Athens and the initial reaction from all sections of Greek society was exuberance.

One of those arriving soldiers was **John Clarke**, *who had enlisted at 17.*

I wanted to join the Navy, but I was too young. I had no parents, but the recruiter forged their signatures: 'Here's your shilling, you're in the army.' Happy days ... Athens was an emergency trip. We'd been fighting non-stop in Italy for nine months, and we were supposed to be going to Palestine. Then word came that ELAS were marching on Athens and that the royalists weren't very good at defending, and that's why we got sent there. Although our advance party were actually in Palestine, the rest of us had to go in a bit of a rush, and we didn't know who was who, who we were fighting.

The civilians would say hello during the day, then at night time they'd attack us. The old ladies used to have grenades in their bras. One time, I grabbed hold of one – she was shouting and raving, and I just grabbed hold of her. And instead of getting hold of her breast, it was a grenade. And there was this young kid, I'll never forget

John Clarke.

it: eight years of age, he was. We were actually billeted in houses near the Acropolis. This young kid starts waving, so we're waving back. All of a sudden, he rolls a grenade at us – and by the time we see it coming it's too late to run.

Zozo Petropoulou-Kritzilaki

After the Germans retreated, the British came, and they were acting as if we were a protectorate. And this was something that we couldn't accept because we considered them allies. Since we were allies, why were the British firing in Athens? The whole thing had to do with the fact that the left didn't want a King. This was the main thing, because Churchill wanted to force the monarchy on us. Until the liberation, I was a member of EPON, but then I joined ELAS, and I was following my unit as a nurse for ELAS.

We knew that EDES [Ethnikos Dimokratikos Ellinikos Syndesmos/National Republican Greek League] was sponsored by the British, and this was not something the other organisations had. Napoleon Zervas and the officers of EDES were getting paid with golden pounds. This wasn't something that was happening in ELAS. There was a story that at some point the British dropped packages for ELAS, and it was only right pairs of shoes – no left pairs.

Nicholas Rizopoulos

By the end of October 1944, Communist elements were trying to impose their views by having bigger rallies and louder shouting. I remember being encouraged by my father to walk through Athens with our housekeeper, to go and see what was going on. I didn't really understand the subtleties, but I could see that I was supposed to be on the side of the good guys who called themselves Nationalists, rather than the Communists. The Communists were planning some kind of military upheaval to take over Athens. There was this creeping sense of anxiety and fear again.

What happened on 3 December was that the left held a monster demonstration on Constitution Square, forbidden at first but it went ahead. My father encouraged our housekeeper and myself to take a stroll from our little apartment towards Constitution Square to experience one more of these events for my general education. And as we approached, my housekeeper and I heard the first explosions. We never got to the square itself – we were literally less than 100 yards away, and then we saw a crowd rushing in our direction, away from Constitution Square. I heard the noises, I saw the crowds, I felt the excitement and saw the fear in people's faces as they were running away from Constitution Square in our direction …

After this, my father was in and out of the apartment at all hours of the day and night, and he was filling me with news. Essentially he said a battle for the control of Athens had started between the bad guys, as far as he was concerned the Communists, and the anti-Communists. And we didn't know how it was going to turn out, but we hoped for the best. He said again and again to me: 'I am basically optimistic, because I think the British will make sure that the Communists don't take over the city.' He also said that we are lucky to be living where we were, two blocks away from the British embassy, because this was going to be a very well-protected part of Athens.

So for the next two or three weeks, while the Battle of Athens raged, mostly I was under lock and key in the apartment. What I could see when I looked out of the window was the most reassuring sight of all: the RAF Spitfires, doing reconnaissance work and dropping bombs in key positions that were occupied by the Communist guerrillas. Inside our little apartment, I could hear mortar explosions, cannon explosions and non-stop gunfire – on and on and on, for the first couple of weeks.

In normal times, it was a 20-minute walk to my mother's house, but during the battle there was no way that I could safely visit her. The area that we lived in was entirely under British control; the area where my mother lived was okay as well, but in between there were certain parts that were dangerous. Communist snipers had penetrated these areas and were taking potshots at people walking in the streets. So I was not allowed to visit my mother. She, on the other hand, being a brave woman, went back and forth and lived to tell the tale.

Eventually, my father allowed me to go out for a walk, and we stopped to see the sight of a lot of wounded policemen who were arriving at the hospital. My father said these were the people who were trying to protect us. My father pushed me towards one of the open-backed lorries, which were bringing in the bodies from the outskirts of Athens, the bodies of policemen and gendarmerie who had been attacked by the Communists. Some of them were dead and, as I was pushed forward to see these mangled bodies with my own eyes, I saw that there were a couple who were still alive, moaning and groaning in pain. Then all hell broke loose. It was no longer just conversations – I've seen with my own eyes things which are shocking.

Towards the end of December, when, unbeknownst to me, the Battle of Athens had already turned against the Communists, we had the famous visit of Winston Churchill.

Nicholas Rizopoulos and his father
on the balcony of their apartment.

John Clarke

I was there because I was a registered stretcher-bearer and they wanted someone with medical experience in case anything happened. There was Anthony Eden, Churchill himself, bodyguards and the Archbishop, a big fella. Oh, and Churchill was in Air Force uniform, like overalls.

From nowhere, this bullet came. It flashed by me, and I could hear it hit flesh. I knew what it was right away. And this poor woman in the back of me, her name was Erula, she was about 40, I think she was a schoolteacher at one of the colleges there … Well, they took her body away right away. The airborne troops were out in the street nearby, that's how they captured the sniper. They spread out and – I think it was about 20 minutes, half an hour later – they came back with this woman. They showed her to one of the military police officers and they took her away in a jeep. She was a Bulgarian girl. I don't know her name. She was 19 years of age, and she was trying to kill Churchill.

He got up, and he laughed. I'll always remember: 'That'll get me a medal,' he said.

It wasn't just Winston Churchill who came under fire during the Dekemvriana. *The entire city was a potential death trap, as* **Nicholas Rizopoulos** *found out when he visited a friend's house.*

As I was waiting for the door to be buzzed open, I heard this funny noise. *Psst*, something like that, very near my head. I spent the afternoon playing with him, then I came home that evening and I was told that a sniper had taken a potshot at me. A couple of days later, my father said, 'Come with me,' and he pointed at the frame of the door of my friend's house and there was a bullet hole at about the height of my head. I was amazed, but that was it – I don't remember feeling suddenly heroic or scared or proud or anything. By this point I'd lived through three months of hysteria in Athens, so somebody taking a potshot at me and missing ... Well, I'm glad he missed, but otherwise it's no big deal.

Zozo Petropoulou-Kritzilaki

Fights were taking place in Athens, from Syntagma [Constitution] Square to Omonoia Square. All the other areas, from Omonoia to Patissia, there was nothing. In all these areas ELAS was operating. ELAS was responsible for Athens. Even though there were combat units outside of Athens, they weren't brought to Athens at the time of the *Dekemvriana*. At least, I never saw an insurgent of the regular army.

At the time of the *Dekemvriana*, I was at Kaisariani with the Ilioupoli Unit. In Kaisariani, there was a battalion, but the second day of the fights, there were so many injured and dead that it needed and asked for backup, and that's when the Ilioupoli Unit came. I stayed at Kaisariani until 29 December, when Kaisariani fell. The British planes were firing at people. It was a huge massacre.

On the second or third day after Kaisariani fell, the administration of the unit sent me to Athens, to Ilioupoli, the 6th area, to check what was happening. There were rumours that the injured had been slaughtered, but this was not the case, not yet. I went on my own from the mountain of Imitos to Ilioupoli and from there to Pagrati three times, gathering information. Afterwards, the unit moved outside the Athens area, so they didn't need me any more. I stayed in Athens until March.

John Clarke

Being involved with stretcher-bearing and wearing the Red Cross, I was walking through the streets of Athens and a gang grabbed me. They must have thought I was a doctor. They took me to a house, and outside the house there were five or six bodies, all dead. They appeared to have been attacked by ELAS, and some of the wounds there ... they were unnatural. I'm not one who dreams about these things, I've seen too many horrible things in my time, but now and then I sit down and I think about what I saw there ...

Nicholas Rizopoulos

In mid-January, when the fighting was definitely over and it was safe to walk around Athens, my father said that he wanted to spend a whole day with me because he wanted to show me some things that were important to know. So we did a grand walking tour of the centre of Athens that took us from our part of the city to other parts that had been taken over by the Communists, parts that had been fought over by the Communists and the British troops, and other parts that had been protected by the Nationalist forces. What he was doing was showing me some of the shocking destruction of the buildings – we walked through parts of Athens that I had known as a child, and I now saw them almost completely destroyed. I was shocked because I'd never seen anything like that, except on newsreels.

After the armistice, all kinds of ugly news began to reach us of people who were not lucky enough to live in a part of Athens that was protected by the British forces. They lived in suburbs and outlying areas that were taken over for at least a week or two by the Communists. When the Battle of Athens started going badly for the Communists, on orders from whom we will never know, they took hostages – hundreds and hundreds of hostages. They took them out of Athens and marched them up and down. They killed some

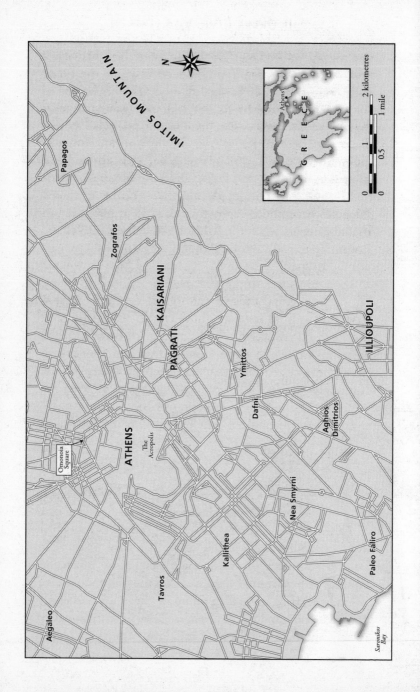

of them on the way and killed others later and committed some horrible atrocities.

When news of this reached Athens in mid-January and the first photographs were available of these mistreated human beings, this became the focus of conversation, just discussing these atrocities and what they meant and how lucky we were that we had escaped. Once again, I was invited in to just sit and listen, and I was obviously horrified listening to the details and then also being shown some of these photographs that then were published in the newspapers.

In February 1945, the Treaty of Varkiza was agreed among the different Greek parties, the various paramilitary groups were disbanded, and an amnesty was declared for political offences committed during and after the Nazi occupation. Many former members of those groups were, however, now classified as criminals.

Zozo Petropoulou-Kritzilaki

I was arrested one morning out of the blue. I was going to work, and you needed ID to enter. I had ID, and at the time I wasn't even operating. But they caught me and they asked me to sign a political belief statement. Of course, I didn't, and I was sent to Chios, which was the first region where a women's camp was created. I was arrested on 1 March, and on 10 March I was sent to Chios in the second 'shipment'. When we arrived, we found a few women there. After this, the boats were going back and forth every day, and more women prisoners were arriving. The camps were full and a lot of people were outside, including me. Inside, it was really packed, and by June it was really hot. Rooms that were meant for 30 people were holding 60 to 70.

We stayed in Chios for 13 months, then we were moved to Trikeri. There were around 200 children in the camp at the time. There wasn't enough water, but there were some wells where they had put some water pumps. We would get water, filling the jugs, and we would walk with that for 200 metres. We had a song: 'Every woman before dawn goes for water and at night she returns with an empty bucket.'

Then we were moved to Makronisi. They sent the men there first, and they treated them very badly. Some died from the beatings, from the bad conditions. In order to get out of the beatings, some men swallowed their spoons so that they would be sent to the hospital. Thousands of men were sent to Makronisi. A very small percentage survived without signing the political belief statement. A very small percentage. They ordered the army police to take children from their mothers. In order to make them sign, they would take her child, and they said, 'We are not going to give your child back unless you sign.'

Even though we went through all these awful conditions, I think that it was worth it. We had such strong ideas that we felt that at the moment we were part of something really big.

The fighting continued in the north of the country, and in 1946 the civil war re-erupted. Concerned by the growing Soviet influence in Europe, in 1947 US President Harry S. Truman announced a programme of military and economic aid.

Nicholas Rizopoulos

Soon thereafter the Brits were gone, the Truman Doctrine was in place, and a lot of Americans started arriving in Athens. And the conversations are: 'Well, it's too bad the

Brits have left, but thank God the Americans are coming. And with the help of the Americans not only will our freedom be preserved, but also as the main part of the Civil War is taking place up in the north we have a much better chance of defeating this last and most serious phase of the Communist Civil War with American help.' And so my whole family and most of my friends were deliriously in favour of the Truman Doctrine.

'The Iron Curtain was in place'

The Communist Coup in Czechoslovakia (1948)

For many citizens of Czechoslovakia, the Communist takeover of their country in February 1948 came as a surprise. For sympathisers, it was the 'Victorious February'. For those who feared the Communists and their Soviet backers, it was a *coup d'état*. With hindsight, it was a key strategic move in the Cold War, a brazen effort by Moscow to ensure that Czechoslovakia fell into the Soviet bloc, marking the final piece in the jigsaw that ensured decades of Communist rule across Eastern Europe.

It also serves as a timely reminder to us today that for a big power to subvert another country's destiny it is not always necessary to intervene with tanks and troops. Behind-the-scenes manipulation, to influence public mood and promote the appearance of democratic choice while at the same time undermining it, can also disrupt an established order. We talk now of 'hybrid warfare' – the combination of military clout, political manipulation and information techniques – as something new. What happened in Czechoslovakia in 1948 shows that it is not new at all.

According to the Yalta agreement of 1945, the three big Allied powers – Britain, the United States of America and Soviet Russia – had pledged to allow the liberated countries of Eastern Europe and the Balkans to determine their own fate through free elections. But reality proved otherwise.

To protect the Soviet Union from any future attack and to extend Soviet influence into Europe, Stalin wanted a constellation of reliable 'friendly' allies to act as a buffer zone along the Soviet Union's post-war borders in Europe. The division of Europe into 'spheres of influence' first discussed by Stalin and Churchill in 1944 was quickly becoming a reality. The 'liberation' of Romania, Bulgaria and Hungary from the Axis powers by Red Army troops in 1943–4 had left them under virtual Soviet occupation, vulnerable to the installation of regimes subservient to Moscow. Before long, Stalin had also engineered a pro-Soviet government in Poland. In the Balkans, Yugoslavia had a Communist government, under Josip Tito, as did Albania, under Enver Hoxha. By 1948 (apart from Greece, as we saw in Chapter 1), only Czechoslovakia out of the Eastern bloc was still led by a democratically elected government.

At the end of the Second World War, by no means everyone in Czechoslovakia feared the Communists. As in Greece and elsewhere across Europe, they had been important in the country's anti-fascist resistance. Like the Soviet armies who liberated part of the country in 1945 (and then withdrew), they were welcomed for their role in ending Nazi rule, and Communist Party membership surged accordingly, from 40,000 in 1945 to 1.35 million by 1948. Central to their appeal was that they appeared to embrace Czech traditions both of nationalism and of democracy. 'The next goal is not soviets and socialism,' said their party leader, Klement Gottwald, in 1945, but 'a really thorough democratic national revolution.' And so in the election of 1946 the Communists won 38 per cent of the vote and were the largest party in a coalition government that looked both East and West.

But by early 1948, the atmosphere was beginning to change. Post-war economic conditions were already grim and had been made harsher by a bitterly cold winter followed by a poor harvest. Under pressure from Stalin, who suspected an American ploy to weaken and isolate the Soviet Union the Czechoslovak government was effectively forbidden by the Kremlin to accept an offer of US economic aid through the recently announced (but not yet formally ratified) Marshall Plan, and was relying instead on Soviet grain to keep starvation at bay. In retrospect, it was one of several moves ahead of the coup that showed the Kremlin's determination to ensure Czechoslovakia was under its sway. Some voters were also perturbed by talk from leading Communists who, in an echo of Stalin's Soviet Union, called for the collectivisation of agriculture and for industrial workers to compete for ever higher outputs with no increase in wages. All of this alienated many people, and it looked as though at the next election, set for May 1948, the Communists might lose ground.

Recognising that their popularity might be slipping, the Communists in Czechoslovakia began to assert themselves. Spurred on by Moscow, they claimed a reactionary plot was being hatched to seize power. 'Spontaneous' demonstrations were organised to 'express the will of the people'. Thousands of workers were bussed into central squares to take part in Communist rallies, building up a head of steam.

Tensions came to a head when the Communist Interior Minister made a move to purge non-Communists from the police force and turn it into a Communist security apparatus.

Those members of the coalition government who did not have links to the Communist Party threatened to resign in protest. In response, the Communist Prime Minister Klement Gottwald called workers and armed police on to the streets. Pockets of organised dissent emerged as if from nowhere, driving the unrest towards revolution. Communist activists and trades union militias took over the streets of Prague. The army was confined to barracks. Workers threatened a general strike.

On 25 February 1948, worried about civil war and a possible Soviet military intervention, President Edvard Beneš capitulated: accepting the resignation of the non-Communist ministers, he allowed Gottwald to form a new government dominated by Communists and Social Democrats, all with close ties to Moscow.

Now in control, the Communist leadership moved quickly to consolidate power. Arrests became commonplace. Thousands of people were fired from their jobs. Those who refused to cooperate were threatened with prison or worse. Some were made an example of and subjected to show trials. In a shocking development, one of the few remaining independent members of the government, the Foreign Minister Jan Masaryk (the son of Tomáš Masaryk, the founder of the country after the First World War) was found dead below a third-floor window. Initially it looked like suicidal despair. Subsequent records showed that he may have been deliberately thrown to his death.

What had happened was nothing less than a Communist takeover. In the Cold War years to follow, the pattern would become familiar: the trappings of a democratic state, masking what was effectively Communist one-party rule, taking its orders from Moscow. And if you weren't on the side of the Communists, you risked being seen as a traitor.

Whether in the Czech capital, Prague, or the Slovak capital, Bratislava, those who feared that their political affiliations or lack of enthusiasm for the new Communist order might put them in danger joined a mass exodus, fleeing the country while it was still possible. One escape route that was still viable was across the border into Austria. Before long (except – as we shall see later – in divided Berlin), making that hazardous trip from East to West would become all but impossible – the stuff of Cold War thrillers.

The coup in Czechoslovakia sent ripples of alarm through the Western world. It raised the spectre of the shameful Munich agreement of 1938, when Western powers had acquiesced in Nazi Germany's annexation of parts of Czechoslovakia. Now, for the second time in a decade, the West was watching Czechoslovakia being appropriated by a totalitarian power. Soviet Communism no longer looked like a wartime ally but like a new and dangerous aggressor. In France and Italy, it put Communist parties on the defensive and ultimately weakened them.

In Washington, President Truman told the US Congress that 'the tragic death of the Republic of Czechoslovakia has sent a shock wave through the civilized world.' Congress moved swiftly to approve the Marshall Plan to pour economic aid into post-war Western Europe, fearing that without it more of the continent would fall to the Soviets. The first shipments of food aid arrived within weeks.

The Czech coup also played to those in the US administration who wanted a military as well as economic containment of Communism. President Truman wasn't the only one in Washington who voiced fears that a new and dangerous confrontation with the Soviets was looming. At the Pentagon, an emergency war plan was drawn up in case of a Soviet invasion of Western Europe. Within a year, in 1949, a new Western military Alliance was to be established to deter further Soviet inroads into Europe: the North Atlantic Treaty Organization, or NATO.

At the beginning of 1948, Czechoslovakia had been the only parliamentary democracy left in Eastern Europe. By the end of the same year, it was part of the Soviet bloc. Not through the invasion of Soviet tanks – that would come later, in response to the Prague Spring in 1968 – but through the actions of local Communists, drawing on their post-war popularity, paying lip service to the process of democracy but in fact stealthily mobilising their supporters from below and with the influence of the Soviet Union lurking in the shadows.

In many ways, the Communist takeover of Czechoslovakia also concluded the partition of Europe and marked the final rupture between the United States and the Soviet Union. Two years earlier, in a speech in Fulton, Missouri, in March 1946, Winston Churchill had warned that 'an iron curtain has descended across the continent'. Now it had become a reality.

Sylva Šimsová was living in Prague with her family at the time of the coup. She was 17 and was beginning to take an interest in politics.

After the war, my father became a politician, and he was the head of the State Planning Office. When the war ended, it was like the happy ending of a fairy tale. We really thought everything was going to be all right for ever. And so 1948 came as a big surprise to us.

I loved the Russians. Russia has a great culture: I loved their music, I loved their folk dancing, and I was slowly finding my way through the political side of things. You see, we were not quite sure what to think of the Russians. I started finding out what Communism was. And I started finding it out by meeting Czechs who were Communists. And they were strange people. They were sort of looking at me and saying to each other, 'She doesn't understand,' and then pointing to a picture of Lenin on the wall. And they were stupid. And gradually I realised they were not just stupid but also dangerous. But I underestimated the danger, so that actually, when February 1948 came, I was surprised because I thought that democracy was something that would protect us, but it didn't.

Karel Janovický, a year older than Sylva, was in his last year of school and wanted to study music at university.

I applied to university. At the interview, there was a group of these youngsters. They asked me what sort of papers I read, and did I read the Communist papers and did I read the left-wing music magazine *Tempo*? And I sort of went, 'Uh?!' Because I didn't, I hadn't. And that meant that I was not suitable for further education.

My father was persecuted because he was not working class. He was a member of the local opera, but he was thrown out. He eventually became a travelling accountant – he went from one state-run restaurant to another and did the accounts.

Almost a year before the coup, Jan Masaryk returned from a trip to Moscow and announced on the radio that Stalin had refused to allow Czechoslovakia to accept the Marshall Plan. And the whole country was shocked. This was something that would have hugely benefitted the country. There was a well-educated force of people who could have got the country up on its feet with this help. This was one of the acts that made people doubt what was said officially later on.

Sylva Šimsová

I heard about the death of Jan Masaryk on the radio. The radio was broadcast through amplifiers on the square where we lived – there was music, and there was the morning news, and among it that he had been found dead. It just said that he was 'found dead'.

My generation was very worried. On the day of Masaryk's death, we went to school and we were all extremely disturbed. Our history teacher was just about to give us a lesson, and we interrupted her and said, 'How can you be so calm when such horrible things are happening?' And she said, 'But girls, that's history, and history is not always pleasant to experience.'

People were emotionally shocked because Jan Masaryk was a very liked person, and he belonged to a family who to us were great heroes. I think people just simply assumed that somebody killed him, and I don't think people believed the story about him committing suicide.

Karel Janovický

It was preceded by so many acts of betrayal and skulduggery on the part of the Communist politicians that nobody really believed any official announcements. Some people assumed that he might have committed suicide out of desperation, and other people assumed that this was another dastardly act of the regime. And the Soviets had to approve anything that the Czechoslovak Communist regime did.

I remember the coup very well, because it was such a shock. We went to school as normal, and a group of our schoolmates – who we'd known all those years – suddenly burst in and presented themselves as a revolutionary committee. They berated the professor in front of us, finished the lessons and said, 'There's a revolution in the country.' They had been training for all those years, clandestinely, and none of us, their closest friends and schoolmates, had known about it. The same thing was orchestrated throughout the school.

It was very worrying because there were workers' militias marching down the streets. They were armed, and they had all been trained, again clandestinely – none of us knew that this was going on. They really looked frightening. And marching with them and shouting and running around were groups of activists of all ages, young, middle-aged and old. These were Czechoslovak citizens. One of the women among them, shouting abuse at the elected government, was the wife of our family's doctor.

John Palka *lived with his family near Bratislava. He was nine years old at the time of the coup – too young to follow such events. The first thing he knew about it was an absence.*

My father disappeared. I don't remember what my mother might have told me about where he was. He was just gone from the family.

He was the owner of a medium-sized leather factory, which had been the family business for generations. After he returned from the war, he put all his energy into reviving that business. He took me to the factory several times to see what it was like – I have all these memories of giant machines and drive belts that went on for 50 or 100 feet. There was a racket everywhere, and out came these glorious leather products like fancy women's purses and elegant bags for me. He spent most of his days in the factory.

Over the years, my father and I had developed a shared love for the family car. It was an American car, and he taught me how to sit in it properly, and how to start it, and so on. One day in April 1948, a group of four men, complete strangers, came over to the house. One of them asked me about the car. I was very pleased to show him how to start it. A few days later, my father vanished and the car was confiscated. That car was an object of enormous jealousy on the part of the power structure. How many people in remote Slovakia had an American car to drive around in? Hardly any. So, if they could get their hands on this status symbol then their star would rise.

After a while, I started to receive postcards from him. There was a series of eight, written from prison. They were written in pencil and addressed to me, although they were really intended to convey information to my mother.

He wrote: 'Dear Pikulik. Maybe I will be home soon. I just have to wait for a man who said various things about me that he has to explain, but he won't be here until Wednesday. I really want to be home so we can play together again. Your daddy.'

A week later, he wrote: 'I thought that the man who said all these things about me would be here last week but he still hasn't come. Nobody has come to see me – not the lawyer, not Mama, not Aunt Ludinka. I hope that someone will come to visit me this week.' They had tried frantically to see him, but they had been denied.

He had been caught up in a broader political intrigue and process. What the Communists did was pick somebody to arrest, somebody from the bourgeoisie. They would fabricate charges against that person, oftentimes totally out of thin air, put pressure on them, threaten them with prison, torture and actually physically torture them. And the way out for many of these accused people was to accuse somebody else – to spread the net, so to speak. And that's what happened to my father.

Many of our family and friends had been at the centre of the anti-Nazi resistance during the war and had been the leaders of the Slovak national uprising in 1944, so they were prime targets for the Communists. So they were either escaping across the border or being arrested. My own grandfather, who was a staunch proponent of a united Czechoslovakia, nevertheless over the years came to see with greater and greater persuasion that the Czechoslovak problem was a real one that would need to be addressed in one way or another over time. During the war, when he was politically active among immigrant groups in the USA, that was a major part of his political platform: he was pro-Czechoslovakia, he was for the West against the Russians, he was a strong anti-Communist, and he was a strong proponent of redressing the balance and restructuring the country so that the imbalance between Czechs and Slovaks would be ameliorated. This was absolutely central to my parents, but they didn't let me know any of this at the time.

Karel Janovický

Before the war, I joined the Boy Scouts as a Wolf Cub. We had a very good leader, a remarkable man, and as soon as the war ended he started reorganising the Scouts. By then, I was a teenager. We decided that we were going to help with the harvest, so a group of us went to one of the farms in a village near my home town of Pilsen, which was in the Russian zone. When we walked through the village in our improvised Scout uniforms, the Russian soldiers all stood to attention while we passed. It was so different from the behaviour of the Americans – you couldn't think of a sharper contrast.

Sylva Šimsová

I was also a member of the Scout movement. I always felt that it was a movement that cared for young people. I always had this feeling that serving the community was very important. Eventually, of course, after February 1948, we realised that the regime didn't like a movement like this; they preferred the Pioneers, who had completely different ideas. The Pioneers were supposed to educate youngsters for the future Communist world, which did not appeal. The question was, what was going to happen to people like Karel and me, who belonged to this sort of movement.

There was a man, a former priest, who decided that he would group together people from the Scout movement who, like me, wanted to keep the ideas but could not fit into the organisations that were being offered by the Communists. I was invited to join a group that wanted to keep doing the work we had been doing in the Scouts. I wondered if I would be going into something that was almost an underground movement under Communism. I realised that it wasn't an underground movement. Its aim was to educate people and preserve civilisation, because the Communist movement was destroying many aspects of our traditional civilisation. We were expected to do a lot of voluntary work; I was working in forestry, cutting down trees, and I was very proud. This gave us some consolation, because there was hope that civilisation would be saved. So that is how I met Karel.

People like us were at risk of persecution if we continued the work we were doing. There was a lot happening in the offices and schools. 'Undesirables' were being excluded. My father was a social democrat. To start with, the social democrats were not persecuted, but they were expected to join the Communist Party by the summer. And those who didn't sign up were then the undesirables. Eventually, a list was made of them, to send them to prison. My father learned that his name was one of the names on this list. And that is the reason why we left the country.

By the time we left, they were already building these watchtowers and they cut out the trees for a certain width of the ground on the border, so it would be absolutely clear who was crossing. And later explosives were put into this land, and then the fences were created. In my office, I have a bit of wire from one of the fences which was given to me in 1989 by somebody who went around collecting this and making it into memorabilia.

The idea that I would leave the country and not take Karel with us ... it would have been very difficult for me. We had been a couple for about six months. But my father said that Karel could come with us if his parents approved.

Karel Janovický

I don't think I felt it was a difficult decision to leave. It was another of those disasters that kept coming upon us every five to ten years, and you simply did what was best. Looking back, we must have been exceptionally lucky.

Sylva's father got some help from someone who had knowledge of the local situation. We were split into two groups to cross the border into Bavaria. We had to be because of attention at the border – special measures had been put in place by the Czechoslovak police. My group went first and Sylva and her parents a couple of days later.

They arranged for us to be taken by car, attracting as little attention as possible. We were actually stopped at one of the checkpoints, but we were allowed to go on. We ended up on the edge of the 20–30-kilometre zone that had been thrown up all along the border. That zone had to be crossed during the night, because nothing was allowed to move through that zone day or night, but at night you couldn't be seen. So we had to walk through this zone and ended up in Bavaria, where we reported to the nearest frontier post. The Americans sent a jeep and an armoured car and we were taken to an American base. Then we went through one or two weeks of interrogation before we were sent on to the refugee camps. I ended up in Munich.

Sylva Šimsová

The whole thing was organised by my father's assistant at the university. I'm still trying to work out exactly how he did it, but he knew a reliable guide across the border. This man was very careful. We never knew his name.

Are you afraid? No. When you are surviving, there is no room for fear. Because when you are surviving, you think about what needs to be done: right foot forward, left foot forward, right foot forward, left foot forward. For 12 hours, we started at seven in the evening, finished at seven in the morning. And we got through.

We thanked the man, and my father paid him. But there was no car waiting for us. Somehow, the local American commander, to whom we would have been taken for screening, had decided that my father was a Communist. So we were sent to a special refugee camp for people who were politically undesirable. We got bread to eat and a bed to sleep on, but it was a very poor existence. And we didn't know where Karel was.

Meanwhile, in Bratislava, **John Palka**'s *family was also preparing to flee.*

The Iron Curtain was in place. There had been a no-man's-land ploughed along the border. There was a barbed-wire fence down that no-man's-land. There were watchtowers every so many yards, and people were shot if they were caught escaping or, if they weren't shot, they were imprisoned. So how did you get across? The way most people did it was they hired a guide. How did you find a guide who will reliably take you across and not instead report you to the secret police? You had to be very, very circumspect in finding a reliable person, and you had to pay him a fortune to do it. My father had been released from prison, but he was still being watched, so he had to stay well away from any of these arrangements.

We put on multiple layers of clothing, because it was March and it would be the only clothing we would have for some time. We couldn't carry anything conspicuous with us – no suitcases, no backpacks, no valises. My parents put in my mother's purse and my father's briefcase an array of things that were small and valuable: watches, jewellery, a couple of small cameras – anything that could be carried without calling attention to itself and that would be saleable on the black market. That was how the family would live in Austria, if we made it successfully across the border.

It was one of the classic under-the-barbed-wire escapes. What my mother said to me as we were getting ready to go out into no-man's-land was: 'We're going to be like Indians, and we're going to follow the leader who will guide us across. And we won't talk, we won't say anything, so that nobody can hear us. So it will be like Indians making their way as quietly as they can through the forest.' Well, I loved American Indian novels; there's a German novelist by the name of Karl May who wrote a whole series of books about them – completely invented and quite unrealistic, but they were very popular and I devoured a whole bunch of them. So this was a very real world for me, and she tapped into it and thereby kept the immediate danger out of my awareness, while setting it up in such a way that I understood that I was absolutely not to make any noise.

The guides strung a long rope between the two of them, and those of us who were being guided held on to the rope as they crept towards the barbed wire. That rope was our lifeline. There were also all these watchtowers with searchlights. We would run forward when the light was pointing away from us, and we would drop to the ground when the light swung in our direction. Even the footing was difficult because it was ploughed up and it was heavy soil, so there were very large clods of earth that my little feet had to somehow negotiate, while we were running forward and then dropping.

So then we were on the other side and still in a ploughed-up no-man's-land, so we weren't safe. We had just crossed the barbed wire, so then we had to continue this entire process until we got to the woods on the Austrian side. From there we were taken to another safe house. This was the Russian zone of Austria. We had forged papers that identified us as an Austrian family, living in the Russian sector of Vienna, but working in the American sector. So then we were in the American sector of Vienna, surrounded by the rest of the Russian zone of Austria, and we had to repeat this forged paper process going westward into the French zone, where we stayed in Innsbruck for nine months while our papers for the US were put in order.

Karel Janovický
We didn't know whether Sylva and her family had in fact managed to come across unscathed. And she didn't know whether we had managed to get across or not. Her father tried to find out from the authorities, and all he managed to glean was that we'd been sent to this refugee camp in Munich, but nothing more. After four weeks, he travelled to Munich to find us. And after four weeks, I was walking

Karel and Sylva in refugee camp Valka, near Nuremberg, on 21 May 1950, the day before their wedding.

down the street in Munich and I met him. It was pure chance, one in a million.

When we had established who was where, they were eventually allowed to come and spend some time in the refugee camp in Munich. Then we were moved to a camp for students in Ludwigsburg, and they were moved to another camp. I hitchhiked from Nuremberg from time to time to see them, and in their camp I met my favourite uncle, my father's brother – they had also escaped. My own parents had not.

The refugee camps were already full of Latvians, Lithuanians, Estonians, refugees from all over. And now there was this new influx from the expansion of the Soviet empire. So every day there were incidents. A friend of mine had all his immigration papers arranged for America, and then it was stopped. He had to stay in Germany. After about five or six years, he managed at last to talk to somebody at an American embassy and they told him the story. Somebody had sent an anonymous letter to the American authorities saying that he was a criminal on the run. So they automatically stopped his immigration because there were so many people wanting to go to America. It was the secret services of the Communist countries who were doing these things to prolong the chaos in West Germany.

I can feel my first physical relief of being safe at last came when I disembarked at Harwich. When I finally stood on British soil, at last I felt that I was out of it. But up until then it could all have gone pear-shaped.

'There were no weapons, only arguments, ideas'

The Italian Election of 1948

Three years after the end of the Second World War, Europe's division was taking shape. Winston Churchill's warning of an Iron Curtain descending across the continent was becoming plain for all to see, with the Soviets occupying Eastern Europe. And when, in February 1948, Communists took power in Czechoslovakia, it became clear that Italy's election, two months later, would be the next test.

The Italian election in April 1948 was a defining moment. For Moscow, it was an opportunity to harness left-wing and anti-fascist sentiment in Italy to try to extend Communist influence further into Europe. For Western powers, already alarmed by what had just happened in Czechoslovakia, it was of utmost importance not to let the Communist 'contagion', as they saw it, spread further west.

In Washington, in a speech to Congress on 17 March 1948, President Truman warned that 'in Italy a determined and aggressive effort is being made by a Communist minority to take control of that country'. The US State

Department's top Soviet expert, George Kennan, who had already in his co-called Long Telegram of 22 February 1946 laid out a policy of Soviet containment, warned that 'Italy is obviously a key point. If Communists win elections there, our whole position in the Mediterranean, and possibly in Europe as well, would probably be undermined.' 'If Italy goes red,' wrote one State Department adviser, choosing his words pithily, 'Communism cannot be stopped in Europe.'

And so the Italian election of April 1948 became something of a Cold War propaganda contest. But on this occasion, the manipulation of public opinion to ensure the required political outcome was above all orchestrated not by the Russians, but by the Americans.

After years of Mussolini's fascist rule, Italians embraced free elections enthusiastically. In 1946, nearly 90 per cent turned out to vote for a republic to replace the monarchy. Italy's Communist Party was the largest outside the Soviet bloc. There as elsewhere in post-war Europe, the Communists had benefitted from being instrumental in the wartime resistance movement. They argued that their conservative opponents, the Christian Democrats, included those who had compromised themselves by their failure to fight fascism.

But while many voters backed the left as the best chance for a new start for Italy, the support was split between the Italian Communist and Socialist parties, leaving the right-wing Christian Democrats as the largest single party. So in 1948 the Communists and Socialists joined forces. The new coalition, the Popular Democratic Front, was this time determined to win outright.

It was a fight between two competing visions, pitting Communists against Catholics. The left portrayed the Christian Democrats and their allies in the Catholic Church as conservative and capitalist, riddled with collaborators and former fascists. The Church demonised the Communists as godless revolutionaries whose rise to power would unleash a bloodbath.

To promote their anti-Communist cause, the Catholic Church established a network of *Comitati Civici* (Civic Committees) connected to local parishes – a powerful tool in such a Catholic country. Priests preached against the sins of Communism. Propaganda leaflets and films equated Communism with the devil and warned Italian voters that in Communist countries 'children send their parents to jail' and 'people eat their own children'.

This was a battle waged not through a civil war – as in Greece – or the manipulation of politics and protests – as in Czechoslovakia – but through a propaganda campaign staking Italian Communists (with some Soviet backing) against Christian Democrats (amply assisted by the Americans). It was an early instance of the information war so characteristic of the Cold War years to come.

What it was most notable for, though, was the highly effective covert operation to swing the election against the Communists, orchestrated by the United States' newly established Central Intelligence Agency, the CIA. In fact, it was only partly clandestine. Frank Sinatra was one of several Italian-American Hollywood stars enlisted to woo voters over the airwaves. A massive letter-writing campaign from Americans of Italian extraction bombarded friends and relatives in Italy with ten million pieces of mail, including picture postcards, cablegrams and mass-produced letters. The message was always along the same lines: that a Communist victory would ruin Italy, and the United States would cut off aid, and a world war would probably follow. But some of the language was more colourful and personal, with relatives threatening to stop sending money home.

Daily short-wave radio broadcasts also warned of what could happen if the Communists won – including the withdrawal of American aid through the Marshall Plan. The US State Department let it be known that any Italian discovered to have supported the Communists would not be given permission to emigrate to the United States. Meanwhile, the CIA also quietly delivered bags of cash worth millions of dollars to bankroll the Christian Democrat campaign, as well as other organisations and parties opposed to the Communists.

The Soviet Union funded their side, too, though probably to a lesser extent. As in the Greek Civil War, it seems that Stalin was not prepared to overreach himself in Italy, perhaps wary of how the West would react, and also because, according to the post-war agreements of Yalta and Potsdam, Italy was clearly supposed to be in the Western sphere of influence. But still, the competing propaganda polarised the country and ratcheted up tensions. What began as a general election turned into a political proxy war between two emerging superpowers, Soviet and American.

In the end the Christian Democrats won with 48 per cent of the vote, against 31 per cent for the left – not quite a majority but a clear win, which delivered them outright control of Parliament. The Communist share of the vote was almost half what it had been in 1946. The election defeat was a shock for the Italian Communists, who had never seen themselves as Soviet puppets. In the decades to come, they would continue to insist that their brand of Communism was different from that sponsored by Moscow. The American government greeted the result with relief: it meant Italy had resoundingly voted to stay in the Western camp and reject Communism. As promised, American economic aid under the Marshall Plan was immediately despatched to accelerate Italy's post-war recovery.

But perhaps most significant was the precedent the election set for future American covert action elsewhere, as the Cold War contest between capitalism and Communism spread to other parts of the world. The success of the CIA operation in Italy in 1948 laid the groundwork for a pattern of covert American intervention for decades to come. It prompted the National Security Council in Washington to expand the remit of the CIA so that, in the words of a directive dated 18 June 1948, it explicitly included 'propaganda, economic warfare, preventive direct action including sabotage', as well as 'subversion against hostile states' and 'support of indigenous anti-Communist elements in threatened countries of the free world'. All these activities were to be carried out in a way that, if need be, the US government could 'plausibly deny responsibility'.

No longer was the priority to be seen to be winning the moral high ground. Covert action, sabotage and subversion were justified too. Serving the national interest and protecting the 'free world' from Moscow's influence were becoming more important than being right. The necessity to contain the Soviet Communist threat trumped all other considerations.

*The writer **Sergio Romano** was 19 years old when Italy went to the polls.*

After the referendum on the constitutional form of the state – won by the republic – the problem was what to do with the Communists. The Communists and the Socialists had an alliance which strongly resembled the

Popular Front in France in the 1930s, and everybody – the middle class, of course, and the Church in particular – was frightened. They were afraid that they would win the elections, so we witnessed a large mobilisation of priests and nuns and everybody in the field trying to make sure the Christian Democrats would win the elections.

Reconstruction had already begun, and the Marshall Plan was already there by 1948, and people wanted to lead a normal life. From that point of view, the possibility of a Communist victory cast a shadow on the future of Italian politics. Everybody knew that, should the Communists win, well, the future of Italy would be quite different.

The appeal of Communism for a part of the country was strongly linked to the Resistance. In other words, the Communist Party was particularly strong in the centre of Italy and the north, where there was resistance and war against the Germans and the army of the fascist republic. Because the Communists were organised, they did a good job as Resistance organisers, they were brave. In other words, they created an atmosphere of esteem, of admiration even, especially in the lower middle classes, the workers, the farmers; even in the countryside, even the rural community was attracted in certain areas by the Communists.

Journalist and politician **Aldo Tortorella** *was 21 years old at the time of the election in 1948.*

Life after the war was a great ferment of ideas and proposals, but also great discussions and great fights. The thing I remember most, and that was immediately required, was a big battle against the conservatism of the Catholic Church and the party that represented it, the Christian Democrats. It was a very closed world, very reactionary, very conservative. It was a time of many battles and many cultural disputes.

In Naples in the south of the country, the future Italian president **Giorgio Napolitano** *had been a Communist for three years.*

My memory is of destruction and of chaos in the city of Naples. There was, of course, much poverty and there was much disorder. Anyhow, the American occupation was a friendly occupation and we can say that there was a mixing of American soldiers and Neapolitan people. There was, of course, corruption, there was prostitution, but there was also a very friendly feeling. But much poverty and even hunger.

I became a member of the Italian Communist Party in November 1945. I was 20 years old. I had many hesitations about the ideological plan, but I must say that my motivation was fundamentally a moral and political motivation. I was terribly impressed by poverty, by inequality, by the poor condition, the deprived condition, on the part of Neapolitan people, so I felt the need to do something to take my place in the battle for social justice.

Aldo Tortorella *also joined the Communist Party at that time.*

There was no subscription then. I was 17, I had finished high school and entered university. I was introduced to the idea of Communism by a young professor of philosophy. At the university, I went to another great teacher, a great philosopher and scholar of the history of philosophy named Antonio Banfi, also a Communist. So my membership of the Communist Party had an essentially cultural and intellectual character. I thought it was necessary to repair and rebuild a world that was wrong; so much so that we were in the midst of a catastrophic war.

At that time, it also meant being on the side of Stalingrad, because Stalingrad in 1942 was a tremendous epic event for a young man. I was a bit ahead in the studies, so I was informed of the facts. My father used to listen to Radio Londra, of course, like almost all the bourgeois here in Italy. Stalingrad had been, for all of us, a breath-taking, epic story and the beginning of the Nazi defeat.

Giorgio Napolitano

The Soviet Union was the country which gave a fundamental contribution to the victory against Nazi fascism; it was a loyal ally of the United States and of Great Britain and, to my eyes, such complete demonisation after the Second World War was absolutely unjustified. Clearly for young Communists in Italy at that time, the nature of the brutal dictatorship and of Stalin's Soviet Union was not clear, so there was a big mistake in the way to appreciate the Soviet Union by our side. But at the same time, I think that the most dangerous consequence of the Cold War was not to understand the importance of the European project, because also the European project at the beginning was seen by the left as a projection of American imperialism. That was really a very blind position, and we paid for that mistake for decades.

Sergio Romano

In particular, the British were definitely worried at one point, because the Greek experience was very, very close and they knew what was happening in Greece. But the Americans – let's not forget that the very first meeting of the Security Council (recently established in the United States) and the CIA was on the Italian elections, and they studied what measures they would take

Giorgio Napolitano (front row, arms crossed) as an Italian delegate at the World Students Congress in Prague, August 1946. Next to him is Giovanni Berlinguer, brother of Enrico, later Secretary-General of the Italian Communist Party.

if the Communist Party won the elections, if there was a Communist government in Italy, and they discussed the possibility of covert operations. That has been studied by historians, it's fairly well known. But there was no doubt that, in a sense, the Americans were more worried than the Italians.

There was a national discussion about the Marshall fund. The first time, I remember there was a certain amount of scepticism. People hadn't seen the money yet, they didn't really know how the system would work. But it began to work rather quickly, and it was obvious when we understood that the business people, the business community was very eager to take part and was anticipating great advantages from the finance coming from the United States.

Aldo Tortorella

The Marshall Plan was launched in 1947. At first, we didn't speak about it so much, then it appeared to those who thought like me as a proposal – because in the beginning it was a proposal by the US government – to exert a strong influence on the countries of Western Europe, and this view is the one that established itself in the Communist Party, for which there was opposition. Today, I think this decision was probably a mistake. Although the Marshall Plan consisted in total of 14 billion dollars that were certainly convenient for Europe, it also served the United States to exert its hegemony.

Giorgio Napolitano

The Marshall Plan was a great idea for Europe, not only for Italy, of course. According to me, it was the first experience of European integration, due to the initiative of the United States of America. Well, it became very soon an object for distinction and opposition.

Sergio Romano

There was a large percentage of Italian society that sided with the Communists and that really expected a great deal from a Communist revolution, but there was also a very widespread sympathy, liking of the Americans. Also because in a sense the American occupation had been lighter than the British occupation. The American occupiers, many of them were Italian-Americans, and that made the relationship of Italian society with American soldiers considerably easier in many cases. And then Roosevelt had forced the French to abandon that part of Italy on the north-western frontier with France, that the French had at one point eyed as a possible piece of Italian territory to become French – and Roosevelt had asked the French to go, so there was a great deal of liking for the Americans.

The French papers gave a great deal of importance to the announcement of the Western Allies to return the Trieste territory to Italy, and that was done, if I'm not mistaken, between February and March, and it was obviously done to persuade the Italians that they should vote for the West rather than for the Soviet Union in the Italian elections. It was a propaganda move: at the time, Trieste was a free territory and a great deal of territory east of Trieste was occupied by the Yugoslavs and nothing could really be moved, but it was done because they felt that this was useful for the elections.

Aldo Tortorella

There was an extraordinary interest, never seen again. Participation in elections in Italy has always been very high. At that time, there was also a feeling of a very decisive, almost definitive choice. The streets were covered with posters up to the first floor and above. Billposters fought each other for space and there were no regulations or means to enforce them. The rallies were huge: those of political leaders such as the Communist Togliatti or the Christian Democrat De Gasperi kept the central square in Milan fully packed. None of them were demagogues, the kind of speakers you get today. They were both reasonable, with calm words – and yet the crowds were huge. So there was great participation, but there was also a very strong feeling of confrontation.

Sergio Romano
There was a mood of great expectations in a sense. It was obvious that people knew that that election would have a determining effect on the future of the country. At the time, of course, electoral campaigns were made with public meetings and radio; television did not exist, of course.

Giorgio Napolitano
It was a climate of confrontation. It was the first tough confrontation between the left and the Christian Democrats, and there was, I think, very much exaggeration on both sides in the propaganda, which was very aggressive against Christian Democrats and at the same time from Christian Democrats against the left.

There were meetings and there were squares filled with people. That didn't mean very much about the outcome of the election, because, according to the socialist leader, in that epoch you could have the squares filled up with people and the ballot empty.

Aldo Tortorella
The Church entered the election campaign with both feet together, as we say in Italy, with excommunication

for anyone who supported the Communists. Even the churches were mobilised to disrupt rallies, which were held in front of the churchyards out of necessity because the central square in Italy is usually the church square. They rang bells to disrupt the speakers.

Sergio Romano
The Christian Democrats were not terribly united, because there was also within the Christian Democratic Party a rather strong left wing, but for the election of 1948 some sort of unity was accomplished. And then there was a Pope, Pius XII, who had been in Bavaria in 1919 and 1920 at the time of the Soviet-Bavarian republic, so he had made a personal experience at that time. He had been a prisoner in his own palace, threatened with death, so he was definitely an anti-Communist Pope, there was absolutely no doubt about it. And so the Church was very militant at the time.

Giorgio Napolitano
The Church was very active in supporting the Christian Democrats. There was a special organisation called *Comitati Civici*, which was not a political party, but it was a strong element beside the Christian Democrat Party throughout the campaign. Of course, *Comitati Civici* was violently anti-left and anti-Communist, and they based their propaganda on the pillars of family and religion, and they gave a big contribution to the victory of the Christian Democrats.

Sergio Romano
Comitati Civici had been organised by a medical doctor who had really managed to create propaganda against the Communists that was working; there was no doubt it was

working. And the parish priests were very helpful from that point of view, because they made shameless propaganda from the pulpit.

Giorgio Napolitano

There were no weapons in that confrontation. Only arguments, ideas, propaganda, but at a very high level of aggressiveness. And people were divided, because also the squares for the meetings for the Christian Democrat Party were filled with people. So there were, I don't say two halves because the outcome of the elections, as you know, gave 30 per cent to the left and gave almost 50 per cent to the Christian Democrats, but it was a very deep and relevant division.

Aldo Tortorella

The strongest memory is of defeat. The election result was a shock. Not all of us were expecting to win, but we weren't expecting to lose so badly.

Back then, you were either on one side or another, and then the feeling that we had was that a long period would begin. I remember someone said, 'We'll have 20 years of it.' And more than 20 years was not long because then the Communists could again appear between the country's ruling parties.

Giorgio Napolitano

For me, and for all the young people of the left, it was first of all deception, a very deep deception, and it was an absolutely unforeseen result. Because there was the illusion that the Popular Front uniting the left could win the election. For all young people of the left, it was a very deep deception. So: shock, deception and concern for the future. Although some more experienced leaders of the

Communist Party, I remember, were more calm and more confident in the future.

Sergio Romano
There was relief in a good number of people, and I think that, as a result, it was much easier to go back to work the day after.

Aldo Tortorella
I was by then directing the political service of the Milan newspaper *L'Unità*, which was an enormously popular daily at the time. *L'Unità* was the party organ of the Italian Communist Party, but it was not a party bulletin; it was an information paper, and was becoming the second largest newspaper in Italy. So, I was directing the Milan Political Unit [...] and I remember that on the day the election results were announced, our headquarters were besieged by a mob, with its insults and screams against the Soviet Union, which was at the time treated as if it was the same thing as us. We already considered ourselves something different to the Soviet Union. In the years that followed, we were faced with an image of Communism that did not belong to us. Our idea of a progressive democracy which is open to the people was contradicted by what was happening in the Soviet world.

Giorgio Napolitano
It became a destiny of opposition, because it was inconceivable to have a Communist Party participating in the cabinet, and for several years that was the same also for the Socialist Party, until the second half of the 1950s.

Aldo Tortorella

For my generation, one indelible image is that photograph taken in Yalta of Roosevelt, Churchill in the middle, and Stalin – the anti-fascist alliance. Then we saw this alliance break apart, and the United States and the Soviet Union became opposite poles of a world conflict.

Giorgio Napolitano

The Cold War was practically the world split in two. Two blocs and two superpowers. The Soviet Union and the United States were the evil or paradise. It was a complete impossibility to dialogue seriously on the role of great powers – you were with one side and against the other.

Sergio Romano

Of course, we had a clear idea of the Cold War. To begin with, 1948 was also the year of the Siege of Berlin and the air bridge that was organised by the Allies to feed the city during the siege, so we knew there was the possibility of a clash. We did not know yet how close the Soviets were to the atom bomb; the news of the Soviet atom bomb came a year later, in 1949. But then, of course, the possibility of another war was present in everybody's mind at the time. We were not hysterical about it, but everybody thought that the possibility existed.

'We were suddenly shut off'

The Berlin Blockade (1948–9)

Nowhere in the world symbolised the ideological rupture between East and West more than the divided city of Berlin. The Berlin Wall, that archetypal emblem of the Cold War, did not go up as a physical barrier until 1961. But from early on, negotiations between the Allied powers on how to administer occupied Germany and its ruined capital were uneasy, underscoring the conflicting ambitions and fears in Washington, London and Moscow.

At the end of the war, the Yalta and Potsdam conferences of 1945 led to an agreement that Germany, the defeated enemy, would be divided into four military zones, each occupied by one of the Allies – the United States, the Soviet Union, Britain and France. Deep inside the Soviet zone, the capital, Berlin, was further quartered into four sectors, each controlled by one of the Allies. Free access to Berlin through Soviet-occupied territory was allowed along specified road, rail and air corridors. The idea was to ensure that Germany could never again represent a threat to the rest of Europe or attack Russia. The Americans in particular wanted Soviet cooperation over this so that, with Germany tamed, the US Army could go home.

The Berlin Blockade of 1948-9 is the story of how that early prospect of post-war collaboration finally collapsed, as mutual suspicion turned into outright hostility, dividing both the city and the continent for nearly half a century.

In 1945, it had been the Soviet Red Army that delivered the final crushing blow to Hitler's totalitarian regime by entering and occupying Berlin. What those in the city went through next was horrifying. The conduct of some of the conquering Soviet forces was brutal. Berliners who had survived the Nazi regime and wartime bombing were now being subjected to the ravages of a new occupying army. Whole districts had been razed and many buildings were barely habitable. The German currency, the Reichsmark, had become worthless. Impoverished citizens were reduced to bartering or clearing the rubble and cleaning up bricks for reuse. When troops from Britain, France and the United States arrived to set up their separate zones, many Germans cowering in their destroyed city must have felt it was a godsend. But it soon became clear that, depending on which sector of the city you found yourself living in, life was becoming very different.

Stalin's government wanted a weakened Germany not just so that it would pose no future threat, but also because Moscow felt justified in demanding reparations worth billions of US dollars given the devastation left by Nazi armies across wide swathes of its territory. So, in their zone in the East, the Soviets set about stripping the German countryside of anything of value they could lay their hands on. Any useful industrial equipment was dismantled and extracted. They even removed railway tracks and washroom taps to be transported back by train to the Soviet Union. In their zone of occupation, the Soviets also installed a de facto Communist-led government, tightening their political grip after a poor result for Communists in Berlin-wide city elections in October 1946.

The British and American governments had a different view. They were worried that if Germany were stripped of its assets and not helped to recover, it would once again, as after the First World War, become a breeding ground for resentment – even for a revival of Nazism. Their preference was to rebuild Germany into a democratic state with a strong industrial base, to create a new pro-Western ally at the centre of a future prosperous Europe.

Through 1946 and 1947, it became increasingly clear that the gap between the two visions was growing. Western powers watched with alarm as, one by one, countries of Eastern Europe were being turned into Soviet satellite states. For his part, Stalin observed with mounting suspicion that American influence in Europe was not lessening as time went on, but increasing, as Washington announced the bold Marshall Plan and other moves, such as currency reform to boost the German economy.

By February 1948, the West's patience with Soviet Russia was wearing thin. The shock of the Communist coup in Czechoslovakia deepened a conviction that Germany's uncertain status needed urgent attention. At a conference in London, the Americans, British and French laid the groundwork to merge their three zones into a new federal state of West Germany, with a new currency – the Deutschmark. The Soviets had not been invited to the conference and were furious. A month later, at the last ever meeting between all four Allied occupation powers, the entire Soviet delegation walked out in protest, claiming the Potsdam agreement had been breached. In the months that followed, the noose around West Berlin gradually tightened, as Allied access into the city through the Soviet-occupied zone became more difficult. Then, in June 1948, tensions came to a head.

The trigger was the announcement by the Western powers on 18 June that a new Deutschmark would start circulating in their zones to replace the Reichsmark. It was the final straw for the Soviets. They declared that the new Western currency contravened what had been agreed at Potsdam, and banned it from East Berlin and the wider Soviet-occupied zone. Instead, a new currency would be introduced – the East German mark.

In the early hours of 24 June, the Soviet occupying powers closed all transport links between the two halves of the city, including all road, railway and water traffic into and out of Western sectors of the city. Even electricity into West Berlin, which came from generating plants in the Soviet zone, was cut off. The Berlin Blockade had begun.

At the time, West Berlin had only 36 days' worth of food and only 45 days' worth of coal. The city, over 70 miles inside the Soviet-occupied zone, was surrounded by one-and-a-half million Soviet military forces. The Western Allies faced unenviable choices: they could surrender their sectors of Berlin to the Communists; they could let the city starve; or they could respond aggressively – and risk provoking another world war. The final option was to try to break the blockade by bringing supplies in through the air corridors into Berlin, which – unlike the ground routes – were protected by an international agreement.

At first, the idea of an airlift looked hopeless. Berlin's two-and-a-half million stomachs needed 2,000 tons of food a day to survive; most of the available planes carried just 2.5 tons. The city also needed coal for heating, plus everything from tools to medicines.

Stalin's move had made Berlin a testing ground in the emerging Cold War. If the West abandoned Berlin, what would stop the Soviets absorbing the rest of Germany, just as they had swallowed up Czechoslovakia only months before? The first Western transport plane landed in West Berlin on 25 June 1948. The Allies expected the Berlin airlift to last three weeks. Instead, it continued for almost 11 months, ending on 12 May 1949.

Keeping such a big city continuously supplied with even the bare minimum was hazardous. There were not enough American and British planes; the air corridors were constrained; there were treacherous summer fogs; and Soviet pilots buzzed them regularly. To keep the airlift going, pilots were flying until they were exhausted, which often led to accidents and fatalities, and local fire officers at Tempelhof Airport had to be constantly on the alert with fire extinguishers.

But the supplies were a lifeline. Even powdered egg and dried milk were welcome to those who otherwise faced running out of food. One American pilot was so struck by the Berlin kids' stoic acceptance of the blockade that he started dropping chocolate, sweets and chewing gum into the city in handkerchief parachutes. It caught on, and the US Air Force was soon dropping 6,000 consignments of confectionery each day. This was the same US Air Force that only a few years before had been dropping bombs on the city. The irony that the same pilots were now risking their lives to drop food parcels was not lost on some of the locals who expressed their thanks to the Americans.

As the blockade intensified, the Soviets did not try to stop the airlift, but they did attempt to lure West Berliners over to their side with offers of food. However, most refused to give in to Soviet pressure, even though they had no way of knowing how long the Western Allies would keep the airlift going.

A leading Social Democrat, Ernst Reuter, who had been elected Mayor but was prevented by the Soviets from taking up the post, emerged as a champion of the idea that Berlin must stay free. On 9 September 1948, he addressed a huge rally in front of the charred shell that was all that was left of the old Reichstag building. His emotional appeal to 'you people of this world, all you people in America, in England, in France, in Italy! Look upon this city ... and see that you should not and cannot abandon this city and this people!' helped stir sympathy around the world for the besieged West Berliners.

Meanwhile, the Soviet sector was still not cut off from the other sectors of the city. Some Germans in the East even risked the journey across town to take food to their relatives in the West. By the end of 1948, the barrage of technical and logistical problems was slowly being cleared, and the airlift became tenable. Luckily, it was a mild winter. By May 1949, after more than two million tons had been flown to West Berlin and – after 54 deaths in accidents – it became clear that the Berliners and the West together had held out and won a major propaganda victory.

Finally, the Soviets announced that the blockade was being lifted. Stalin had failed to thwart the creation of a West German state. All he could do was respond in kind and sponsor the creation of an East German state – a Communist dictatorship.

The blockade of Berlin transformed the early Cold War. It turned the Americans, British and French, so recently Germany's foes, into its friends. It forced the Americans to realise they could not turn their backs on post-war Europe. And it was yet one more pressing reason to galvanise the war-weary and fractious Western democracies into forging a common military defence pact – which in 1949 became one of the fundamental pieces of Cold War architecture: NATO.

The formation of NATO was momentous for the United States, a country that since the days of its Founding Fathers had preferred to avoid 'entangling alliances', but now found itself committed to a leading role in Europe's collective defence. The emergence of NATO also fuelled suspicions in Moscow that the West, under US leadership, represented a military threat to its interests in the region, suspicions that have persisted to this day.

But that was all still ahead. What emerged from the Berlin Blockade was that a single Western military bloc now stood on one side of Europe against a Soviet bloc on the other, each with its own set of post-war German allies. And any early hopes of German unity had been frozen – it would take another 40 years for that dream to be revived. Meanwhile, the tense, divided city of Berlin would remain the Cold War's focal point for decades.

Gerhard Bürger was a teenager when the war ended.

When the Americans, British and French arrived in 1945, it was like awakening from being half-dead. Berlin had been captured by the Russians, and the city was scared stiff by them. As long as the Russians were there, one couldn't do anything. Everybody had to report to the *Kommandantur* and hand in their radios. Everyone between 16 and 60 had to report for work. The Russians dismantled everything that could be dismantled, from the big factory to the small enterprise. All machinery, whether it was usable or broken, was all sent as far as Białystok.

Then, when the Americans arrived, people went out to greet them. Freedom as opposed to dictatorship. The Russian and Western occupations could not be compared. The Americans started to work with the teenagers, and they set up youth clubs. Life got a meaning again, although we were still poor.

There was a shortage of butter, fats, flour, sugar ... We had ration cards for butter and meat, for example. Those who dealt on the black market were doing well, but the majority of the people were not well off.

There was a disused square – now the Platz der Luftbrücke – directly in front of Tempelhof Airport, where about 1,000 people would meet to trade and bargain, Americans among them. Those who still had rings and bits of jewellery would exchange them for food. Then the police would raid it, and everyone would disappear again. That happened practically every day.

Life was buzzing at the time. There were the girls who flirted with the American soldiers – the so-called Frolleins. When the Americans came to Berlin, there were notices on the bulletin boards that hung at each unit: 'No fraternisation.' Then, shortly before the airlift began, they changed to: 'Fraternisation is first class.' But there were some for whom we remained the enemy. In the American pocket guides, it said: 'Be careful, there is no German who was not a Nazi.' Events proved that the leadership were Nazis, but the majority of Germans were not.

The contrast between the defeated regime and the city's liberators was especially striking to six-year-old **Jürgen Blask**.

It was an extreme change. The Americans came with chocolate, they were so friendly, they didn't need to pounce on the women. They had their cigarettes, the Lucky Strikes, and that was a kind of currency. Life changed completely.

There was a cinema in the street where we lived. The Americans moved in there, and my mum was lucky that she got a job there as an usherette. I was allowed to sit next to her to watch the Allied films, which the Americans wanted to see. Partly, these were war films, because America was still fighting a war with Japan.

Before the blockade, hunger, hunger, hunger – there was no refrigerator, nothing. There were a few Russians who had a sense of social responsibility, and there were places where you could get soup. And if one had a watch or a radio, for example, one could exchange it for something from a garden. Valuable items were exchanged for food. My mum was already working at the cinema and there was one farmer who took cinema tickets from us and in exchange for that we got potatoes and carrots.

One time, there was a dead horse on the street, and some men in our building decided to bring it in. It had already been dead for three days. They butchered it and then people from the neighbourhood who wanted some of the dead horse came too. I remember that I was disgusted, but then it did not taste that bad. My mum said that hopefully there would soon be peace and then there would be bananas and chocolate again.

Gisela Bilski, who was 13 when the Berlin Blockade began, lived with her family in the Soviet sector. She remembers the time before the blockade.

Everything was pretty low. We had ration cards. We could also buy things in the Handelsorganisation's shops, but that was more expensive: a pound of butter was 5 marks instead of 1 mark on the ration cards. We were a big family, and so now and again we sold something in the West in order to shop more cheaply.

The division of Berlin was very obvious to us. In the East, there was no school on Wednesday afternoons. Instead, we had to walk across Berlin, from Ostkreuz to the border of Wedding [in West Berlin], where they were building a big stadium. It was our job to clear away the rubble from the ruined buildings. That was our 'free' afternoon.

The black market had to flourish as we were short of so many things. I used to knit a lot. I took scraps of wool and knitted gloves and socks, and since there was no material to heat with and all the houses were cold, it was easy to sell them. And then you bought something else for that.

Berlin's post-war deprivation was set to worsen, suddenly and starkly, after 24 June. **Gisela Bilski** *had always taken food when she visited her relatives who lived in the Western sectors. And just because the emerging Cold War was cutting their city in half, Gisela's parents saw no reason for her not to continue this tradition. So she became a smuggler.*

It happened overnight and we heard it over the radio. The Russians blocked the streets that gave access to West Berlin, so we tried to provide, as far as possible, for our relatives in the West. Then they installed controls at the borders. At first, Berliners were employed at the controls, and Berliners stuck together and often turned a blind eye. So Saxons were brought from the villages, and they were happy to get their own back on the Berliners. We used to call them our 'fifth occupying power'.

At Friedrichstrasse Station, when one goes west, there is an exit, and behind that exit they built a shack. There, everybody who was pulled out of the train was frisked. Controlled down to the soles of your shoes. I stood there with my apples, and everybody was already eyeing them greedily. So they would not have passed them on but eaten them themselves. I would not have cared. In any case, up there, there was a window open and when the train pulled

Gisela Bilski as a child in East Berlin.

out of the station, I threw the apples in front of the train. The conductor must have got a shock.

The second time, I had five lumps of coal in the bag next to me. Well, they took those off me, too. The third time was when I travelled to see my cousin. I took a pound of butter. This they also found and that was the last straw. So, off with the whole pack of us who had been arrested, into the 'green Minna', as we called the police cars, and I spent the weekend in a room somewhere with those other people who'd been arrested.

At that age, it's all still an adventure. I wasn't really afraid. I was just worried: how soon would I get out, and what would my parents do if I don't return? I was more concerned about them than about myself. When I was released, I wasn't allowed to talk about what had happened. They threatened me.

Gerhard Bürger

The Russians had always harassed people using the three access routes into Berlin, and they would sometimes block them two or three days. But when the complete closure came, that was a shock. The radio and newspapers were full of it. We were suddenly shut off. On the other side, of course, the Russians in the East sector were beckoning: 'Everyone, come to us.' A few did go, because they could go to the Handelsorganisations, the state shops in the Soviet zone. But most did not want to do that.

When the blockade started, no one knew what would happen. There was a whole week of suspense, and of fear. It seemed possible that the British, French and Americans would leave again, and we would become Russian again. That was the potential consequence and, until the decision was made that they were going to stay, you were palpitating with fear. That lasted a few days, until the first aircraft landed.

I was already working for the Americans at the time, in the fire brigade at Tempelhof Airport, and they had no more idea what was going on than we did. We were all puzzling: 'What is going to happen?' Then suddenly the first plane landed. We watched as it came to a standstill then opened its doors, and we saw that it contained food and coal. 'What does that mean?' An hour later, the second plane arrived. 'Boy, does that mean everything is okay again?'

It slowly trickled through that the Americans planned to feed Berlin from the air. People were sceptical. We thought it was not possible, but you can see it worked fantastically. They sustained the whole city with food and coal.

Even after her weekend in prison, **Gisela Bilski** *continued to smuggle goods over to the West.*

Back then, there were also so-called plated socks. These were lady's socks which were a bit warmer, and they were terribly expensive in the West. My mum and I bought some in the East and sold them in the West, so that we could also buy products in the West.

Once, just before Christmas, I came back from West Berlin, and I had chocolate for the children. I was stopped. They asked, 'Where did you get this from?' I said, 'My aunt is ill, and I helped her with the Christmas preparations so she gave this to me as a present. I did not buy it!' Then I was allowed to take it as a present.

Gerhard Bürger

The Americans got planes from all over the world, and also pilots: people from the army, from Canada, from New Zealand – adventurers. We rejoiced that they came and that the pressure from the Russians came to almost

Gerhard Bürger at Tempelhof Airport during the Blockade.

nothing. They must have been cross that this solution was found. We didn't know how long the Russians would put up with it, but that almost didn't matter. The Allies would remain in Berlin – that was the important thing.

When the airlift was up and running, the planes would be emptied at lightning speed. The workers competed with one another to see who could get the plane emptied first. Some of the coal was taken to the power stations and factories, and the rest went to normal people, so they could heat their homes. One American pilot brought cows, and they had relieved themselves in the plane. The pilot was ranting about it.

The airlift went on around the clock. Imagine, at peak times, a plane was arriving every three to five minutes. It slackened a bit at night; perhaps there was a plane only every ten minutes. My hair went white back then because the responsibility was enormous. There would be a line of 120 planes and, each time one took off, we had to be ready with fire extinguishers because the petrol was leaking and it could ignite.

They built an observation point which oversaw the whole airport. We always had a vehicle ready on the Neukölln side, that is the east side of the airport. If they said, 'Smoke in the cockpit,' sometimes an electrical cable was actually smouldering. We had radio contact with the planes, so if they said, 'Smoke in the cockpit' we had to get out there quickly … We had no deaths at Tempelhof, no casualties. The only time when a plane crashed was in the Friedenau [district of Berlin], with two people dead. They crashed into a house. But that did not have anything to do with us. Tempelhof was exemplary.

The boys there were really good, and there were no glitches or breakdowns. There were a few small disasters. There was a C44 where the front wheel broke off, then it slid on its nose through the fence at Tempelhof station and then, thank God, came to a stop. Another got off the runway, but then the undercarriage broke off. The wing got torn off another; it burned, but not the plane itself.

There were always crowds of people by the fence around the airport, looking in curiously. One side was the children's domain, as there were rubbish heaps they could climb to have a good view of the runway.

Jürgen Blask

In 1949, I lived next to Tempelhof Airport. There was a house on the flight path that had been set on fire, but it was still standing, and one could go up the stairs and sit there and watch the air traffic. That was not allowed, of course, but no one paid any attention. For me, it was fascinating because I was a fan of planes. We all wanted to become pilots. We knew all the different types of airplanes. The ones I can remember are the Rosinenbombers [the 'raisin' or 'candy' bombers]: the Skymaster, the four-motor ones, and then the one with two motors was the Dakota. When we sat upstairs in that house, we could tell by the sound of the motors what type of plane it was.

Gerhard Bürger

Some of the pilots were good businessmen. In the back, they would have loads of food, and at the front 30 kilos of coffee or 20 cartons of cigarettes to flog to the workers. The problem was getting it out of the airport. There were military police at the gates, and they frisked everyone. So if you bought a carton of cigarettes from a pilot, the guards might take it off you again as you left.

Then secret passages and tunnels were built, so we could get stuff out. We were quite well off in the fire brigade because we not only looked after the airport, but also the private homes of the Americans in Berlin. If something caught fire in a cellar, we were called and one of our cars drove us there. That was a good opportunity to get things out!

If people did not obey the rules, they got *Alliiertenverbot* – their identity cards were marked and they were not allowed to work for the British, French or Americans. That was a real punishment. The work was much in demand because every bit counted.

Maybe there were some people who made a connection between the planes that had attacked Berlin during the war and the planes that were saving it now. But the main subject after the war was the dispute between the Western Allies and the Russians, who couldn't reach an agreement. The important thing was it was stable and the Allies didn't allow themselves to be pushed aside.

When the planes dropped sweets for the children, **Jürgen Blask** *remembers them flocking to the parachutes.*

We were a bit arrogant, perhaps because we were a bit older. We didn't want to rush there at all costs to get the sweets. Perhaps the grown-ups had given us the feeling that the Allies were still not very well thought of: they were our enemies, and suddenly children were running when they dropped sweets. But that wasn't our problem. We were just excited to see the planes.

The Americans brought us food, and it was exotic food that had an appeal. Pom, that was dried potato purée, which had to be mixed with milk, but that wasn't there, so we used water. Cake, which came in tins. Everything came in plastic and tins, and everything was dried. Peanut butter was for us a sensation – it tasted like heaven. And chewing gum. That's what the Americans distributed, and whenever the Americans came we were blissfully happy.

Gerhard Bürger

Suddenly we heard that the Russians had reopened the roads, then the lorries started coming through. You can imagine the scenes on the streets then. When the blockade ended, I personally was happy because I got rid of an enormous responsibility. By then, I was chief of the fire brigade, so I had the responsibility to make sure everything ran smoothly. Finally, I could relax. The Russians had tried to get the Western Allies out of Berlin, but they had to accept that that would not work. The planes kept getting through, and eventually the Russians had to give up.

If the airlift hadn't happened, then we would have gone back to the Stone Age, from democracy to dictatorship. We had always come last; we were second-class people. And we only got rid of that feeling when the Federal Republic was founded and the first statute came. Then we could finally say, 'It's getting better, and this all has meaning again.'

*Years later, **Jürgen Blask** wrote a letter to the pilots to thank them for what they had done for his city.*

'During the Berlin Blockade in 1949 I lived next to the airport. As a 9-year-old boy, I ran with my friends to the airport every day to watch where the planes landed and took off. We were the most delighted spectators of this kind of air traffic. We were so fascinated to see so many airplanes flying in the shortest time to our airport to bring food and stock to us. So we built toy airplanes with cardboard wings and acorn engines and ran with them through the whole area.

'Each and every one of us wanted to become a pilot like you, some girls as well. Great unhappiness about the end of the Berlin Blockade. Goodbye candy bombers, goodbye dried food.'

Jürgen Blask as a child.

'Then fear replaced pride'

The Fall of Shanghai
(1949)

It was not just in Europe that the end of the Second World War led to a new reckoning and a new beginning. In Asia, too, the tide was turning and new political currents were coming to the fore. In 1947 an exhausted post-war British government began divesting the country of its over-extended empire, starting with colonial India.

Elsewhere in Asia, other governments found that – as in Europe – their assumption that they could revert to the pre-war status quo and return to power as before, relying on a mixture of corruption, cronyism and repression, was no longer a given. As in Greece and Yugoslavia, left-wing resistance movements, which had fought against invaders and in the end defeated them, felt they had earned the right to decide the political shape of what came next. And in Asia, none felt more entitled to a part of the new peace than the Chinese Communist forces led by Mao Zedong.

Mao had first led his Communist insurgents to challenge the Republican government of Chiang Kai-shek in 1927. It was an ideological split between Mao's Communists and Chiang's Nationalists that ended five years of earlier collaboration and launched China's protracted on–off civil war. In 1937, the two sides put aside their differences to forge an uneasy common front against Japan, which had launched a full-scale invasion of China, occupying parts of it. After the Japanese attack on Pearl Harbor in 1941, this Sino-Japanese war merged into the greater conflict of the Second World War. But in 1946, one year after the Japanese surrender, China's civil war resumed with renewed vigour, this time with the balance of power shifting in favour of the Communists.

By 1946, 'Liberated Zones' controlled by Mao included one-quarter of mainland China's territory and one-third of its population, including many important towns and cities. His People's Liberation Army (PLA) numbered 1.2 million troops and a further 2 million under arms in militias. He could draw on further support from millions of desperate peasants who he promised would get their own land once the war was over.

By contrast, Chiang Kai-shek's Kuomintang (KMT, Nationalist Party of China) armies, overstretched and weakened by the Second World War, lacked the same unity and resolve. The United States government, already alert to the Soviet Union's inroads into Europe and under pressure from the pro-Nationalist 'China lobby' in Washington, was concerned about another major world power 'going red' and poured in billions of US dollars of military aid and despatched tens of thousands of US troops including Marines to train, equip and transport KMT forces and to guard strategic sites.

But not all officials in Washington saw Chiang Kai-shek and his Nationalist forces as the best bet. In 1946, after an abortive US attempt to broker a ceasefire in China, the US Secretary of State, General George Marshall, assessed that the Nationalists were unlikely to win the civil war. His successor, Dean Acheson, warned against predicting events 'until the dust settles' and referred to Chiang Kai-shek's government in a document on US China policy as 'a regime without faith in itself and an army without morale'.

On their side, the Chinese Communists enjoyed some Soviet support, but Moscow also signed a Treaty of Friendship with Chiang Kai-shek after the Second World War, apparently believing that the Nationalists were more likely than Mao and his largely peasant army to keep the peace inside China and on the Soviet Union's southeastern border. Whether Stalin underestimated Mao or conversely was wary of him as a potential Communist rival is unclear. But Mao's forces did benefit from captured Japanese weaponry, supplied in part by the Soviets, and over the next four years the People's Liberation Army slowly won the upper hand.

By the spring of 1949, a succession of decisive campaigns had resulted in astronomical casualties on both sides, but had allowed the Communist forces to capture the KMT's capital, Nanjing. With the Nationalists on the back foot, the focus of the civil war moved to the city known as 'the Paris of the East' – Shanghai.

The largest and wealthiest city in China, Shanghai had a population of six million people and accounted for about a third of the country's economy. It had been under Japanese occupation, but control reverted to the Nationalists after the war, a major prize that Chiang Kai-shek could not afford to lose. It was also a trophy that Mao Zedong and his People's Liberation Army were determined to take, as they edged towards their goal of turning China into a Communist state.

By May 1949, the prime concern for many residents of Shanghai was the terrifying economic collapse under the corrupt and incompetent KMT government. The unemployment rate in the city already stood at over 37 per cent. For these people, the notion of Mao Zedong's Red Army taking over the city did not seem such a bad prospect.

What they did not see was what life was like out in the countryside, where Communist officials and the People's Liberation Army had already taken control and were confiscating private property as part of a promise to redistribute land. Impoverished peasants were encouraged to vent their anger and take revenge on 'rich landlords' at public meetings. One estimate suggested that, between 1947 and 1952, as many as 2 million so-called landlords may have been executed and land redistributed to some 300 million peasants.

The Nationalists, still nominally in control of Shanghai, knew that they were heavily outnumbered. But they mistakenly assumed that too much was at stake in global politics for them to have to fight Mao's army alone. They believed that if they could hold out against an initial attack, Western allies were bound to intervene with a counterattack to prevent a Communist takeover of such an important stronghold. So their plan was to station forces to defend the city and wait for help to come, and if necessary fall back on an escape by sea, torching the city behind them.

But the People's Liberation Army pre-empted them. In mid-May, it moved in with a pincer movement that took over the city's suburbs and cut off any escape route by sea. What's more, the Nationalists, perhaps cynically without regard for life or perhaps to avoid panic, had neglected to tell the population to evacuate the city. When residents learned of their leaders' plan to torch the city and flee, they were outraged. They organised themselves to protect buildings, banks and other parts of crucial infrastructure. Some Nationalist commanders still managed to escape by sea, but many were blockaded by Communist forces and had no option but to surrender. Within days, the city centre was in Communist hands.

The fall of Shanghai was an important victory. It paved the way for the pivotal moment just a few months later, in October 1949, when the Nationalist hold on China finally crumbled and Mao Zedong proclaimed a new People's Republic of China, the PRC. China was now the most populous Communist nation on earth.

In Washington, there was consternation, and a blame game began over who had 'lost' China. The pro-Nationalist 'China lobby' argued that the fight against Communism had gone global, and the United States and its allies now faced not just one, but two great Communist powers in Europe and Asia: Soviet Russia and Red China.

But some US officials mused that perhaps Mao Zedong would turn out to be an independent-minded 'Asian Tito' and that, like Yugoslavia's Marshal Josip Tito, also a former guerrilla fighter, he would resist being pulled into the Soviet orbit. Dean Acheson argued that an American rapprochement with Mao's government might help drive a wedge between China and the Soviet Union.

As a short-term prospect, that looked unlikely. Already, in a speech on 30 June 1949, Mao had unequivocally aligned Communist China with its Soviet 'Big Brother', dismissing Britain and the United States as capitalist imperialists and declaring that 'we must lean to one side ... Sitting on the fence will not do ... The Communist Party of the Soviet Union is our best teacher and we must learn from it.' In December 1949, he accepted an invitation to meet Stalin in Moscow, and during his two-month stay there they worked out a new common strategy, including a 'division of labour' to promote world revolution in both Europe and Asia.

They also signed a Sino-Soviet Treaty, which appeared to be a deliberate echo of the treaty to establish NATO, just signed by the Western Allies. As with NATO, this was a mutual defence pact in case of attack on one of its members, forging a new defensive link between the world's two global Communist powers.

By now, Chiang Kai-shek and the Nationalists had established a government-in-exile on the island of Taiwan, where they had fled the previous year. Mistakenly, they hoped that it would be a temporary stronghold until foreign support arrived to help them take back the mainland. In fact, the exile would be more or less permanent. Communist China would still be in charge of the mainland more than 65 years later, outlasting the Soviet Union, in time growing in stature to challenge even the United States for global clout.

And in the Cold War decades to come, and the post-Cold War years that followed too, the clash of titans – American, Russian, Chinese – would become triangular, a story of shifting alliances and tensions that encompassed the globe, as each played one off against the other.

*In 1949, **Eddy Hsia** and his family were living in the remote countryside south of Shanghai, where they had moved several years earlier to escape the worst of the Japanese occupation during the Second World War.*

After the war, many of the KMT government officials were corrupt, and their corruption spread all over China. So they gradually lost the people's support and confidence, and that was one of the main things that promoted the Communists' success. I didn't know much about the situation – I only knew that the Communists were coming. At that time, I had heard so much about the bad side of the Communists, I just wanted to be away, so I went to Canton and then to Taiwan. I did not have my family with me; I was alone.

The Communist forces, wherever they went, their first so-called struggle was against the landlords, and they killed a lot of landlords. Some were real landlords. Some just owned a small piece of land, but they classified them as landlords. They killed them, without justice, without trial. They had the right to kill whoever they wanted. People were afraid of the Chinese Communists. So we knew, if they came, we'd better escape.

Some things I try to forget. My mother was killed by Communists. She was considered a member of a landlord's family. But that was not true: she did not have any land herself. We were not rich people, but we had some land in the countryside, in a very remote village up in the mountains. There was no highway; you had to get there on foot. In the remote countryside, you cannot have anything like a rich farm – it's impossible. The Communists just wanted to kill as many people as possible, for whatever reason they could find. So then definitely I had my personal hatred about the Communists. She was an innocent woman. Why did they kill her? She did not do anything wrong. She was just a housewife. She was killed, shot. One bullet. During those years, when the Communists killed someone, they asked the family of the people they killed to pay for the bullet. I cannot understand, I cannot forgive, I cannot forget.

When I arrived in Taiwan, I had no family, no support, no job. So what could I do? I joined military service. We did not know how long we would stay in Taiwan – maybe three months, and then we'd go back to mainland China. At that time, people would say, 'Maybe at most a year, you'll be back to mainland China.' I remember some of my relations also went to Taiwan from Shanghai. And their parents told them to enjoy their holiday in Taiwan: 'When the Communists settle down, you can come back.' Nobody realised the Communist government would be in place for ever.

*Betty Barr Wang was born in Shanghai in 1933; her father was a missionary teacher from Glasgow, and her mother was from Texas. Her future husband, **George**, was also born in Shanghai, in 1927, and was working in a newspaper office in May 1949 as the Communist forces approached the city.*

George

After 1945, in a way we were just enjoying the victory over the Japanese, so we didn't know there was a civil war. The first time I heard there was a civil war was in October 1946, and during 1947 things got worse and worse. I knew a driver who had been punished by the Kuomintang: he was a driver for the government, but he was accused of carrying somebody who was a Communist Party member. He was imprisoned and lost his wife and child. The aim of the civil war was to liberate the people from the Nationalist government.

Betty

Things were so bad under the Nationalists, mainly because of the extreme inflation. For example, there's a photograph of my mother holding a tray with a huge pile of cash on it – this was a month's salary – before they had to rush to the bank with it to buy silver or dollars to preserve the value of it.

George

I had to change my salary into silver coins or US dollars. Every month when we got our salary, our office allowed us to go out for half an hour or so because we had to change our salary into silver coins or US dollars through the black market in the street, because if we took our banknotes home, by the time we arrived in the evening our salary value was cut in two.

Betty

That created great uncertainty and so I think people thought anything must be better than this. At that time, I was a teenager attending an American school in Shanghai, and so I really was not very aware of what was going on. Except that in 1948–9 our school year began with quite a number of students, and many left during that year because people were afraid of what was going to happen when the Communists came. The Communists were coming down from the north – Peking was already in the hands of the Communists, and there were stories circulating. There were many rumours, but nobody really knew what was going to happen.

At the end of May 1949, we were taking our final exams. One morning, we got up and looked out on to the street and we saw one lone, young PLA soldier wearing rubber shoes, holding a rifle, standing there, guarding our school.

George

The first time I saw a PLA soldier, he seemed to be like an officer, and he just told people, 'Don't stand near the road, just stand inside of the pavement, otherwise you might be killed.' So to me it was not like fighting, it was like making a film. I crossed the road to the other corner, hoping to see more clearly. By the time I got to the middle of the road – *whooo!* – a bullet over my head!

A small number of people were afraid, but they were the upper class. But all our neighbours welcomed the liber-

Betty and George Barr Wang.

ating army. They arrived about ten o'clock in the morning and, when I went home in the evening, the soldiers were sitting on the pavements. They never bothered the neighbours. The only thing they asked for was fresh water. They were so polite.

Betty

The PLA soldiers made a very good impression on the local people when they arrived in the city. The *North China Daily News*, the English-language newspaper at that time, had several articles about the good behaviour of the soldiers.

I saw the victory parade. Before it took place, some of my father's students, boys in a boys' secondary school, came to my father and said, 'Mr Barr, can we please borrow your hat and your walking stick?' He said, 'Certainly, with pleasure.' We went to watch the parade and I can remember it to this day. It was a very long procession and suddenly coming along in this very long procession were two figures: one was Uncle Sam, and one was John Bull; they were being caricatured at that time by the Chinese Communists. And there on the head of John Bull was my father's hat, and he was carrying my father's walking stick. So we saw them go by, and after the parade my father's students came back and returned them and said, 'Thank you very much, Mr Barr.' Up to that point, they were not thinking of him as an imperialist enemy; they liked him, and they admired him. Personal relationships endured, in spite of big movements.

George

The first thing the Communists did was set up a monetary committee to get rid of the speculators and stamp down on inflation. So people felt their money was safe, and the majority of people loved the new government. Our living standards were certain now.

Betty

Within a few days, the problem of inflation was solved, so they had planned it all.

I was in Shanghai for the first year after the Communist victory, until the spring of 1950. A lot of missionaries and businessmen stayed at first, because nobody knew what was going to happen, and so my parents stayed until late 1952. There was a point, they told me later, when they were denounced by the Chinese teachers in the school, who surrounded their house and shouted slogans. But that was about the worst thing that ever happened.

My parents were given a farewell banquet, Chinese-style, when they left. My mother told the story of how, with great ceremony, a big melon was brought in – usually it had soup inside and had a Chinese dragon carved intricately on it. This time, it was carved with the words 'Down with the American imperialists', and they put it on the table right in front of my mother.

George

Because the Communist Party wanted to run the city, they had to educate people to know what their aims were. Mainly they wanted people to understand their policy, and their policy was just one sentence: Serve the people wholeheartedly. At first, only those working in government offices had re-education.

Betty

I was taking pipe-organ lessons in the Anglican cathedral, and suddenly we heard a plane overhead. My teacher was very frightened, so we went down into the crypt to hide. It was the Nationalists, coming to bomb the city. Shanghai was blockaded, so no ships could get in to bring imported food and goods like that. That was very difficult for the city, and gradually there were no more imports and exports, and therefore the foreign businesses had to close down, and therefore the foreigners gradually left.

George

The whole country was blockaded. The main idea of the bombings was to destroy the power stations. The Nationalist slogan was that the Communist Party would only hold Shanghai for three months. China has only 7 per cent of the world's land, yet China had to support 25 per cent of the world's population. Without enough cultivable land and without enough fresh water, how could China grow enough rice to support the people? For a long time, China had to import rice from south-eastern countries. So once the country was blockaded, there was starvation. It was nothing to do with who was leading the country – it was the blockade. So, just think how difficult it was for the new Communist leaders of Shanghai to ensure that the people had enough food. There was a song praising Mao Zedong, and I came to understand why people sang this song.

You pray that you will go to heaven. I am in heaven. When I was a child, my mother often sighed, 'Oh, they are so lucky, [they] don't have to worry about clothing and food.' Now everywhere in China, even the poorest area, do they worry about these two things? No. So that's why we are in heaven. But not many people in the West understand this.

Betty

As I see it, yes, many unhappy things have happened since 1949, but I think the proof of the pudding is in the eating, and what George is talking about is the raising of so many people out of poverty. I think it's 500 million. It's an astonishing thing that has happened in China, in spite of unhappy things which have happened, and we feel that many Westerners don't give credit to the Chinese government for that.

Liliane Willens was a 21-year-old of Russian descent, who was born and raised in Shanghai.

I was born in Shanghai in 1927. My parents had met in Shanghai, as they had both fled separately from the Bolshevik revolution, my father from Kiev and my mother from Siberia. They knew that Shanghai was controlled by the three powers – the British, the Americans and the French – and they felt safe. My two sisters and I were born there, we lived in the French concession, and we went to a French school. There was no reason to learn Chinese; we all lived in a bubble. In 1924, the USSR had denationalised all those who had fled Russia, so we were stateless.

During the Second World War, we lived through three-and-a-half years of Japanese occupation, and when they left there was euphoria. But Chiang Kai-shek's regime was very dictatorial and very repressive. China was helped by the Americans, but when the money was received it went into the pockets of the Chiang Kai-shek clique. Things were getting to be very difficult in Shanghai at that time. There was utter corruption. There was poverty. When I was riding my bicycle to go to school we used to see straw bundles: these were children who had died of famine or starvation or cold during the night.

Things had deteriorated to such a point by 1948 that many foreigners had left and many Chinese with passports had emigrated. People heard about the Communists, a little propaganda: that they were very good, they were very

Liliane Willens.

decent, they never robbed the peasants. So it got to the point where people were waiting for the Communists to come. We believed that they were not Soviet Communists, they were *agrarian* Communists.

The People's Liberation Army walked into Shanghai on 25 May 1949, and things started changing. For the first six months, from May to October, it was a honeymoon. The new government was saying, 'We are here to help you. We are here to make a better life for you.' This was the first time in 5,000 years of Chinese history that the government ever did something for the people. There was entertainment in the streets – the soldiers were parading, there was dancing for the public. The only thing you couldn't do was walk behind a soldier when they walked in the streets, because you had to always walk in front.

I was quite shocked to see that they were poorly dressed, because I had seen the Kuomintang soldiers all equipped by the USA with guns and beautiful uniforms. They were poorly dressed and very quiet, walking in singing 'Down with imperialism'. And also when they were tired they slept on the sidewalk and they didn't take anything from the people. These were peasant boys, gawking, walking around. I remember seeing one in front of a store with refrigerators; they didn't know what a refrigerator was. There was a joke going around that when they washed their rice they washed it in the toilet. There was total illiteracy; I think 85 per cent of the Chinese population was illiterate.

They were very smart when they walked in. First, there was re-education. They realised nobody could read, so they had free comic books in the streets. This is how it started, little by little: 'We are here to help you. We are your family. Forget about Confucius; Communism is your family now.' The propaganda was very strong, very serious: 'You better behave.'

When Mao declared the establishment of the People's Republic of China on 1 October 1949, the USSR recognised the PRC the following day and things started changing. The laws became more restrictive. You had no right to criticise the People's Republic or Communism. They were very shrewd about saying: 'If you have properties, we'd like you to register them.' This was a ploy: during the Chiang Kai-shek era, it had been very difficult to collect rent, but if the properties were registered they could collect rent and taxes.

We still had a nanny in our house, and they wanted her to report on what was happening in our house. Every week, she had to attend a propaganda meeting. She told us about an ambulance arriving at a house – they had been into the house and shot a Kuomintang follower, but they didn't want anyone to know, so they carried the body out on a stretcher as if they were collecting someone who was sick.

You had posters of the good Communist soldier stomping on the belly of the – usually American – imperialist. I saw one rather scary situation where they had demonstrations, and they had a show trial of a so-called guilty party. Usually, their crime was to have been a Kuomintang spy, or you had criticised Communism. And the cadres were there, telling the people, 'He's guilty, he's guilty,' and they yelled, 'Hit him, hit him,' and you knew that person would be found guilty, given a dunce's hat and then taken away and probably shot. The big word was 'Fear' – fear settled in the country.

The Chinese were very proud. Finally, the country was united. No foreigners out there, no more fighting, the warlords had disappeared, and you had one country – and it was China.

First time. So there was a lot of pride at the beginning, no question about it. And then fear replaced pride.

Things were tightening. And that was the first time I realised what it means not to have freedom: it's like you no longer can breathe. And *you* can't talk about freedom which you have in England and elsewhere unless you lose it. It's like love: unless you fall in love, you don't know what love is.

'The trap shut'

The Korean War (1950–3)

From 1910 until the final days of the Second World War, Korea was under the harsh rule of imperial Japan. In August 1945 Moscow declared war on Japan, and Soviet troops began advancing through Manchuria towards Korea's northern border.

Fearing Soviet expansion, the Americans proposed dividing Korea along the 38th parallel. Soviet troops could have occupied the whole country but, taking the United States aback, Moscow agreed to the division. The deal placed 16 million Koreans in the American zone and 9 million Koreans in the Soviet zone to the north.

The original plan was to work towards a unified administration, so that within five years Korea could be free and independent. But mounting antagonism between the rival Korean governments put paid to that. Korea was to become the focus of a new tug of war in the geopolitical battle for influence.

Soviet forces withdrew from the North as agreed in 1948, and the bulk of US troops left the South the following year. Yet for ordinary Koreans, the end of occupation brought not liberation but a country split between two unsavoury regimes, each vehemently and ideologically opposed to the other, with frequent clashes along the border.

In the South, a brutal anti-Communist, Syngman Rhee, carried out wide-spread repressions to keep the lid on rebellions blamed on Communist guerrillas. In the North, an even more brutal leader was in charge: Communist Kim Il Sung had trained with Soviet troops in Manchuria and was to be the first in the dynasty of isolationist and despotic leaders who continue to rule North Korea.

In 1949, Kim Il Sung tried to persuade Moscow to support an invasion of the South to reunify the country and bring it all under his control. At first, the Soviet leader, Joseph Stalin, was cool to the idea. But by April 1950, the outlook was more promising. US troops had completed their withdrawal from South Korea, the Soviets had detonated their first atomic bomb, and the Americans had been unable or unwilling to prevent a Communist victory in China's Civil War. So Stalin gave Kim Il Sung permission to mount an invasion, promising Soviet military aid and advisers but not combat troops, so long as the Chinese agreed to send reinforcements if needed.

On 25 June 1950, the first North Korean troops advanced across the 38th parallel, sweeping south so fast that they overwhelmed all opposition. The South Korean army was unprepared, and most large US garrisons in the region were stationed in Japan. Within days, the South Korean capital, Seoul, was captured and the North Korean army was pressing further south towards the key port of Busan on the country's south-eastern tip.

In Washington, there was considerable alarm. If Stalin was prepared to use his proxy, Kim Il Sung, to go to war in Korea, where would be next? Japan? West Germany? President Truman was also worried about the Middle East.

'Korea is the Greece of the Far East,' his adviser George Elsey later recalled Truman as saying. 'If we are tough enough now, if we stand up to them like we did in

Greece, they won't take any next steps. But if we just stand by, they'll move into Iran and they'll take over the whole Middle East. There's no telling what they'll do if we don't put up a fight now.' Despite fears that a conflict in Korea could trigger another world war, this time with both sides armed with atomic weapons, the Truman administration decided it had to act.

The forces that came to the aid of the South Koreans were under United Nations auspices and included troops from 22 nations – from Greeks to Indians, Turks to Thais – and equipment from 25 more, but 90 per cent of the troops were American. On 5 July, US troops came face to face with the Communist North Korean advance, but their positions were overrun and they were forced to flee southwards in disarray.

North Korea's decision to invade – and the Americans' decision to send in troops in response – was a pivotal moment. It meant the United States and its allies were no longer just manoeuvring and shadow boxing to contain Communism; now they were caught up in a vicious shooting war, fighting Communists face to face. And the fighting was not in Europe, the main focus of tensions to date, but far away in Asia. The Cold War had exploded into a bloody conflict with potentially global ramifications.

Three months after the invasion, the tide began to turn. Reinforcements, now under a UN umbrella, arrived to defend a North Korean attack on the southern port of Busan. Meanwhile, General Douglas MacArthur decided to outflank the North Koreans and cut off their supply lines. On 15 September 1950, he launched a daring American landing behind enemy lines at the port of Incheon, halfway up the peninsula on Korea's west coast, to seize Seoul back. The North Koreans were trapped and forced into a hurried retreat, with the US-led UN forces in hot pursuit.

But there was another factor to contend with. Across the border to the north, Mao Zedong proclaimed a giant new Communist power: Red China. The mammoth People's Liberation Army represented a far more formidable foe than Kim Il Sung's forces. When China decided to come to its Communist brethren's aid and enter the war on North Korea's side, the Americans found they were up against an enemy in a different league.

On 25 October 1950, China's counter offensive unleashed its armies across the border from the north, expelling US and South Korean troops southwards. For the second time in six months American and South Korean troops were forced to beat a rapid and chaotic retreat southwards, and once again the battle front shifted. By mid-December, the embattled UN troops, most of them American and South Korean, were in serious trouble. President Truman declared a national emergency and ordered a massive evacuation from the North Korean port of Hungnam, on the north-east coast of the peninsula, to get them out.

But not only military personnel wanted to leave. The cost of the war was counted not just in the casualty figures – some two million Koreans were killed before it was all over – but in millions of desperate refugees. They criss-crossed the country as they fled the fighting, evacuating their homes, seeking protection from bombing raids, and dodging the press gangs searching for new recruits for the North Korean army. First, they streamed northwards to escape the American advance, and then south to avoid the Chinese arriving from the north. They carried babies, pushed handcarts and tried not to lose track of family members. American servicemen who witnessed it remember a biblical exodus.

So when local North Koreans heard that American warships were arriving for an evacuation, they flooded to the port of Hungnam too, hoping to be allowed on board. Many of them were in a woeful state, with almost no personal belongings, shelter or food, in a freezing, snowy winter.

And now one of the most extraordinary episodes of the Korean War unfolded. When the flotilla of naval and merchant vessels arrived, along with the US and Korean troops they had come to evacuate, they allowed tens of thousands of Korean refugees on board too, in an act of compassion and mercy. The SS Meredith Victory, a freighter licensed to carry only 12 passengers, even jettisoned its military cargo to make room for 14,000 refugees, all packed like sardines, including five babies delivered by the first mate during the voyage. All in all, 100,000 troops and as many refugees were transported to safety, in nearly 200 shiploads, finally reaching the South Korean port of Busan after several days at sea. It felt like an astonishing escape. And it was almost Christmas. No wonder the evacuation from Hungnam in December 1950 became known as the 'Christmas Miracle'.

It took two-and-a-half more years for the war to end. And even then, in July 1953, no peace treaty was signed, just an armistice agreement, which brought about a cessation of hostilities and the creation of a demilitarised zone between the two sides, to be patrolled at all times.

The Korean War had important outcomes. South Korea, along with nearly two-thirds of the population, was saved from Communist rule and would in time become a remarkable success story. North Korea remained trapped in the clutches of a stifling and oppressive dictatorship. The Americans had been given a sobering taste of what could happen when Cold War posturing and politicking turned into a hot war. They were also awakened to the idea that Communism was as much a threat to their interests in Asia as in Europe, and in response they ordered an unprecedented military build-up.

Well over half a century later, the division of the peninsula has become entrenched. The front line between North and South is the most heavily guarded in the world and is seen by many as the most dangerous potential flashpoint on earth. It is a legacy of the Cold War that persists unresolved to this day. And for those whose families were torn apart, it remains a trauma yet to be healed. The refugees who spoke to us made it to safety in 1950, but they paid a price.

Schoolgirl **Lee Hoo Ja** *fled with her father and older sister but had to leave her mother and younger sisters behind in North Korea. They made it out on a later evacuation, but the grandparents did not.*

I was born on 11 June 1936. My family consisted of my grandfather who was 78, my grandmother who was 64, and my father who was the eldest of his siblings. I had an elder sister who was six years older, an elder brother who was born three years before me, a sister who was two years younger, a nine-year-old brother, and finally a five-year-old sister. We lived comfortably in Hungnam at the time. There was farming, prosperous fishing and light manufacturing – fertiliser, a wide range of shoes, alcohol, a tremendous amount of rice. The fishing grounds were so rich that, when we went out to the beaches, we could easily discover huge clams in the sand.

I was just an ordinary schoolgirl. School was my life and my ambition was to become a politician or a diplomat. I was the class president at the time and all of my classmates would assemble in the morning in the front yard of my house. Following my lead, they would all stand in a straight line and together we would shout, 'One, two, one, two,' as we marched together to school.

Lee Hoo Ja's primary school graduation photo. She is in the
second row, eighth from the left. The portraits of Stalin and Kim Il
Sung that hung from the school walls were later erased when she
was living in South Korea.

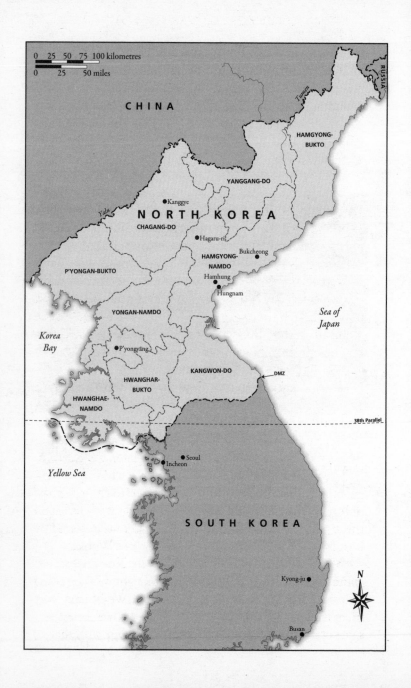

Whenever the school headmaster called out my name in the morning assembly, I would instantly know that I was in trouble again. My family was often targeted because my uncle had earlier fled to the South, and the authorities would come around to our place to inspect the bookshelves. Any books that were deemed ideologically inappropriate were taken away.

On 15 September 1950 there was the Incheon landing by the American and South Korean forces, and by 18 September the South Korean flag was flying once again in Seoul. Later, I learned the same unit had pressed northwards, and later some of the soldiers ended up near where we lived. One of the soldiers came to our house and asked our family if we could cook for their group, three meals a day. They didn't require a place to stay, but only help with their meals. About 70 soldiers were in the group altogether. Every three days or so, they would bring butchered beef and we would cook it for them.

Norman Deptula *had his 21st birthday while serving in Korea as part of MacArthur's invasion forces.*
The invasion actually began on 15 September with the 1st Marine Division, and then my company landed at Incheon on 25 September. A short time later, we moved to […] Yeongdeung po. We were there for a while, and then eventually MacArthur wanted to move us to the east coast of Korea. So one day, early in the morning, we were given the word to get in our trucks, and we were transferred by boat from the west coast to the east coast at Wonsan.

When we first entered the area, the Koreans put up white flags, ready to surrender – they thought we were going to invade and imprison them. We didn't! We became very friendly with them: they gave us fresh eggs; we gave them some of our rations, and they were quite happy with that.

Elsewhere in North Korea, before the war broke out, **Sohn Dong Hun** *wanted to go to university, but he says the regime forbade it as his family was too middle-class.*

My family was not rich, but we did live comfortably on a medium-sized farm in Bukcheong, and we had a separate farm growing fruit. After liberation in 1945, Kim Il Sung entered the North, the land reforms were initiated, and our family land was all taken from us. I graduated in 1949, and upon my graduation I earned my licence as a state veterinarian. I was placed at the national veterinary research centre in Pyongyang.

When the Korean War broke out in 1950, I was working at the research facility. After the UN forces landed at Incheon in September, the retreating North Korean army arrived in Sariwon on 10 October. That day, the research staff at our institute were told to evacuate north, to Jagang Province, to an area called Kanggye. I went east instead, over mountain after mountain, passing Hamhung and finally reaching Bukcheong after two weeks of trekking over hills. When I got home, my parents were stunned to see me because they thought I was already dead, and that I had been reborn from the dead.

Norman Deptula

We got word that my radio relay team was to break up all our gear, load it and report to a company at Hamhung. The next day, four people from our team were to move to the Chosin Reservoir, to the hamlet of Koto-ri, 70 miles from the Manchurian border. We left early in the morning, and it was a beautiful sunny day. We went higher and higher, and we reached an elevation of 4,000 feet. The wind was howling, and it was very cold, bitterly cold. The truck we had had been manufactured for duties in the desert: it had no sides; it had a canvas top. Eventually, we found our hill.

Another relay team was already there, and they had their tents set up. We heard a lot of noise that night – gunfire – but nothing happened.

What we didn't know until later was that there were about 120,000 Chinese, and only about 16,000 of us. I heard about a Chinese general who told his soldiers to 'kill those Marines as you would snakes in your home'. But we just knew that we were pretty well surrounded. As we were driving up into the mountains, Chinese troops were looking down on us. We had troops getting in, but they were fired on if they tried to get to our area. So we were there, trying to supply communications.

On 27 November, the trap shut. We had a radio terminal team at Hagaru-ri, and we tried to contact them. We could hear our terminal team at Hungnam, and we could hear them north of us, but we couldn't transmit our messages to them. The answer to that was to move our equipment to a higher location – there was one right across the road at the bottom of our hill – but it was held by the Chinese. On the first night, we sat there expecting the whole Chinese army to attack us. We tried again and again and again to make contact.

We were supplied by air. I remember the planes would come in at the northern end of our valley, swoop low then – as they reached our hill at the southern end – they would swoop up, and all these parachutes would come falling down on plywood panels. The parachutes were different colours: white for medical supplies, red for ammunition. As they came down, the colours made it look like a bright spring day.

Then we got word that our troops to the north, the Marines to the west and a regimental combat team to the east, under fire, had withdrawn to Hagaru-ri, where there was an airstrip where they could send out casualties and bring in supplies and replacements.

We had a group coming from Hagaru-ri, and we left the hill and set our tents up in the valley, and we took turns waiting for our team to come in. There were trucks coming through. I was waiting by the side of the road with one of my buddies, and he told me to look in the back of a two-and-a-half-ton truck. We saw boots stacked on top of each other – they were the bodies of those that had been killed. And as the truck hit a bump in the road, these frozen bodies would bump up and down.

Then came the big push from Koto-ri to Hungnam port. We had troops on either side of the hills to provide protection from ambush, and we slowly went along. It was a 40-mile trip, but it took 26 hours to get there. And then around 20 December we were told to report to the dock at Hungnam for evacuation.

Sohn Dong Hun
After about 40 days of relative happiness, talk about the need to retreat and evacuate surfaced. The thinking was that we could get away for just a couple of months and wait for the UN troops and South Korean forces to return. So the men in my family – my father, my uncle and myself – decided to go away, just as other men over 20 years old were doing. Everybody else stayed behind: my grandmother, my mother and my younger brothers and sisters. The plan was to get to Hamhung and stay there for just a couple of months. Then we were hoping to go back.

As we travelled towards Hamhung, we were struck by how many refugees were fleeing south. There were so many people that I even got separated from my father and my uncle; I later learned from my father that he success-fully fled south on his own on a small boat, to Pohang. I was lucky enough to get a ride on a South Korean army truck, and I made it to Hamhung. I found temporary refuge at a relative's place there.

When we realised we needed to head south, going to Hungnam and getting on a ship seemed to be the best option available. But because the port there was so small and there were so many people, the whole area had become almost paralysed. No matter how quickly you got there, you weren't going to leave any time sooner. Only once the UN and South Korean forces had finished their retreat did they take on the refugees. On 15 December General MacArthur and General Almond gave permission for refugees to get on the ships as well. By that time, most of the military had already left, apart from a minimal presence that had stayed behind.

Lee Hoo Ja

When we heard that American ships had arrived in Hungnam, everyone started to head for the port. It felt at the time that there were several hundred thousand people there. I heard later that there were 98,000 people, but it felt like more. People were clustered very tightly together. There were some campfires here and there in the snow, but nothing substantial enough to do any real cooking. I saw people using huge aluminium pots to cook. It was so cold that it felt like minus 30 degrees, maybe even lower than that. The cabbages were frozen, so people had to rip the leaves off one by one. Some were eating rice that was frozen over.

My family didn't suffer too much because we had a relative who ran an inn near Hungnam harbour, so we were able to stay comfortably there, and we were provided with hot meals as well. Before the evacuation, when we offered to cook for the South Korean soldiers, we ate really well with the meat that they'd brought.

The reason I had come along was to help carry the blankets. The plan for me was to head back home. In our group was my father, my older sister, myself and my younger brother, as well as my uncle's family. The night before the evacuation, I challenged my father: 'Dad, aren't our lives equally precious? Why are you planning to take only the older sister? Why can't I come along?' My sister kept on pinching me and told me I needed to go back home. I was a bit dismissive of my sister at the time, and I thought that she was being selfish about her own survival, and I hadn't thought of how irresponsibly I was acting, not thinking of my sister and mother back home. My father was silent.

The area near the port was divided into separate territories for different families. The ones who came alone would look on, trying to join other groups as they tried to find any food.

Sohn Dong Hun

When I reached Hungnam, I had no personal belongings. The only thing I had with me was my high-school diploma. I had no rice or food, and I was completely on my own. There was a snow storm, and it felt about minus 20 to minus 30 degrees. The clothes I had on were inadequate: no coat or jacket. During the daytime it was bearable, but at night the cold and wind were so severe I could not cope.

Most of the homes in Hungnam were destroyed by the bombing and only a few houses remained. I didn't have any luck getting into any of them. Eventually I managed to find some shelter in the kitchen of a stranger's house. Probably there were 100 people in that cramped space. I stayed there for about four days, from 16 to 19 December. I barely had anything to eat. I ate out of an empty rations food can.

Lee Hoo Ja

On 18 December, I saw ships out at sea. There were make-shift wooden bridges from the harbour to the smaller boats that would take people to the larger LST ['Landing Ship, Tank', a military vessel designation] landing ships. People were already getting on the boats. I ran back inside to report the beginning of the evacuation.

When we got ready and came out to the port, the lines were already packed. People were walking tightly together to board the smaller boats that were taking people to the larger ships. I urged my family that we should get on board too.

Sohn Dong Hun

I boarded the ship on the night of 19 December. I had seen soldiers leaving days before, and I remember wanting to be on the ship as well. On 19 December, people were asked to get in line in groups of 100. There were several ships wait-ing, a Japanese cargo ship and the LST landing ships. The *Meredith Victory* was not there at the time; that arrived a few days later, on 24 December, I believe. The ship I was on was the *Tobadamaru*, a Japanese cargo ship. The bottom areas were full of cargo like army tanks and fuel. The people were taken to the top deck. I think there were several hundred people, possibly several thousand.

Lee Hoo Ja

I was kept busy looking after my younger brother, and trying to feed him. The daily routine would be going up to the top deck and collecting rice and toffee candy for him. I remember him saying that the next trip we went on as refugees, we should remember to take lots of food. It makes me laugh when I think of that, but my brother always got embarrassed when I told the story. My father had brought lots of things along in his carrying pack, rice and toffee, and

40,000 won of South Korean currency, which we got from the South Korean soldiers we'd cooked for back home. The soldiers cooked food for themselves, and I would trade my toffee with their rice. I don't know how the days passed by, but I think going to the toilet was the hardest thing.

I can't remember ever seeing my older sister going to the toilet. She sat motionless. She was already all grown up, so she would have been thinking of home, regretting having to leave behind gifts for a wedding that had yet to happen, thinking of our mother back home and already missing her. My sister just sat stoically, not moving at all during the whole four-day trip, not going to the toilet, not eating.

Sohn Dong Hun

On board the *Tobadamaru*, I still had no coat. It was a bit better during the daytime because of the warmth of the sunlight. But at night, as the ship began to roll and pitch and the winds began to pick up, the temperature dropped, and I could barely stand it. We had to stay there night and day for five days. I think the hardest aspects on board were the cold, the hunger, the vomiting and not being able to sleep. So for five days I was out in the cold without anything to eat, viciously cold, and my only wish was to get back on land.

There were no toilets on deck. There weren't even any cans, so people had to relieve themselves on the floor of the ship. The excrement would freeze over because of the cold. And the ship was rocking so much that I vomited everything I had eaten. The conditions were so atrocious I can't describe them.

I never saw it with my own eyes, but I learned that some elderly people passed away on the ship. I believe four people had died on board. I heard later that their bodies were thrown into the sea.

Lee Hoo Ja

Something I often saw when I went to the top deck was soldiers throwing the bodies of those who had died overboard. Many died on board of hunger and malnutrition, regardless of age. If the height of the top deck was that of a 10-storey building, the waves that would crash down felt like they were 20 storeys high. My father and his younger brother were sitting on wooden planks at the top and the water was even hitting them.

Sohn Dong Hun

I felt I could survive if only we reached land. Then I could eat something, even if it was tree roots. Out at sea, there was nothing to eat. When we arrived in Busan on 24 December, our ship had not been authorised to enter the port, so we moved on to Geoje Island and we arrived there just as the clocks struck midnight on Christmas Day.

As we were coming ashore, I saw a church on top of a hill. That's how I knew it was Christmas – from the sound of the church bells: 'Dong! Dong! Dong!' That's when I realised I had survived. I'm not a Christian, but it felt to me that the sounds of the bells were signalling my being born again. I was originally born in North Korea on 8 April, but I had almost died during the Korean War, and again on board the ship at Hungnam. That's why Christmas Day of 1950 really feels like my second birthday.

Norman Deptula

When we arrived at Busan, the southernmost port, the place was bustling – ships were coming in, people going back and forth, troops here and there. I remember carrying my heavy duffel bag, my pack and weapon, and these little Korean boys would come up and ask if we would let them carry our gear. We were all tired and we hadn't slept all

Norman Deptula photographed while serving in Korea.

night long, and I let this little kid carry my duffel bag, and I paid him for it in Korean won.

We left there as soon as possible; they didn't want us staying in Busan as there were other ships coming. We walked a short distance, then got on a train. It had wooden benches, which weren't comfortable, and I ended up next to a broken window. I remember spending that night trying to patch the window, but I couldn't find anything – the wind howled through that window, and I didn't get much sleep. [I was] tired, unkempt, dispirited.

There were so many people there. They sent us to a town, Kyong-ju, 70 miles north of Busan, and as soon as we got there they assigned us a place to set up our tents and get organised.

I was Catholic, and word went around that there was a Catholic church there and they would be having midnight mass. We were finally given permission to get a truck and get there. It was a cold, clear night, and I was singing 'I'll Be Home for Christmas'. I wasn't; my parents were observing Christmas 10,000 miles away. We entered the church in our torn uniforms; we were dirty and unkempt. There were big chunks of the ceiling where the plaster had fallen down. It was very close to the action in the first part of the war. It was unheated. And I noticed they had a nativity scene, and a Christmas tree, and signs in Korean. In deference to us they wanted to put up a sign in English, but it came out, 'MAHRY CHRISTMAS'. They played Christmas songs and sang in Korean, and we sang in English. At the end the priest, Father Kim, spoke in Korean, and then he turned to all of us and gave us his blessings.

Sohn Dong Hun made good on his rebirth with a PhD in pharmacy and a career as a university lecturer. He gives ironic credit to the dictator under whom none of that would have happened.

I feel very grateful that events happened as they did. If Kim Il Sung had not started the war, I would have continued to live in North Korea and would have suffered pain, hunger and loss of freedom. So I'm thankful until this day for being allowed on the ship back then.

Lee Hoo Ja

I thought at the time we would be able to go back home up north soon. I don't think we would have travelled on the ship if we had thought we were never to return again. Some of my friends have said that if I had stayed behind in North Korea, I would have ended up as a senior party official. I don't agree with them; they don't know how much stress I had been burdened with before leaving the North.

Later, the remainder of my family was evacuated too, including my aunt's family, my mother and my younger sisters. My grandfather and grandmother couldn't travel with them, though. If I had been there, I could have helped them, but it felt as if they were left behind because of me. I'd been such a good child until then, but because I'd been so insistent on going with my father and older sister, I wasn't able to help my grandparents escape as well.

Sohn Dong Hun

We live divided, with separated families on either side of the border. And for myself, I will never get to see my mother or my younger siblings again. My wish has been to be able to return home for a visit, but in the years since then my mother has passed away. Before I die, I hope I can pay [my] respects at her gravesite. That's my final wish, to be able to go back to our home in the North.

'The world became a hostile place'

McCarthyism (1950–4)

By the start of 1950, the United States' near panic about the Cold War was mounting. Stalin had tightened his grip on Eastern Europe, adding Czechoslovakia to the list of countries in the Soviet bloc, and responding to the West's decision to create a new federal West German state by imposing a year-long blockade on occupied West Berlin.

Communism was spreading across Asia, too, with first Mao Zedong's takeover of China and then, in June 1950, the war between South Korea and Communist North Korea. And the Soviets had also tested an atom bomb – far earlier than had been anticipated – partly as a result of the Communist spy rings, which were only now being uncovered.

In January 1950 a senior State Department official called Alger Hiss was accused of being a Communist spy and convicted of perjury when he denied it. At the same time, the United States discovered that Klaus Fuchs, a German-born British physicist, had been spying for the Soviets while working for the Manhattan Project, the top-secret collaboration between the United States, Britain and Canada that developed the first atomic bomb. Then a Communist couple from New York, Julius and Ethel Rosenberg, were arrested on charges of passing atomic bomb secrets to the Soviets.

All this fuelled fears that Communist infiltrators must be intent on subverting the United States from within. Everyone from Hollywood screenwriters to academics and government officials came under suspicion. In 1947, with right-wing accusations about 'red' infiltration already stirring, President Truman had countered the charge of being soft on Communism by ordering loyalty reviews of federal employees. His Attorney General had made public the government's list of 'subversive' organisations. But then in 1950, a much more aggressive right-wing figure emerged.

The involvement of Joseph McCarthy, the junior senator from Wisconsin, began on 9 February 1950, when he raised the spectre of a network of traitors in high places during a fiery Lincoln Day speech in Wheeling, West Virginia. Warning that the United States was engaged in a war between two diametrically opposed ideologies, 'a final all-out battle between communistic atheism and Christianity', he launched a full-blown attack on the Truman administration for failing to stop the spread of Communism, first in Eastern Europe and then in Asia, and accused the State Department and its Secretary, Dean Acheson, of harbouring Communist traitors: 'I have here in my hand a list of 205 ... a list of names that were made known to the Secretary of State as being members of the Communist Party and who nevertheless are still working and shaping the policy of the State Department.'

The State Department immediately denied the charge and Joseph McCarthy never made the list public, but the speech caused a media storm. Together with the FBI under its director, J. Edgar Hoover, the ominously named House Un-American Activities Committee (HUAC) in the House of Representatives and several subcommittees in the US Senate, and even self-appointed private-sector publications such as *Counterattack*, McCarthy spearheaded the hunt for Communists. He took every opportunity to warn that Communists and Communist sympathisers were seeking to undermine America, claiming alleged conspiracies inside government, throughout Hollywood and on Broadway, in universities, schools and libraries, and even inside the US armed forces. This was the era of the right-wing anti-Communist backlash known as 'McCarthyism'.

Anyone who was actually a member of the American Communist Party was immediately a target. Some activists were charged with conspiracy to overthrow the US government under the Alien Registration or Smith Act of 1940, which made it illegal for anyone to teach or advocate the violent overthrow of the government. Those who could went underground to escape arrest. Others, among them journalists and academics who had visited the Soviet Union or China or written about Communism, were hauled before Congressional hearings or visited by FBI investigators, even if they insisted that they were not members of the Party. McCarthy and his followers didn't stop there. They persecuted people on the basis of guilt by association, of suspicion, hearsay and conspiracy theory.

In Britain, the most pressing Communist threat was seen to be the Soviet Union. But in the United States in 1950, 'Red China' was just as important. During the Second World War, China under the nationalist leadership of Chiang Kai-shek had been an ally of the West. But when Mao Zedong and his Communist army marched into Beijing in October 1949, many on the American right were incandescent and demanded to know who had 'lost' China. McCarthy accused President Truman, and the late President F. D. Roosevelt before him, of having long been soft on, or even in league with, Communism, calling it 'twenty years of treason'. The search for scapegoats was on.

Accusations of Communism had become a weapon to wield against a wide range of enemies. For years, the American right had felt marginalised. Now, they could give full vent to their suspicions: about the real aims of civil rights supporters, and about anyone who expressed a non-hostile approach to the Soviet bloc, even if they were not Communists. In a brutal irony, the McCarthyites' approach to evidence and due process echoed the methods of the very Communist dictatorships they were so worried about.

Hollywood actors, writers and directors were also grilled about their alleged Communist affiliations. One of the earliest manifestations of the so-called Red Scare was the interrogation by HUAC in 1947 of eight screenwriters, two directors and a producer who refused to say whether or not they had ever been Communist Party members. The 'Hollywood Ten' had, in fact, all been Communists at one time, and some still were. But as the McCarthyite mood gained momentum, not just card-carrying Communists were tarred with allegations. The notorious era of Hollywood blacklisting began.

The crusade spread throughout the entertainment industry. Alleged subversives were suspected of being part of a secret campaign to exploit American popular culture by colouring it with Communist propaganda. HUAC confronted those it subpoenaed with an invidious choice. One option was to plead privacy of belief under the First Amendment, but the Hollywood Ten had tried that and the Supreme Court ruled in effect that they could be sent to prison for contempt of Congress. After the Ten were jailed, very few went this way. Many chose instead to take the Fifth Amendment against self-incrimination, but that meant being black-listed. Hundreds of talented professionals ended up on the blacklist and were blocked from working, some of them well-known directors, writers and performers. Some emigrated, some worked under pseudonyms, and some did not appear on screens or on stage until the 1960s. Others chose to cooperate and undergo HUAC's prescribed ritual for 'clearing' their names – to repudiate Communism and name people they knew who were or had been Party members. Motives varied from desperation and fear to a genuine desire to thwart the Communism they had once embraced. Many of these people were burdened with guilt about 'naming names' for years.

But by 1954, increasing numbers of Republicans and American conservatives were becoming impatient. They feared that McCarthyism was becoming a liability to the Republican Party and to the cause of anti-Communism. Finally, the McCarthy bubble burst. During live televised hearings to investigate his claims that the US Army had been infiltrated by Reds, McCarthy's unsubstantiated allegations and evidence of increasingly heavy drinking failed to impress. An army counsel dared to defy him publicly: 'You have done enough. Have you no sense of decency, sir? At long last have you left no sense of decency?' McCarthy's popular standing plummeted, and by the end of 1954 the US Senate had voted over-whelmingly to condemn him for bringing the Senate into disrepute.

The Cold War was often claimed at the time to be a moral crusade by the freedom-loving West against the evils of Communist dictatorship. But the era of McCarthyism shows that it was not as simple as that. The lasting impact of McCarthy's methods was not to weed out Communist spies – that required a rather more professional approach to evidence. Rather, it was to sow distrust in American society and undermine the West's claim to be the champion of liberty and tolerance. The hunt for enemies had gone too far. McCarthy and his kind handed an effective weapon to the very people they supposedly opposed.

The doubts, though, lingered, marring the careers of the thousands of innocent Americans who had come under suspicion, and blighting the lives of families who suffered the stigma and strain of having their loved ones harassed and ostracised. And for some, the memories of how their parents became victims of the Cold War's Red Scare colour their lives still.

*In 1951, **Kathryn Jackson** was living in New York. She was just three years old when her father, a black civil rights activist, disappeared. Having taught classes on violent revolution, he had been indicted under the Smith Act of 1940, which outlawed conspiracy to teach or advocate the violent overthrow of the government.*

I was born in 1947, at the beginning of the Red Scare. My parents were college-educated African-American Communists, and they both worked in the South as early civil rights activists. After the war, my mother went to London and Stalingrad, and she talked of the struggle of being a pacifist after seeing the horrors of the war and yet

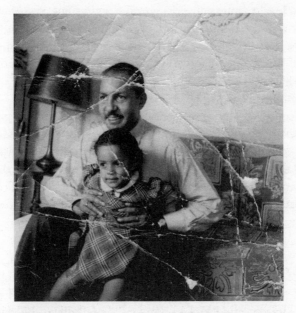
Kathryn Jackson with her father before he went into hiding.

also having some allegiance to political beliefs. My father was charged with 'conspiracy to overthrow the government', and he went underground. He disappeared for five years, and resurfaced when the threat of McCarthyism had somewhat abated. He left when I was three; he came back and was jailed briefly when I was eight. Then he went on trial. He was given a suspended sentence, which was eventually thrown out when the Smith Act was found unconstitutional. So I grew up very aware that there is always a struggle between the sometimes bad outside world and the sometimes very good inside world – that was a struggle I had to make sense of.

I was in nursery school because my mother was working – not in a professional job, she was an assistant to a politically friendly doctor. I went to a public state nursery, and apparently they were told that my mother had more money than she was saying, that she might even have Russian money, so they said I would have to leave. But she was able to organise people, and a petition was sent, and I wasn't expelled. There was trauma, but there were also moments of great love and great care.

We were always followed by the FBI. An FBI agent once came to the house, and my mother said that I kicked him down the stairs! He tried to open the door, and I put my foot out and I kicked him, and he fell down the stairs. They always followed us. We would go to the Botanic Gardens in Brooklyn, which I loved, and I was always aware that there were FBI men there. Later, when I was in graduate school, one of the topics of conversations would be to talk about hip psychological concerns: when a person thinks that someone's following them, that's a sign of paranoia. And then I would think, 'Wait a minute, that actually happened to me!' The FBI *did* follow me, and it was a constant source of fear.

I was very, very close to my father before he went underground, and I do have some memories of him then. My mother had this ritual of bringing out his photo every night and telling a story about him. What I remembered of him then was a hero who had left, so there was obviously a lot of loss and pain around that. As a child I missed him. Even though, logically, I was given a reason for why he was away, I was always afraid that I would never see him again. So it was almost miraculous that he was able to 'resurface'.

I guess I always assumed that 'underground' meant being away. I know that there was one survivor of the Smith Act who thought that 'underground' meant actually dying. But for me, it always just meant being away, being absent.

I didn't want to cause my mother any trouble. I tried very hard not to be a typical child who might be rebellious or question rules because I thought her life was so difficult. She was incredibly open to me. In nursery school, I always wore three or four undershirts every day – that was obviously some way of giving myself some protection, some comfort. And my mother let me do that; she never said, 'This is crazy. You can't go to school wearing four undershirts.' Her ability to be sensitive to some of the things I needed was very important.

My mother always seemed very heroic to me. The only time I remember seeing her with tears in her eyes was when a journalist came from an African-American newspaper to interview her. And that always stuck with me: there was this heroism, but there was also an intense pain that wasn't spoken about.

I remember when she called up to me and said that Dad was back, and I said, 'Well, where is he?' And she said, 'He's in jail, and we need to raise money to release him.' I was excited that he was back, but also somewhat unnerved that he was in jail. I wondered how friends who were not part of the community would react to me and to my father, knowing he had been in jail.

The first time I saw him again was just a few days after he resurfaced. It was quite traumatic going to a jail with my mother and sister to see him. A reporter came with us to photograph us going in, and then my dad was brought out, and that was really hard. We talked about what we had been doing, and he said he was happy and didn't know what to say. I was overwhelmed and felt the same. He was sat behind a glass screen so we couldn't touch him. Years ago I wrote a poem about the experience, and how I really wanted to hug him. It was painful, too, just to have this glass there, and then the guards coming to take him away again. That was scary.

Probably a month later, when the bail was raised, we went to court and he was freed. His trial hadn't occurred yet but he was free to come home.

I still had the fear that he could be taken away again, but the intensity of worry and fear was removed. We attempted to be a typical family again, but there were still pressures. My father became the Editor of the *Worker*. He came home once, and his office had been bombed, so I was worried and scared. There were events all through my life with him, some difficulties and some struggles. But there were also good times: I always loved going to summer camp in Vermont, a 'progressive' camp there, where people knew about my family, but feeling safe and protected in the mountains.

For my parents, the idea of Communism was tied in with thinking about a broader world. My parents had both worked in the South before I was born and had worked with other young, primarily African-American and some white activists, and they were mostly Communists. There was this contradiction of hearing in school that Communism was bad, and at home being told that Communism was the ultimate good. Trying to make sense of that was not easy as a child.

I think there was more of an accepted demonisation of Communism then. It wasn't really until high school that there was more of an acceptance of having different political viewpoints. Because of the stark belief that any beliefs outside of the normative ones were bad, I kept quiet in school. I remember once watching the news when my father was still underground, and his picture came up on TV, and I was shocked but I realised I couldn't tell anyone, and I was very scared. My mother put my father into a context of heroism, and [slave rescuer] Harriet Tubman and the Underground Railroad, and the fight against Nazism and the Holocaust. But the news was talking about a bad man, who was against the law. At home, he was one person, and even though in the outer world he was considered an enemy by some, I guess what I was taught at home was stronger than what I was learning outside.

In 1950, **David Lattimore** was a sophomore student at Harvard University when his father, Owen, a scholar of China and Central Asia, was first hauled before a Senate committee.

My father originally came from a Southern abolitionist family that had settled in Washington with Lincoln. My grandfather was a Latin teacher in a Washington high school. Then he went abroad, to China – not as a missionary but as a secular professor in schools founded by the Chinese empire after the wars of the end of the nineteenth century. My father grew up there; he was schooled in Switzerland and England, but went back to China as a businessman. He spoke Chinese fluently, and he travelled in the interior for his import and export firm and eventually got fascinated with the north-west frontier of China. He took off with my mother across the country for a year and a half by caravan and carts and yaks, over the mountains and into India. He wrote travel books, which caught on in Britain, then in the USA, so he got himself into an academic career by the back door. He was sent to Harvard on fellowships, but he settled in Peking. He edited a journal for the Institute of Pacific Relations (IPR), which Communist-hunters of the 1950s believed might have been a Communist-saturated organisation that had influenced the American State Department to abandon Chiang Kai-shek and his Nationalists, thereby giving carte blanche to the Chinese Communists. China was 'lost' in 1949, and it was a temptation to find someone to blame that loss on. That, of course, presupposed that the USA 'owned' China.

In 1950, McCarthy started his vendetta against supposed Communists in government on whom the various trepidations of the period could be blamed. In January 1950 hearings in the House Un-American Activities Committee led to one official, Alger Hiss, being convicted of perjury, because they couldn't get him on treason charges due to the Statute of Limitations.

McCarthy's technique was to say that he had the names of 250 spies or 57 spies or at least *one* spy, but not divulge who it was. I was beginning to suspect that he might be targeting my father and, when I talked to my mother on the telephone, she said she had the same thoughts and had already made overtures to a Washington lawyer. McCarthy's first idea was to characterise my father as the 'boss' of Alger Hiss in a spy ring – a Soviet espionage outfit centred in the US State Department. The only difficulty with this as a storyline was that my father had not been *in* the State Department, nor had he been a Communist.

There was no credible evidence, but that didn't deter McCarthy. When it was clear that the spy charge wasn't going to stick, he shifted to one of *influencing* the State Department. Accusations to this effect were brought up by McCarthy before a Senate subcommittee. At the time, my father was in Afghanistan, but he asked to be allowed to reply to these charges. He returned home and had three days in which to get to know his lawyer and concoct an opening statement of 42 pages. Their strategy was that my father would never at any time plead the Fifth Amendment, which permits refusing to testify on grounds of possible self-incrimination. He had nothing to hide, so he would answer any question. But in exchange for that, he was resolved to defend himself by attack.

It was the spring vacation, so I went to Washington to help out, and I was present for the first hearing at which my father spoke. It was a crammed Senate conference room with newsreel klieg lights glaring. McCarthy himself was there for the first half; he wouldn't meet anybody's eye. My father spoke for a couple of hours, then answered questions for many more hours. He spoke with great vehemence, a sort of grating anger. He attacked McCarthy just as vigorously as McCarthy had attacked him. He referred to 'this man McCarthy' and 'his base and contemptible lies', who was 'either a fool or an enemy of his country'.

That particular Senate committee agreed with my father and concluded that McCarthy's charges were a fraud and a hoax perpetrated on the US Senate and people. My father had a lot of support in the audience and in the majority of the subcommittee, and near the end there was a great round of applause for his remarks about the necessity of not falling into a situation where the country was cowed by demagoguery. A lot of people were cheering my father on. In a way, it was a triumph. It didn't last forever as he later found himself in worse trouble with another Senate committee.

It went on for more than five years, well into 1954. There were hearings in front of the McCarran Committee [the Senate Internal Security Subcommittee]. Unlike the previous committee, this committee was totally unfriendly and had put together a subcommittee that was of the unanimous opinion that there was a Communist conspiracy behind the loss of China and there was a spy web, whose centre had been in the State Department and originally in the Institute of Pacific Relations. They had seized the archives of the IPR – some 1,800 documents – and taken them to Washington. There was a lot of correspondence involving my father and the director. The Senate people apparently didn't know that the FBI had already been through these papers at the invitation of the Institute, and had found only five documents of any significance – none of which implicated my father as a spy or even as a sympathiser of Communism of any sort.

That didn't stop them. They went through these papers. Of course, they didn't find any evidence of espionage either, but they decided to run the hearings as a perjury trap. My father was asked questions to which the committee already knew the answers, from those documents. My father was not allowed to consult the documents. They were looking for instances where something in the documents, no matter how trivial, had been remembered differently by my father. There were half a dozen inconsistencies about names and dates, none of them suggestive of sedition.

Then the committee demanded of the Justice Department an indictment for perjury, as had happened in Alger Hiss's case. The Justice Department came up with this, but the federal courts in Washington refused to try this indictment; they said it was ridiculous, in effect. The committee came back with a second indictment, which was almost the same as the first, but they attached an opening charge, which was that my father had lied when said he had never been a sympathiser of Communist causes. They knew darned well he had not been a Communist, so they said he had lied when he said he hadn't been a sympathiser.

The same judge dismissed the indictment twice. The committee appealed it. The superior court backed up the district court judge each time. There were four court sessions, but the Justice Department was left with the tattered remnants of an indictment that they knew they couldn't make stick. So in effect he was exonerated, and they said they had no case. But it took five years to get there, and it really put a brake on his career.

My father lost half his income. He had earned half his income from his academic salary, and half from authorship and journalism. There were some jealous academics who had gone along with the concocted tales and testified against him and said they had known him in the Communist Party. Now, Harvard was the only university that continued inviting him to lecture. It was, in a way, isolating but it also mobilised a lot of support for him among academics. He was not fired, although some of the trustees of his university were in favour of firing him. It would have been a fight, as he had tenure. But they dissolved the institute he had been the head of, and sent the money back to the donors. He was put on leave, with pay. It was difficult.

I spent the summer of 1951 at Johns Hopkins University, and it was evident that some of the supposed students were actually FBI or CIA. One was a nephew of Walter Bedell Smith, who was the director of the CIA. In seminars in my father's garden, there would be these strange people writing notes with a very hard pencil on grey paper so you couldn't see what they were saying. A car from the Baltimore office of the FBI was parked in the roadway, just out of sight of my father's house, evidently listening in and apparently recording.

My father was not one of those people who went to school in the USA and absorbed Marxism in college or in the labour movement. He had no contacts with any of the 'usual suspects'. He had grown up in China before there were Communists in China. He was a scholar of history and geography, and he didn't believe in the Marxist view of history, or any other ideological sort of historical perspective. He didn't like ideologies. He wasn't an ideologue and didn't want to be marked as one. He didn't read any Marx until late in life. He wasn't interested. He thought the idea of history as a grand march towards Communism was idiotic.

Sian Snow's father, Edgar, was an American journalist and author, known for his bestselling book on the rise of Communism in China: Red Star Over China (1937).

In the 1940s, both of my parents were enjoying successful careers in New York City. My father, Edgar Snow, was a seasoned journalist and well-known author who had lived in China and travelled extensively in the Far East and Europe. He was the first Western reporter to reach Red-held territory after the fabled Long March and to interview Mao Zedong. My mother, Lois Wheeler, was a Broadway, film and TV actress who supported progressive causes, including the civil rights movement – a fact that was duly noted in her FBI file.

During the Second World War, my father worked as a foreign correspondent for the *Saturday Evening*

Post. On his return to the USA, he became Associate Editor of the *Post* and continued to write about the Far East, the Soviet Union, India and Europe. He was able to express his opinions freely until the early 1950s, when Red-baiting cowed the publication's managers. After they adopted increasingly right-leaning views, he resigned rather than submit to censorship. That was in 1951, the year I was born.

At the height of the McCarthy era, I was still a little girl. In fact, I thought the Senator's name was 'Bacarthy'. I knew people disliked the man, but I didn't understand exactly why. I did feel, though, that danger lurked for my family and our friends. My parents were never formally accused of 'un-American activities' or called upon to testify, but they were questioned by the FBI and they were blacklisted, as were many of their acquaintances and colleagues.

My father repeatedly stated that he was not a Communist. As a reporter who had lived in China and witnessed the historic events unfolding there in the 1930s, he was naturally interested in how and why Communism had attracted so many followers. He had witnessed misery, oppression, hunger and destitution under Chiang Kai-shek's regime and was intrigued by the Communists' twin goals of improving the lives of average people and resisting Japanese aggression. On the other hand, he was horrified by the excesses of the Stalinist regime. I think his aim was to report the facts as accurately as possible in the hope of fostering mutual understanding and peace amongst countries at a time of nuclear brinkmanship. He believed that the West should seek more constructive ways of interacting with Communist nations if further war was to be avoided.

After my father resigned from the *Post* in protest over censorship, he found it increasingly difficult to earn a

Sian Snow with her father, Edgar, in 1953.

living. With two young children to support, he turned to writing his autobiography, *Journey to the Beginning*.

My mother continued to work for TV, but offers dwindled despite her talent. She eventually found out by chance, at a party, that she had been blacklisted. The director who told her this said that, if asked, he would deny it. He had tried to cast her in several shows, to no avail. She then approached a TV executive who at first feigned ignorance, but finally dug out a file on her. Among other falsehoods, it claimed that she was hiding her true identity, supposedly that of a Jewish woman named Miriam Oppenheimer. When my mother heard this, she laughed out loud. She informed the man that she played the role of 'Miriam Oppenheimer' every evening at the Cort Theater from 8 to 10pm, and invited him to come and see for himself. Much later, when we got hold of my father's FBI file under the Freedom of Information Act, we saw that it too contained gross errors.

We moved to New Jersey when I was two or three. On the first day in our new home, someone threw mud all over our car. During the 1950s, my parents were the victims of malicious gossip. My mother ran for the Board of Education and lost the election because of unfounded accusations that she was married to a Communist. When my father decorated our porch with Japanese lanterns for my brother's birthday, a rumour went around town that we were flying Communist flags.

As I grew older, I became aware that the Soviet Union was considered an 'enemy' of the USA, but my parents felt that it was wrong to vilify other nations – this would only lead to further warfare. To demonstrate their opposition to Cold War policies, they kept my brother and me home from school when air-raid drills were scheduled. I was proud of my parents for upholding their principles but, like children everywhere, I worried about being 'different'.

Although the situation was confusing to me, I knew that my parents and their friends were facing some sort of danger. I remember FBI investigators coming to our house. They did not accuse my parents directly but attempted to pry information out of them that might incriminate people they knew. My brother and I were told to go to our rooms and, as I turned to walk upstairs, I saw two men in dark overcoats and hats silhouetted in the doorway, and I was very frightened.

After that, I had nightmares. I dreamt that our house was surrounded by enemies on all sides. I didn't know who they were or what they wanted, but I knew that it was dangerous to leave the house. The world had suddenly become a hostile place.

'When I saw the light, I had no idea what was happening'

The H-Bomb (1950s)

For children growing up in the United States of America in the 1950s, the possibility of nuclear war felt very real. At school, nuclear air-raid drills were commonplace. Schoolchildren were taught to 'duck and cover' if they heard a siren, seek shelter in a basement and climb under their desks. Booklets offered suggestions on how to survive an attack. Shops sold underground ration packets, do-it-yourself bomb shelters and fallout protection suits.

The Soviet authorities publicly scoffed at the Western information campaign as a cynical ploy to reap capitalist profits from the sales of inadequate shelters, but the Soviet Union had its own extensive civil defence programme, which trained millions of volunteers, built bomb shelters and issued protective clothing including, apparently, gas masks specially designed not just for humans but also for farm animals.

The spectre of nuclear Armageddon hovered. The Cold War was no longer confined to politics and ideology. From 1950, the Korean War had turned it into a military

135

confrontation, all the more terrifying because the year before it had emerged that both superpowers, American and Soviet, had nuclear weapons.

The first Soviet atomic explosion took place on 29 August 1949 at a remote testing ground in Semipalatinsk in northern Kazakhstan. Specially constructed buildings and caged animals were placed near the site to measure the impact of the blast. The 20-kiloton explosion destroyed the buildings and incinerated the animals.

The Soviet test was top secret. News of the detonation reached the world courtesy of the Americans. They got wind of it when an American spy plane picked up signs of the radioactive fallout. On 23 September 1949, President Harry S. Truman went public with a declaration that 'within recent weeks an atomic explosion occurred in the USSR.'

In Washington, the US administration was shocked. After the atom bombs dropped on Hiroshima and Nagasaki in 1945, the United States had assumed it would remain the sole nuclear power for some time. Now Moscow had demonstrated that it too had the capacity to detonate nuclear weapons and could already be making headway on a more powerful device – the hydrogen bomb. When the physicist Klaus Fuchs confessed in January 1950 that he had been passing atomic secrets to the Soviets, paranoia in the United States soared and the Americans became determined to get ahead of the Soviets again. They gave priority to new research to develop a new and more powerful weapon. Thus began what over the next few decades would become the defining feature of the Cold War: a spiralling nuclear arms race, astronomically expensive and terrifyingly destructive.

The idea of a hydrogen bomb had been around since 1942, but initially there was little American commitment to its development. The A-bombs dropped by the United States on Japan were powered by nuclear fission. The initial theory behind a hydrogen bomb was to use fission as a trigger, but derive much of the bomb's energy from nuclear fusion reactions between isotopes of hydrogen.

Also known as a thermonuclear weapon, the H-bomb worked in stages: when the initial fission bomb was detonated, it heated fusion fuel to thermonuclear temperatures, releasing the energy to induce a further fission stage with a far greater explosive yield. In theory, this could lead to another fusion stage after that. A thermonuclear bomb was therefore extraordinarily powerful, hundreds of times more destructive than the bombs dropped on Hiroshima and Nagasaki. It was a nuclear weapon on an entirely different scale. But at the beginning of the 1950s, it was still just a theory.

The American project to build a hydrogen 'super-bomb' was carried out at the nuclear facility at Los Alamos in New Mexico, assisted by 'Project Matterhorn' at Princeton University. The highly classified final design was based on an idea developed by a Hungarian-born theoretical physicist, Edward Teller (known as the 'father of the H-bomb'), and a Polish-born mathematician, Stanisław Ulam. About two dozen young American scientists worked on the project, motivated by a sense of patriotism and the challenge of solving very difficult theoretical physics problems. By the autumn of 1952, the team was ready to test the 'proof of principle' for the first prototype of a hydrogen bomb, to see if the thermonuclear theory would really work.

The large, unwieldy, two-storey contraption looked more like the inside of a small factory than a bomb. Given the codename 'Ivy Mike', it was transported thousands of miles to Enewetak Atoll, part of the Marshall Islands in the

South Pacific, to be put to the test. There, on 1 November 1952, an explosion proved that the theory could work. Ivy Mike generated a fireball more than 2 miles wide and released energy about 700 times that of the Hiroshima bomb. The island of Elugelab, on which it was detonated, was completely vaporised.

Within two years, that initial American test had been translated into a usable H-bomb. The Americans detonated it on 1 March 1954 at Bikini Atoll in the Marshall Islands, under the code name 'Castle Bravo'. The bomb proved to be unexpectedly powerful, the largest bomb the United States ever exploded. At 15 megatons, it was about 1000 times more powerful than the bomb dropped on Hiroshima, and left a crater 6,500 feet wide.

The fallout from Castle Bravo spread over hundreds of miles and was the worst case of radiological contamination in American history. Over 200 local islanders were endangered. Many of their island homes were too contaminated to be inhabited again. Their plight led to a decades-long fight to get adequate compensation from the US government.

American personnel involved in the test were also exposed, although when they realised that the wind was unexpectedly carrying hazardous fallout in their direction, they took shelter in bunkers for several hours. But some of them, too, were subjected to dangerous levels of radiation.

Even more unfortunate was the crew of a Japanese fishing boat, *Lucky Dragon*. They were supposed to be outside the danger zone but, because the blast was twice as powerful as expected and the wind blew the radioactive ash over a wider area, the crew members were exposed and fell ill with radiation sickness. On their return to Japan, one died within six months and several others in the coming years, and the whole crew experienced severe effects for the rest of their lives. It took years to agree a deal on modest compensation for the surviving fishermen.

The Americans were not the only ones developing a hydrogen bomb. Soviet scientists were working on their own secret research project. The lead physicist was Dr Andrei Sakharov. In later years he was to become a prominent Soviet dissident and Nobel Peace laureate, but in the late 1940s and early 1950s he was the driving force of the Soviet research team and, like his American counterparts, focused above all on solving the puzzle of how to make a thermonuclear bomb work.

The first Soviet attempt, in August 1953 – nine months after the first American test – was less powerful than the American version. But the following year, only a few months after the American Castle Bravo test, the Soviets successfully tried out a new design. Like the Americans, Sakharov and his colleagues had concluded that the key to making a thermonuclear explosion of enormous energy release (or 'yield') was to use the principle of radiation implosion, in which radiation from a fission bomb acts as an enormously powerful 'piston' to compress the thermonuclear fuel.

Several intensive years of above-ground nuclear testing followed, carried out mainly by the United States and the Soviet Union, but also by Britain, France and China. It raised the stakes ever higher in the nuclear arms race, and the tests harmed local environments and populations. The United States continued to use the Marshall Islands, as well as a dedicated test site in Nevada, where tests were conducted above ground until 1962, and thereafter underground. The Soviet authorities used what was called the 'Polygon' testing ground at Semipalatinsk, as well as a second site on the archipelago of Novaya Zemlya in the Arctic North. In October 1961 the Soviet Union conducted a test in the Arctic of the most powerful bomb ever deployed, with a yield of 50 megatons. Nicknamed 'Tsar Bomba', it was dropped from altitude and attached to a parachute to slow its fall, so that the specially adapted Soviet 'Bear' bomber that released it stood a chance of getting away in time. The explosion produced a mushroom cloud seven times the height of Mount Everest and caused damage hundreds of miles away, prompting an international outcry.

Two years later the USSR and the United States agreed to stop aboveground testing altogether, but it was not until after the collapse of the USSR in the 1990s that the two sides reached a deal to stop underground testing too. By that time, over 1,800 nuclear explosions had taken place. Bikini Atoll, where the first hydrogen bomb exploded, has been designated a UNESCO World Heritage Site to commemorate this and other tests that marked the dawn of the nuclear age.

Over the following decades, diplomatic attempts to ban all nuclear testing and implement an agreement to phase out nuclear weapons failed to make headway. Having acquired them, it seems that few nuclear powers are prepared to relinquish them. Today, at moments of high international tension, the threat of nuclear war remains a potent propaganda weapon. As relations between Russia and the West deteriorated over the Ukraine crisis in 2014, one prominent pro-Kremlin TV journalist reminded viewers that Russia was still the only country in the world that could reduce the United States of America to radioactive ash. When tensions escalated further in 2016, the Russian government ordered a nationwide civil defence training drill involving 40 million people and warned its population to prepare for possible nuclear war with America.

Over half a century on from the drills at the dawn of the nuclear age, it seemed that the wheel had come full circle and the pattern of Cold War behaviour was repeating itself.

Kenneth Ford was a graduate student in physics at Princeton University in New Jersey, United States, in the spring of 1950.

I had just turned 24. I'd finished my coursework and qualifying exams for my PhD, and was ready to start my dissertation. So I approached the professor with whom I wanted to work, John Wheeler, and I asked him if he would guide my dissertation work. He said he would be happy to do so, but he also said, 'You need to know that I'm going to Los Alamos on leave of absence for at least a year to work on the development of the hydrogen bomb.' He then invited me to join him.

Edward Teller was visiting Princeton, and Wheeler had told him that I was a graduate student of some promise and that he had invited me to come. There was no such thing as a soft sell for Teller – he was an intense person. He had been focused on developing a hydrogen bomb since 1942 and, triggered by the explosion of the first Soviet bomb in 1949, there was a new fire and a new impetus to the idea. So Teller and I sat down together on the steps at the Institute for Advanced Studies on a warm May day, and he gave me the pitch of why I should join.

Number one, probably, was the fear of Soviet domination, Soviet expansion, Soviet threat to the rest of the world – I think that was the principal motivation. And it was, in fact, the reason why I accepted the invitation and decided to go to Los Alamos. I was pretty naive about politics, paid no attention to it really, but I had the general idea that the United States was a moral nation, a nation that could be trusted with great power, and the Soviet Union was not – and that all in all it would be better for the world if the United States got the hydrogen bomb before the Soviet Union did. They had now shown, just four years after us, that they could set off an atomic bomb, so surely they were already working on a hydrogen bomb. So we had to mobilise and build an H-bomb.

That argument did not resonate with United States physicists, with the exception of John Wheeler – it did resonate with him. He was moved, I think, by an anti-Soviet feeling that he and Teller shared, and with simple patriotism: when your country calls on you and asks you to do something, you do it. That argument did not work very well with most American physicists. They felt that they'd done their duty: they'd spent the war years developing radar and the fission bomb, and now they wanted to get back to their research and to their students. So very, very few senior people were moved to join the effort to build the H-bomb; it ended up being junior people such as myself who did most of the work.

If we had been able to prove that it would not work, I guess we would have been happy. But I put behind me a sense of worrying about whether this was the right thing to do; I stopped worrying about it. I had made a decision, I went to Los Alamos, I joined the project. From that point on, it was simply a very, very challenging physics problem. And actually one wanted it to work. Our whole sense was we wanted this to succeed.

The hydrogen bomb was developed almost entirely by theoretical physicists, and a very small group of them – there were no more than two or three dozen of us. The concept, in its simplest terms, was that you put a whole lot of deuterium into some kind of container; you explode an atomic bomb next to that container, which provides so much heat and pressure that it brings the thermonuclear fuel, initially assumed to be deuterium, up to ignition temperature, and that yields a large multiplier on energy over what the fission bomb itself released.

At the time I joined the project, in the summer of 1950, a lot of calculations had been done about whether or not this would work. Would the needed temperature of tens of millions of degrees Celsius be achieved, and if so would the thermonuclear explosion actually take place? Up to that point, most of the theoretical calculations were disappointing: so much of the energy produced by the thermonuclear reaction was radiated away – wasted, so to speak – in the form of electromagnetic radiation that there wasn't enough left to keep the fuel itself hot enough to burn.

But we were still exploring a lot of options. We were anything but pessimistic. The calculations were pointing towards pessimism but we as young researchers kept saying, 'Well, there's got to be a way to do it. Let's keep after it.' We were exploring a lot of different ideas. It wasn't until March of 1951 that what turned out to be the key idea, the idea that led to success, was advanced by Edward Teller and Stan Ulam: radiation implosion. If you could get enough compression – enormous compression – you could create thermal equilibrium. You would reduce the amount of energy that was in the radiation and increase the amount of energy that was in the fuel itself, which would allow the thermonuclear reaction to proceed. We didn't rejoice instantaneously, but as we did more calculations, it looked more and more promising. By May or June of 1951, the implosion route clearly seemed the way to go.

Once the configuration of Ivy Mike as a physical object – a huge cylinder, about 20 feet long (not counting its fission 'trigger') and about 7 feet in diameter – had

Kenneth Ford in 1952.

been settled, all of our calculations were based on that given physical model. The question was how would it play out, in terms of the microseconds under which all of this would happen, and the temperatures of tens of millions of degrees that would occur – all conditions very, very remote indeed from anything that had ever been encountered in a laboratory. That required that we calculate based on our extrapolations from what we did know into these unknown realms.

I did not attend the test. Edward Teller did not attend either, but he went to a geophysical lab at the University of California, Berkeley, and watched the seismometer, very cleverly figuring out how to tell if the test had been success-ful. John Wheeler did attend it; he watched from a ship about 30 miles away. Back in Princeton, where Wheeler's group had been working since the summer of 1951, we didn't know the precise time that the test would take place, and we knew that we wouldn't be notified right away anyway. There'd be no way for us to find out instantly whether it had been a success. So, I think we went about our normal busi-ness, and I may have gone back over to Palmer Laboratory, the physics building on the campus, and thought a little about pure physics instead of about bombs.

I had actually carried out the calculations on a computer called the SEAC in Washington, DC, during the summer of 1952 that led to the prediction of what the total energy release would be. The final number that I came up with was 7 megatons. It turned out to be 10 megatons, even more than we had forecast. Ten megatons, for perspective, is about 700 Hiroshimas.

I felt … well, elated might be too strong a word, but a sense of satisfaction. We'd worked on a hard physics prob-lem for two years. We had succeeded, we were successful, it worked. So, of course, the first reaction was one of pleasure and satisfaction, not one of regret, not one of apprehension for the future. Such thoughts came later.

I feel no regrets. Later on, in 1968, moved in part by my opposition to the Vietnam War, I made a pledge never again to work on weapons. I and many other people felt strongly that the only long-term course of action for the world was to eliminate nuclear weapons altogether. The only suitable goal for the world is zero. One nuclear weapon in any arsenal is one too many, and I have to hope that – if not within my lifetime, but within this century – that goal will be achieved, and nations will come to their senses and see that nuclear weapons make no sense. But, looking back to 1950–2, I don't feel I made a wrong decision. I don't feel regret about it. I do even now feel that the world was indeed made a slightly safer place by the United States getting that weapon before the Soviet Union did.

Matashichi Oishi was a 20-year-old fisherman when his boat the Lucky Dragon *was caught within the danger zone of the Castle Bravo H-bomb test on 1 March 1954.*

I was 14 years old when I dropped out of second grade at junior high school to become a fisherman. I didn't know anything about the world. We were a defeated country, and there was no food. We looked for protein sources, and fishing was a good business. Compared to ordinary people, we made a lot of money and we lived in quite a grand style. I had a hard time, but I learned a lot. We didn't have machinery like there is now, so everything was done by hand, and the *Lucky Dragon* wasn't sturdy at all. It was built after the war when there was nothing. I get scared to think now how we managed to sail on the Pacific Ocean..

The fishermen of the *Lucky Dragon*.

From the test site to where we were was 160 kilometres, so it was quite far. The captain and the chief radio operator knew there was a US military test site nearby, and they had been warned not to get close to it, but we didn't know anything about it. I didn't know anything about America's important confidential experiment, so when I saw the light, I had no idea what was happening.

That day, we finished putting the long line into the sea, and the crew members were catching a little sleep. About three hours – that was the only sleep we would get. The dawn hadn't completely broken, and it was a darkish sky, so the light looked so vivid. The colour was a little lighter than the colour of sunset. It emerged from the horizon, from the west and the east and every direction. It wasn't flashing, it was like the light was flowing and covering the whole area. I thought it was some kind of natural disaster. Everybody on the boat was anxiously watching what was going to happen next. The light was there for one or two minutes, then it gradually changed colour and disappeared.

We were all asking each other, 'What was the light about?', but no one had a clue. We just knew something extraordinary was happening beyond the horizon, so we decided to pull out the long line in the ocean as soon as possible. Before we started pulling out, the crew went to eat breakfast in relays. We ate at stern, at the very back of the boat. A big wooden container for cooked rice was served with miso soup and simmered fish. We always had fish. And as we started eating, the sound struck.

It was far beyond the horizon, so we couldn't see what was happening. Only the sound and the light reached us. When the light flashed, everyone had just gawped, but when we heard the sound everyone dived to the deck and crawled into the cabins and hid themselves. It was a huge rumbling that came up from the bottom of the ocean.

Everyone was stunned by the sound. It was not a bang, like the explosion of a bomb. It was the earth rumbling, from the bottom of the ocean to the surface. I couldn't tell from which way this big sound was coming. Everyone was stunned by it. Something extraordinary was happening, and we wondered what would happen next. We waited and waited, but nothing happened. That was it. Nothing happened, and it became calm.

Everybody was worried because we had no idea what had happened. But our long line was still in the ocean. Fishermen cannot run away leaving equipment behind, so we started pulling out the long line. We were pulling out the long line at the opposite direction from where the light had emerged, so we were moving away from it. It took more than six hours to pull everything out, and the sky became brighter before we finished. I saw a big fluffy cloud, something like a thundercloud, on the horizon. I don't know why, but I couldn't get it out of my head. I kept looking back at it.

It was coming towards us at great speed. The sky had been clear, but it became cloudy, and the rain started sprinkling. A little later, stark white powder started falling. On the southern ocean, there was no way it would snow and we wondered what this white stuff was, but I didn't feel any danger, because the white powder was falling all over my face but it didn't leave any mark. We picked it up, licked it and nibbled it. If it had been snow, it would have melted in our mouths, but it didn't melt – it was crunchy like eating sand. It didn't smell either. We couldn't understand it. More and more things we couldn't understand. The powder went under my shirt and underwear, and inside the gloves I was wearing. It was itchy, and it kind of hurt. The boat was covered by it; it piled up on the deck, we left footprints in it. We had no idea, we had no clue. We were not scared. If it had been hot or if we had felt any real pain, we would have been scared, but it wasn't like that at all. We just kept working, and the time just passed by. I kept doing my job for six hours, and in the meantime death ash kept falling down.

Professors at the University of Tokyo investigated the white powder when we got back to Japan, and they found that it contained tremendous radiation. You can't see radiation; you feel nothing if you touch it. You have no idea if you are hit by it. So we were not aware at the time but, when that ash was dropping down on us, there was radiation equivalent to the radioactivity within the range of 800 metres of the atomic bomb dropped on Hiroshima. It's been reported that we encountered a hydrogen bomb which was 1,000 times more powerful than the atomic bomb dropped on Hiroshima, and people imagine how awful the damage must have been, but it wasn't like that. It was completely different from Hiroshima. In our case, white powder was falling down like snow on us, and it contained radiation, and we only found out later. That's how we were exposed to radiation.

We started seeing a change in ourselves on the evening of that day. There were no external injuries, but we were dizzy, and some people started having diarrhoea. There was only one crew member who was confined to his bed; the rest of us were tough, so we just went to sleep that night. From around the second day, we started seeing real visible changes: the places where white ash landed started swelling. Ash had been piled up around my stomach, around my wrists and ankles, and lots of large blisters began appearing. If they had been regular burns, they would have been sore and tingling and they would have turned red, but it didn't hurt that much.

Then, after four or five days, our hair started falling out. One of the crew was combing his hair, and lots of it came off. Then everybody pulled at their hair, and it didn't hurt but whatever hair we pulled at came off our heads. I said we should not tell anybody what had happened to us. We thought that it was probably a secret US experiment, and if the US military found out we might be taken to America, and they would experiment on us. We were frightened. All of us kept our mouths shut.

We believed our hair would grow back again. But somebody collected his hair and had it checked at Tokyo University Hospital, and it was a mass of radiation. Then it became a big deal. It was reported that we had been exposed to radiation, and the news spread from Japan out into the world.

We didn't know what we'd experienced until we came home. I'd never heard of radiation at that time. Most ordinary people, except special cases, had no idea about it. After it came out on the news, people got scared and wouldn't come near me. People thought they would be infected by radiation if they came close to us. They thought their hair would fall out. It was a strange time. I felt somehow that death was approaching because people were making a lot of noise about it, but our bodies moved without difficulty. At that time, people didn't know about internal exposure – that came out 30 or 40 years later. At that time, people had no idea. A lot of harmful rumours were circulated, so nobody came close to me. It was a strange time.

Mr Kuboyama was the oldest man in the crew, and the radiation had a greater impact on an older person, or that is what I think, at least. Mr Kuboyama fell into a critical condition after about six months. The doctors thought those with fewer white blood cells might be in danger, so they kept an eye on us, and gave us blood transfusions every day. The blood had hepatitis C virus and all of us were infected. Mr Kuboyama ended up developing liver damage and met a tragic end. His bed was next to mine, so

I saw everything from the beginning until he died. At first, we were laughing together, then he got brain fever. Toxins from his liver had reached his brain, and he went insane. It was pitiful and sad.

Like the others from the boat, I got infected with hepatitis C and I had the same diseases. I got liver cancer and had an operation at an early stage, and I survived, although my companions died. I don't know why. I might have had the devil's luck, but I didn't die. My first child was born dead with a birth defect. They say radiation can produce babies with birth defects, so I think it's linked. I didn't get over it, but I just carried on.

I've been thinking about it and talking about it for all these years, but the US will never admit it and the government of Japan supports what the US says. They'd rather save the US's face than listen to our claims. There has been no progress in the talks. They are so powerful, and we have no chance against them, whatever we do. More than ten of my friends died at half my age, in their forties or fifties – in the prime of their life. But our words are not taken seriously. I write and sometimes talk about the resentment and bitterness, but the government won't talk to me. The Japanese government doesn't want to touch it.

I didn't have much education, and I didn't know anything about the Cold War. Now, 60 years later, I have studied hard and gained some knowledge. I think it wasn't just a conflict between America and the Soviet Union, it was humanity's karma. In the history of humanity, the wars never end. And there's no effort to abolish nuclear weapons. It is human stupidity.

'Now it was going to be different'

The East German Uprising (1953)

By 1953, post-war Germany was a tale of two states. The Federal Republic of Germany had been forged by the Americans, British and French out of their combined occupied zones in the west. The Soviets had responded by turning their occupied zone in the east into a socialist alternative: the German Democratic Republic, governed by the Socialist Unity Party (Sozialistische Einheitspartei Deutschlands, SED). And whereas the United States was using its Marshall Plan to pour aid into the new West German state, East Germany had been stripped for war reparations and was in the throes of an economic crisis.

The difference was most stark in divided Berlin. After the hardships of the blockade of 1948–9, West Berlin was awash with imported goods, shipped in to transform it into a shop window for Western democracy and capitalism. East Berlin, like the rest of East Germany, was by contrast becoming increasingly grim. Food and consumer goods were in short supply, there were frequent power cuts and, although crossing from one side of the city to the other was still possible, East Berliners were under instructions to stop consorting with Westerners.

In Moscow, the ailing Soviet leader, Joseph Stalin, had become increasingly paranoid. The division of Germany in 1949 had put paid to his hopes of the whole country eventually becoming part of the Communist bloc. Now he was worried that the new West German state would join NATO, rearm and pose a direct military threat to Soviet interests, right on its East German doorstep.

To pre-empt this, in 1952 Stalin floated the idea of a new united Germany, which would be neutral and demilitarised. When the West rebuffed that offer, he changed tack and ordered the East German leadership to push for rapid Sovietisation.

East Germany's leader was a hard-line Communist whose close ties to the Soviet Union went back to the 1920s. Walter Ulbricht even sported a goatee beard apparently modelled on that of Vladimir Lenin. He eagerly complied with the order to transform East Germany into a Stalinist command economy and set about collectivising agriculture, ramping up industrial and military production and tightening political control. It pushed the East German economy to the limit and created a backlash of popular frustration. The number of people emigrating to the West escalated. A crackdown on dissent by his Stasi secret police created a high number of political prisoners.

Then, on 5 March 1953, at his country house outside Moscow, Stalin died.

It was a turn of events that left the Soviet population bewildered and uncertain. The Soviet Communist Party leadership announced that it would henceforth rule collectively, but behind the scenes a bitter power struggle was unfolding. As the rivals jockeyed for power, the last thing they wanted at this delicate moment of political transition was trouble in Eastern Europe.

They had reason to be worried. In mid-May, the East German leadership announced that from 30 June 1953, Ulbricht's 60th birthday, all East German workers would have to meet higher production quotas without any increase in pay.

In late May there was a brief flicker of industrial unrest in Czechoslovakia in response to a similar push for higher prices and wage cuts, so the Kremlin was concerned about the reaction in East Germany. The new leaders summoned Ulbricht and his East German colleagues to Moscow and warned them that they must ease up on the pace of enforced industrialisation. The reprimand did not have the desired impact, and the East German government went ahead with the new targets anyway.

East German workers were incensed at the prospect of what was essentially a compulsory pay cut. On 16 June 1953 several hundred construction workers in East Berlin marched through the city to the main government building to complain about the planned hike in production targets. It was an unprecedented show of defiance against the authorities.

When a government minister came out to try to reason with them, his appearance had the opposite effect. The protest mushroomed into political demands and a general strike was declared for the following day. News of the planned strike spread quickly, not least because it was all reported in detail by the American-run RIAS (Rundfunk im amerikanischen Sektor) radio station in West Berlin, which could be picked up across most of East Germany. After years of increasing hardship and restrictions, for many East Germans it was an exhilarating moment.

The following day, a huge demonstration of striking workers gathered in East Berlin calling for political prisoners to be released, for free elections, for the government's resignation and for the 'Goatee' (Ulbricht) to go. It was as though a dam had been opened. Protests broke out in many other East German cities and towns including Dresden, Leipzig and Frankfurt an der Oder, and in the Baltic port of Rostock. Overall, an estimated one million people joined in. For the East German authorities, it was a profound shock and an embarrassing setback: their attempt to establish a workers' state had instead provoked a workers' uprising.

Walter Ulbricht was determined to crush the rebellion by whatever means necessary. He asked Moscow to send in Soviet tanks and troops to help him. In East Berlin, the area where demonstrators were gathered was cordoned off with barbed wire to stop Western military observers who had the right to enter East Berlin from seeing what was going on. Then Soviet tank units and East German police confronted the crowds, opening fire in some places. The demonstrators responded by throwing bricks and Molotov cocktails, but they were outgunned and outnumbered. A brief moment of heady euphoria had turned into a nightmare.

The East German authorities imposed a state of emergency and a curfew, and eventually were able to restore control. Some protestors managed to flee for their lives, in some cases making it over the border to the safety of West Berlin. Others were surrounded and loaded on to trucks to be taken off for interrogation or even mock executions. In a couple of days, it was all over.

The crackdown led to dozens of deaths; hundreds of people were injured and thousands arrested. Hundreds of workers deemed to be ringleaders were given long prison sentences. Links with West Berlin were cut off until the situation calmed down. There was one victory, though: Ulbricht's government did agree to the original strikers' demand for an easing of work quotas.

Outside Germany, there are probably few people today who remember the East German uprising of 1953, but it was the first widespread public revolt against Communist power in Eastern Europe and it did in fact set an important precedent. A pattern of uprisings against dictatorial party rule would be repeated in various parts of the Communist bloc in years to come: in Poland and Hungary in 1956; the so-called Prague Spring in 1967–8; the Polish ship-yard workers who in the 1980s instigated the Solidarity movement; and the coal miners of Russia and Ukraine whose strikes in the late 1980s contributed to the internal collapse that destroyed the Soviet Union.

The uprising caused a fundamental shift in the way Moscow viewed East Germany. Before 1953, it was treated as a vestige of the old Germany, in debt to the Soviet Union for the damage and destruction caused by the Nazis during the war. Now it was a frontline state, cheek-by-jowl with the West's capitalist showcase in West Germany, an important part of the Cold War propaganda stand-off. Instead of bleed-ing East Germany dry, the Soviets wanted to see it prosper. Instead of keeping a distance from Walter Ulbricht's hard-line regime, Moscow now needed to bolster it to ensure that it survived, whatever the cost of the project.

In local newspapers, the East German authorities claimed that the unrest had been orchestrated by 'Western agencies' seeking to undermine the country from within. They condemned the corrosive influence of American popular culture seeping across the border from West Berlin. For eight more years, disaffected East Germans still had an escape route via West Berlin, until the Berlin Wall was constructed in 1961 to stop them.

Meanwhile, the East German police state tightened its grip. The people would not risk rising up once more against their Communist masters for another 36 years –

not until the mass demonstrations of 1989 that began in Leipzig and led to the fall of the Berlin Wall.

*As part of his National Service, **George Flint** was dispatched to Berlin to be a driver for BRIXMIS – the British Mission in the Soviet Zone. This gave him, at just 19, an extraordinary close-up view of the troubles of East Germany that led to the uprising.*

The Soviet zone was very downtrodden. There was no greenery, because all the trees had been cut down and burned for fuel. The shortages were terrible – the shop windows were empty, and there were great big queues outside the butcher's. One lady came out with a big news-paper bundle in her hands and, as she came past me, it burst open and there were hoofs in it. She was going to boil them up for jelly. If any bread came in, they all some-how knew and everyone ran to the shop.

You couldn't talk to any of the East Berliners as they were scared to be seen talking to Westerners. The West Berliners were loving it, though; they loved being Westernised. They'd just had the Berlin airlift, so they were getting coal and heating. They were starting to get back to normal. But in the Eastern sector, it was very hard.

The East Berliners didn't have a lot to do with the Russians if they could help it. The Russians wandered around going into shops wanting to buy watches and silly flashy ornaments – they were like big kids. But after what happened when they took Berlin, the German people were very dubious about any fraternisation with the Russians. When I first went there, the non-fraternisation law was still in. And even if you made friends with any Russian squaddies, they would be looking out for their commissars – they had eyes and ears everywhere.

The commissars were very persuasive, and they had good techniques. They'd get their cigarettes out and use them as bargaining chips – swap them for the Russian cigarettes, which were half cardboard, half horse shit. They'd be saying that the Americans wanted war, but the Soviets didn't. They thought they would turn us.

In areas where the Russians had exercises and things they didn't want anyone else to see, they had signs up in three languages: 'British, French, USA prohibited'. These signs were nailed to trees or up on gates, and there'd be rolls of barbed wire. But it wasn't a deterrent – it spurred them on. The idea was to get past them and see if anything was happening. Officers would argue that they hadn't seen any of the signs. Some of the lads nicked them and put them in their cars.

Hardy Firl was a young driver working in East Berlin, capital of the German Democratic Republic.

It was not nice in the GDR, and we were constantly told what to do at work – to join organisations like 'Free German Youth' and so on – but I didn't join any of them. You faced a lot of disadvantages if you didn't want to join the party.

Everyone had work, but we earned very little and there wasn't much, unlike West Berlin that had everything. The rent was cheap, but without central heating, you had to heat your home with an oven. I earned 600 marks per month, so I could not afford a rent of 500. There were delicatessens where you had to pay 10 marks for a tin of pineapple. But no one could afford that apart from high-ranking men.

From the end of the war to the early 1950s, it all got worse. There was hardly anything to buy any more. My parents wanted a few nails, and even those were not available.

Hardy Firl.

Joachim Rudolph didn't think much of life in East Germany either. He was a 14-year-old schoolboy – too young to work – but he was excited to hear about the upcoming strike.

A few days before 17 June, there was another 'raise of the norm', which meant that the builders had to work faster and harder in order to receive the same wage. It was not the first time, and the builders were very indignant. They gathered and discussed going to the authorities to protest about it. So they went to the Housing Ministry to speak to someone responsible for this, but they were not given access to him and were sent home again. They could hand in a petition, but nothing more.

They met up again and decided to go on strike – not only the builders but the whole of East Berlin. Ideally, the whole population of the GDR would go on strike. That reached the Western media very quickly, and therefore it also reached everyone in the GDR. That's how there came to be strikes and demonstrations in several hundred towns.

We heard about it in the evening, and I agreed to meet with a friend, who had the same political attitude as me, in the morning about eight or nine o'clock at my house, as we wanted to see what was going to happen. When we stepped on to the streets, we saw the demonstration coming from Weissensee towards the city centre. Everyone was trying to get to Marx-Engels-Platz, where the population had to march past representatives of the GDR government every bank holiday.

On the morning of the strike, 17 June 1953, Carla Ottmann was looking forward to her seventh birthday party, which was coming up in just two days' time.

The atmosphere shortly before 17 June had been very tense for me. My birthday is on 19 June, and I was looking forward to all the guests and all the presents – and a richly laid birthday table with relatives and friends. I did not notice the threat that my parents sensed but, looking back, it was there. The looks between them became more anxious. There was a sense of unrest, but as a child one is not really aware of it.

On 17 June, my parents woke me up because there was noise on the street. We lived on a street that had a little promenade in the middle, and normally there was not much traffic. And suddenly there was the sound of many, many vehicles and that, of course, was confusing. So we looked out of the window and there were Russian soldiers who drove up in vehicles, big and small, occupied the promenade in the middle of the street, erected tents and made their presence felt so that we all wondered what was going on.

It chilled me to the bone, mainly because I saw the frightened looks of my parents. My father was wounded at Stalingrad, my mother had to run with her sister out of a bombed and burning house … These were all things I knew but could not put them together. And suddenly, it hit me that my birthday was in two days. What was going to happen with my birthday?

That was in the morning. We children were not allowed to go to school, and we were not allowed to go on to the streets. Towards midday, we heard other sounds. I lived on Schönhauser Allee in Prenzlauer Berg, and that was the street that led to Berlin Pankow, where the government of the GDR was situated, and on that route were tanks. The sound of the tanks gave me goose pimples; I can remember that very clearly. That was very frightening, seeing the tanks and hearing the terrible sounds that they were making.

The teenage schoolboy **Joachim Rudolph** *joined a huge demonstration, marching towards the city centre.*

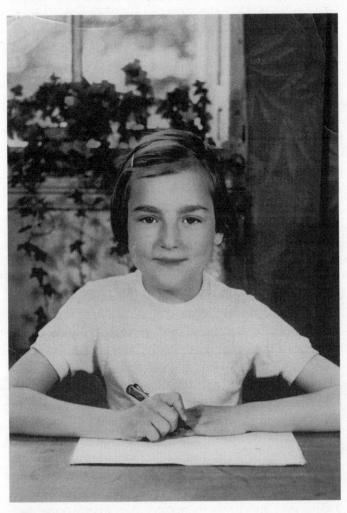

Carla Ottmann in the early 1950s.

We passed a shoe factory. Many women were leaning out of the windows, looking and waving and cheering, but you couldn't hear what they were saying. Then the march, which was already very big, stopped, and we went to the gate, which was closer to the windows, and we called: 'Come down! Join us! You can see and you know that the national strike is today.' And they said: 'Yes, we would like to but the management has locked all the doors and gates. We can't get out.' Then someone climbed over the steel gate and managed to break the gate open, and then the doors. Many women came down and joined the march in their work aprons.

At the corner of Dimitroffstrasse, there was a tram, which was stopped by the march. The organisers went straight to the conductor and the ticket collector, and they said: 'Come along, you know today people are on strike.' The conductor and the collector refused, saying they were not allowed to. And then the organisers said, 'You'll join us, you won't drive any further.' Then they simply took away the pull rod that the conductor used to adjust the points. 'You can't get any further, you don't have a pull rod any more.' I am not sure if they joined then, but the tram did not go any further.

Hardy Firl left his job and joined the march, too.

I was given a banner to carry and it just said: 'We Want Free Elections'. I'm stressing that I did not touch a stone. I did not attack one policeman. I saw with my own eyes how policemen were attacked. They were defenceless; they didn't dare do anything any more. There was a radio car from the People's Police in Warschauer Strasse, and I went over and I told them to give me the microphone. They didn't want to, but I told them, 'Even if I don't like it, I can also act differently. I would advise you to give it to me.' And with the microphone I repeated our slogan: 'Free elections!' And then we shouted, 'The Goatee's got to go!' – meaning Walter Ulbricht. And then we demanded the resignation of the government. Always the same slogans.

At the same time, protests and riots broke out in cities across the country – including Dresden, Leipzig and Frankfurt an der Oder, where **Alfred Wegewitz** *was a young law student on placement with the Communist-appointed People's Judges.*

My fellow students who belonged to the Communist Party went to a builders' camp and tried to talk to the builders, saying that they should give up the strike and go back to work. The workers refused. Everybody who was visibly from the party was rejected.

At court, there was some commotion. The judges were intimidated by all these events and did not dare to voice other views towards us than what the party line said. As judges, they were employed by the state, and if they deviated from the party line they would be fired. These were simple people, who only had a little education; they were the so-called People's Judges. We were told: 'It's a very bad business, a counter-revolution, and for our protection we have been given weapons.' They showed them to us: 'Look, we are not completely defenceless.'

Although I saw the weapons, I knew these people and assumed that they would not have the courage to use them. I didn't see it as a serious attempt to fight against the counter-revolution. I think they just wanted to calm everyone down.

We only knew that there was a state of emergency from the papers and the broadcasts. More than five people were not allowed to stand together, and there was a curfew from when it got dark. I can't remember if it affected me in any way, but I had little reason at that time to be outside.

I was worried that the intervention of the Russian army would lead to casualties among the civilian population. We were so intimidated by the Russians that we said to ourselves: 'Let's wait. Hopefully this will all resolve peacefully.' There was also a lot of propaganda from West Berlin, an attempt to heat up the situation. That did not resonate with everyone; some people said to themselves, 'Why should we give away our skin for goals we do not quite know?'

Back in East Berlin, **Joachim Rudolph** *and his fellow marchers reached a building belonging to the SED – the Socialist Unity Party.*

It was locked, of course. The march stopped and they shouted threats up at the windows. We went up some stairs and knocked on one of the window panes – we wanted to get in. And there was a roller shutter, which you couldn't tear out or break open. In front of these bars, there was a disabled ex-serviceman who had lost a leg in the war. He was beside himself with anger and ranted on the steps and stabbed with his crutches through this roller shutter and smashed all the glass panes behind it with his crutches.

When I returned to the street and looked up, I could see the outlines of men's faces behind the net curtains in some of the windows. It was the SED-party bigwigs, also afraid, and looking out of the window to see what was going to happen. The whole time, I did not see one policeman or a border guard. I did not see one uniformed person on the street that day, at least until the Russian tanks came.

When we got to Marx-Engels-Platz, it was full of people – I had never seen anything like it before. A great atmosphere. There were people with banners – 'Freedom Not Socialism', slogans like that. There was a euphoric mood, and they really believed that now the system was overthrown. Now it was going to be different. It couldn't go on like that. But before long, there was a dull rumble. And then, immediately, it passed from person to person: 'Russian tanks are coming!'

We stood there as it got louder, louder and louder. And suddenly we saw that from Rathausstrasse, the East Berlin Town Hall, the first Russian tank was coming with a gigantic blue cloud of smoke from its exhaust pipe. There was an extremely loud noise, and I recognised that noise from my reservist training courses. And on top of the tank there was a high-ranking officer, who had a cape and a steel helmet on his head, and he was shouting at the crowd. But, of course, we did not understand a word – it was extremely loud. We could just see from the movement of his mouth that he was shouting, making threats and waving his fist. Then, at a distance of 10 or 15 metres, the next tank followed around the corner. And they just drove into the crowds.

George Flint and his British military colleagues had been driving around monitoring what was going on. But the Soviet Army didn't want an audience.

Some people had Molotov cocktails, and some were using bricks as weapons. But they couldn't really do anything against the might of the Russians. You're not going to fight a tank with your bare hands, are you?

When the riots got going, people were getting killed. The Russians had people out dragging barbed wire across to stop Brits looking, so we would try and get in through another place. Sometimes we were lucky and got through. Mainly, though, the Russians kept us away – they were very efficient at that. Tight on security.

Eventually, there was calm. People were now too frightened to come out on to the streets. And it was all covered up very quickly. They covered up whether any fighting had gone on – they had plenty of men to do that.

They muffled it all down – that was a favourite thing with the Russians.

As a state of emergency and curfew were imposed, **Joachim Rudolph** *tried to get home.*

We were mighty frightened. We didn't know how many more tanks would come, and we thought a lot might come. I don't know how many there were – perhaps six to eight, I don't think it was more.

We tried to get home as soon as possible, because we knew that from now on it wouldn't be possible to demonstrate much further. We walked back towards home and reached Königstrasse, and we had to get past the East Berlin police headquarters. We suddenly heard, perhaps 100 or 200 metres in front of us, extremely loud bangs, like gunshots. 'Man,' we thought, 'now they're even shooting at people.' We were all very frightened and went into the entry halls of houses, and we crouched in the hallways and waited, wondering what would happen next, and hoping that the shooting would stop soon.

Joachim finally made it home, to an almighty scolding from his mother. **Hardy Firl** *wasn't so lucky.*

We got to Andreasstrasse, and then the Russian tanks came. Many people continued, and they managed to get to Potsdamer Platz, but we were surrounded. We were ordered to put down the banner, and we put it down. We went down Andreasstrasse, and there were ten lorries of the People's Police with dogs. The tailgates were lowered, and everybody was ordered on to the lorry, men and women alike.

They drove us to Friedrichsfelde East, where there was a former stockyard from the time of the emperor, where cattle was brought in and slaughtered. So we all got off from the lorry. There was one officer who would have liked to shoot me. He had a weapon in his hand. Five of us had to go and stand against the wall, hands up, legs apart, faces facing the wall. Behind us were three men from the Stasi with machine guns pointing at us. It was a mock execution. I said to the man next to me, 'They're going to shoot us in the back.' And he said, 'They wouldn't dare.' Luckily they didn't, otherwise I wouldn't be here.

After an hour, we were taken inside the hall, and made to lie on a stone floor, covered in a very thin layer of straw. On the right side were the men; on the left, the women. Then they came and took away our identity cards. There was one who needed the loo and they shot – not the people, but into the air. There were still casualties, though, from the ricochet of the bullets.

Someone called my name, and then it really started. I was handcuffed and put into a car, then they drove me to a police station in Lichtenberg. They put me into a cell, and took away my shoelaces and belt. They didn't want anyone hanging themselves. I was left in the cell, alone, then they came back and drove me – handcuffed all the time – to Glinkastrasse. There I had to go up five flights of stairs, with two policemen at my side. This was the head-quarters of the People's Police, in the Interior Ministry. I went into a room, where a high-ranking officer was sitting behind a desk. He told the police officers to get out so that he wouldn't have any witnesses.

He looked up and down at me and then he said, 'American jeans.' One could buy those in the West – there wasn't a wall yet. I didn't say anything. Then he said, 'Who sent you to the uprising?' I said, no one had sent me. 'But you are also with the CIA.' I said, 'No, I am not with them.' He kept asking, and I kept denying. Then he said, 'But you were with the demonstrations.' I didn't say anything because I thought he would need to prove that. Then he brought out a big photograph and he said, 'Look, that's you.' And there was my head, marked with a white circle. We had been photographed.

I couldn't deny it any longer. He went to a cupboard, he unlocked it, and there were truncheons in there. He took one out, came up to me, and said, 'If you don't sign – I can act differently.' Then he hit me, not in the face but in the chest. Then I did sign a confession that I had been at the demonstrations. Then it was quiet. He pressed a button, and two policemen came in and took me away, back into the car to the remand prison in Dircksenstrasse, where I was kept in solitary confinement.

That was 17 June. On 30 June there was the trial. I was handcuffed again, driven to Littenstrasse, and taken into the courtroom. I had a show trial. I had a defence lawyer who didn't say a word; it was just to show that they had someone acting for me. There were at least 30 spectators, but not from the public – they were all high-ranking officers from the People's Police. The judge reeled off my details, where I was born, and so on, and that I had signed that confession. Whereupon I said, 'Yes, but under duress.'

He looked puzzled: 'What do you mean "under duress"?' I told him that I had been beaten. A murmur went through the officers: 'Who does he think he is?' The judge leaned forward and said, 'Our government bodies do not beat defenceless people.' And I said, 'But that is the case.' The charges were causing unrest and being a ringleader. I was sentenced to three years' Zuchthaus. Not prison, there is a difference. Zuchthaus is harder.

They drove me back to the remand prison and two days later to Berlin-Rummelsburg. I had to undress completely, everything; they checked if you were smuggling anything into the prison. Then they gave me some basic clothes and a yellow stripe – that was for those from 17 June. They shaved all my hair off, which was humiliating. There were four men to a small cell, with two bunk beds. And I was given one blanket. No mattresses, but bags of straw, pillows too, filled with straw. During the day, we were not allowed to lie down.

*And what about **Carla Ottmann**'s seventh birthday party, planned for 19 June 1953?*

School started again a day or two later, but our parents kept us children at home. When our parents were not at home, we children secretly went to that middle promenade, where the Russians cooked fragrant soups in their field kitchen, and they picked us up in their arms. The Russian soldiers were known to be very friendly to children; they gave us sweets and suddenly this wasn't dangerous any more. When I got upstairs with my sweets, my mother scolded us terribly. And we responded: 'But the soldiers were very friendly, they gave us sweets and sang us songs.' To us it all seemed very merry.

My birthday completely fell through, though. I'm not even sure if my mother was able to bake a birthday cake for me. But no visitor could come from the West. Friends and relatives who lived in other parts of East Berlin didn't come either, because everybody was afraid, so my birthday was celebrated very quietly in a very small circle at home ... It was a sad birthday.

'Democracy and freedom became a memory only'

The Iranian Coup (1953)

By the early 1950s, Iran had become a focus of concern for Western powers. The Korean War, the emergence of Communist China, the extent of Soviet domination over Eastern Europe and the news that the Soviet Union had tested an atomic bomb had all intensified fears of a Cold War confrontation in some 'weak spot' in the world, or even of a new global war being triggered. Oil-rich, strategically placed and engulfed in political turmoil, Iran looked a likely candidate.

The Americans were particularly worried about the potential spread of Soviet influence in the Middle East. During the Second World War, British-led troops and Soviet forces had jointly occupied Iran to prevent its oil fields and supply routes from falling into German hands. But after the war, although the Western Allies complied with the agreement to withdraw, the Soviets did not. Soviet forces remained in northern Iran to channel military support to two breakaway regions of local Azerbaijanis and Kurds respectively, which were fighting Iranian government forces. It looked as though Moscow was deliberately using the enclaves to set up pro-Soviet footholds in north-west Iran.

For a short while, the flare-up looked as though it could escalate into an early Cold War conflict. Eventually, American diplomatic pressure led the Soviets to withdraw, but Washington remained suspicious of longer-term Soviet intentions in the region.

The British strategic interest in Iran was, above all, about oil. It was a British company that had first discovered Iran's lucrative oilfields in 1908, and Britain still retained a controlling interest. In the early 1950s, the Iranian oil industry was in the hands of the British-owned Anglo-Iranian Oil Company or AIOC (one of the antecedents to British Petroleum or BP), with only a modest percentage of the profits going to Iran. For many Iranians, this foreign control of their main economic asset aroused intense nationalist anger and looked like British imperialism in economic guise.

In 1951, a European-educated lawyer and committed nationalist called Mohammad Mosaddegh was elected Iran's Prime Minister. To the alarm of the British, he declared his intention to bring the country's oil production under national control. First, he asked the AIOC to allow its books to be audited, to check whether the Iranian government was receiving its due share of profits. When that request was refused, he asked the Iranian Parliament to pass a law to nationalise the oil industry. This move was hugely popular in Iran, but put him at loggerheads with the British government, which in response instigated a world-wide boycott of Iranian oil.

By 1953, Mosaddegh was beginning to run into problems. He had broken off diplomatic relations with the British government, and the British-led oil embargo was beginning to take its toll, causing increasing economic discontent and raising political tensions. He was also in open conflict with the Shah of Iran, Mohammad Reza Pahlavi, whose executive powers he considered too extensive for an unelected monarch.

Then, in August 1953, Mosaddegh made a move that probably sealed his downfall. He decided to dissolve Parliament, giving himself and his cabinet complete power to rule. The move stripped the Shah of his powers and led to accusations that it was Mosaddegh, once a champion of democracy, who was now acting like a dictator.

By now, the United States had elected a new President – General Dwight Eisenhower. The previous American President, Harry S. Truman, preoccupied with the war in Korea, had refused an earlier British request for help to depose Mosaddegh. But countering the Soviet threat had been a key issue in Eisenhower's election campaign in 1952, and his White House professed worries that Mosaddegh was becoming too dependent on the pro-Soviet, Communist Tudeh Party, and could become a conduit for a Communist takeover in Iran. Whether this was the main reason, or whether the United States, like Britain, was also concerned not to lose control of Iran's oil and the waterways of the Persian Gulf, the Eisenhower administration agreed to undertake a joint effort to oust him. The Shah was also persuaded to play a role.

The first attempt to remove Mosaddegh failed. On the night of 15–16 August 1953, an army colonel was sent to deliver a royal decree signed by the Shah, ordering Mosaddegh to step down. But Mosaddegh, who had been tipped off by sympathisers within the armed forces, refused to accept the message, promptly arrested the colonel and ordered other coup plotters to be rounded up. The Shah, fearing retribution, immediately fled abroad.

In the days that followed, tensions rose as large crowds took to the streets, initially in favour of Mosaddegh and of turning Iran into a republic; later (after the first demonstrations were dispersed by the police) with some demonstrating in support of the Shah and against a 'Communist revolution'. It is generally accepted that various agents were sending in paid infiltrators who were encouraging the mood of mounting confrontation, and trying to inflame the crowds and increase the likelihood of conflict, though exactly who was trying to orchestrate events remains unclear.

By 19 August, the stage was set. On the streets of Tehran, not far from the house of Mosaddegh, the day began with groups of demonstrators gathering, as though primed for trouble. By the middle of the day, street unrest had turned into a full-scale riot and troops and tanks had been deployed, with fierce fighting taking place outside Mosaddegh's house. A mob descended on his house to ransack and loot it. By early afternoon, the radio was broadcasting that Mosaddegh had been killed and the government had fallen.

In fact, Mosaddegh had not been killed but had left the city to escape the violence. A curfew was imposed, and soldiers conducted house-to-house searches and barricaded off sections of the city as they looked for him. Within a day, he had turned himself in and, although he had been the democratically appointed Prime Minister of Iran, he was put on trial, imprisoned for three years and then lived under house arrest until his death in 1967.

The Shah was chaperoned back from exile by the Americans and within a year had signed a deal to give American as well as British oil companies a stake in the oil industry, in return for extensive aid to bring Iran back from economic collapse. Mosaddegh's associates, including many Communists from the Tudeh Party, were rounded up and imprisoned. Some were sentenced to death and executed. The Shah remained an absolute ruler and loyal Western ally until he was overthrown in the Iranian Islamic Revolution of 1979.

For many years, the role of American and British secret services in what were termed 'Operation Ajax' and 'Operation Boot' remained shadowy. For decades, the CIA refused to comment officially. But in 2000 the US Secretary of State, Madeleine Albright, went on the record to admit that American involvement in the coup had been a setback for Iran's political development and fuelled Iranian resentment against the United States. In 2013, declassified CIA documents confirmed that the coup had been 'carried out under CIA direction as an act of US foreign policy, conceived and approved at the highest levels', though the extent of official American involvement in the coup that successfully removed Mosaddegh is still disputed. The British have still not formally acknowledged their role. It has also been suggested that, whatever the activities of the CIA, the key factor may not have been foreign intervention at all, but unrest stage-managed from within Iran by those, including senior clerics, with their own reasons for wanting Mosaddegh gone.

Whatever the truth, Operation Ajax set a precedent. After Iran came a secret CIA operation to topple the government in Guatemala the following year, then the less successful Bay of Pigs invasion of Cuba in 1961. All were covert actions that helped to fuel a powerful anti-American backlash in later years.

In Iran, the coup of 1953 cemented deep-seated suspicion of the American and British governments. When the Shah was overthrown in 1979, secret CIA involvement in the coup of 1953 served as a rallying point for anti-US protests in Tehran. And as late as 2016, the Iranian government was still trying to sue the United States for compensation.

Mohammad Mosaddegh's nephew **Farhad Diba** *was 16 at the time of the coup.*

I was a schoolboy in England in 1953, but I was in Tehran for the summer, spending the holidays with my parents. My father was the half-brother of Dr Mosaddegh, and I was very close to my uncle. I followed the events very closely. I was a little bit wild, so far as my parents were concerned; there were constant riots and disturbances in Tehran in those days, and I would go out on to the streets to see what was happening.

In Iran, Mosaddegh began by being very popular on all sides of the political spectrum. As time wore on, certain sections took sides and he had quite an active opposition. The newspapers were freer than they had ever been in Iran at that time, and there were some vituperative articles in the papers against him. But he made his mark by saying that they should be free, they should not be censored, and for that, of course, he was admired.

The relationship between the Shah and Mosaddegh was fraught. The Shah had American and British support, but they could not come to terms with the character of Mosaddegh. He was thought by the West to have possible tendencies to lead Iran to Communism, whereas for the Russians it was quite the opposite: they rejected him because he was a landowning aristocrat, and could never think of him being a Communist. But Mosaddegh wanted to re-establish the terms of the 1906 constitution, under which the Shah was just a nominal monarch – he could not interfere in the workings of the government, which the Shah had begun to do by influencing elections and influencing the army. He tried to interfere in the governing of the country. It came to a head when Mosaddegh insisted, the second time he became Prime Minister under the Shah, that he himself had to choose the Minister of

War. In fact, he took that position himself for a while. Those supporting the Shah refused to accept this, saying that the army and the Ministry of War should be under the control of the Shah. This was a serious falling-out point between them.

On the other hand, Mosaddegh was a royalist, he was a monarchist, and it is false to say that he wished to be rid of the Shah. When the Shah fled in 1953, Mosaddegh really had the carpet pulled from under him because there was a vociferous section of the National Front which wanted to declare a republic. But he, being of a legal mind, said, 'No, this is not correct. We have to have a regency, and the regency has to then decide how to treat the monarchy in Iran.' By then, the point was moot, because he fell within hours.

After the failed first coup, everybody was jittery. Nobody knew the second coup was coming, but there was unease and there'd been very serious demonstrations against the Shah, so there was a lot of movement on the streets on 17 and 18 August.

At nine o'clock in the morning on 19 August, there was some noise in the streets. I went out with my camera. I went out and walked southwards and there was a huge crowd, marching northwards. They had come from the bazaar – they were the people who had been gathered by the agents of the coup: hooligans, with batons and sticks and so on, all shouting 'Long live the Shah!' They were moving northward, therefore moving towards the Park Hotel, where I was coming from. I must say I was a bit scared: I was 16. I ran up to the Park Hotel, the gate was shut, banged on the door, the doorman let me in, and the crowd marched past.

After they had passed, I went out again and, rather than following them, I went out and turned left towards my uncle's house to see what was happening there. In

Farhad Diba with Mohammad Mosaddegh, 1962.

that part of Tehran there was not much happening – it was concentrated on the Parliament building. By the time I got around to my uncle's house, near enough midday, already huge, huge crowds were gathering there, and it was quite tense. People were shouting this way and that way, pro- and anti-Mosaddegh slogans. I think their policy was to get a movement going, to gather as many people as possible and descend on Mosaddegh's house with such voluminous slogans against him and to get him to resign – that was their intent.

There was one photograph I took, a horrific one, when I left the hotel and approached the huge crowd. On the ground, I saw the tyre marks of a lorry which had gone over a body. I don't know how the body had been killed, but it was very gory.

Another person in those same Tehran streets that day was **Homa Sarshar**. *She remembers unusual activity on the afternoon of the coup ...*
On that day, I was just a shocked seven-year-old girl who didn't know what was going to happen. We lived very close to where Mosaddegh's home was – it was walking distance to his residence. I vividly remember that day: everybody was telling us to stay inside the house. We were watching through the window. I saw people running around, and I heard gunshots. My parents and my uncle were very scared and confused. I was scared. My brothers and I were just watching, wondering what was going on.

There was a construction site between our house and Mosaddegh's residence. This site was only at the first stage of construction. We saw a lot of people coming to this construction site, many of them workers, construction workers. We knew them a little bit because we would see them working every day from our balcony. And I saw many of them having furniture, dress, radio – you name it, they had it in their hand. And they were just running around, coming up to the first and second floor of the construction and putting them down. And I also saw my dad asking one of them, 'Why are you doing this? What is all this? Where did you get them?' And one of the construction workers told my dad, 'They are forcing us to do it.' And my dad asked, 'Who?' 'The police. The police are forcing us to loot the house, and take whatever exists.' And I remember the last pieces that they were bringing inside that construction site were Mosaddegh's rose trees that were in his garden. So, they even looted the garden; they even looted the plants that were there.

Farhad Diba

It was getting quite dangerous, so I left at just past noon and went to my sister's house. I wasn't allowed out again until we heard the news on the radio at two o'clock. They stopped playing music and announced that Mosaddegh had been killed and the government had fallen.

At that time, my father sent a driver to collect me. He said, 'You have to go out of town, go up north to our house.' On the way up, we were stopped maybe ten times. It's about 16 kilometres. Each time we were stopped, there was a crowd of ruffians shouting pro-Shah slogans. They stopped the car, and we had to take out a currency note with the Shah's face on it and put it on your windscreen and put your lights on, and with that you went on, as if you were supporting the Shah.

I thought Mosaddegh had been killed, because I had been there – I had seen the crowds building up. I thought they must have rushed his compound and gone into his house and killed him. It was horrifying, and we were in a state. But by the evening, my father received a message that he was safe.

A crowd gathers around a body outside the Park Hotel.
Photograph taken by Farhad Diba, 19 August 1953.

We stayed at home that day and the next, but the next day two lorry-loads of soldiers came to our house and ransacked the house, saying that Mosaddegh was hiding there, at his brother's house. Having found no Mosaddegh, they said, 'You can't leave,' and posted a lorry-load of soldiers at the gate. We were basically under house arrest. And there we were until Mosaddegh turned himself in.

When he was in solitary imprisonment, I visited him as many times as I could. And when he was in internal exile, for the rest of his life, I would go every Friday that I could to see him – it was about 140 kilometres outside Tehran, a compound guarded by the secret police. Nobody could go in except with special permission; they gave permission to the family, but they would quiz you at the door, they would take down your number plate and they would want to know everybody that was in the car.

He was more than an uncle, he was a father to me. Whenever I had a problem with my father, I would go straight to my uncle because he was the elder brother and his word went, and usually he would take my side against my father. We were close, we were extremely close. But after those events, he was an extremely broken man.

If you read the American archives, one after the other people who were writing policy said, 'Mosaddegh is not a Communist.' Early on, the British Anglo-Persian Oil Company decided that they could not and would not negotiate with Mosaddegh. I think the whole question was not Mosaddegh or the Shah. It was a three-letter word: oil. That was the crux of the matter.

Homa Sarshar
The day that they ousted Mohammad Mosaddegh, our Prime Minister, was really a *coup d'état*. They ousted him with the help of some of his friends. I believe those were

the last days and months of having the ecstasy of experiencing freedom and democracy in the country. Slowly, slowly after that, democracy and freedom became a memory only. A lot of people would remember him as a Prime Minister who was running a democratic government. After that, the country did not experience any of those glorious moments that we had with Mosaddegh.

'It was the beginning of freedom'

Khrushchev's Secret Speech (1956)

The death of Joseph Stalin on 5 March 1953 paved the way for a sea change in Soviet politics. To Western powers, Stalin, once a wartime ally, was seen by the early 1950s as a dangerously paranoid arch-rival in a global struggle between two ideologically opposed camps. News of his demise generated cautious optimism in Western capitals that Cold War tensions might subside.

For Soviet citizens, the situation was more complicated. Some privately saw Stalin as a monster at the heart of a brutal police state, whose ruthless policies had destroyed lives and ravaged the country. They remembered the upheaval of the early 1930s, when millions of peasants had seen their land seized and been forced into state-run collective farms. They recalled the terrifying purges of the late 1930s, when millions more were denounced as traitors and executed, imprisoned in brutal 'gulag' labour camps or banished to remote outposts.

But others looked up to Stalin as an icon of Soviet power who made the country a force to be reckoned with. They saw him as a war leader who had steered the Soviet Union to victory against the Nazis despite extraordinary suffering, and a strong ruler who over the past quarter of a century had successfully transformed the country into a formidable empire, equipped with industrial and military might. For these people, Stalin was revered as a father figure who was virtually a deity. Life without him was almost unthinkable.

The popular reaction to Stalin's death was one of shock. There was widespread consternation at what would become of the country without his leadership. His funeral was the biggest state occasion in the Soviet Union since Lenin's death in 1924, and the crowds on the streets of Moscow were so great and impossible to control that in places some people were crushed to death.

Inside the Kremlin, Stalin's death created a power vacuum. Almost immediately, the main figures at the top of the Communist Party hierarchy moved against the hated head of the secret police, Lavrentiy Beria, who was arrested and executed as a traitor. They then declared their adherence to the principle of 'collective leadership', while behind the scenes engaging in an intense battle over who would inherit the mantle of supreme leader.

Nikita Khrushchev was not an obvious first choice, but he managed to side-line his opponents and consolidate his own position to emerge as the front runner. To dissociate himself and the party from the worst excesses of the Stalin years, he ordered millions of political prisoners to be released from the gulag camps and launched an investigation to collect evidence of repression.

The formal 'rehabilitation' of Stalin's victims involved a commission examining the circumstances of each arrest and exposing trumped-up charges. Before long, horrific testimonies began to emerge, collated by the commission, which shone a spotlight on the dark side of Stalin's Russia. This evidence was one factor that contributed to Khrushchev's plan to break definitively with the Stalinist past, both to revitalise the party and to secure his own position as Soviet leader.

The place he chose to set out his new stand was the Congress of the Soviet Communist Party in 1956, the occasion when the leadership from around the country gathered in Moscow to set a new course, and to update Communist guests from across the world on policies and ideology. This 20th Party Congress in February 1956 was the first time these top officials had come together to take stock since Stalin's death. But what the delegates might have assumed would be a routine political gathering turned out to be anything but.

Late at night on 25 February 1956, Soviet officials were instructed to assemble for a private, closed meeting, with all foreign delegations and other guests excluded. Then Nikita Khrushchev rose to address them and for the next four hours delivered one of the most remarkable speeches of the Soviet era: a denunciation of Stalin's excesses and the personality cult that surrounded him, in a deliberate attempt to destroy the Stalin myth, only three years after his death.

It was an extraordinary change of tack, given the reverence with which Stalin had been treated until then. The assembled delegates listened in bewilderment. Some reacted with applause and laughter, apparently too shocked or confused to take it in. Others were so stunned, they collapsed and had to be helped out of the hall.

Not everyone wanted the speech to be made public. Some of Khrushchev's more conservative colleagues insisted that it was too incendiary to be released. The text was treated as a top-secret document. But, inevitably, before long the gist of it leaked out, first in reports based on hearsay, then after versions of the text made their way into

Western newspapers. The speech was eventually distributed in printed form, so that Communist functionaries could take it back to their regions and read it out for discussion at local – and sometimes turbulent – party meetings.

It became known as the Secret Speech and ushered in several years of relative liberalisation, in politics, in culture, in a new focus on consumerism, and in an opening up to Soviet Russia's old Cold War enemies in the West. The period became known as Khrushchev's 'thaw', named after a 1954 novel of the same name by the Soviet writer Ilya Ehrenburg.

Among practical measures that eased daily lives was a massive housebuilding programme. This, for the first time, gave many families the chance to live in small individual apartments where they could talk freely, instead of having to share communal flats with neighbours who might be informers. In the cultural sphere, the works of some previously banned writers, musicians and composers, including some from abroad, were allowed to be published and performed.

In 1957, a World Festival of Youth and Students was held in Moscow, bringing 34,000 young foreigners to the city, an unprecedented event. In 1959 millions of Soviet citizens flocked to see the *American National Exhibition* in Moscow, which gave them a glimpse of what life in the West might be like and fuelled their appetite for more and better consumer goods. The exhibition also provided the backdrop for an extraordinary exchange between Khrushchev and the visiting American Vice President, Richard Nixon, during which the two sparred in front of television cameras over the relative merits of capitalism and Communism. A few years later, Khrushchev personally approved the publication of Aleksandr Solzhenitsyn's story about life in the gulag camps, *One Day in the Life of Ivan Denisovich* – a publishing sensation.

But the liberalisation was inconsistent and only went so far. There may have been more cultural exchanges with the West and a relaxation of censorship, but the Soviet Union was still a dictatorship, controlled by the Communist Party and a powerful KGB state security network that monitored both foreigners and Soviet citizens alike. And Khrushchev had no intention of dismantling the Communist system or its control over its satellite states. Only months after his Secret Speech, in late 1956, an uprising in Hungary, which turned into a nationwide revolt, was brutally put down by Soviet tanks on orders from the Kremlin.

In the longer term, Khrushchev's speech did little to ease international tensions and Western suspicions of Communism. But inside the Soviet Union, the shift away from the repressions of the Stalinist period marked a dramatic turning point in Soviet politics at the height of the Cold War. And though the thaw did not last long – Khrushchev was deposed in 1964 – the process of de-Stalinisation that he began sowed the seeds for some of the thinking that would later be taken up in the 1980s 'perestroika' reforms of Mikhail Gorbachev.

Tatiana Baeva's father was one of many millions denounced as traitors and executed, imprisoned in brutal gulag labour camps or banished to remote outposts.

I was born in 1947 in the small village of Norilsk. We had some political men like Nikolai Bukharin, and this Bukharin had a secretary, and this secretary had a little philosophy society. My father participated in this philosophy society. In 1937, Stalin banished Bukharin, and Bukharin was killed and all people who worked with him were arrested. They were all arrested and killed, except my father. He was arrested, and stayed a prisoner for seventeen-and-a-half years. Sometimes he was in prison; sometimes he was out of prison but could not move to any place. I was born when he was out of prison but could not move to any other place. Before Norilsk, my father was a prisoner in a famous place, Solovki, but Solovki was closed and my father moved to Norilsk, and he worked there like a dog. It is a place close to the North Sea – it's tundra. No trees, no nothing, no food. Only snow, and half a year it's night, half a year it's day. But it was a very healthy place. I like everything what I have in my childhood. Of course, my father was not happy, but I was absolutely happy. Thank you, Stalin, for my happy childhood. It's a paradox.

In The Gulag Archipelago, *the writer Aleksandr Solzhenitsyn described the beating of a priest imprisoned in the Soviet labour-camp system. This was the father of Tatiana's future husband,* **Alexei Shipovalnikov**.

My father was a priest, and it was punishable to be a priest. My father was very friendly with [Solzhenitsyn] at that time, and I was too. He wrote a story of my father: how he was in the army during the Second World War; how, after he became a seminarian, he made a big mistake – he went to Bucharest, but he was so Russian he couldn't stay there. He went back to Russia, and he was arrested and put in a gulag.

I was born in the city of Rostov-on-Don, after my father was freed from prison, but after 13 months we had to escape very fast from Rostov-on-Don because some people came one morning and told [my parents], 'You will be arrested again.' During the night, we fled. After that, we travelled.

Nikita Khrushchev's son **Sergei Khrushchev** *vividly recalls the moment when he heard the news that Stalin had gone.*

When Stalin became sick and had a stroke, from the very beginning the doctors said there was no chance of survival. They published this medical bulletin, which showed there was no chance of survival. So, we had this feeling that he would die.

I knew it the same evening it happened. Stalin died about nine o'clock in the evening, and they had this final meeting to elect the new leadership. And then my father came home, sitting on the sofa, very tired, because they'd had two shifts at Stalin's bedside: day, it was Beria and Malenkov; night, it was Khrushchev and Bulganin. So he sat there and then he told us, without any real sorrow, 'Stalin died. I'm so tired, I will go to sleep.' I had the same feeling about Stalin as everyone because I knew nothing about the truth. So I thought, 'How can he say this?' Stalin died, and he said, 'I will go to sleep!' I went to another room and tried to cry. I couldn't cry, but I tried.

And next morning I went to the university, and there with the other students we were told we had to go to the Hall of Columns, where Stalin lay, and say goodbye, so we went there. It was crowded, you couldn't move, just move with the crowd, left and right. I was standing there, they had closed the exits, so you could not disperse, could not go back, could not go forward, from maybe eight in the evening until six in the morning.

My parents were very nervous when I came home late, maybe seven o'clock [the next morning], and they said, 'Where were you? We looked everywhere, in the police station, in the hospitals.' We went to say goodbye to Stalin, but we couldn't do it. My father looked at me and said, 'If you want to see him, go to sleep, and later I will take you with me and you will look at him as long as you want.' You had this stream of people who walked beside the coffin. There were many interruptions because the delegations came there with wreaths and flowers. The leaders and members of the family could go through another door, and they had chairs and were told, 'You can sit here and look as long as you want.'

Alexei Shipovalnikov

When I was almost three-and-a-half years old, I was in the children's hospital. I had diseases from travelling in the very dirty trains. In front of me across from my bed was a huge portrait of Stalin, and when news came that Stalin was dead I started crying, 'Rah! Rah! Rah!' I was so happy that Stalin was dead. The reason was very simple: first of all, life was very tough and in my little brain all these travels over Russia from the KGB were personal with Stalin and to live months in the hospital exactly across from the portrait of Stalin, I came to hate him.

The pianist and conductor **Vladimir Ashkenazy** *was a teenage prodigy at the time of Stalin's death, studying in Moscow.*
It so happened that on the day of Stalin's funeral I had a lesson with my piano teacher. I had to walk through an absolutely silent and stopped Moscow. There was no transportation, not even the Metro, the underground. And so I had to walk for my lesson for about 45 minutes across Moscow to my teacher's apartment. And I remember seeing lots of old ladies sitting and crying: 'Oh, our father is dead,' they were saying. 'Our father is dead.' Stalin. To me, it was a bit strange because I couldn't understand why the attitude was to have such a depth. I couldn't understand it. I got to my teacher's apartment. She was Armenian, and I said to her, 'What do you think will be now with this situation, seemingly such a tragedy for a lot of the population?' She, in her apartment, whispered in my ear: 'It will be better now.'

Then those people who were in the Politburo next to Stalin became the government, with Khrushchev probably already being more important than others. I think Malenkov and some others tried to become number one but, in the end, Khrushchev won. We weren't aware, of course, of all the goings on between the important people at the top.

Sergei Khrushchev
During the Cold War, if you had your adversary, you created an image that you thought would work for you. So, to the West, especially in America, it was confrontation: Khrushchev was an unpredictable, emotional, very aggressive person. But in reality that was absolutely wrong. He was very warm. He was emotional, like all of us. He was enthusiastic about this own country, like any good politician. He said that his goal was not victory in the Cold War: he wanted to make the lives of the Russian people better. So in politics he was focused on agriculture, on housing and on consumables. He was a good family father; we loved him and he loved us. He liked culture. He visited theatres maybe two or three times a week. He liked opera; he didn't like ballet – for him it was too boring. He liked nature, going walking in the woods, picking mushrooms in the autumn, or just swimming in the Moscow river. It was very different then: there was no wall of bodyguards. His mansion was the official residence; there was an old wooden fence with a small gate. He would open this gate and go out, and all the Muscovites would be sitting on the grass around there, and he would be saying, 'Hello, hello, how are you?'

His relationship with Stalin was different. They grew up in politics together. At the time of the revolution, Stalin was a bureaucrat. My father was not in the movement

Sergei Khrushchev with his father Nikita in Crimea, 1960.

before the revolution, so he was not affected by Trotsky. When Stalin started to fight for power, my father was in Moscow because he wanted to study to be an engineer, and he supported Stalin strongly. From his point of view, Stalin was the most reasonable person, because all these revolutionaries were so theoretical and didn't really have an interest in the real economy, in the real things that happened in the country. In the late 1930s, he became very negative towards Stalin, and this negative feeling grew during the Second World War because it was clear to him that it was Stalin's fault – it was not the generals who were not prepared for the war. Stalin thought that he knew better than his generals. After that, he was very critical about Stalin.

Tatiana Baeva

When Stalin was dead, my father was immediately freed, and we went to Moscow. It was the first time I saw cars and big buildings and culture and movies. We have nothing but what the government gave to our family and another family: a flat, and some possibility for my father to begin work as a scientist.

At Moscow, I had some problems at school because the teacher asked me, 'Where were you born? Who is your father? He was a prisoner – he is guilty.' Slowly, I began to understand.

Alexei Shipovalnikov

After Stalin, the Communist Party decided, 'Okay, you can go – go, you're rehabilitated now, go.' But in the community, you're forever Stalin's prisoner. Can you imagine, you're back to an apartment and you figure out that the man next door is the person who put you in prison 20 years ago? It happened all the time. It was sometimes the price for freedom. People understood what they were doing: they wrote a letter about somebody; they knew exactly that this person did nothing, but it was the price for freedom.

Sergei Khrushchev

After Stalin's death, my father said, 'We have to tell the truth to the people. If we want to build the best society in the world, where everybody will be equal, you cannot live in paradise surrounded by barbed wire.' So, he exposed Stalin's crimes, and I think that was his big mistake in domestic politics.

The main thing that Khrushchev did was transform the structure of power from a police state, where you rule through the secret police, to a normal bureaucracy, like it is in any democratic or even authoritarian state. It is the beginning of freedom. All these new poets like Yevtushenko and others, the new composers emerged then, the writers. It was the beginning of the boom in science; at that time, there were more Nobel laureates in Russia than before and later. It was the beginning of development in chemistry, in agriculture, in missiles industry, in aircraft industry, in everything. The level of life started to grow. More than half the population of Russia improved their living conditions. Before, they lived in rooms, like this, 20 square metres with six, seven, eight people. And then people started to live in their own apartments. Small apartments, but their own apartments. It is difficult for you to understand what does it mean if you live ten families in one apartment, with one bathroom, and in the morning you are waiting and waiting and waiting and waiting until you can access the toilet. So, it was the beginning of the boom in the new families.

Vladimir Ashkenazy

When Khrushchev made his famous speech after Stalin's death, it was 1956 – I was 19 years old. At that time, being already quite a well-known young musician, I was not terribly interested in other things. I understood that this was a Communist country where I lived and the rest of the world was quite, quite different, but I never gave it too much thought. I was a musician, and a successful one, and they sent me abroad, I was very happy and pleased that I had seen the world a little bit, and it never entered my mind to think what could happen and what should happen and what my country was like. It came later.

I wasn't terribly aware of the history of the Soviet Union because the availability of material from which you could learn the truth of what really happened wasn't there. When I went abroad, I could learn a little bit, but not very much because I was very busy practising and playing concerts. So my knowledge of the past of the Soviet Union, how the system came around in 1917, all the details and all the unbelievable executions and everything – I wasn't aware of everything. But in 1956, it looked like life was a little bit freer, people could talk to each other a little bit more, not afraid to say this or that – that I could feel.

As **Sergei Khrushchev** recounts, at the 1956 Party Congress, the assembled Communist delegates listened in stunned and bewildered silence to Khrushchev's speech.

It was emotional. He told them, 'We committed these sins, all of us, so we have to confess. And then, after, if we're forgiven we can go forward with clean hands, though we will live with these sins all the time.' So, he had this feeling from his soul that we have to say the truth.

So, they kept the speech secret, and I learned about this only when it was exposed and all these rumours began. I saw this small red brochure on my father's desk in the apartment, and I looked at it, and my father saw me and said, 'If you want, you can read it.' And I read it, and it was a shock.

I was with my father in London in April '56 and I was shocked because Stalin taught us that all of [the people] are very poor, and then I saw it was a very different picture. In one reception, a man asked me about [the] speech, and I was young, and he asked what the reaction of the people was? And I said it was different, but not so different; I answered diplomatically, so I thought. And then I told my father next morning, 'This gentleman asked me this question, and I answered.' And my father said, 'Ah, you did the wrong thing, you mustn't talk about this at all,' because at the time it was still secret. 'You're not thinking about the subject, you're thinking that it was exposed, and then someone will report and then hard-liners will say your son just discussed this secret speech with some capitalist in Great Britain.' So he thought more about me than about the secrecy of the speech.

Alexei Shipovalnikov

First of all, it was a secret report of Khrushchev and the extra last day of the Congress of the Communist Party. We didn't know about it – it was secret because it wasn't public. When it happened, in 1956, nobody knew. It was about 1957 the rumours started: something had happened upstairs, in the Politburo, in the Communist Party. But everybody was guessing only – nobody knew what had happened. Until, I believe, 1959 or 1960, some information started leaking. It was again leaking information;

it wasn't a real share of this information from the top. Finally, the secret report of Khrushchev about Stalin became public.

Somebody found this text. But there were big suspicions that it was not real. First of all, the language was very 'high'. Khrushchev's language was usually very low-level, not intelligent language. It was very strange – it was not Khrushchev's language. So people didn't trust this paper when it was found. Some dissidents very famously said, 'No, it's not real.' But when it was finally published, the people who found this copy were right – it was real. So, who wrote this for Khrushchev? We still don't know. But this secret report did something good for us.

Tatiana Baeva

It was very important because it was like a great revolution. People changed their minds, and there was more freedom. Khrushchev did a very important thing. Beria was the KGB chief and right hand of Stalin, and he was very close to succeeding Stalin. But Khrushchev was very smart: he talked with people and they arrested Beria immediately. If Beria had stayed, it would have been a bad story for Russia.

Alexei Shipovalnikov

I don't think that Khrushchev was so smart – I think he just cared that Beria would be first. Khrushchev was absolutely equal to Stalin in power but not in the brain. When Khrushchev became a dictator, it became a very tragic time for the Church to which I belonged. In 1957, yes, of course, a lot of people were freed from prisons and concentration camps. Although, of course, people could be happy they were free, but we were very poor, absolutely poor. To understand what it means to be poor, for example, when my sister and I were at school we had only one coat for two of us, one pair of shoes for two of us. We had two shifts in the school: she had afternoon shift and I had morning shift, and when I came home from school I had to give her the coat and the shoes.

I had a lot of problems. Problems started in school immediately because my father was a priest. 1961 was a terrible time for the Russian Orthodox Church. They not only closed the churches, they started to blow up the churches. A lot of very famous churches were destroyed at this time. And that's my memory about Khrushchev. There was a lot of trouble, not only for the Church. There was the time when Solzhenitsyn and others were published, but it was a very brief time. After, it became a very tough time again.

It was only ten years after the war, and the country did not recover so fast under Khrushchev like was expected. After the coup in 1964, when Khrushchev was dismissed and Brezhnev became leader, at one point it was a healing. But after it was stagnation. Life was in the middle – not perfect, but not worse.

The Soviet Union was still a dictatorship controlled by the Communist Party, and a powerful KGB state security network monitored both foreigners and Soviet citizens, as the young pianist **Vladimir Ashkenazy** *found out.*

In 1958, when I was 21, I had my first American tour as a pianist. I had good reviews. It was unbelievably successful for a chap of 21. I couldn't travel alone; at that time, people who went for tours of this type would have to have a companion from the Ministry of Culture, or whatever ministry it would be – basically, of course, a KGB chap. This chap who went with me had no idea, had never heard the name of Beethoven or Mozart – he was an absolute moron. But he had to watch me because he would have to report on our return how the tour went. The tour was very successful, but he wrote a negative report about my behaviour. He said that I never expressed in my interviews or in contact with Americans pride at being a Soviet citizen. Can you imagine? He submitted his report to the Ministry of Culture. I was called to the ministry a few weeks later and I was confronted by this chap, and the head of the Department of Foreign Relations read his report to me and said, 'Well, what do you say to that?' I didn't know what to say; I was taken by surprise. I said, 'I can't understand. I think I behaved very well. I never did anything that would be considered damaging to the image of the Soviet Union, so I can't understand why this chap wrote such a report. I had a successful tour, I made many friends with American musicians, and I can't understand why he has written this.' The chap said, 'Well, whatever it is, we have decided now you don't go abroad for a few years. You might as well play your recitals for the workers and peasants of our country.' That's what he said. Just a slogan. What could I do?

The chap who was the head of the party department in the conservatory was there at the meeting too. His name was Kurpekov. He was a bassoon player and a very nice man. I had played with him. He came out of the ministry with me, and said, 'Don't worry, don't worry, I don't think it will be that bad. What could I do? I couldn't say anything. But you know it will improve. Don't worry, I will always support you.'

In 1962, when John Ogden and I won the Tchaikovsky Competition – we shared the first prize – we were asked to attend a reception in the Kremlin, with the presence of Khrushchev and Brezhnev and all the party members. It was quite an experience. Imagine, we are in the Kremlin, and Khrushchev and all those important people are coming and shaking hands with us … I'll never forget it.

I married a 'capitalist' in 1961 – an Icelandic 'capitalist', can you imagine! Then the Ministry of Culture told me quite officially, 'If your wife doesn't become Soviet, you will have no career.' So two days after we married on 25 February, after the weekend, she applied to become a Soviet citizen.

Because of my first prize in 1962 (the Tchaikovsky Competition), I was allowed again to travel abroad to perform concerts. In 1963, I was invited for the first time to England. My wife had lived in England with her family from 1946 onwards, and naturally we wanted to go together with our young son on this trip.

As we had already discussed the possibility of remaining in the West back in Moscow (outside in the middle of the street), when she said, 'I'm not going to go back' I was fully supportive. I was granted permanent residency in the UK by the British authorities, based on my wife's having been resident in London for fifteen years, so when we decided to stay in England, it was a shock to the Soviet authorities.

My wife and I decided to come back from the UK to Moscow for what was initially supposed to be a ten-day trip, but we decided to leave our very young son in London. That was a very wise thing to do! When we arrived in Moscow, my international travel document (foreign passport) was taken away (my wife refused to give hers up) and I was left with my local Soviet identity card only. We had to spend about six weeks in Moscow, I played some concerts, and we just didn't know if we could leave or not.

At the Ministry of Culture, quite by surprise, a very nice secretary said to me, 'I know you are getting a little anxious, waiting to see Furtseva (the Minister of Culture). Don't worry, it should be alright in the end, but you never heard it from me ...' Apparently, Furtseva went to the top, to Khrushchev himself, who decided it was right to let us go. Finally, I got the call from Mrs. Furtseva's secretary, saying that the Minister of Culture wanted to see me. When I saw her, she said to me, 'So when are you leaving?' Just like that! I was amazed. I realised that she had been given the okay from Khrushchev personally. I went to the passport office. 'My passport,' I said. The officer looked at me as if I were an enemy of the people. Five minutes later I had my passport back. So of course we left for England. In his memoirs, Khrushchev mentioned this particular incident and said that he remembered meeting me at the Tchaikovsky Competition and he thought it just about the right time for our country to make some of its citizens much freer, and in this case I should go back to London. We didn't go to the Soviet Union for 26 years after that because I didn't trust them.

After he was deposed in 1964, Nikita Khrushchev lived in internal exile until his death in 1971, shunned by the authorities, and undisturbed except for the occasional visitor – such as **Tatiana Baeva***, who in 1965 knocked on his door with a friend.*
It was 1 May, a year after he lost power; 1 May was a great Soviet holiday, and some people went to Red Square, but some people stayed at home and drank vodka. I was with the people who drank vodka. We sat and talked and drank and talked about history, and suddenly somebody said, 'Let's go to Khrushchev's dacha.' Probably he worked at *Pravda*, and he called somebody, the KGB, I think. And we went to Khrushchev's dacha.

He met us at the front door, double security there, and invited us into the house. It was huge territory, but the house was small, regular. We sat down in his dining room. Inside the room were two KGB security men, and Khrushchev told us that they stayed all the time in his house, they never went out. And we talked with Khrushchev. I just saw a very small man who looked like – you know in the English garden, you have some small statue with a big head? – he looked disappointed. He had lost all friends, he had lost everything. I asked him about the secret paper and about how many secrets were open, and Khrushchev said, 'Oh, it's many secrets we have, but I cannot talk about this.'

I asked him about Pasternak. He wrote *Dr Zhivago*. Khrushchev was against *Dr Zhivago* – he forbade it being published. I asked him about it, and he said, 'Oh, I was wrong. I was against it, but I never read *Dr Zhivago*. Now I have read it and understand that it's a good book, and I'm very sorry about this.'

I am against revenge. My father was against revenge. Many KGB people now in prison helped my father. When you have tyranny in your country, people help each other a lot.

'We are not your comrades'

The Hungarian Revolution (1956)

The Hungarian Revolution began on 23 October 1956 and lasted long enough for its supporters to believe, at least for a short while, that it had succeeded. It was not the first popular uprising against Soviet rule in an Eastern European country. But whereas in East Germany in 1953 unrest was extinguished quickly, in Hungary it grew into a larger rebellion. Thus, when it was finally crushed by Soviet tanks, the suppression was all the more violent.

Hungary had been under what amounted to Soviet military occupation since the end of the Second World War. As elsewhere in Eastern Europe, the regime installed with Moscow's help during 1948 and 1949 was in the process of transforming the country along Soviet lines to increase state and party control over all aspects of society. And because Hungary had been one of the Axis powers, allied to Nazi Germany and involved in invading the Soviet Union, the clampdown was particularly brutal.

Part of the control was political. After the war, Hungary went from being – briefly – a multiparty democracy to becoming a Communist authoritarian state in just a few years, although the ruling Communists went under the name of the Hungarian Working Peoples' Party. Before long, candidates stood unopposed in elections, education was heavily politicised, and Western culture such as American films and jazz music was banned as subversive.

Part of the control was economic. Like East Germany and Romania, Hungary was obliged to pay draconian war reparations to the Soviet Union and help finance Soviet troops garrisoned locally. Added to this was a disastrous Five Year Plan based on the Stalinist model, which focused on building up heavy industry and state-run collectives taking over private farms. All this contributed to food shortages, a dearth of other consumer goods and general economic mayhem. Any prospect of alleviating the catastrophic economic situation through Marshall Plan aid from the United States was blocked when, in 1949, Moscow created a rival Eastern trading bloc. Alongside the Warsaw Pact, which was designed to be a counterweight to NATO and from 1955 bound Eastern European countries militarily to Moscow, this euphemistically named 'Council for Mutual Economic Assistance', or Comecon, tied them economically.

But worst of all in Hungary were the series of purges that targeted anyone suspected of being an enemy of the state, as an anti-Communist, a former Nazi sympathiser or a member of the 'bourgeois' classes. Even some leading Communists were not exempt, if deemed unreliable or a threat to rivals. As in Stalin's Soviet Union, citizens were encouraged to report to the authorities anyone they thought might be suspicious. Overnight disappearances of neighbours, colleagues and family members were commonplace. Some were put in prison, some were subjected to show trials and some were put in front of a firing squad for execution. By the early 1950s, Hungary's government was one of the most repressive in Europe. Stalin's death in 1953 and Khrushchev's 'Secret Speech' in 1956, however, raised a ripple of anticipation that perhaps the lid of tyranny might be lifted in Eastern Europe.

In Poland, Khrushchev's speech roused expectations that the country might be given leeway to pursue its own destiny, instead of slavishly following Soviet orders. In June 1956, protests by Polish workers in Poznan were violently suppressed by Polish troops. Over the next few months, the rebellious mood escalated and on 19 October a popular moderate Communist leader, Władysław Gomułka, took the helm.

Worried that the situation in Poland was becoming unstable, Khrushchev ordered Soviet troops already in Poland to start moving towards Warsaw to put pressure on the Polish government. Meanwhile, he flew into Warsaw, uninvited, to block Gomułka. There followed a tense confrontation, during which Khrushchev threatened armed intervention by Soviet forces and Gomułka responded that Khrushchev himself was partly responsible for what had happened, because of the signals sent in his 'Secret Speech' condemning Stalinism earlier in the year. Gomułka also warned that Poland would 'not permit its independence to be taken away'.

In the end, Khrushchev thought the better of risking a nationwide Polish uprising. He ordered Soviet troops back to barracks and allowed Gomułka to remain in charge, on condition that Poland remained a loyal member of the Warsaw Pact. The concession to Poland was in marked contrast to the rigid crackdown in East Germany three years before. In Hungary, those hoping for a more flexible approach were now also emboldened.

A few days later, on 23 October 1956, excited Hungarian students decided to march peacefully to show their support for the Poles. At first, they expressed their hopes tentatively, chanting patriotic poems and songs. As the crowd swelled, the demands grew bolder until the demonstrators began directing their anger at the continued presence of Soviet troops in Hungary, blatantly chanting: 'Russians go home!' They then marched to Parliament to present a set of 16 demands, including the withdrawal of Soviet troops, free elections, free speech and the installation – as in Poland – of a reformist leader. Their choice was Imre Nagy, the popular Prime Minister who had been ousted the year before.

But that evening, the hard-line Communist Party chief Ernő Gerő went on the radio to reject the demonstrators' demands and accuse them of deliberately making trouble. The furious students were not prepared to take no for an answer. Some went across the city to join workers engaged in cutting down a giant 30-foot statue of Stalin, leaving just a pair of empty bronze boots. Others massed outside the heavily guarded state radio station, hoping to get inside to broadcast their demands. There, when the ÁVH – Államvédelmi Hatóság, Hungary's notorious State Protection police (formerly the ÁVO, Államvédelmi Osztálya), who were guarding the building – opened fire on the crowd, the demonstration turned violent and became a wider insurrection. Workers from factories joined the fight, armed with weapons and ready to use them. Some protestors broke into armaments factories and helped themselves to guns and ammunition. Police cars were set ablaze and some Hungarian soldiers tore off their badges and sided with the protestors.

Alarmed that a serious rebellion was now under way, Hungary's Communist authorities asked Moscow to intervene. Between 23 and 24 October, Soviet tanks and troops entered Budapest overnight to guard the Parliament and other key strategic locations in the city.

The arrival of Soviet troops only galvanised the resistance and turned the revolt into a nationwide revolution. Armed protestors set up barricades and took over buildings. Thousands of people joined makeshift militias. A Hungarian tank commander went over to the rebels; some Soviet troops refused to turn their guns on civilians. Schoolchildren joined the fighting and peasants from the countryside helped by bringing food into Budapest to feed the rebels.

With the shift of power came a new reckoning. Former political prisoners were released and newspapers exposed the privileges and excesses of Communist leaders. Those seen as loyal to the Communist regime or security forces were now in danger. Several dozen were arrested and executed, or even lynched on the streets. The corpses of some were hung from lampposts.

By 29 October, it looked as though victory for the rebels was in sight. The Soviet army had agreed to withdraw to garrisons outside the city. In place of Communist committees, new revolutionary and workers' councils were setting themselves up to take over the functions of local government. The government had collapsed and Imre Nagy had been brought back to lead a new national government. He went on the radio to declare an end to one-party rule, and pledged to turn Hungary into a multi-party social democracy with neutral status. Before long, he also made it clear that the intention was to open negotiations with Moscow for Hungary to withdraw from the Warsaw Pact and for Soviet troops to leave the country.

The prospect of Hungary pulling out of the Warsaw Pact, a crucial bulwark in the Soviet defence against any possible aggression from the West, may well have been a step too far for Moscow. At first – as with Poland a few days earlier – the Kremlin leadership had been wary of inflaming the situation. But under pressure from hard-liners in the Soviet Politburo, Khrushchev changed his mind and ordered an invasion to put an end to what was now being seen in Moscow as a counter-revolution. On 4 November 1956, Soviet tanks rumbled back into Budapest, this time in huge convoys, accompanied by 15 divisions of armed forces, and began an attack backed up by airstrikes and artillery.

Over the next five or six days, Budapest was smashed to pieces. By the end of it, the city looked worse than it had after the wartime bombing. According to Hungarian archival researchers, 2,700 Hungarians were killed in the fighting, with nearly 20,000 more wounded. On the Soviet side, around 700 troops were killed or missing and some 1,450 wounded. Imre Nagy, the revolution's figurehead, was tricked out of hiding, and later hanged as a traitor.

By January 1957, the new pro-Soviet government under its new leader, János Kádár, had suppressed all opposition. In the months that followed, the Hungarian army was purged of those seen as disloyal and Soviet troop levels in the country were stepped up. There were also mass arrests, with some 35,000 people imprisoned or interned and at least 230 executed for their role in the revolution. Some 200,000 Hungarians fled into exile.

The message from Moscow was blunt: any attempt at rebellion among its client states would be crushed. It was to be the last uprising against Soviet rule in Eastern Europe for 12 years, until the so-called Prague Spring in Czechoslovakia prompted another Soviet crackdown.

A United Nations report from 1957 described the suppression of the Hungarian uprising as 'a well-equipped foreign army crushing by overwhelming force a national movement and eliminating the Government'.

The version in *Pravda*, the official newspaper of the Soviet Communist Party, reported that 'fascist, Hitlerite, reactionary, counter-revolutionary hooligans, financed by the imperialist West, took advantage of the unrest to stage a counter revolution' and 'the honest Hungarian people ... appealed to Soviet forces stationed in Hungary to assist in restoring order.'

The events in Hungary caused ideological ruptures in some Western Communist parties. Some backed Moscow, arguing that the insurgents were not true Hungarian nationalists, but counter-revolutionaries and former Nazi collaborators trying to stage a comeback – even though those students who had sparked the revolution were still children when the Nazis were defeated. Other European Communists condemned the Soviet intervention and resigned their party membership.

But the uprising was also significant for what it said about the attitude of Western governments to Eastern Europe in the mid-1950s. Aside from expressing their outrage and registering a formal protest at the Soviet invasion through the United Nations, the Western powers chose not to come to the aid of Hungary's beleaguered revolutionaries. This Western failure to respond decisively to the crackdown was a sobering lesson. It showed that, for all the American Radio Free Europe broadcasts that had urged the revolution on, the West's willingness to back a popular revolt against Communist power in Eastern Europe only went so far. Britain and France were distracted by their abortive plan to seize back control of the Suez Canal – a separate crisis that was unfolding simultaneously. The Americans were reluctant to provoke anything that might lead to an all-out war with a Soviet rival now armed with nuclear weapons.

The unwelcome conclusion for the people of Eastern Europe was that the Cold War had sunk into a stalemate. If countries wanted to stage revolutions against their Soviet overlords, they were on their own. They could not assume that the West would risk upsetting the new Cold War global balance of power and come to their rescue.

Péter Pallai knew the Communists had taken power when, aged ten, he found he could no longer go to see Tarzan movies – the new government had banned American films, jazz and listening to Western radio. In fact, there were many things you weren't allowed to do in Communist Hungary in the 1950s.

Membership of the Young Pioneers was compulsory. Learning Russian was compulsory. At secondary school, we were given state-issued textbooks. As an 11-year-old, my favourite subjects were geography and history, and when we were given textbooks at the start of the school year, I read them like a novel – from beginning to end. Then, suddenly, in the autumn of 1948, we were asked to hand back our textbooks and we were given new ones. I leafed through the new ones and found that they no longer called Tito a hero and a great friend of the Hungarian people – now he was an imperialist stooge and an ex-Gestapo agent! They changed the textbooks to say that the steam engine, the radio and the aeroplane had all been invented by Russians.

I had been learning classical violin, but quarrelled with my teacher and stopped playing. I started fiddling with the radio and, in 1951, I heard a guy singing on a German station. At first, I was outraged – how can anyone be allowed near a microphone with a horrible voice like his? But something in it caught me. I described what I heard to an older guy at school. He said it was jazz, and that you weren't meant to listen to it. And then he told me which stations I could hear it on, although they were sometimes jammed deliberately. There were the US Army stations broadcasting from Germany, Yugoslav stations and eventually in 1954 *Voice of America Jazz Hour*, presented by Willis Conover. I carried that first tune in my head – it was 'Ain't Misbehavin'' by Louis Armstrong.

I was 18 years old in 1956, a first-year law student at Budapest University. I wasn't overly political, but I did follow events and it was a year that brought some easing of the dictatorship in Hungary and there was a great deal of hope that summer. Intellectuals and writers felt freer than before to express themselves. And everyone was watching what was happening in Poland – there were riots in Poznan, which we heard about on Radio Free Europe and the BBC.

In the early autumn, the students at another university decided to quit the official Communist Party youth organisation, of which membership was practically compulsory, and the second- and third-year students at Budapest University were considering following that example. A meeting was held in October, which I turned up for, and I got very excited about it. It was decided that we would march on the streets on 23 October to give emotional support to the Poles.

That morning, we heard that the Ministry of the Interior had banned this demonstration, and we debated whether to go ahead or not – and the decision was made that we would. Two or three years before, we would not have made that choice because we'd have expected to be

Péter Pallai, summer 1956.

Mátyás Sárközi.

shot at, but now we weren't expecting that, and, by the time we started, they had lifted the ban.

So, we went on the streets, a few thousand students on both sides of the Danube, and we headed for the statue of a national poet who had taken part in the 1848 uprising against the Austrians. It was a really emotional moment and people were amazed because it was the first non-government-organised demonstration in the city. People were joining us from the pavements. An actor from the National Theatre recited a poem from [the revolution of] 1848, and we all sang patriotic songs, which had been very much frowned upon before. Then we decided to head for the statue of another hero of 1848, a Polish general who had fought for Hungary. And the crowd just swelled spontaneously. There must have been 100,000 people there, if not more.

The first demands were simply for the reformist Prime Minister Imre Nagy to be reinstated as head of the government. Then it all sort of ballooned. There was a very funny slogan: roughly translated, it meant 'Soldiers of all lands go back to your homelands.' It was a thinly veiled reference to the Russians getting out of Hungary. Some people started shouting 'Give back the uranium mines', which were used by the Soviets as well. In the end, they were simply shouting 'Russians go home!' and people started to cut the Soviet-style emblem from the Hungarian flag.

I didn't see any security police there at the beginning. The ordinary police were quite supportive, and they let us through. There was such a huge crowd that I couldn't hear the speakers or see anything.

There were rumours that Imre Nagy would be speaking, and people started saying, 'Let's go to the Parliament.' So, we went over to the other side of the Danube, and a huge crowd was waiting there for Nagy to appear. It was getting dark, and my friends and I got fed up waiting. We heard that people were knocking down the statue of Stalin, and that sounded much more fun than waiting for a Prime Minister-designate, so we set off for that part of town. On the way, we passed the trade union building and someone was knocking the Red Star from the top. I thought, 'There's not going to be much teaching at the university tomorrow!'

Mátyás Sárközi *was a young reporter, aged 18 at the time of the Uprising. He watched the growing crowd begin to direct their anger at the continued presence of Soviet troops in Hungary.*

On 23 October 1956, I was told by my editor that there was going to be a march by university students. As I was the youngest on the paper – not even 19 then – he thought that I would probably know some of the students involved. I thought it would be boring: there'll be a march, a speech about how we sympathise with the Polish workers' demands and how Hungarians are their great friends, and then I'd go home and have coffee with my mother.

Instead, I saw an enormous group of people, filling the width of the Grand Boulevard. They were shouting slogans like 'Russians go home!' That was very brave. It was a sentiment from the East German Rising in 1953, and I think we took it over from the East Germans. They had a list of demands, as there had been during the Hungarian Revolution in 1848 – Why is only Russian taught as a foreign language in school? Why is it compulsory to join the Hungarian Communist youth organisation? and so on. The students wanted to take these demands to the national radio station, and read these demands to the nation.

The news came that Imre Nagy was in the Parliament building, so people decided to go there and ask him to come out and talk to us. So, five or six thousand marchers gathered in front of Parliament and started shouting for Imre Nagy. By this time, it was quite dark. The authorities switched off the street lights, so we were standing there in pitch darkness, but people were lighting cigarette lighters, and making little torches from the Party newspaper. In this blackness, a single light came on in one window of the huge edifice of the building, and Nagy came out on to a balcony and told everyone to go home!

*18-year-old student **Sándor Váci** had also made his way to the demonstration.*

Nagy addressed the crowd as 'comrades', and he was shouted down: 'We are not your comrades!'

Then somebody shouted, 'Let's go to the radio!' That made sense, as the radio was the only way of communicating with the whole country. Around 100 of us marched up there. By the time we arrived, there were already people there. The radio station was already occupied by the security police, and they started throwing out tear-gas bombs to disperse us. It's a really quite terrifying experience – you think you're going to choke to death.

They opened the door, and a whole contingent of uniformed security personnel marched out. Then somebody threw a bin at them, and it rolled along their caps, like on cobblestones. One of them was injured, and blood was running down his face. That's when I thought it was all getting out of hand, so I left and went to my aunt's house nearby. Soon after that, shooting started.

Mátyás Sárközi

Ernő Gerő – a hated member of the Hungarian Muscovite group of Communists – made a speech claiming that fascists were taking over Hungary. When the students

Sándor Váci in the 1950s.

heard they were being called fascists, they got very angry and marched on the radio station. I went with them. The radio station was in a very narrow street, and there were so many of us that I really felt uncomfortable – I was shoved and knocked, and my jacket almost came off because people wanted to get closer in. So I went to a house opposite, went up to the third floor and rang the bell of a private flat and asked to be allowed in so I could watch from their window. The family let me in, but asked me not to switch on the light, and not to stand visibly in the window. So, half-hiding behind the curtain, I had an opera-box view on what was happening.

They didn't let the students into the radio building. Green army buses began to arrive, with Hungarian soldiers with guns. Their order was to clear the streets, so they started shoving people. I saw one 'civilian' in a brown hat and leather coat, and that always meant the secret police, the ÁVO. He had a pistol and he was giving orders to the soldiers. The soldiers were not regular army; they were national service conscripts, and they were not very happy to be shoving people off the streets, and they kept apologising! Some of the soldiers came into the house I was in and asked for civilian clothes, or at least a jacket, so they could get away.

Meanwhile, **Péter Pallai** *was on the other side of the city, watching an assault on another major symbol of Communist power.*

We got to the Stalin statue, and there was a very happy carnival atmosphere there. Workers were using blow torches and chains and trucks to pull the statue down. I didn't see it fall because somebody came on a motorcycle and said that the security police were shooting at demonstrators outside the radio station building. We got on to trucks and were driven to the radio station. We heard the shooting and we ran into the street, which was pretty stupid because we had no arms. While we were running in, one girl was shot next to me. She was probably no more than 14 or 15. We were in a terrible state of shock.

We turned heel and ran for the safety of the Grand Boulevard. There were Hungarian soldiers there, and we asked for their arms. They wouldn't give them to us, but they weren't against us. We asked the ordinary police for their arms. As we were waiting and trying to think of ways to get arms, trucks arrived carrying workers with arms from the armament factories at Csepel Island. They wouldn't part with their weapons – they went in and started fighting with the security police.

Mátyás Sárközi

Workers on the night shift from the Csepel arms factory just outside Budapest came into the city in trucks, and they were armed. When they saw the turmoil, they pointed their guns at the soldiers. A contingent of AVÓ men started shooting at them. I saw the first dead body lying on the cobblestones – not a soldier or a worker, but a student. That was the first bloodshed of the revolution. In a couple of hours, this peaceful demonstration had become a revolution. Within a couple of hours, trams were stopped in the streets, cars were turned over, windows were broken.

Péter Pallai

Someone suggested going to the barracks and demanding arms from the soldiers. We went there, but the gates were locked. We started banging on the gates, and people were using a wooden pylon as a battering ram. When we got in, there was a line of soldiers with rifles with fixed bayonets, and a first lieutenant shouting at us to withdraw or they would fire on us. Most of us didn't believe they would do that as they were ordinary soldiers, but we couldn't turn back anyway as there was such a huge crowd behind us. The soldiers didn't obey orders – they let us in and showed us where the armoury was. We got rifles but no ammunition.

Then someone suggested we go east to another arms factory and get bullets there, which we did. We returned to town and tried to get to the radio building. But we were told that there were many armed people there by that time so we were not needed. We were told to go to the printing works, which were printing the students' demands. We went there, and we were attacked by the security police, who occupied the house opposite and opened fire. That was the first time I fired at another human being. We had had military instruction at university three times a week, so I knew how to handle a rifle, thanks to the regime! We fought through the night, but were beaten and driven out. We had to escape because the security police and the Russians were controlling the streets.

Sándor Váci

Stalin's statue was cut down on 23 October. The next day, my aunt locked me in her flat. She was protecting me by locking me in – when you're 18, you don't have a proper measure of danger, you're reckless. There were bars over the kitchen window – I tried to get hold of a screwdriver to undo the screws. But I couldn't get out. In the afternoon, my aunt came back and I persuaded her to let me out, but she said she would come with me. We walked towards the shooting. There were fewer and fewer people the closer we got, and I'm afraid my fear overcame my curiosity, and we eventually turned back.

On 25 October, the shooting had stopped. I was let out of the flat again, and I walked towards the Astoria Hotel. There was a whole line of Russian tanks there, with young Russian soldiers standing awkwardly on the tanks. A demonstration came from the east, holding Hungarian flags with the Communist insignia cut out. That became the symbol of the revolution – the flag with a hole in it. Nearby, there was a bookshop and books by Lenin and Stalin and the Hungarian Communist Party had been taken outside and burned in a huge pile.

The Russian soldiers saw the demonstration was coming, and they got into their tanks and lowered their guns. That was the most dramatic moment of my life. You think they're going to shoot, people are going to be killed, and there will be blood and bones on the pavement. The demonstration came closer and closer.

Then the people standing near the tanks started chatting to the tank crews. They offered them cigarettes, and the situation mellowed. The demonstrators arrived and surrounded the tanks. The tank crews were fine – the hate changed. The demonstrators climbed up on the tank and one of them put a flag into the barrel of the tank's gun.

Then a whole crowd of us followed the tank to Parliament Square. We were on foot, so it took perhaps 25 minutes. By the time we arrived, the tank was already stationed with its back to Parliament, the flag still in its gun barrel. There was quite a good-humoured crowd filling the square, waiting for something to happen.

And then my mother and my aunt turned up, and forced me to go home with them! So, we walked to my aunt's flat, and within 15 or 20 minutes we heard shots being fired and saw lorries filled with the injured and the dead, going slowly past.

Protestors in University Street, Athens, 3 December 1944.

A huge crowd of Czechoslovakian Communists mass in Old Town Square to back the demands of Premier Klement Gottwald in Prague, Czech Republic, 23 February 1948.

Communist supporters marching in Rome, April 1948.

West Berlin boys stand on a rubble mountain to wave at a transport plane bringing supplies during the Blockade.

The last coal bags are loaded on to a plane heading from Rhein-Main Airport, Frankfurt, to Berlin, 30 September 1949.

Queues outside a Shanghai rice shop as food prices in the city rise under Nationalist rule, December 1948.

North Korean refugees crowd on to the decks of fishing boats at Hungnam, December 1950.

The Hollywood Ten in front of the District Building in Washington, DC, where they pleaded not guilty to Contempt of Congress charges, 9 February 1948.

A line of Soviet tanks rolls through East Berlin's Leipziger Strasse, 17 June 1953.

A demonstration for Iranian Premier Mohammad Mosaddegh, c. 1951–3.

Protestors wave a Hungarian flag atop a Soviet tank captured in the main square in front of the Houses of Parliament in Budapest 1956.

People watch from their apartment windows as an East Berlin policeman puts bricks in place to heighten the Berlin Wall, 9 September 1961.

A family from West Berlin waves at relatives from East Berlin, 10 September 1961.

US Marines fortifying the Guantanamo Naval Base in Cuba, 16 November 1962.

*Despite the violence, **Péter Pallai** remembers those days with fondness.*

It was a fantastic time, even during the fighting. For the first time in my life I saw a spirit perhaps like that during the Blitz in London. These are my most vivid memories. In several places, official state-owned food shops had their windows broken but there were signs: 'The Revolution doesn't steal' and 'The Revolution is not for criminals.' There were boxes to collect for those who had fallen – containing banknotes, not just coins – and nobody touched them. That was unique to those times. People were helpful. Peasants came up from the collective farms, and they brought food and gave it out from the backs of trucks to anyone who asked. So they were gorgeous days, and I have very happy memories of it. We firmly believed – as we'd heard on the radio, which had stopped lying for a change – that there would be talks with the Soviets about withdrawal.

The withdrawal of the Russian troops was very liberating, and I was young enough to believe that it was our military might that had made them turn back. We thought it was a huge victory.

*Once the Russian troops had withdrawn from Budapest at the end of October, **Mátyás Sárközi** was beginning to feel that, maybe, just maybe, Hungary might get away with it.*

By Sunday 4 November, it looked as if everything was going to settle down: Imre Nagy was going to be Prime Minister; there would be a coalition government. There were even rumours that, for first time since 1946, Western films would be back in the cinemas – we would get to see Donald Duck, and British films. There was a genuine feeling of hope and happiness.

All of a sudden, at three o'clock in the morning, the news went round – people telephoning each other: the Russians are coming, the Russians are coming. People had seen them in huge convoys of tanks, coming towards Budapest.

Péter Pallai

I went to sleep quite happily at my parents' on 3 November. At dawn the next morning, I heard the gunfire, and I knew it was up. I didn't go back to fight.

The revolution was broken, but we still went on leafleting. Teaching didn't resume at the university, and we were having meetings about what to do – some people thought that we could start again in March. By then, though, it wasn't a military struggle. The workers went on general strike, and the workers' committees had begun a very successful passive struggle against the new regime that the Russian tanks brought in.

On 22 November, I was going home from leafleting, and my dad was waiting on the corner. He said, 'Don't come home, get out, they've been looking for you.' I had been reported by someone from the neighbourhood for taking part in the fighting. Someone must have seen me carrying arms. My best friend, who lived four streets away, was in the same position. His mum had talked to my dad. We had to escape.

My father arranged fake documents for us that said that we were 'Grain Supervisors' accredited to the western part of the country. Although there was a general strike, the railway workers were still getting trains out to western Hungary. So, we got out of Budapest by train, then set off on foot. By 27 November, at night, we'd got to where we thought was near the border. We found a farmhouse, knocked on the door and offered money to take us across the border. He refused, but directed us south-west towards the marshes. The Russians had come in huge numbers to seal the border, but they didn't know the terrain and were scared of the swamps. We said, 'So are we!' He told us to go as near as we dared to the border guard barracks. He told us we had to flatten ourselves to the ground as the searchlights swept past and to go south of the Russians so the wind would carry their voices to us and not the other way round. So that's what we did. I don't think I've ever been so scared. As far as I was concerned, it took days, though it wasn't anything like that. We crawled through. On the Austrian side, there were people with searchlights helping us to get across. So, we made it into Austria.

Mátyás Sárközi

My mother and I knew a Hungarian army officer, Major-General Béla Király, who had sided with the revolution and formed the National Guard – armed volunteers to keep order and prevent crime and looting. On 4 November, when the Russian army returned to Budapest, he wanted to escape and organise a resistance force. He managed to gather around 300 freedom fighters, but by this time the Soviet army had made a ring around Budapest.

Major-General Király came to see us to say goodbye, and gave me three letters to deliver if there was a possibility of armed resistance. I delivered the first letter to an ex-army officer, but when I went to deliver the second letter the address was already surrounded by the secret police. Then our neighbour reported that freedom fighters had been coming to our house at four in the morning. This neighbour thought it was their national duty to report this. That was what finally prompted me to flee Hungary and head to England. Eventually my mother was arrested and held for three days. She said she knew nothing about it – it was all between General Király and her son, who was now in London.

Péter Pallai

For 28 years, I wasn't allowed to visit Hungary. The first time I was allowed back as a visitor was 1984. I still don't know what exactly the charges against me were. The first freely elected government after Communism collapsed decided that they would partially release security police papers and reports, but only from the department that dealt with internal subversion. We were subject to counter-intelligence abroad, and those papers – reports by Hungarian agents on Hungarian émigrés – have never been released. I still don't know what is on my file.

'They were leaving with only their suitcases, they lost everything'

The Congo Crisis (1960–1)

The first two decades after the Second World War were not only marked by the emergence of the Cold War. This was also a period of intense decolonisation. Between 1945 and 1960, three dozen new states in Asia and Africa won limited or full independence from colonial rule, in parallel with and sometimes shaped by deepening superpower enmity. In fact, an aversion to colonial rule was one thing that the Soviet Union and the United States had in common: both were keen to see exhausted post-war European powers like Britain, France and Belgium relinquish their colonial possessions.

Moscow backed decolonisation for ideological reasons (to liberate oppressed peoples from their colonial masters), but also for geopolitical ends (the hope that it would allow the Soviet Union to extend its influence and cultivate new allies). The United States, a former colony itself, was likewise sympathetic to the principle of national self-determination. It was also keen to see the emergence of potentially profitable new markets.

But as the 1950s progressed and Cold War rivalry increased, first the Truman and then the Eisenhower administrations began to worry that the withdrawal of European powers from their colonies would limit access to precious raw materials, and might also prompt takeovers by pro-Soviet Communist parties, shifting the international balance of power in favour of the Soviet Union.

One case in point was one of Africa's most strategically important and biggest states, the country then known as the Belgian Congo. The so-called Congo Crisis was an early example of the type of proxy war, driven by local tensions but exacerbated by Cold War competition, that in later years would become all too common.

The Congo had been under Belgian control since the late nineteenth century, subjected to a rigid colonial regime with a high degree of racial segregation. By the 1950s the *évolués*, as the growing ranks of Europeanised and educated urban middle class were called, were becoming impatient. A nationalist movement, made up of different and opposing factions, was gaining momentum.

In 1959 protests by Congolese nationalists demanding an end to colonial rule descended into violence and put Belgium into a panic. In January 1960, the Belgian government convened a Congolese Round Table Conference in Brussels to discuss the country's future. The Congolese nationalists present pushed for new elections and an early date for independence – 30 June 1960 – but the meeting left unresolved tricky issues, such as the balance of power between central government and key provinces.

One attendee – released from prison to join the conference – was the charismatic left-wing leader and one of the founders of the National Congolese Movement or MNC (Mouvement National Congolais), Patrice Lumumba. Several months later, in May 1960, his coalition having won the largest number of seats in the National Assembly, he was elected the country's new Prime Minister, having campaigned on a nationalist platform for an independent Congo that would be a unitary state, sovereign and in charge of its own resources.

These were contentious issues. One of the largest countries in Africa, the Congo was rich in highly prized mineral deposits, including the uranium needed to produce nuclear bombs. This made it an attractive prospective ally for either of the two superpowers, both of them now armed with nuclear weapons. Who controlled the mines was also a delicate political question. The resource-rich provinces of Katanga and Kasai, and their allies in Belgium, the United Kingdom and the United States, were worried that Lumumba's central government might nationalise the country's valuable mines and deny them access to a crucial part of the local economy.

On 30 June 1960, Independence Day was marked by a grand ceremony in the capital, Leopoldville. But when the guest of honour, King Baudouin of Belgium, rose to speak, he shocked some of the Congolese politicians present when he praised the 'genius' of his ancestor King Leopold II for colonising the Congo and depicted the handover to independence as the successful end of a 'civilising mission', glossing over the millions killed and oppressed during the years of colonial rule.

The new Congolese President, another nationalist leader called Joseph Kasa-Vubu, duly thanked him. The more radical Patrice Lumumba, the new Prime Minister, was not so diplomatic. He delivered an impromptu and scathing rebuke to the Belgian King, pointing out that the

Congolese had fought for independence 'to put an end to the humiliating slavery which was imposed on us by force'. His speech, broadcast on the radio, was greeted enthusiastically by many listening across the country.

But not everyone was a fan of Lumumba. In the far south-east of the country, Katanga Province was already agitating for more autonomy from central government. And it took only a few days for more general discontent to emerge, as high expectations of immediate change were not met and swiftly turned into frustration.

The Congo Crisis began with a mutiny in the security forces, initially among units who had expected that independence would translate into instant promotion and higher pay for Africans and were angry to find themselves still being commanded by the same white colonial officers. The mutiny soon turned into a wider revolt, which Lumumba's new government was unable to contain, and the country descended into chaos.

On 10 July, without seeking permission from Lumumba's government, Belgium sent in paratroopers to protect fleeing white civilians. Before long, Congolese government troops were clashing with Belgian forces. Adding to the mayhem, Katanga and South Kasai provinces – both keen to stop Lumumba's government taking control of their assets – declared they were seceding, offering lucrative mining deals to Belgium in return for its backing.

Lumumba appealed to the United States and the United Nations. The Americans declined to side against Belgium, a NATO ally. The United Nations sent in peacekeepers but refused to help Lumumba suppress the secessionist provinces. At this point, Lumumba took a bold – and with hindsight fatal – step and turned to the Soviet Union for weapons, training and other military support to launch an offensive against the separatists.

There is no evidence that Lumumba had ideological sympathies with Soviet Communism, or was doing much more than trying to enlist help from the only quarter where he could find it. In any case, the practical assistance given by the Soviet Union turned out to be minimal. But the United States was not happy. This was just months after Castro's revolution in Cuba. The worry was that the Congo might be next on the list to become a Soviet client state. A cable from the CIA station chief in the Congolese capital described what was happening as a 'classic Communist takeover'.

The country was now dangerously split. In the secessionist areas of Katanga and South Kasai, Lumumba supporters were no longer welcome and many fled to avoid trouble. In the capital, President Kasa-Vubu was under mounting pressure from Western powers to remove Lumumba from office.

By September 1960, less than three months after Congo's independence, Lumumba's 81-day term as Prime Minister was over. After violence by Lumumba's troops in Katanga, he was dismissed by President Kasa-Vubu, a move he contested. But when he fled the capital he was arrested by the recently appointed Army Chief of Staff, Colonel Joseph-Désiré Mobutu, a staunch anti-Communist who five years later, with US backing, was to take over in a bloodless coup, change the country's name to Zaire, and become one of Africa's longest-serving despots.

Once in captivity, Lumumba was despatched to Katanga, one of the provinces that had battled him for autonomy. When he was handed over to local forces, it was to all intents and purposes a death sentence. On the night of 18 January 1961, he was shot by firing squad and his body reportedly dissolved in acid to erase any remains. News of the execution was not made public for weeks, for fear of rousing public anger.

As well as his Congolese rivals, Britain's MI6 and the American CIA were all thought to have been involved in the events leading up to his death, an extrajudicial killing of a democratically elected African leader who was seen to be too close to the Soviets and therefore, as so often during the Cold War, necessary to remove to stop the spread of Communism.

In the decades that followed, the Soviet Union hailed Patrice Lumumba as an anti-colonial socialist hero and martyr. They even named a university in Moscow in his honour. Elsewhere he served as an inspiration for independence causes. But in the Congo the upheaval that led to his early death halted the prospect of a peaceful transition to democracy when it had barely begun. What followed instead were decades of bloody military dictatorships and a country still ravaged by conflict today.

Georges Nzongola-Ntalaja was born in 1944 and grew up in the post-war period in what was then known as the Belgian Congo.

I was born in a Presbyterian mission station close to Laputa in the Kasai Province of the Belgian Congo. I grew up in that mission station until I was 14, when I went to another mission station for secondary school, close to the town of Luluabourg, now Kananga. We were kicked out because of inter-ethnic strife between Lulua and Baluba – actually people of the same ethnic group but divided through history. I went back to my own region and attended secondary school there for two more years.

We were extremely politicised. The struggle for independence started basically in 1956, and I went to secondary school in 1958. The missionaries gave us access to a radio, where we could listen to the BBC, Voice of America, Radio Moscow and so on, and we had all of the major newspapers published in the Congo delivered to our school. So, we were very up on what was happening, not only in the Congo but what was happening in the world. We knew, for example, what was happening in Vietnam and Laos and Cambodia. We knew about the independence of Sudan, Morocco and Tunisia in 1956, the independence of Ghana in 1957, the independence of Guinea in 1958 – so you can see why the Congo wanted to become independent like the other African countries. And, for that matter, countries in Asia which were also becoming independent. We felt that we could administer ourselves just like any other country in the world. I was extremely political – as a matter of fact, I was expelled from my secondary school in April 1960 for 'independence activities'.

Our missionaries were American Presbyterians, almost all of them from the Southern states of the USA. They had a very arrogant attitude, very condescending – in a sense, probably racist – and they said that we Congolese could simply not rule ourselves, we were too backwards and too behind the times to be able to do that, and so we took outrage at that. So, one time there was a demonstration by students which got out of hand: some irresponsible students torched the library of the school, and somehow I was designated as one of the ringleaders, which wasn't true. I was a participant. I didn't participate in the burning of the library or anything like that. I was simply doing peaceful protest, but some of our comrades got out of hand. So, when the college did its evaluation of what happened, I was among the people chosen to be expelled from school.

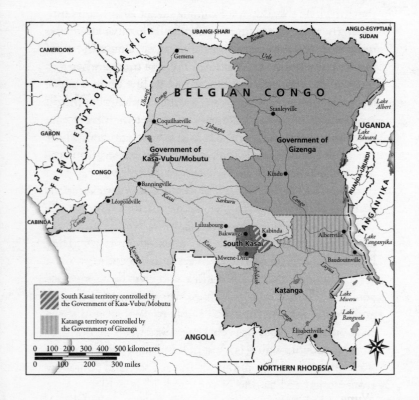

The Belgians had set up a very good train system in the Congo, and I lived 10 kilometres away from a major railroad station, so we travelled a lot by train. The trains had four classes of cars: first, second, third and fourth. Blacks were allowed only in the fourth and the third, which were the most elementary. The fourth class had only wooden benches. The third class was a little better – they had cushions. The second and first were basically luxury cars. Those were reserved for Europeans and those Congolese who attained the status of the *évolués*. And, of course, when you went to the train station, blacks had to line up in a queue to buy a ticket; a white person could simply walk straight up to the counter and buy her or his ticket. So, discrimination was everywhere. I lived in a mission station where we were segregated. We lived through segregation and discrimination and oppression on a daily basis.

We didn't like the Belgians. The Americans, we could excuse them. The Belgians, we didn't like them at all. They were extremely rude, they were very racist. They called us *macaques* – monkeys. They whipped people in public: every day at 6 o'clock and 12 noon, when the Belgian flag would be raised, prisoners would be whipped publicly. Those of us walking to the train station had to witness these prisoners being whipped. We lived under a very, very harsh colonial rule.

Wung'a Lomami Onadikondo *was a schoolboy in Katanga Province in the far south-east of the country.*

There were schools for black people and schools for white people. I attended what was called at that time a Metropolitan school, a white school, because my father applied. There were conditions to accept children: they had to give evidence that they had the same life standards as the people who normally attended that school. They would come and visit the family of the child to see if they were living as white people were living. Then there was the medical condition to make sure you had no contagious diseases. You had to undergo a lot of medical research – blood and urine and faeces and everything. You had to pass an exam to check if you were speaking French and had the level to attend that school.

People didn't live in the same places. There were places for white people and places – *cités indigènes* – for black people. I was in between. When I was attending that school, my relations with my mates where I was living were not very normal because they considered me as somebody who attended the white children's school.

There were municipal elections in 1957, and my father went for the municipal council. My brother and me helped him to run his campaign, door to door. We knew that some change was coming. I was aware of everything which was happening, because my father's friends used to come and listen to the radio at home and to make their comments, so I knew what was happening.

Georges Nzongola-Ntalaja

Almost all of us in secondary school were supportive of Kasa-Vubu's advocacy of immediate independence. And, of course, when Lumumba became the pre-eminent leader of the independence movement, we supported Lumumba. Probably the great majority of our students were Lumumba supporters.

All we knew about him was through his speeches on the radio or articles in the party's newspaper, the newspaper of his National Congolese Movement, which was one of the most popular newspapers among students. Basically, we liked the fact that he was a very advanced person in his thinking: he was for national unity, against those parties that were advocating federalism or secession and so on. We liked very much that he wanted to see an independent Congo that was unified, that was truly sovereign and that was going to use Congolese resources to benefit the people of the Congo.

Jacques Brassinne was a Brussels-based Belgian diplomat who was to become deeply involved in the process of Congo's independence.

In 1959, we had a few problems with the Congo. We had very big troubles in January 1959, with a lot of deaths in Léopoldville. In Brussels, we decided to take the problem of the Congo seriously. It was decided that in January 1960 a big conference would be held in Brussels with African leaders and members of our government: *Conférence de la Table Ronde*, Conference of the Round Table. I was involved in that conference because my minister was its president. I was the only man in his cabinet who had a diploma in African political science, so I became at that time the specialist on the Congo, although I had never been there at that time.

I met all the African leaders when they came to Brussels for the conference. I was the secretary of the conference, so all of them came to me to ask questions, to pay taxis, to pay hotels, to pay expenses, so I got close to most of them.

The first time I went to the Congo was two days before independence, and I stayed at the Belgian embassy in Léopoldville for six years. I was there when King Baudouin was making his speech.

Georges Nzongola-Ntalaja
Joseph Kabasele, who was one of the leading figures in Congolese popular music, composed the song 'Indépendance

Cha Cha' in Brussels on 27 January 1960, the day that the Round Table Conference decided that independence would take place on 30 June 1960.

I followed the ceremony of independence on the radio. King Baudouin of Belgium basically insulted us in his speech, telling us that the independence of the Congo was the culmination of the civilising mission started by King Leopold II – King Leopold, the *butcher* of the Congo, the man responsible for ten million Congolese lives lost during his reign. For this guy to tell us that this was our civiliser, it was simply insulting.

Jacques Brassinne

I knew Patrice Lumumba from before, and I was there when he delivered his speech. I saw Lumumba writing on his knees, so he adjusted his speech after hearing King Baudouin. He had a very clear voice, and we were very upset to hear what he said about the Belgians, and the way the Africans had been treated by the colonial imperialists. He was not very kind to Belgium.

The speech he delivered was to the people of the Congo, it was not directed to the people of the Assembly. He said, 'We have been slaves, we have been put in jail, we have been hungry.' It was really not very acceptable for the people who were present.

Georges Nzongola-Ntalaja

Kasa-Vubu made a speech but made no sense. We were very, very excited by Lumumba's speech, which told it like it is. We loved it. We loved it because it told the truth. It was probably not very diplomatic. One of the problems we have with the Western press is that you guys never criticised King Baudouin's speech, which was patronising and insulting to the Congolese, so it wasn't diplomatic either.

They criticised Lumumba's speech because he wasn't very diplomatic, but what he said was completely the truth. No one could quarrel with the facts; the facts he told were extremely correct.

Jacques Brassinne
At that time, we believed that Lumumba had done what he had to do, because we knew him very well and we knew the position he had taken before independence. We knew that the way he behaved was to win the election. He became Prime Minister – that was not our choice, but Belgium believed in democracy. Lumumba had a majority at the Chamber of Deputies and at the Senate. He was Prime Minister – we accepted it. We would like to have had another one, but it's like that. So, at that time things were clear and we were not nervous at all. We said, 'Well, we have Lumumba, we will deal with him, it's just a matter of time, he will certainly understand that he will need us.'

Wung'a Lomami Onadikondo remembers how the festive mood after the proclamation of independence changed quickly.

It was a very big feast, a very big celebration. The independence was proclaimed on 30 June 1960. It was a Thursday. So it was a very long weekend. And the first day people had to work, there was a mutiny of the army. Before independence, the Congolese leaders were discussing with the Belgian authorities to promote some Congolese in the army because there were no Congolese officers. When independence came, the soldiers saw that everything changed in the administration but all the officers in the army were still white.

Georges Nzongola-Ntalaja
The people of the Congo followed everything on the radio. The major event that occurred was the mutiny of

the armed forces, which took place only five days after independence, on 5 July. What happened was that the military were extremely displeased with the fact that we got independence and then kept the army structure exactly the same way as it was under colonialism: not a single Congolese officer. During the colonial period, the highest-ranking Congolese in the military until 1959 was sergeant-major. In 1959, some sergeant-majors were sent to Belgium for training; they became warrant officers. We didn't have a single lieutenant or sub-lieutenant, which meant the Belgians kept control of the military.

The soldiers had made their displeasure known to Lumumba and other politicians. Lumumba took the technocratic position that, 'Yes, we know that you need promotions but we're going to train you first before you get officer appointments.' Then the soldiers replied: 'What training did you have to become Prime Minister? Your ministers – what training did they have?' The Belgian commanding officer of the armed forces knew very well all the discontent in the armed forces because he had excellent intelligence services. So, on 5 July, he called a meeting of soldiers in Kinshasa and wrote in capital letters on a blackboard: 'BEFORE INDEPENDENCE = AFTER INDEPENDENCE'. He said, 'Independence is for civilians. For you, things are not going to change. Discipline will be maintained as before, under Belgian officers.' So it was very provocative. So the soldiers went to the ammunitions depot, took up guns and ammunition, and disarmed all of the Belgian officers. They communicated to all other military camps around the country. This was the event that led to the flight of most of the Belgian civil servants, military officers, technicians, engineers and so on.

And this is what brought about the Congo Crisis. Belgium intervened on 10 July with Belgian troops stationed

THE CONGO CRISIS (1960–1)

in the Congo and then brought in reinforcements from Belgium. And then on 11 July, the Katanga Province seceded, and this was the beginning of the real confrontation which led eventually to the assassination of Lumumba.

Mostly, people were very supportive of Lumumba. Kasa-Vubu was President – at the beginning, he sided with Lumumba. They went around the country together to pacify soldiers and to restore order. They also went to the American ambassador and asked for US intervention. The ambassador told them that the United States could not intervene – the USA, being an ally of Belgium in NATO, would never intervene against Belgium. The ambassador advised them to go to the United Nations. So they asked the United Nations, and the UN agreed to send troops to the Congo.

Through radio, we could tell what the criticism of Lumumba was in Western capitals and how badly he was seen by the Western powers. They were calling him all kinds of names: lunatic, Communist, Communist sympathiser, unstable, all kinds of stuff, which simply amazed us. We had no such conception of Lumumba, no such perception that he was that kind of person, but that's how he was described.

Jacques Brassinne

Lumumba was not a Communist. He had contact with Belgian Communists when he went to Brussels, but he was not close to those kinds of ideas. He had maybe read a few books on Communism, but he was not a Communist. Some people thought that. But to be frank with you, the secret service in Belgium followed Lumumba for months and months; they knew everything about the contacts, about the kinds of people he met. If somebody can prove that he was Communist, let them say that, but they will have to prove it. What he wanted was very clear until he got it. He wanted independence for the Congo. He wanted to have all the very important ministries in his government – security service, ministry of the interior, ministry of propaganda – so he got what he wanted. But he never really formed a kind of programme. His programme during the year before 30 June was to have independence and then we'd see after. So, you won't find any papers about what kind of policy he wanted to make.

During July, there was quite a lot of trouble all through the Congo. At that time, Lumumba had the support of the Americans, of the CIA, and also from the Secretary-General of the United Nations, Dag Hammarskjöld. Hammarskjöld really thought that the problem of the Congo was the Belgians – he thought that if you got rid of the Belgians you wouldn't have any problem with the Congo. It was completely false. After that, Lumumba went to the United States and to the United Nations and had lots of contact, and they came to believe that Lumumba was not exactly as they thought. Then he had a lot of contact with people who were close to the USSR, like Guinea and Ghana. Those people were examples for Lumumba. He wanted to change the political system of the Congo to a kind of dictatorship. That was the development of his thinking.

I was in Léopoldville until the end of August, and we felt at that time that Lumumba was changing his mind. And then Dag Hammarskjöld changed his mind, and Eisenhower and the CIA changed their minds, saying, 'We are going to have not a Cold War but a warm war in the Congo.' Nobody wanted to help him apart from the Soviet Union and its allies. At that time, the Russians made a lot of promises to Lumumba, but in fact they did very few things. They promised trucks and aeroplanes and so on, but they only gave him some very old machines. I had the opportunity to speak to him, but he was not able to trust any more.

One consequence of the spiral towards anarchy was white flight, including from newly autonomous Katanga, where **Wung'a Lomami Onadikondo** *grew up. Wung'a's father – a Lumumba supporter – had to flee to avoid arrest. The rest of the family would follow.*

Where I was living, it was on the road to Rhodesia [now Zimbabwe] and when white people began to flee to Rhodesia they were leaving only with their suitcases, they lost everything. A boy of my age I know went to see them flee and he was shot dead.

We left during the night because our neighbours were Katangese. We were friends before independence but from 11 July, when Katanga proclaimed its independence, things didn't go well any longer. We knew there were things we had not to say because it could endanger our families, so when we left it was at three o'clock in the morning to go to the airport and then we left.

Georges Nzongola-Ntalaja

In December 1960, I was at my second secondary school, not far from the secessionist Kasai Province. I was now in an environment where the majority were anti-Lumumba. I was more or less at risk because we were identified by the principal of our school as young people who were pro-Lumumba and we were very, very scared because we had to be very careful about what we say, fearing that they might arrest us and send us to be killed.

What we knew for sure was the fact that Lumumba was dismissed as Prime Minister by Kasa-Vubu, the President, on 5 September 1960, and this dismissal was totally illegal in our view. Here was a Prime Minister in a parliamentary democracy, where he had majority control of both Houses of Parliament, the House of Representatives and the Senate. And, of course, the two Houses rejected Kasa-Vubu's decision, saying that Lumumba was still Prime Minister. Then, on 14 September, Colonel Mobutu – who used to be Lumumba's protégé – staged a *coup d'état* against Lumumba.

We knew about the main events, and we followed them: Kasa-Vubu's dismissal of Lumumba, Mobutu's *coup d'état*, and then Lumumba's attempt to run away from Kinshasa and go to Stanleyville, and his arrest, and then his being sent to Katanga, where he was killed.

Jacques Brassinne

I was in Élisabethville [in Katanga] when Lumumba arrived around a quarter to five in the afternoon. He came with two other prisoners. All of the Belgian consulate was against his arrival. Lumumba gave troubles to all the rest of the Congo, and we were for the independence of Katanga, so if Lumumba came to Katanga we knew perfectly well that he would be killed. We knew that because the Minister of the Interior had said several times that if Lumumba came to Katanga he would be killed right away. He was sent there by his worst enemies: Mobutu, Kasa-Vubu, Bomboko. They were not able to keep Lumumba in jail because he had a lot of partisans, so they decided to get rid of him, and the way was to send him to Katanga. And so the problem was solved. To be frank with you, when Lumumba arrived in Élisabethville, I said to my friends from the Belgian consulate, 'This is the end of Lumumba.' And it was true.

Georges Nzongola-Ntalaja

We didn't know about the killing until February. He was killed on 17 January, but the Katangese authorities kept the information secret. It was only in mid-February that they announced that Lumumba had escaped from prison and he and his two companions had been caught and killed by villagers – which was a total lie. He was killed by an execution squad of Belgian soldiers and police.

Jacques Brassinne
Don't trust the people who try to see Lumumba as a prophet. He was not a prophet. He was utilised by people who wanted to make the kind of policy he had in mind.

Georges Nzongola-Ntalaja
He remained extremely popular in most of the country. Even in areas where the politicians were against him, among ordinary people he was very much admired. And, of course, Mobutu followed the popular mood in the country by naming him a national hero in 1966.

Wung'a Lomami Onadikondo
They say that he was unpredictable. That means he was not submissive.

'If one went, one couldn't return'

The Berlin Wall (1961)

The Berlin Wall epitomised the Cold War division of Europe. When it was breached in November 1989, Soviet control in Eastern Europe collapsed virtually overnight. But the simmering tensions that led to its construction had brewed more slowly.

From the outset, when East Germany was first established as a separate socialist state by Stalin in 1949, its 900-mile border with West Germany was a problem. With no physical barrier to prevent traffic between the two, it was difficult for the East German authorities to stop those citizens who chose to flee westwards. At first, the East German government did not try to stem the exodus, in part calculating that emigration would get rid of those awkward types who might hinder the building of socialism. But in 1952 'deserting the republic' became a criminal offence and the main border between East and West Germany was sealed with barbed-wire fencing and watchtowers. The exception was Berlin, still ruled jointly by the four occupying powers of Britain, France, the United States and the Soviet Union, where the border remained open.

The city of Berlin was unique. Whereas the remainder of the Eastern Bloc was increasingly sealed off from the rest of Europe, Berlin remained a transit point, a Cold War gateway between Communism and capitalism. And West Berlin became an extraordinary display of Western capitalism and democracy, linked by road and rail corridors to the West, but – as the Berlin Blockade of 1948–9 had shown – also a precarious enclave, surrounded by Soviet-controlled territory. For many citizens in the East, continued access to West Berlin was a precious outlet, a means of temporarily escaping the stifling rhythm of daily life under a Communist regime and sampling Western prosperity. And for those who wanted to leave permanently, it was the one place they could still cross to the West relatively easily. Once they were safely in West Berlin, they could then transfer to West Germany, where all Germans had the automatic right to become citizens. West Germany even paid for many refugees to fly out.

As early as 1952, East Germany's leader, Walter Ulbricht, had wanted the Berlin loophole closed. But the Soviet leadership in Moscow was reluctant to hand the West a propaganda victory. Putting up a wall to keep its citizens from escaping, it was argued, would be tantamount to admitting that Communism could not compete. So, Ulbricht was instead told to take steps to boost the East German economy and prove to both his own citizens and the West that life in a Marxist-Leninist state was a better option.

But the flood of émigrés kept streaming westwards. By 1956, over a million people had left, most of them young, well-educated professionals and skilled workers, the lifeblood of the East German economy. East Germany was in fact the only state in Europe during the 1950s to experience a net loss of population. In contrast, West Germany was economically booming and was now under a German Chancellor, Konrad Adenauer, whose aim was to create a free, united Germany. For the Soviet leader, Nikita Khrushchev, the nightmare scenario was of a revived capitalist Germany, backed by the United States and armed with nuclear weapons, challenging a much weaker East German state, and ultimately posing a direct threat to the Soviet Union.

What is more, 13 years after the end of the Second World War there was still no formal German peace settlement. So, in 1958 Khrushchev tried another tactic. He warned the Western Allies that unless they signed a peace treaty recognising the existence of two German states and agreed to end the post-war occupation of Berlin and transform it into a free, demilitarised city, he would sign his own peace treaty with East Germany and turn over control of all lines of communication and access rights to the East German authorities. In essence, it was an ultimatum and a threat: either agree to withdraw, or be forced out of Berlin in any case.

It did not work. Led by President Eisenhower's administration, the Western powers stood their ground and, as they had a decade earlier, refused to abandon West Berlin. Meanwhile, the brain drain of those opting for a new life in the West continued.

By January 1961, the authorities in East Germany and in Moscow realised that it was imperative that something be done. Between 1949 and 1961, at least 2.8 million people had left East Germany – one-sixth of the population. Not only was it causing a serious labour shortage, East Germany's claim that socialism was superior to capitalism was beginning to ring decidedly hollow.

By now, a new American President had taken office, the young Democrat John F. Kennedy. At their Vienna summit meeting in early June 1961, Khrushchev once again demanded that the Western Allies relieve the pressure on East Germany by agreeing to withdraw from West Berlin and sign a peace treaty to recognise East Germany. But like Truman and Eisenhower before him, President Kennedy refused to cave in and the summit ended in acrimony. As the political temperature rose, both sides moved to hike their military spending.

Khrushchev decided that the only way to stop the haemorrhage was to give Ulbricht what he wanted: the green light to dust off long-laid plans and start secret preparations to build a wall around West Berlin. The plan was kept under wraps, although Ulbricht declared at a press conference in June 1961 that 'no one has any intention of building a wall' – a rather too vigorous denial.

The first stage of the Wall went up under cover of darkness, in the early hours of Sunday, 13 August 1961. East Berliners awoke to find East German police and army units digging trenches and unrolling bales of barbed wire to cut off their access to Berlin's western sectors. Before long, concrete blocks were added, and eventually a 12-foot-high concrete wall was zig-zagging through the city, reinforced with steel-mesh fencing and watchtowers. Parallel to the Berlin Wall was the so-called death strip, open ground policed by armed border guards who were under orders to shoot anyone who tried to cross over. And ringing the city, a few miles outside, were Soviet troops and tanks, poised to intervene if needed. No longer was it possible to travel freely into West Berlin by train or on foot. Some East Berliners, desperate to escape, jumped from windows that faced the newly sealed-off west, or raced across the Cold War's new no-man's-land.

Soon, crossing from inside East Berlin became too dangerous. Some sought more indirect routes, trekking out into the East German countryside to approach West

Berlin from outside the city, where there was less intense scrutiny from border guards.

Those who made it safely into West Berlin could start again, creating new lives for themselves in the West. But their freedom came at a cost. Relatives left behind in the East were now unreachable, and for the next 28 years they would be on the other side of the Iron Curtain. During that time, the Berlin Wall would stand not just as a physical barrier cutting the city in two, but as an emblem of the Cold War division of Europe.

At a political level, leaders on both sides concluded that the new status quo was hardly an ideal arrangement, but it was better than the alternative of a conflict that might go nuclear. Officially, the East German government called it the 'Anti-Fascist Protective Wall', constructed to protect the East German state from the aggression of Western 'fascists'.

Khrushchev was franker. He admitted that the wall was a 'hateful thing', adding that 'you can easily calculate when the East German economy would have collapsed if we hadn't done something soon against the mass flight. There were, though, only two kinds of countermeasures: cutting off air traffic or the Wall. The former would have brought us to a serious conflict with the United States which possibly could have led to war. I could not and did not want to risk that. So the Wall was the only remaining option.'

For the Americans, the Wall was, as the US Secretary of State Dean Rusk proclaimed in 1961, a 'monument to Communist failure'. But there was also relief that the new arrangement did not appear to jeopardise West Berlin's access to the outside world; and while there was now a de facto partition of Berlin, it was hoped that it might ensure more international stability. In a letter to the Mayor of

Berlin, Willy Brandt, written not long after the Wall went up, President Kennedy warned that he too was anxious to avoid at all costs a confrontation that might lead to war with the Soviets.

'Grave as this matter is,' he said, 'there are ... no steps available to us which can force a significant material change in this present situation ... This brutal border closing evidently represents a basic Soviet decision which only war could reverse. Neither you nor we, nor any of our Allies, have ever supposed that we should go to war on this point.'

Nonetheless, the building of the Berlin Wall did ramp up friction between East and West. Western garrisons in West Berlin were reinforced, as were Soviet troops on the other side of the border. In October 1961, an incident at the Berlin crossing point of Checkpoint Charlie led to a stand-off between Soviet and American troops. For 16 hours their tanks faced each other on full alert before both sides backed down and a confrontation was avoided.

Leslie Colitt *was an American student who went to West Berlin in 1959 to see for himself what this Cold War gateway between Communism and capitalism looked like.*

One could sense that it was a divided city, politically, but in human terms it wasn't ... People flowed back and forth between East and West Berlin. I had the feeling that it was still one city – which politically was divided, but it didn't really matter much in terms of people being able to meet and get together, families and all that sort of thing.

The atmosphere in East Berlin was very raw. In the streets, there were more holes between the buildings than there were buildings: so much had been demolished during the war that the sight of a whole building was quite something. People would come over from the East to buy almost everything in the West that they could afford.

They had to exchange money at the rate of four East marks for one West mark. So that means that things were four times as expensive [...] They came over to buy fabrics. The women would buy textiles to make up into dresses in the East. Mechanical things, tools, all kinds of things like that they would buy in the West. Things for their car and women cosmetics, cosmetics, cosmetics. There was nothing like that in the East. Stockings ... You just name it, and they would buy it, if they had the money.

In the student village where I lived in West Berlin, about 20 per cent of the students living there were from East Germany. And because they came from families which were considered bourgeois, they couldn't study in the East, or at least not the subjects they wanted, so they came to the Free University of Berlin or the Technical University in West Berlin.

On the other side of the city, **Joachim Rudolph** *was a young East Berliner who had taken part in the uprising against the Communist government in 1953. For him, the saving grace of life in the austere, stifling East was that Western prosperity was just a metro ride away.*

We went to the Kurfürstendamm and looked at the great cars which stood on the streets and photographed them. My friends were into cars. And then they developed the photos in a big bathtub. We very often went to West Berlin, and two of my closest friends were already studying there. We had done A levels together, we knew each other well, and we completely trusted each other.

I knew people who fled; I even helped one family, our neighbours, to flee. I helped them carry things over the border because the borders were not controlled and, if one didn't carry suitcases that were too big, one could walk past the policemen at the border on the East side.

The numbers of refugees from East to West Berlin rose and fell. But in July and August of 1961, the numbers rose again, and there was an enormous shortage of workers in the East. It was said that the GDR wouldn't put up with it for much longer, especially because it was mostly young people who had a good education that went to the West and did not come back.

In 1960 **Gisela Nicolaisen** *was a student in Leipzig; she watched as, day by day, people eerily vanished around her in her hometown of Weissenfels, south-west of the city.*

Suddenly a couple would be gone, or a whole family, or the GP, or the boyfriend of my sister, or a former classmate ... Rumours would spread very quickly through the town, and one knew that they weren't there any more. I was happy that they managed to do that. And I started to ponder: 'Should I not go myself? Is it still possible? How long is it still possible? When will they shut the door? Then I won't be able to leave at all.'

But there was also a case of a music teacher who suddenly wasn't there any more, and that was very much condemned as a betrayal of the state. She came back, though, because she couldn't make her way in the Federal Republic. She was welcomed with open arms and given money so she could find her feet again.

One had to apply for a place to study and one had to answer a lot of questions, and the study places were then allocated. That was determined by your background, depending on whether you were a worker's child or a farmer's child or a child of the intelligentsia. Workers' and farmers' children were given preference, and they could basically choose to study whatever they wanted, especially from professions that were traditionally occupied by intellectuals, such as doctor, pharmacist, lawyer or judge. Those positions would not be given to children of intellectuals.

In addition to your school record, there was your social-political work – how you had applied yourself to the building of socialism, whether you held a position in the Free German Youth [Freie Deutsche Jugend (FDJ)] and so on, and whether you had any family who had already fled the GDR. I was the child of an ordinary employee and I had fairly good marks, but I couldn't show much social-political work, and I also had a sister who had left the GDR four years earlier and now lived in Switzerland, so I had very bad prospects. I applied to study pharmacy and food chemistry and, of course, I did not get a place; if I wanted to wait for them, I would have to have proved myself by working for two years in production, or I could have studied to become a teacher of maths and chemistry. At first, I rejected that because I never wanted to become a teacher in the GDR, because it was a highly politicised profession. But my father told me it was the only opportunity to actually get to university so I should take it – and who knew what might be done with it later. That convinced me, so I accepted the offer and went to university in Leipzig..

For the duration of my two years' studying, I could not assess how my fellow students were politically oriented – except for those who wore the party badge, of whom there were quite a few. They never expressed themselves privately. We always spoke in party jargon in front of the teachers, at political gatherings and in front of those with party badges. So, for two whole years, I could not find out who thought as I did, who was critical of the regime. That situation was very depressing.

Pretty soon, our seminar group was declared a socialist collective. This meant that we not only studied together but also learned together in the remaining time, that we drank beer together, that we went to the theatre together, that, at the weekends, we went on outings together. It was a controlling measure. A private life was not desirable.

One day, the Free German Youth secretary came to us and ordered us to call in pairs on those farmers who had not yet consented to join the state cooperative farms. I was on the side of the farmer who refused to give his farmyard to the cooperative, but had to lecture him that he should join it. The farmer was so pale and so unfriendly. As soon as he said, 'No', I got up and left. My fellow student didn't say anything. It was an excruciating situation. But I was always afraid that if I opposed all this – if I said anything against it – I would be summoned and interrogated. That's what I was most afraid of because I didn't know if I would be able to stand my ground. Out of that fear I did what was expected of me. And inside, I was always torn.

When I was 18, I hadn't felt able to leave home by myself, forever, because if one went one couldn't return. I knew already that I wanted to live and work in a Western country, but it was simply too early. So, when I started university I was struggling with what would be the right decision: to leave or to stay. That is something that my father got out of me.

He came into the hallway and said: 'Do you really want to go? Do you really want to go?'

'Yes, I really want to go!'

'Then go now.'

That was like a kick. It was like a liberation. And then the decision was made.

We had to ensure total secrecy. No one was to hear of it. We played out every situation I could run into on the

Joachim Rudolph in the early 1960s.

Gisela Nicolaisen in the late 1950s.

way to Berlin. We drafted carefully phrased letters, which I would then send from Berlin, to the university, to my seminar group – and to my parents, who officially would not know anything about it. We thought of everything so that no one could prove that they knew of it; that would have been a criminal offence. They also wanted to be on holiday when I left, so that it looked like I had used their absence to secretly head to Berlin.

I had asked at West German universities whether I could continue my studies there and they said yes, if I could prove my previous studies with the relevant course material. I couldn't have any course material in my suitcase – that would have been very suspicious. So, we took photos of my course material, and hid the negatives in the spines of books, which I then sent to my sister in Switzerland.

Gisela *eventually headed West on 5 November 1960.*

It was a Saturday and, like every Saturday, I went to the train station. Usually, I would be going home, but this time I was going in a different direction. You can plan as much as you like, but there are still some situations that you can't calculate in advance. I bumped into a fellow student at the station, and I had to get rid of her because I wasn't buying a ticket home but to Berlin – under no circumstances could she be allowed to hear that. I remember that I was not nervous at all. I thought completely clearly about what I could do to get rid of her. I told her to stand in line in the other queue and we'd see whose turn it was first. That's what she did, and she could not hear what ticket I bought. I then sat on my train and between my platform and hers there was another train that was waiting to leave. My train left first, so she would not have been able to see me board.

I was very lucky at the border control. A group of young nurses had got on and taken over the whole compartment. They were in high spirits and, when the guard came in to inspect passports, they started to flirt and joke with him. He came to me, and I also smiled at him. He looked at my passport, turned around, made a few more jokes with the others and left. And that was it.

I had been to West Berlin before, and I knew my way around. I knew what to say at the ticket booth – that one had to buy a return ticket – and I moved confidently through the stations. I think that was an advantage because there were hundreds who went that way every day. If I could move like a local, I wouldn't stand out so I would not be noticed. I sat close to the door, the train stopped, I got off and then I was on Western ground. It had happened.

We never said that I had left for political reasons; that would have made things very difficult for my parents. We said that I had fallen in love with one of my pen pals and had gone to join him in West Germany. That was believed because my fellow students knew that I had a pen friend. And my parents got off lightly. They suffered no real reprisals. When I met my former fellow students almost 40 years later, they all believed that I had married that pen friend.

Leaving is a decision that I have never regretted. It was the best decision in my life.

*Soon it would be much more difficult to flee through East Berlin. On 13 August 1961, **Leslie Colitt** awoke to the news that East German soldiers were enclosing West Berlin in barbed wire, backed up by Soviet tanks in case of trouble.*

When the refugee crisis reached its peak, something like two to three thousand people were coming over every day from East Germany or East Berlin. And one knew, something had to be done [...] We thought, if the East would do something radical, like trying to seal off the city, that the Western powers, the US, Britain, France, would react in some strong way, militarily or so, but of course, that never happened.

I was away on a vacation with my parents in southern France on 13 August. In the morning, we heard the radio and the main news item was that a wall was going up in Berlin. Partition. Partitioning of Berlin.

I immediately sent a cable to my fiancée in East Berlin saying I would be arriving as soon as I could get there and that we should meet outside the Pressecafé in the Friedrichstrasse.

And the first thing we discussed, of course, was how she was going to get out of East Berlin, which was no easy matter because the Eastern sector had been severed physically from the West for the first time.

One went through all the possibilities. Friends who might know somebody, who could smuggle her out, that was too dangerous. I knew some Americans who claimed they might be able to help, but in the actual event, they couldn't, or didn't want to.

So, in the end, we were left with our own resources and the thing that came to mind first was my sister. She was much younger than my fiancée but nonetheless her passport would have to serve. I immediately cabled my parents to send that passport to me as quickly as they could. Four days later, I got it. With that in hand, I realised, my God, it doesn't have an entry stamp from West Germany. That means if a controller from the East looks at it, he would wonder – how did she get to East Germany in the first place?

This was just one of these things one had to go with.

And I smuggled the passport in under my clothing into East Berlin. My sister had brown hair and my fiancée was blonde, so she had to dye her hair in order to fit the picture.

We set a date when we would have to do this because we were afraid that the controls would stop being so lax. At any date they could start issuing coloured slips together with the passport with a stamp on them that would render our passport useless.

Joachim Rudolph *was also away from Berlin when he heard the news.*

We were on a camping site by the Baltic Sea. And there we learned via the loudspeakers that the borders were closed in Berlin. Not only that, but they also played heroic marching music all day, alongside announcements: how, at last, the German Democratic Republic could build up socialism without obstruction from evil agents and West German and American saboteurs.

We thought they were making a fuss to try to boost socialist morale. Nobody believed that the border closure could last for long. We thought that it might be like the uprising on 17 June 1953, when the borders were closed for a week or ten days and then they were reopened again and everything continued as before.

After a few days, those who were studying in West Berlin began to worry that they'd not be able to continue their courses. So, we decided to return to Berlin and see what was happening.

It was dark when we arrived back in Berlin, and we drove straight to the border at Bernauer Strasse. Now, instead of the two border policemen who usually stood there controlling the pedestrian traffic, there were five or six soldiers, with steel helmets on their heads and Kalashnikovs around their necks, guarding the border. As our car drew closer, they called from a distance that we should go back at once; we had no business being there, and we were to leave the border area.

Now we realised that the situation was serious. We met up every evening in the pub and discussed what we were going to do. And what did we want to do? We needed to be back in Dresden on 1 September to continue our studies. One friend of mine had already intended to leave at the end of 1961 or early 1962 to go to West Berlin and stay there because his father was already there. He said if he succeeded in escaping to West Berlin, then he would try to fetch his mother and his brother over too. And that was also going round in my head.

Those who lived in the GDR or East Berlin but worked or studied in the West now had to be registered, so we went along with my friends who had to do this. They came out and told us that they could not continue their studies in the West; starting the next day, they had to present themselves at a construction company on the outskirts of Berlin.

I returned to university in Dresden. There, we now had to agree in writing to be on standby to join the People's Army for an unknown duration. We also had to bind ourselves in writing to wear the blue Free German Youth shirt to all seminars and training courses until a peace treaty between the Western Allies and the Soviet Union was signed – and I knew that there would never be a peace treaty on Soviet terms.

I went to the enrolment office and asked to be allowed to leave, and then I returned to East Berlin, because I wanted to be with my friends to discuss how we would proceed.

After two or three sleepless nights in East Berlin, I was ready. When we met up again, I said to my friend: 'We are going to do it together. We find an escape route, and we will try to get to West Berlin.'

We got on our bikes and, beginning in the south of Berlin, we rode along the border. We tried to get as close to the border as possible to see how it was secured. We often heard and saw on Western broadcasts that there were people who had tried to flee by swimming across the River Spree. We thought that could work. But then we tried swimming at night on the outskirts of the city and immediately broke it off because it seemed far too dangerous. It was great weather, a starlit night, but we knew by then that the border soldiers had a duty to prevent the escape. We knew that on 20 August 1961 the first refugee who tried to swim from East to West was shot. He was killed.

Leslie Colitt's plans were further advanced, but when the day came it wasn't quite as straightforward as he had hoped. Moving his fiancée's luggage across the East–West Berlin border involved complicated subterfuge – and began to bring him unwelcome attention.

I went over to West Berlin, then back to East Berlin and at that point in Friedrichstrasse Station, the controller looked up at me and said, 'Didn't I see you here once before?'

'Yes, I was here earlier.'

'Aha! – what are you doing here?'

Well, I had to think of some reason quickly and I said: 'My father's due on the train from Leipzig.'

This happened to be at the time of the Leipzig Fair, when Westerners were able to go into East Germany freely. I wasn't sure if the controller believed me, so I decided not to use that station on our way to West Berlin.

I had agreed to meet my fiancée at the Pressecafé, which was just across the street of the station. And to my horror, my fiancée had not gotten her hair dyed at all, because all the hairdressers in her area had been closed and therefore she had tried to get an appointment at the Friedrichstrasse Station hairdresser, which she did.

There was only one thing that we had overlooked. She didn't speak a word of English! We each had a double vodka in front of us and I was trying to give her a snap English lesson on the questions I thought she might be asked.

Had we known all this we would never have done the preparation in the Pressecafé because it was teaming with informers for the Stasi. The place was known as a meeting point for potential escapees.

We didn't know this, so we left the café and walked up Friedrichstrasse towards what would become known as Checkpoint Charlie, the crossing point to West Berlin. It was dusk, and I could just make out the figure of a uniformed East German, standing there, alone – I will never forget the last steps up to him. We stood right in front of this very young man, and we took out our passports; I took out mine and my fiancée took out my sister's passport and at that moment she fumbled and the passport fell to the ground. And we all dived down to the ground to pick up the passport. All at the same time. We virtually knocked heads and we laughed actually and the border guard laughed too.

I knew at that point that we were safe.

Joachim Rudolph and his friend were still looking for a safe escape route.

We had three. Two fell through because those areas of the border had been reinforced.

The third involved cycling from East Berlin into the GDR, very close to the border until we were out of sight of the border guards. Then we turned and cycled back in the direction of West Berlin into an area called Schildow. We found warning signs: 'Border area. Keep out!'

We ignored them and carried on until we reached a field, which sloped then rose again on the other side. Our map showed that the border was at this lowest point, a small river.

On the other side we could see tractors, and my friend identified them as West German tractors – not GDR or Soviet ones. That seemed to be our ideal escape route.

Then we waited for bad weather. On the evening of 28 September, we finally saw clouds gathering.

We went home and fetched the things we wanted to take on our escape: a plastic bag with our important papers, A-level certificates, skilled worker's certificate, birth certificate and so on, and clothes in a small briefcase.

At around eleven o'clock we were at the edge of the field, and by three o'clock in the morning we were at the river. It was 150 to 200 metres at most, but we needed four hours to cover it because we took turns to crawl. One of us crawled 10 to 15 metres, then the other followed, then the first worked his way forward. We reached the river and until then we had not seen any more indications of the border. But the map showed it. We were surprised: there was no barbed wire fence, no signs, nothing at all. We thought the border must be 50 or 100 metres after that, at the most, so we would have to cross the river.

As we dipped our feet into the river, there was a loud noise. We thought at first it was an explosion or a machine gun, but it soon turned out it was only a flock of wild geese we had startled, which had spent the night at the riverbank. They rose up and you can imagine to our ears the flapping of the wings made a terrible din. We both got a terrible fright and thought: 'What do we do now?' But it was clear that going back would be pointless – it would take too long, and a patrol of border soldiers might come to see what had disturbed these wild geese. We realised we just had to go on. And that's what we did.

The river was not deep, about knee-deep, but the bottom was a bit boggy, so we had to be very careful that we did not fall down or get our papers wet. On the other side, we ran, half-crouched, to get out of sight of the river.

It was still dark, and we couldn't see further than 15 or 20 metres. We continued running in the direction of the tractors we had seen. By then it was morning, four o'clock. When we saw the first houses, we had still not seen any signposts. We thought, 'Are we in East Berlin? Are we in West Berlin?'

There was a blue-lit window – it was a fire station. Behind it, there sat a young man. He had his head propped up in his hands. He was dozing. We knocked. He started and said, 'Boys, where do you come from?'

Well, where did we come from? We did not know. Were we in East Berlin, were we in West Berlin? We could only stammer.

'Yes, yes, boys,' he said. 'I can imagine where you come from. Congratulations! You managed it! You're in West Berlin.'

*Joachim had made it. He went to a West Berlin camp set up to screen refugees and weed out Stasi spies, and at the end of 1961 he was able to resume his studies. **Leslie Colitt**'s fiancée had left her entire family. Now they were almost unreachable, on the other side of the Iron Curtain.*

She immediately sent a telegram to East Berlin, to her parents, informing them that she had come to West Berlin. So, if the authorities had asked what happened to their daughter, they could say, 'We had no idea she was going to escape.' We only learned in 1994 that her father was demoted at work because of her escape. She didn't see her mother for five years after that.

Leslie Colitt and his fiancée Ingrid in the 1960s.

In those days, West Berliners who wanted to see relatives in the East had only one way of doing this, and that was to stand at a vantage point in West Berlin where they could be seen by their relatives in the East. They could wave to each other. My fiancée saw her parents only as tiny little dots about 500 metres away.

'The world was going to end any time now'

The Cuban Missile Crisis (1962)

The confrontation known as the Cuban Missile Crisis, and in Russia as the Caribbean Crisis, took place over 13 days in October 1962. It was the closest the United States and the Soviet Union came during the Cold War to triggering nuclear apocalypse.

The starting point went back to more than three years earlier and the moment, in January 1959, when a band of rebels on the Caribbean island of Cuba, led by the young revolutionaries Fidel Castro, his brother Raúl and Ernesto 'Che' Guevara, succeeded in ousting the unpopular, corrupt dictatorship of Colonel Fulgencio Batista, following a two-year guerrilla campaign.

To begin with, Fidel Castro's new Cuban government was more nationalist than socialist, and his revolution attracted little attention in Moscow. But when he nationalised American companies in Cuba and the United States retaliated with a trade blockade, Castro appealed to the Soviet Union to come to Cuba's aid by buying up the sugar, which accounted for 80 per cent of the island's exports.

For Moscow, Castro's Cuba was a welcome new revolutionary ally, sympathetic to Marxist doctrine, ready to defy Washington, and whose geo-strategic position only 100 miles off the American mainland was interesting, to say the least.

To Castro, the Soviet Union was the obvious ideological partner and a necessary source of economic support, whereas the Americans were hostile imperialists, working hand-in-glove with Cuban exiles intent on destroying the revolution.

To the United States, Castro had turned Cuba into a Communist threat and given Moscow a foothold in America's backyard. It raised questions about the future viability of the US naval base on the island, at Guantanamo Bay. The US government decided it had to act.

In January 1961, the incoming American President, John F. Kennedy, inherited from his predecessor, Dwight Eisenhower, a plan to invade Cuba and topple Castro using CIA-trained Cuban exiles – what became known as the Bay of Pigs Invasion. But when the operation took place, on 15 April 1961, it was a fiasco. Instead of being welcomed by locals as liberators, when the exiles landed at Playa Girón and other beaches on the Bay of Pigs in Cuba, they were attacked and outnumbered by Castro's troops and tanks. Within three days they had surrendered. It was an embarrassing failure for the Americans and a humiliation for President Kennedy.

In Cuba, it turned Castro into a national hero. But the invasion was also seen as a warning of what the United States might try again. It encouraged Castro to cement his relations with the Soviet Union, and publicly declare his allegiance to Communism and to the Soviet bloc. He also asked Moscow for weapons to protect the island against any new American attack.

The Soviet leader, Nikita Khrushchev, was receptive to the request. He was acutely aware that American nuclear warheads were stationed in the United Kingdom, Italy and Turkey, all capable of reaching Soviet targets. Khrushchev reckoned he could offset this by placing missiles on Cuba where they could reach Washington, thereby giving the Americans a taste of their own medicine and deterring them from trying to intervene either in Cuba again or elsewhere in the Caribbean. As Khrushchev colourfully put it in discussion with his advisers in April 1962: 'Why not throw a hedgehog at Uncle Sam's pants?'

At first, the Americans accepted Soviet assurances that the weapons being shipped to Cuba were anti-aircraft defensive missiles, and looked the other way. But in mid-October 1962, American spy planes seemed to show evidence that missile sites were being constructed in Cuba for offensive nuclear weapons, capable of striking the United States.

The Kennedy administration went into crisis mode. The stakes could not have been higher. This was no longer a quarrel with the Soviets about Europe or a fight against Communists in Asia; it was not even long-range Soviet missiles stationed on the other side of the world; it was short- and medium-range ballistic missiles targeting US cities, being secretly installed on America's very doorstep.

For the next few days, top security officials in the White House weighed up how to respond. A surgical strike on Cuba to take out the missiles and a bigger air offensive were both considered but discarded as too dangerous. Eventually, President Kennedy chose a less risky option and ordered a naval blockade to seal off Cuba by sea. As a precautionary measure, he also put all American military forces worldwide on a heightened state of nuclear alert, ordering all airborne strategic bombers to be armed with nuclear weapons.

Then, on the evening of 21 October, Kennedy went on television to give a nationwide address and put the Soviet Union on notice, grimly stating that the United States would regard 'any nuclear missile launched from Cuba against any nation in the Western Hemisphere as an attack by the Soviet Union on the United States'.

In Moscow, Khrushchev feared that a new American invasion of Cuba was imminent and gave the Soviet commander on Cuba permission to fire tactical nuclear weapons if the Americans attacked. He also sent a message to President Kennedy warning that, while the Soviet Union would not strike first, if the naval blockade meant any Soviet ships were stopped, the American vessels involved would be sunk by Soviet submarines. It looked as though both sides were preparing to go to the wire.

Over the next few days, tensions remained at a level that was unprecedented. The Americans held high-level meetings to talk through a possible invasion of Cuba to destroy the missiles, and concluded that it would lead to catastrophic casualties.

Meanwhile, on Cuba itself, Castro was battening down the hatches. People were told to brace themselves for an invasion. He appealed to Moscow to get ready to respond with a nuclear strike if American troops landed, and ordered his own troops to open fire on any American planes seen flying over the island.

After days of intense shuttle diplomacy to come up with a deal, both leaders stepped back from the brink. On 28 October 1962, Khrushchev announced that he was giving the order to dismantle and withdraw Soviet missiles from Cuba. Kennedy announced that he was standing down the naval blockade and confirmed a pledge not to invade the island. He also privately agreed to a Soviet request to withdraw the US nuclear missiles based in Turkey, so long as this part of the deal was kept secret. They were quietly removed the following year.

Castro flew into a rage when he learned that a deal had been done behind his back, and argued that it was a mistake to have caved in under American pressure and left Cuba defenceless. He laid out five points of additional guarantees he wanted from the United States to back up its pledge not to invade, including that it end its embargo, all 'subversive activities' and 'pirate attacks' against Cuba, stop violating Cuban air space and territorial waters, and return Guantanamo Bay Naval Base to Cuba. His demands fell on deaf ears and, under Soviet pressure, Castro had no choice but to consent to the missiles being withdrawn.

In Washington and Moscow, the outcome was portrayed as a victory. President Kennedy had stood his ground and got the Soviet missiles out of Cuba. Nikita Khrushchev had secured a promise that there would be no American invasion of Castro's Cuba, and no American missiles in Turkey.

But above all the crisis had been a moment when nuclear madness nearly descended, but mercifully was averted. It had shown how easy it would be to trigger an all-out nuclear war, which might destroy humankind. It prompted the setting up of a teletype hotline between Washington and Moscow, and the rapid conclusion of a treaty banning all but underground nuclear tests, because both sides now recognised in their guts that avoiding nuclear holocaust served everyone's interests.

American-born **Frances Glasspoole** *was 14 years old when she and her family went to live at Guantanamo Bay.*

My father was in the navy, and he was transferred there to work, and my family went to the base, as military dependents do. We drove across the United States from southern California in our car to Norfolk, Virginia. It was the early part of 1960 – Eisenhower was still President – and when I was in Virginia, never having been to the East Coast or the South before in my life, it was the first time I ever saw 'whites-only' drinking fountains and bathrooms and separate sections in restaurants for what were called 'coloured' people at the time. It was still segregation, and the civil rights movement had not yet begun.

We flew to Guantanamo Bay on a military plane. It was green and mountainous and the water below was turquoise, and it was just different than anywhere I'd ever been before. It was both different and the same. We lived in a housing area that was not near the main part of the base; it was closer to the fence line. You could actually see the fence line from our back porch with binoculars. I rode a military bus to go to school – everywhere we went on the base, we went on big, grey military buses.

The writer **Ciro Bianchi** *was a teenager living in the Cuban capital at the time of the crisis.*

I was born in Havana in October 1948. My father was a construction worker and my mother was a housewife, so it was a typical working family. Thanks to my parents' sacrifice we were able to study so, despite the hardship, it was a happy upbringing. Life was intense during that period [of the missile crisis] – we lived two days in one. We could have been wiped out, or God knows how many thousands of people could have died. But there was no fear. There is a scene in the film *Memories of Underdevelopment* in which the main character says, 'In this country, before opening the newspaper you have to take an aspirin.' Because the situation was really very tense, with the breaking of relationships, all kind of aggressions, even physical aggressions, and there were comrades who died in plots in Cuba and outside Cuba. It was a relentless war against Cuba and a blockade that cost us millions. So, when you see all of that, you say: 'This is people who sympathise with Fidel and Raúl.' We had to have a great trust in Fidel and Raúl to be able to endure all that.

Frances Glasspoole
When we arrived, it was shortly after the revolution. Prior to that, the gates were open and there was free travel into what we called Cuba-proper. When my family went there, the gates were closed. There was no travel. We called the land on the other side of the fence Castro's Cuba. We were on United States land. There were thousands of Cuban nationals working and living on the base. Some of them were exiles and could not go back home for fear of execution. Some of them commuted freely back and forth every day. There was a United States gate with Marines on duty, and just beyond that was a Cuban gate, and they had set up some kind of financial arrangements for the Cuban workers to change their American dollars into Cuban pesos because American money was worthless in Cuba.

My experience with Cuban people was widely varied. Almost all the military families on the base had Cuban gardeners or maids, so we had Cuban people in our home. We made friends with them, we had social activities with them – I actually had a Cuban boyfriend.

A word that comes to mind about Guantanamo Bay in the early 1960s is that it was ambiguous. On the one hand, it was a simplistic life where everything we needed or

Frances Glasspoole's family Christmas card from 1961.

wanted was made available to us. The lettuce wasn't very fresh, but we had a good life. And yet not very far away there was so much else going on. One of the beaches that we went to was right on the boundary of the base, and you could clearly see Cuban militia on the other side of the fence watching us with binoculars while we were watching them with binoculars.

I think we were pretty well indoctrinated that Castro was bad and Communism was bad and Russia was a threat – I think that came with the territory of being a US citizen. Before we ever left the country, we had a mindset already in place. Living on the base, we did not have a sense of what was going on in the world. Our news was filtered. The base newspaper was a little typewritten newsletter. It talked about American politics a little bit, but we were sheltered in that way. We did not know what was going on beyond our daily lives. There was a radio station on the base and a television station on the base. That was … *censored* is the only word I can come up with. The television station didn't come on until 7pm, and it was just old re-runs of *The Ed Sullivan Show* and *I Love Lucy* and things from several years previous. There wasn't any current information. The radio station played music. I had a portable radio as a teenager, and I remember sitting outside in the backyard at night and dialling around and picking up some rock-and-roll music from the US, because we really didn't have a lot of access to contemporary music.

There were what we called 'war games' every month or two on the weekends. We civilians had to stay home, and then there were tanks and noisy things going on – they did practices with aircraft and helicopters and artillery. If we did have to go out, we were stopped by roadblocks.

In April of 1961, there were increased war games going on but, because that was a standard activity on the base, it was not perceived by those of us who lived there, the civilian people, as anything different than usual. It was only later that we found out that that was in fact the Bay of Pigs. The Cuban people who we knew told us that things were really bad in Cuba and that there had been fighting and that Castro had won, but we had no idea what that was about. We were not insiders at all.

Ciro Bianchi

We lived under the threat of American aggression. They had invaded us in Girón already; the bombing in Havana just before Girón had happened. Before that, we suffered aggression from Trujillo, the Dominican dictator. And there were counter-revolutionary gangs that were very powerful. But we also faced the cut of the sugar quota by the United States, that was basic for the Cuban economy. We lived through the break-up of relations with the United States, the break-up of relations with the Latin-American countries except Mexico – that was the only country that never broke relations with Cuba. So all that was forming you, it was making you stronger; also the speeches of Fidel and other leaders of the revolution, especially Fidel's, were constant and that was very instructive.

I was very involved, not in the military, but in student organisations. We performed guard duties in our neighbourhood, in the junior high school where I was studying at the time – we did all that. People had a strong conviction and great fervour, and I don't think it was because we thought that the Soviet Union was going to help us, but that we trusted the direction of the revolution, especially the leader of the revolution: Fidel Castro.

Cuba was being threatened with an American invasion, the Soviets offered to help with conventional weapons and nuclear weapons, and Cuba as a sovereign country had the right to have those nuclear weapons. That's the way we saw it.

Nikita Khrushchev's son, **Sergei Khrushchev**, *recalls that this attitude of Cuban defiance was much admired in the Soviet Union.*

They became heroes to most of the Soviets, of the youth, who never knew about Cuba before but now they saw these young people fighting against American imperialism.

I remember the tension of the days, but you have to remember – what was the crisis? Khrushchev changed the major foreign policy of the Soviet Union. Stalin accepted the American and Churchill deal: 'You must be kept in your borders. We agree that you will dominate Eastern Europe; the rest is the Western world – it's our world. Don't even put your nose in the Middle East.' But my father said: 'No. I want to be a world power. I want to be respected as an equal.' And Americans don't respect anybody as equal. It was not about the balance of power. It was not about infiltration in the Western hemisphere. Americans pushed Castro from them; Castro visited Washington in April 1959, and the President didn't want to meet with him. And it was a rule of the Cold War that if you can do something bad to your enemy, do it. So, we supported Cuba, but we didn't want to bring them too close.

I asked my father, 'Why not invite Cuba to the Warsaw Pact?' He told me, 'They're too far, we don't know them too well, and if America will attack them we will have to start nuclear war.' It was too dangerous, and he didn't know what Castro would do. After the Bay of Pigs, Castro officially declared that he had joined the Soviet bloc. He told Khrushchev that he had to defend him because the obligation was for the superpower to defend all their allies, good or bad. So, Cuba became to the Soviet Union the same as West Berlin to the United States: small, useless piece of land, deep inside hostile territory, but if you will not defend it, even risking nuclear war, you will lose your face as a superpower.

So, my father decided what he could do. He cannot defend Cuba diplomatically. He cannot use conventional forces because Americans control all communications. So – send there these weapons to show America we're serious.

But Americans are very different. We lived all the time here with enemies on the gates, you in Great Britain, we in Russia. Americans were surrounded by two oceans, they were protected. They were like the strongest predator in the world, like a tiger, but a tiger which grew up in a zoo, and when sent into the jungle they were afraid of everything. So, when they found that it is the missiles in Cuba, the American public started panicking. It was an American psychological crisis: 'If it will be ready, they will launch against us.' It was no logic in this – why not launch them from Siberia? It was only 20 minutes' difference in the delivery. But it was clear to the politicians, and it was creating this panic in the United States: 'We have to remove them at any expense.'

It made the resolution of the crisis very difficult for Khrushchev and Kennedy, and we are lucky that all of them were balanced politicians who decided not to shoot. It was very different because we knew that it was so dangerous, but for the Americans it was unique. Now they found: 'We're also vulnerable. We can be killed.' In the Berlin crisis, if we start a nuclear war, Russia will kill Europeans – Germans, British, French – and Americans will watch it on TV. Now, they saw that they were the same.

Ciro Bianchi

I have very vivid memories of the October Crisis – we've always referred to this as the October Crisis. It's too important and too dramatic to be forgotten easily. But my most vivid memory is – maybe because of our optimism and confidence in the revolution – the tranquillity with which the Cuban people faced the event. I don't remember that there was fear, despite how terrible it was.

Frances Glasspoole

It was a Monday, and the weekend before had been one of those military exercise war-games weekends, or at least so we thought. There was increased military activity, except this time there were jets, and that was different. It seemed like there was a larger volume of military. But other than that, we had no clue what was going on, no idea.

Ciro Bianchi

I remember a headline in the *Revolution* newspaper. It read: 'The nation has awakened on a war standing.' I remember the atmosphere in Havana, I remember the militias on the streets ... I remember trenches at the Hotel Nacional that are still there, because that hotel was built over a system of caves. So they took advantage of the caves to build trenches, preparing for nuclear aggression. They are still there, a tourist attraction. I also remember anti-aircraft weapons around the FOCSA Building, an emblematic building in Havana. So, there was that atmosphere on the streets of Havana: people ready with nursing posts to take care of the injured, people ready to provide food to the population – everybody had a mission. As El Che said, those days were luminous and sad.

Frances Glasspoole

It was business as usual, except on that particular day there was a PA announcement; the principal came on and said that we were supposed to go home: don't ask any questions, just get on the buses and go home, and there would be further instructions. The further instructions were provided by the commanding officer of the base. My mother was handed a piece of paper at her work and also told to go home and follow those written instructions. And what the instructions said was: 'Get your suitcase and sit in your front yard and wait to be picked up.' Period. So that's what we did. We did what we were told.

We were picked up by something called a cattle-car, which was like a tractor or truck, open-ended in the back. There weren't any seats, you had to stand up. We were taken to the docks and turned back – they said the ships were all full. So, we went to the airport and we were put in line to go on to a military transport. I walked away from that line and took a photograph of that aircraft – I probably wasn't supposed to be doing that – and my mother and my brother waiting in line. The military personnel – my dad and the rest of the servicemen that were stationed on the base – were not evacuated. They stayed and did their duties.

My family happened to be on the very first plane that arrived in Norfolk, Virginia, the same day. All the dependents who were evacuated by ship arrived three days later. When our plane arrived – because it was the first plane from Guantanamo Bay to land on American soil – we were greeted by reporters, and flashbulbs were going off. I believe that they thought that the families of the brass, the commanding officers' families, would be on that plane, and that is not how it worked out; we were just ordinary folks.

The most significant thing I remember about that first day being back in the United States was that evening, was John Kennedy's speech on the radio, and it was broadcast overhead in the barracks. I remember sitting on a bed, listening to his voice for the first time. It was 1962. He'd been President for two years, and I'd never heard his voice.

John Guerrasio *was a child in Brooklyn at the time and remembers the fear that ordinary people felt.*

We grew up getting under our desks at school all the time for nuclear attacks. In my childhood, I think it was every Friday the air-raid siren would sound, and we would either practise getting under our desks or we'd all form orderly lines and go down to the basement.

I remember sitting down with the family and watching Kennedy's speech and thinking the world was going to end any time now. And then there was some point in the crisis when it looked like it was very, very bad, and my mother called all of her six children into the kitchen and said, 'We may not see each other again. The world may end this afternoon.' And we said a prayer. And she had found some poem which described New York City in a nuclear attack with the skyscrapers forming canyons that filled with water like in one of these disaster movies. And she read us that poem and kissed us, and we all walked off to school thinking that that was the end of it. And I was pretty amazed when three o'clock came and I got to go home and watch the Three Stooges again.

Sergei Khrushchev

The atmosphere in Russia was the same as in previous crises – we worked, we understood it was dangerous, but we believed that, we *hoped* that the government would resolve this crisis. If not, what can you do? So each morning, I went to my design bureau, working there as usual, then I came back to my residence where I lived with my father, and we went for a walk, and I asked him what was happening there.

He told me sometimes. He answered most of my questions. I asked him, 'What is there? What is America doing?' Sometimes he said, 'I am tired. Let's walk silently.'

Ciro Bianchi
Then came the retreat of the Russians, who decided not to continue. We never knew if in reality the missiles were here or not, if the missiles were here and the nuclear weapons were not, that was never clear, or at least I'm not clear about it. But when the Russians accepted the inspection on the sea and when the American ships blocked them and made them go back, we didn't expect anything else, we just trusted the revolution and its leaders and that is what is important.

I remember the day that Fidel stated the Five Points, when he did not accept the American inspection, when he did not accept that there were missiles on Cuban soil. I was studying in a night school, and I went to school and when I got there I was told that Fidel was going to speak. We started to listen to his speech at school and on our way back home we continued listening to the speech because you could hear it from every house and there Fidel took the position of total defence of Cuban sovereignty, not accepting the inspection of our national territory.

Frances Glasspoole
As a teenager, I believed that Castro and Khrushchev were both maniacs, crazy people. They were both dangerous, and the potential of nuclear war was real. But it wasn't a primary concern, probably because we were so protected.

Ciro Bianchi
We never thought about the Cold War. We had an aggression: financial, economic, military. So, we were in a hot war, not a Cold War. We lived it.

'There was no future'

The Fall of Khrushchev and the Rise of Brezhnev (1964–82)

On 14 October 1964 the Soviet leader Nikita Khrushchev was abruptly brought back to Moscow from a holiday by the Black Sea to attend a specially convened plenum. There he was publicly denounced by former colleagues and stripped of his positions as Communist Party leader and Chairman of the Council of Ministers. The ostensible reasons given were 'advanced age and ill health'. Taking the lead in deposing him was one of his former protégés, Leonid Brezhnev, who had concluded that the process of de-Stalinisation had gone far enough and it was time to call a halt, to protect the Communist Party from further criticism.

Khrushchev's personal style had not helped: the Politburo was, it seems, tired of his restless experiments with agriculture and reshuffles of party personnel. Abroad, Khrushchev's decision to resolve the crisis of 1962 with the United States by pulling Soviet missiles out of Cuba did not feel like a propaganda victory. And his erratic public behaviour, like the banging of his shoe on the table at the

United Nations, looked undignified and unworthy of the Soviet Union's global status.

After the brutality of the Stalin years, when top officials who lost favour might be arrested and shot, the ousting of Khrushchev was relatively benign. He was not thrown into prison or sent to the snowy wastes of Siberia, but allowed to keep his pension and stay on in his Moscow flat and dacha, living out his life as a political outcast. Cold-shouldered by his former colleagues and ignored by the Soviet media, he was left alone to write political memoirs, which, in time, his son smuggled out to the West. With his removal, the reformist period known as Khrushchev's 'thaw' petered out, and a more conservative period that would later be described as Brezhnev's 'era of stagnation' began.

The new party leadership began as a power-sharing collective. Over the next two decades – until he died in office in 1982 – the cautious and conservative Brezhnev gradually strengthened his position in the hierarchy to assume the mantle of Soviet President as well as General Secretary – head of state as well as head of the party – and therefore secure his place as undisputed Soviet leader.

In 1964, the political aim of the leadership was to maintain a conservative status quo and avoid any shocks to the system that might threaten the party's monopoly on power. Being overly critical of Stalin was no longer tolerated, but there was no rehabilitation of him either. The new party policy was to avoid mention of Stalin or Khrushchev altogether, stick to bland, empty slogans and crack down hard on anyone who stepped out of line.

There was also a stronger focus on party cadres, to build up a loyal *nomenklatura* of Communist bureaucrats who had an interest in preserving a system that conferred upon them special privileges, such as elite cars, shops and housing, only available to top party members. This self-perpetuating mechanism of mediocrity looked after those who never rocked the boat and who steered clear of showing initiative. For party officials who remembered the terrifying purges of the Stalin era and the unpredictable zigzags under Khrushchev, it was a welcome shift towards stability. It was also in sharp contrast to the political turbulence in China, where Mao's Cultural Revolution was getting underway.

One big problem for the Kremlin was the economy, which was becoming ever more dysfunctional. Although living standards improved, progress was slow and uneven. Centrally planned targets were set with no reference to demand. Rigid price controls encouraged hoarding. There were acute shortages of consumer goods. Rampant corruption led to shoddy quality. And hopes for rapid growth never materialised. Khrushchev had impetuously promised that the country would outpace the inequalities and miseries of capitalism to move from an interim stage of 'socialism' to the goal of 'full Communism' within 20 years. Brezhnev now scaled back that ambition and talked about attaining a period of 'developed socialism', starting from 1971.

The reality was that the Soviet economy was not delivering what consumers craved. Still recovering from the rebuilding needed after the Second World War, it was now being further undermined by the demands of an escalating Cold War arms race and competition in space too, as the Soviets tried to attain military parity with the Americans and maintain the lead in space, which they had achieved when they put the first man in orbit, Yuri Gagarin, in 1961.

Alexei Kosygin, who was in charge of the economy as Chairman of the Council of Ministers from 1964 to 1980, introduced some modest reforms to increase incentives and quality control, but they made little long-term difference. As a result, the decline in living standards, coupled with a desire to keep alive the spirit of reform from the Khrushchev era, fuelled public and private disaffection and – both inside the Soviet Union and in Eastern Europe – encouraged new voices of dissent.

In Eastern Europe, the biggest problem for the Politburo came in Czechoslovakia, with the political reforms of the Prague Spring and the subsequent Soviet invasion in 1968. This led to the development of the so-called Brezhnev Doctrine – Moscow's self-proclaimed right to intervene in any of its satellite states, if it deemed that their socialist status was at risk.

Inside the Soviet Union, the challenge was a new Soviet dissident movement, made up of those who insisted on their right to speak freely and campaign for human rights and civil liberties, even though in the post-Khrushchev era this could invite severe punishments, including long prison sentences. In response to renewed censorship, the dissidents defiantly set up their own samizdat self-publishing network, to copy and circulate forbidden literature clandestinely.

In 1965, two prominent writers, Andrei Sinyavsky and Yuli Daniel, were arrested and subjected to a show trial for the crime of publishing their satirical 'anti-Soviet' work abroad. They were both sent to prison, and the case marked the start of a concerted effort by the authorities to stamp out the nascent dissident movement.

That did not prove to be easy. Two leading Soviet dissidents enjoyed such international prominence and authority that it was almost impossible to silence them. Aleksandr Solzhenitsyn was a former prisoner in Stalin's labour camps whose books on the subject made him famous worldwide and would win him the Nobel Prize in Literature in 1970. Andrei Sakharov was a distinguished physicist whose ground-breaking work had helped develop Soviet nuclear weapons. He also became a Nobel laureate for his dogged moral stand as a peace campaigner.

In 1967, a new head of the Soviet Union's powerful security agency, the KGB, was appointed – Yuri Andropov. His claim, informed by Cold War suspicions, that dissidents were part of a wide-ranging imperialist plot to undermine the Soviet state would remain a train of thought that still reverberates 50 years on in Vladimir Putin's time. Russian security officials hostile to the West would still denounce opposition activists as traitorous 'fifth columnists' and 'foreign agents' in the pay of the CIA.

Andropov was responsible for an elaborate plan to use psychiatric hospitals to 'treat' political opponents, on the grounds that they must be mentally ill. He also encouraged a policy of side-lining those suspected of being disaffected or potential troublemakers by sending them into emigration. Large numbers of Soviet Jews and ethnic Germans were given visas to leave in the 1970s. And in 1974, on Andropov's orders, the outspoken writer Solzhenitsyn was arrested, stripped of his Soviet citizenship and forcibly deported abroad.

But Brezhnev and Andropov's attempt to keep the lid on alternative thinking only worked so far. For many people, Soviet achievements were still a source of pride. But Khrushchev's de-Stalinisation programme had enabled hundreds of thousands of former prisoners to return from the gulag camps, to tell their families and friends horrific stories of what they had endured. Such was the scale of the Stalin-era repressions that most people knew of someone who had been in the camps. These private testimonies directly contradicted the official version of recent Soviet history, which focused determinedly on the positive and heroic. Some returnees from the camps even sought out jobs as teachers, in order to pass their stories on to the next generation.

For the party to expect that Soviet citizens would ignore that period, and instead take at face value the relentless exhortations about fictitious grain harvest yields and unrealistic Five Year Plan targets that filled the official media, was patently absurd. The result was that, from the late 1950s onwards, true believers in the Soviet Communist dream were on the wane. A substantial number of people were paying lip service to the official Soviet doctrine, but no longer believing it to be true. They lived a twin life of outward obedience and inward dissent. Some just dismissed politics as an irrelevant joke. Others described the process as going into internal exile.

The private dissenters included some who held influential positions in the Communist Party, in government and in the academic world. These closet liberals, who had enjoyed a taste of reform during Khrushchev's thaw, now kept their heads down and bided their time until Mikhail Gorbachev came to power in the mid-1980s, when they would emerge to play important roles in helping to drive through his perestroika reforms.

Pavel Litvinov was born in 1940 in Moscow. His grandfather Maxim Litvinov served under Stalin as People's Commissar for Foreign Affairs from 1930 to 1939.

As a child, I was very impressionable and emotional and I loved Stalin. All Soviet propaganda affected me very much. I was very idealistic and romantic. I dreamed about revolution, being in an underground organisation of revolutionaries against tsarists and capitalists. At the same time, I was very upset when I saw some things in Russian life which are not good. I saw, for example, many people were very poor who went with me into high school in Moscow. I thought, 'The father of that boy was killed during the war and he lives in a communal apartment with one kitchen and one bathroom for six families.' I felt very guilty. But otherwise I thought that it's temporary and people will start living much better.

After the death of Stalin, suddenly people started to talk. I understand that things are not that simple, but in the beginning I [thought], 'Okay, maybe Stalin is not a very nice guy. He made some mistakes.' But we thought Lenin was good. The whole atmosphere in Russia made me a very, very patriotic Russian Communist. I was a member of Young Pioneers, I was a member of Komsomol [the Young Communist League]. But I was so undisciplined that I was expelled from the Young Pioneers. I was expelled later from Komsomol. Although I sincerely felt I belonged, I just couldn't keep up with the discipline and I would always tell the truth. I hated lies. And of course they had lies all the time, not only political but the whole atmosphere.

Of course, we didn't get any information [about what was] going on. But suddenly at the home of my friend we started to listen to BBC, then Voice of America and started to learn about a different life, different information. BBC and Voice of America were jammed. They had noise transmitted on the same frequencies, but we tried. And we learned how to avoid the jamming. You can take a train from Moscow for an hour outside and you can go into the woods and can listen to the transmission much better. Later on, when I was in university, we learned how to improve radio receivers, so we could hear in spite of jamming. We got a lot of information that way.

Friends of my parents came back from a labour camp and among them was a physicist, Mikhail Levin, who really influenced me. Mikhail Levin spent several years in a labour camp, including the special labour camp which Solzhenitsyn described in his book *The First Circle*, the camp for scientists who made secret weapons and secret research for the military. In the 1950s he was released and sent to exile in Siberia. Finally, he returned to Moscow in 1956, already under Khrushchev. He was rehabilitated, and he became a very good older friend for me. He told me a lot about the Soviet regime and labour camps and so on. We were all in the 1950s influenced like this.

In the 1960s, there appeared a very important phenomenon which became known as samizdat, where people typed on a typewriter or took a picture with a camera, of some book which officially was not permitted. You would make several copies of a poem or a book of poems or an article critical of the Soviet Union and give it to your friends. And because you have carbon paper you have several copies; you could give one copy to somebody else; they would repeat this procedure. So those manuscripts started to circulate and it became known, ironically, as samizdat, which means self-publishing house. Samizdat is how we read a lot of books by Solzhenitsyn; that's how we read *1984* by George Orwell, which somebody translated anonymously in Russia and it was circulated and we started to learn about the truth of what's going on.

Change was slow. The early sixties was a relatively free time. Some people were even permitted to travel abroad. That improvement was mixed with some stupid things that Khrushchev did. He didn't understand anything about art, and he was provoked by some advisers to start harassing Russian artists [...] and to yell at writers.

After Khrushchev, Brezhnev and his group decided to stop this independence and free development. During that time they started to restore the name of Stalin. Stalin was already declared to be a criminal and suddenly Brezhnev would say that Stalin was a hero of World War Two, and he was responsible for a very difficult time. They started to restore his cult, his name. And at the same time [they] started to put pressure not to publish this, not to publish that. So it was slowly changing. But my generation, we had already stopped being afraid. We already grew up in a country where we didn't expect arrest every day, and that became a foundation of the human rights movement.

Foreign radio became, in a strange way, a connection between people in Russia. For example, I could meet a foreign correspondent in Moscow, give him a copy of an article. He smuggled it out and it was transmitted back into Russia by Voice of America and suddenly people in Siberia, who didn't have any connection to Moscow, would hear it on the radio, or somewhere in Ukraine, and they would use a primitive tape recorder to record it and then with their own typewriter they'd re-type it and give it to their friends there. People were so hungry for a free press and free discussion.

There was a famous case in 1965: two writers, Sinyavsky and Daniel. Under pseudonyms, they published their books in different languages, in America and in France. They were even published in Russian and smuggled back into Russia and read by Radio Liberty in Russian or Ukrainian or other languages of the Soviet Union. When Sinyavsky and Daniel were arrested after publishing abroad, that only antagonised my generation. During that time, a friend of mine, Alexander Ginzburg, decided to collect all the info about the case of Sinyavsky and Daniel, and I helped him to do that. He made a book, the so-called

White Book of Sinyavsky and Daniel, which also started to circulate. It was smuggled abroad and Alex Ginzburg and some other people were arrested. It became like, you do something, you're arrested and some other people speak up. At that time, I was Assistant Professor of Physics and I decided that I had to do something to help my friend Alex Ginzburg. I met a lawyer who could visit Alex in prison and we got more and more information. I was one of the first who started to meet, openly, foreign correspondents. We exchanged information and it became what later became known as the dissident movement.

In the dissident movement, the first action was the campaign of people of all types of life, mostly scientists and writers, but there were workers and other people, who wrote letters [saying] that they don't [agree with] arresting people because they publish books which they believe are true – there is nothing illegal about that. We were afraid of the return of Stalinism. We were afraid that the campaign of persecution of people protesting in Russia will start spreading and we wanted to speak up. People were arrested for writing those letters, people were expelled from their work, from universities, so there started [to be] a lot of harassment. I lost my job and was under threat to be arrested. I became a 'social parasite' because I didn't work. The only job you can get is the one the Soviet government is ready to give you, because they're the only employer at this time, so it was worse than blacklisting. I was threatened with arrest for 'social parasitism'.

At the same time, I prepared two books in defence of people who wrote in protest at Sinyavsky and Daniel. I wrote a book about the demonstration in Pushkin Square by Vladimir Bukovsky, who became later a very famous dissident. And my books were smuggled from Russia and published abroad. Eventually we hoped there would be changes in Russia because there were changes in Eastern Europe, especially in Czechoslovakia with the start of the Prague Spring. We hoped that if Czechoslovakia would be allowed to slowly develop into a more democratic society that maybe Russia also will change in the same direction. We had some kind of hope that it would change and decided to speak up that it's impossible to live quietly when such violations of human rights happen. They would put people into mental hospitals like my friend, the poet Natalya Gorbanevskaya, and the mathematician Aleksandr Volpin. So, we wrote about that, we published it in samizdat and it was published everywhere.

Eventually, when the Soviet Union decided to reoccupy Czechoslovakia because they were afraid of the example that Czechoslovakia would give to everybody else, at the time I, together with a small group of friends, went to Red Square and spoke up with slogans against the Soviet invasion of Czechoslovakia. It was a place chosen called Lobnoye mesto; it's a famous execution place, where enemies of the tsars in the sixteenth century had their heads chopped off. And Red Square was almost empty – very few tourists because at that time Lenin's tomb was not open. There were eight of us, we were sitting on the steps of Lobnoye mesto and opened our [banners]. Mine was 'For Your and Our Freedom'. Konstantin Babitsky wrote 'Long Live Free and Independent Czechoslovakia' in Russian and in Czech. And we were sitting there. At first, no one understood what was happening. Then the KGB came to us and took our [banners] and started to beat us with their hands and feet. I was beaten by a woman with a heavy bag. Apparently it was full of books, but it felt like bricks. Anyway, they beat us all up, they tore our [banners] and started to yell at us pretending that they are the public who cannot stand our provocation. And during that time, because of the commotion there were 40 or 50 people surrounding us and several KGB people tried to tell them how bad we are. They looked at me and said, 'He's a drunkard, a social parasite.' They knew exactly who we were and they tried to get the crowd against us, so it was [a] pure brainwashing operation. But people were asking us questions and we were explaining. In about ten minutes the KGB brought several cars. And I told everybody, 'Don't resist, but you don't have to go.' So they had to carry us and put us in the cars. Several cars went to the local police station, station number 50 in Pushkin Street, and from there I was brought to my home and they had a very deep search for books and manuscripts, samizdat, and all that. Very late at night, they took me to Lefortovo Prison, the KGB prison in Moscow. I was in a room with another prisoner who definitely had to report about me. He was a prisoner who was involved in illegal activity reselling foreign radios on the street and, of course, they told him that if he gets me talking and reports back they will cut his term.

I was for several months out of touch with anybody but my interrogators. I refused to answer their questions, except to explain that, yes, I wanted to protest against what I saw as an illegal occupation by my country, [the] Soviet Union, of its neighbour and friend Czechoslovakia, and I wanted to use legal means to protest, that I didn't do anything illegal. Of course, they had taken from my home a lot of manuscripts and things like that. I didn't talk about those things. Eventually they tried us, a kind of semi-open trial: they didn't let the public in, although there were several hundred people outside the trial. But they permitted, eventually, my parents and my wife and several other relatives and Soviet official press, which wrote about us that we are drunkards and parasites who tried to make a commotion on a holy place, Red Square. They didn't explain anything about Czechoslovakia, just that we were hooligans.

We were all sentenced to different periods of exile, labour camp, and some people to mental hospital. Then I was transported in a special prison car, which are described very well by Solzhenitsyn, the so-called *etap*: there is a train, a regular train, with a special car where they would put prisoners. In about three weeks, they brought me to a place in eastern Siberia, a very beautiful place. It was fluoride mines; it was a mining village, not a prison. I was told that I have to live there. They gave me a room in a workers' dorm and I had to work in the mines. I started to work as an electrician in the mines. And eventually my wife joined me with my son Dima. We even bought a very primitive house, which I learned how to fix, and we lived in that house for four years. My daughter Lara was born there. It was a tough life. I got very sick and almost died from pneumonia. People visited me, my friends and relatives.

Eventually, after four and a half years, I returned to Moscow. I had trouble finding a place to live because they didn't want to give me so-called *propiska*, which means permission to live in Moscow. They started to harass me and threaten me with a new arrest because I resumed writing letters in defence of Solzhenitsyn. I became a friend of Sakharov. Eventually, I was arrested again, brought to the police station and was told either I apply for an exit visa or I will be put in a prison with much worse conditions. The KGB didn't want to put me in prison, they wanted to get rid of a troublemaker. In March 1974, we decided to go. My wife was very sick at that time and there was a hope that we'll find treatment for her. And basically I didn't want my son, who was 12 years old, to become a dissident and go to prison for many years.

Zinovy Zinik is a writer and broadcaster, born in Moscow in 1945. His early life was lived in one of the communal flats typical of the era.

The most essential aspect of my childhood was happiness, as for every child. And second, the horror of it. There were two families that lived there: my parents, my stepsister and I in a 12-square-metre room, and my cousin's family, his parents, sister, were in a 24-square-metre room. And from time to time the families would swap. Then my grandparents retired and they moved in, and we had to share this communal hell. Parents were constantly quarrelling. My life was full of sound.

When I got married, I moved into a room in the heart of Moscow, next to the Bolshoi Theatre. There were 11 families and they shared a single 12-square-metre kitchen, where about seven kitchen units were squeezed in, and one toilet and one bathroom. You can compare it with hippie dwellings or migrants settling down in a not-very-friendly country. But that was an ordinary, accepted way of life.

Either through the process of growing up or because finally I got different sources of information, I realised that I don't live in a paradise. Until then, I regarded myself as a very happy Soviet child who lives in a paradise. Of course, the outside world does exist, but it's a kind of abyss; it's all submerged in a darkness and in the poverty of the working classes, and the capitalists having a good time by humiliating their populations. It's all Soviet propaganda and I was a proper product of it and, in a way, it was bliss and happiness.

When I was 17, I met people of an older generation who became my mentors and some of them went through the penitentiary system; they were in prison, in psychiatric hospitals and in labour camps. They were not lecturing anyone, but they were exchanging stories, some of them quite horrific, some of them funny. And through them I became aware gradually of what's happening behind this red calico facade of the Soviet happiness.

It was the emergence of technology that absolutely changed the way people communicated with each other. It all started with a couple of festivals: the International Youth Festival in 1957, when Khrushchev invited delegations to send their youth to Moscow and to celebrate this peaceful coexistence of all the peoples on the planet. It was actually the first time the Soviet population met face-to-face crowds of foreigners. It was definitely like meeting Martians. So that changed the vision of the people about the West, that it's not a kind of evil darkness, that normal people do live there.

The American Exhibition [in 1959] was another great shock to the general Soviet population because, for the first time, ordinary people saw fantastic, magic machines, like washing machines and fantastic refrigerators and kitchen equipment – and American abstract expressionism and surrealism. And there was Pepsi-Cola free for distribution. I stood there about ten times in a long, long queue. And after the famous scene in front of worldwide television when Khrushchev had arguments with Nixon about who is the best, the Soviet Union or the United States, and Khrushchev swore to Nixon that we will catch up with and eventually overtake the United States in our industrial progress, and we would have colour televisions too. After that, seemingly from the sheer bragging, he decided to allow the mass production of tape recorders, as well as typewriters. So everyone had them. That was a revolutionary change on an enormous scale, because once you have a typewriter and a tape recorder you could record absolutely everything. You could create four copies of everything you wrote or you liked or were given by your friends. Then you give it to your friend who makes another copy, and eventually it grows in geometrical progression into quite a powerful underground. That created the atmosphere of a certain independence. Then with these tape recorders all kinds of unofficial balladeers emerged. They would record their self-composed songs accompanied by seven-string Russian guitars, some of them political, some of them lyrical, and they started to circulate en masse among the ordinary population.

A group of my friends decided to parody it and it was the first conscious artistic effort in which I took part, reflecting on the life of society around you, the country around you. We produced a parody of these balladeers. And people believed. I had to play, because I did know about four chords and could more or less sing in tune. So, there was a creation of little salons. In a private apartment you were invited, where people would get together. Like in New York in the 1960s. That type of alternative culture created a totally different atmosphere.

I remember Khrushchev exported the whole equipment of an American diner to certain points in Moscow, to create a kind of network of American diners. Some of them were automats, American automats. You were supposed to get a drink by dropping coins [into a machine]. I remember them distributing not tea or coffee or Coke, but beer, or fortified wine, terrible stuff. All these alcoholics would drop their coins and, getting nothing, would start hitting the chrome surface of this automat. Suddenly at one point I heard a voice behind this chrome wall: 'Wait a moment, comrade. I'll fill it in.' So it turns out that the automats had stopped working and there were real people pouring this wine behind the wall. But still, they made an effort to create the illusion that the Soviet Union lives in a progressive, Western-type of society.

One of the geniuses of the [dissident] movement, the poet and great mathematician Aleksandr Volpin, created the so-called Reminder for the Arrested – how to behave yourself when you confront the KGB officer during your interrogation. A wonderful bunch of people started to publish an unofficial 'Chronicle of Current Events'. It just listed, with a brief description, what happened, where there were food riots or somebody was arrested for what. And that was dangerous. People's apartments were searched, people were arrested, dismissed from their jobs, because that was very useful bits of political information.

The official culture was regarded as a dead shell, like a kind of crust that framed the country and framed the life of the country. At a certain point, especially after the mid-sixties, with the fall of Khrushchev in 1964, it was an absolutely dead verbal culture – still administratively functioning, still very much politically powerful with distribution of goods throughout the whole country and the right to publish, to print everything they like. But at the same time, everyone knew that it was totally dead, so people paid lip service. If you fell out, you could end up badly, without a job, or if you were active politically, you are going to be arrested, beaten and imprisoned. If you are not politically active, you could have a decent life, on the verge of impoverishment, but still left alone by the authorities.

Otherwise, you could boil in that soup of alternative culture, which was quite rich and quite varied in its different manifestations, for you to feel some kind of fulfilment, artistically, creatively and emotionally. It was a prison, but the most entertaining prison in the world. And it was a prison because you knew that you could never leave the country unless you become an asset for the Soviet government, a famous musician or famous author like Yevtushenko. But for that you have to be affiliated with the Party propaganda one way or another.

There was a certain type of literature that would expose the horrors of labour camps and the Stalinist penitentiary system. These memoirs were part of the governmental effort to finish off the most horrific, monstrous aspect of the Soviet system under Stalin, which was regarded as a distortion of the norms of Leninism. That literature, brilliant as it is from a literary point of view, was part of the government's effort to get rid of this absolutely unacceptable system that had been developed under Stalin. At that time, indeed, there were quite a few honourable masterpieces of Russian literature published. There was the first publication of the suppressed novel by Bulgakov [*The Master and Margarita*, which] appeared in the magazine *Moskva*, a highbrow literary magazine. It was censored a bit, but still, it was quite an event, absolutely amazing.

There was an upsurge of unofficial, alternative culture. It reached such a level that people became daring and cheeky. And it ended with a wonderful writer, novelist and critic Andrei Sinyavsky. Together with his mate Yuli Daniel, [they] started publishing their prose – which was an outrageous satire on the obsolete Soviet way of life – abroad. It was very daring still. You could give it to a foreigner, who could smuggle it abroad and publish it. And Andrei Sinyavsky was doing it under a pseudonym, Abram Tertz, but finally they were caught and sentenced. That whole trial was a sudden repetition of a Stalinist show trial, with liars, with false evidence, with horrible Stalinist language about 'the enemy of the people', 'traitors', 'slanderers of our beautiful way of life'. That sent shockwaves around Moscow. It was a kind of depression. It created a sense of a kind of comeback of the worst proto-Stalinist tendencies in Brezhnev.

Especially in Brezhnev's time, the language, the ideology, the official way of communication, the mannerisms – mausoleum, platforms, parades, etc. – they all remained intact. There still was this shell within which people could live with more or less security. It gave a kind of stability. There was no future, but at the same time there were no violent changes, there were no crises. The crisis would be if the price of vodka was suddenly raised. But they would drop it immediately because that was the only mechanism to keep the population satisfied – the price of vodka and the price of bread.

Then there were waves of reminders that we still live in the Soviet Union. At every prominent visit of a foreign official, or celebratory days, all dangerous elements were removed from Moscow and put into psychiatric hospitals or temporarily imprisoned, and then released. Moscow was cleaned of all unwanted elements in society. These reminders started to occur more and more frequently in the late 1960s, from the show trial of Sinyavsky and Daniel [in 1965] onwards.

The invasion of Czechoslovakia was a real comeback to something that reminded us about Stalinism. There was a rather daring demonstration in Red Square of a few people, among them the poet Natalya Gorbanevskaya. They unfolded a poster: 'For Your and Our Freedom'. And they were immediately arrested, beaten up and punished severely. So, that was basically the end of Khrushchev's thaw. The total end.

But Soviet power itself was the KGB apparatus. What Brezhnev was emblematic of – the Soviet power on the administrative and propaganda level – was a total joke. Nobody believed in these slogans and in the founding principles or whatever. It was total cynicism. Even on the part of the Politburo, I presume.

I signed a letter of protest because my friend was dismissed. And then I was dismissed. It was a joke of a job. It was a scientific institution, preparing the texts for them. It was doing nothing because it was a state institution, the majority of which were totally fictitious. There was the Institute of Sociology, for example. What kind of real sociology could have been conducted in those years in the Soviet Union? It was all fiction, and theories. It was basically verbal exercises. So it was one of those fictitious institutions that I was sacked from. The KGB visited the place I lived, a communal flat, asking who was visiting me, etc. But I don't believe I would have been arrested or harassed really. Everyone could somehow have got involved with the authorities, negatively on a political level. But you also could have avoided it. But the sense of complicity was there, especially after the Czechoslovakia invasion. This sense of complicity never left me as a Soviet person.

'They could accuse you of anything'

The Outbreak of the Chinese Cultural Revolution (1966–7)

The Sino-Soviet split in the 1960s was one of the key shifts in the Cold War and a turning point in the history of Communism. It turned what had been a binary battle between East and West into a triangular contest. There were no longer two but three global giants – the United States, the Soviet Union and China – all now jockeying for power and influence – and ideological purity.

China's growing disenchantment with its Soviet ally went back to 1956 and Nikita Khrushchev's Secret Speech denouncing the legacy of his predecessor, Joseph Stalin. Mao Zedong had been a dedicated disciple of Stalin's and saw the new criticism of him as a betrayal, a divergence from the true path of Marxist–Leninist orthodoxy. He was also concerned by the uprisings the new policy appeared to have provoked in Poland and Hungary in 1956, and viewed the efforts to deliver prosperity and consumer goods to Soviet society as un-revolutionary.

And he thought Khrushchev's attempts to ease tensions with the United States through visits and summits was misguided.

In contrast to Khrushchev's 'thaw', Mao took a sharp turn to the left and in 1958 announced the Great Leap Forward – a mass mobilisation of China's workers and peasants, herded into huge 'people's communes', with the goal of ramping up heavy industry and agriculture to reach giddy new heights of grain and steel production. It was a monumental disaster, causing chaotic upheaval and a largely man-made famine, which led to tens of millions of deaths.

By the early 1960s, China was rowing back from this ruinous experiment, but Mao's censure of Khrushchev's reforms continued. Before long, the world's two biggest Communist parties were indulging in open polemics, with China castigating Soviet 'revisionism' and 'counter-revolutionary trends'. In 1964, the breach was formalised when the two Communist parties, Chinese and Soviet, broke off relations.

Moscow, meanwhile, had backtracked on a pledge to help China develop nuclear weapons technology. But China went ahead and tested its first atomic bomb anyway on 16 October 1964. It came just two days after the dramatic ousting in Moscow of Khrushchev by his Kremlin colleagues. Even once Khrushchev had gone, the relationship did not improve. Mao dismissed the new Soviet leadership under Leonid Brezhnev and Alexei Kosygin as 'Khrushchev-ism without Khrushchev'.

From the United States' point of view, the Sino-Soviet split was welcome because it divided the Communist world. Washington could sit back and watch from the side-lines as the two Communist giants bickered and undermined each other. But it was also worrying because the various possibilities of flare-ups between any two of the three big Cold War powers had just multiplied and China, now armed with nuclear weapons, was newly dangerous. Mao even made clear that China's population was so big, the country could probably weather the casualties caused by a nuclear war.

The moment had the eerie feel of life imitating science fiction. With the two Communist big powers now at loggerheads, it was suddenly as though the world had edged closer to the tripartite division imagined in George Orwell's dystopian novel of 1949, *Nineteen Eighty-Four*, where the three world powers of Oceania (American dominance), Eurasia (Soviet dominance) and Eastasia (a separate Asian power) all existed in a perpetual state of shifting allegiances and hostility.

There was good reason for Washington to fret about the added hazards that the Sino-Soviet rift might create. In the mid-1960s, tensions were already building up along the Soviet Union's 4,000-kilometre border with China. By 1969, this would lead to clashes between Soviet and Chinese forces and a hint from Moscow that it might consider deploying its nuclear arsenal, raising fears of a full-scale war between the two Communist global giants. In the end, tensions subsided and, a couple of years later in 1972, President Nixon used the fact that Mao could ill afford to stay on bad terms with both Moscow and Washington to 'play his China card'. The fact that Nixon, a conservative Republican, should be the American President who made that first trip to Beijing to mend fences with Communist China was unexpected, and the irony was even more pointed, given that during the McCarthyite Red Scare against suspected Communists in the 1950s, Richard Nixon had been on the side of those on the American right who had vengefully harangued those supposedly responsible for the US 'losing' China to Communism.

But before all that, Mao's new hostility to the Soviet Union was also a factor in his next alarming policy shift – the Cultural Revolution. Introduced in 1966, its stated goal was to purge any remnants of capitalist and traditionalist elements from Chinese society, and reconfirm the country's path towards Communism through 'continuous revolution' and 'violent class struggle'.

In part, Mao hoped to show that, unlike the Soviet Union, China had lost none of its revolutionary purity, and in contrast to those complacent revisionist backsliders in the Kremlin, Mao could claim he was the true keeper of the flame, the guardian of Marxist–Leninist orthodoxy. One Chinese poster from the early days of the Cultural Revolution declared 'Topple the Soviet revisionists. Smash the dog heads Brezhnev and Kosygin.'

In part, this was also Mao's political comeback. The calamitous failures of the Great Leap Forward had damaged his authority. This was a bid to restore his leadership within the party and across the country – helped by a cult of personality that reached near religious proportions – and eliminate or side-line through a mass purge those critics in the party hierarchy whom he saw as dangerous rivals.

The idea of the Cultural Revolution was to involve all strata of Chinese society – workers, peasants, soldiers and officials – to overturn and reshape society and root out 'enemies' from top to bottom. It was spearheaded by a new force in Chinese politics, a youth movement called the Red Guards, made up first and foremost of children and students. These young people responded to Mao's appeal to turn their backs on the norms of school and university and organise themselves into quasi-military units. They proved their revolutionary credentials by attacking anyone they suspected of harbouring bourgeois values or concealing a 'bad' class background, such as a former landlord, rich farmer or capitalist, or indeed anyone, such as a teacher, who had held a position of authority. Their victims were not just those suspected of bourgeois tendencies. Mao's new child army was also, unusually, a tool to take on the Communist Party itself. These fresh-faced vigilantes vented their fury on old party members whom Mao wanted purged from the ranks, making the Cultural Revolution a disruptive political campaign like none that had come before. Armed with the 'Little Red Book' of quotations from Mao's writings as their guide, they marched out across the country to galvanise the masses and lead the revolution 'to make China red, inside and out', as one Red Guard leader put it.

Underpinning the campaign was a mission to wipe out the 'Four Olds': old customs, old cultures, old habits and old ideas. This entailed a wholesale destruction of anything associated with the past, all in the name of the revolution. So, numerous religious and historical sites were ransacked and pulled apart, books and ancient manuscripts were burned, and countless cultural treasures were destroyed.

The revolutionary zeal went to extreme lengths. One proposal from the Red Guards was that red traffic lights should henceforth signify 'go' rather than 'stop'. But infinitely worse than this absurdity was the suffering caused to people.

The fanaticism of the revolutionary zealots was terrifying. Their campaigns involved not just rhetorical denunciations, but physical violence on a shocking scale. In the search for counter-revolutionaries, frenzied crusades rooted out imaginary traitors who were paraded, flogged and spat on, often in front of crowds at mass meetings.

A campaign against a suspect would often begin with them being publicly denounced in a 'big-character poster', handwritten in large Chinese characters and pasted on walls or reproduced in a newspaper for all to see. Then the victim would be hunted down and subjected to bouts of torture, or humiliated and abused in other ways, such as being made to bend forwards while their outstretched arms were forcibly raised behind them in the degrading and excruciating 'jet-plane' position, or having their heads shaved, or being maimed or sexually assaulted, or beaten so hard that they died from their injuries. Those who 'confessed' to their crimes would be taken away, possibly executed, or else despatched to hard labour camps to be 're-educated'.

The campaign atomised society. Children turned on their parents, students turned on their teachers, denounced regardless of guilt or innocence. Some, unable to stand what was happening or in a bid to escape their tormentors, committed suicide.

Foreigners were not immune. Western embassies were attacked. Mao had not only severed links with the Soviet Union. Immersed in its own revolutionary drama, China also cut off contact with much of the rest of the world.

Before long, the campaign spun out of control. There was widespread factional fighting as opposing groups fell out with each other. Some more radical Red Guard units were suppressed by the People's Liberation Army and themselves accused of 'counter-revolutionary' tendencies. Parts of the country were engulfed in what amounted to civil war.

The Cultural Revolution was above all an urban phenomenon, a purge targeting intellectuals, teachers and party officials. The death toll was nothing like the scale of the Great Leap Forward, but it had a devastating effect on the entire country, as economic activity ground to a halt in favour of revolutionary fervour.

In the countryside, primary education for the rural poor expanded, but in towns and cities, schools and universities remained closed for years, not only because students left but also because so many academics and teachers were persecuted and sent to an early death in rural labour camps.

After the initial two-year spasm, in 1968 a policy was introduced that somewhat calmed down the revolutionary turmoil, though in this second phase there were more victims. It required millions of Red Guards, educated urban young people, to go out into the countryside to live and work alongside the rural poor. It meant that an entire generation of Chinese youth never completed their studies.

Mao declared the Cultural Revolution at an end in 1969. But it was not finally laid to rest until after his death in 1976 when the next Chinese leader, Deng Xiaoping, began to dismantle Maoist polices and reverse the damage by introducing a programme of economic modernisation and by opening up contacts with the West.

For some people in China, the era of the Cultural Revolution is still remembered with some nostalgia, as a time of inspiring revolutionary fervour, of pure ideals and a moment when politics really seemed to matter. But for those who remember what their parents, teachers and friends were subjected to during the height of the Cultural Revolution, the memory is of manic madness and the pain is still very much alive.

In August 1966, 19-year-old **Cheng Zhang Gong** *had completed senior high school at Luhe Senior High School in Beijing,* *and his 16-year-old brother,* **Cheng Zhang Rang**, *had completed junior high school. Their father, Cheng Min, 54, was the deputy headmaster of the Luhe Middle School, then called No. 1 Middle School, of Tongxian County. The Cultural Revolution started before the last semester ended, so they didn't have their final examinations.*

Cheng Zhang Rang

My father treated his students as his own children. He was really like a father to them. He really cared for the students and looked after them. I remember once our school had a meeting. My father was giving a speech. He told the students that they should study hard, and every one of them should obtain at least one skill. He meant that people should be able to contribute to the society and they should at least have one skill. You don't need to be developed all around. But you should be able to make contribution to the society.

The policy at that time was that workers and farmers work together. So he took the students to the countryside to do work. My father would go pick up cotton and do farming work in the field. He had a really good relationship with the students.

Cheng Zhang Gong

Before the Cultural Revolution, according to the lines and principles issued by the party, the school had been teaching students about class struggle, enmity between different classes, and hatred between different nations. All schools had to teach that. At politics class or other classes, teachers had been teaching about class struggle. A large percentage of people accepted these teachings. Even I believed them deeply. We truly believed that before the 1949 Liberation everything was bad. The propaganda then

311

told us that all the landlords, rich farmers and capitalists are all bad, even their children. Then, when the Cultural Revolution started, these teachings were deeply rooted in people. The idea that all the exploiting class is reactionary and needed to be overthrown was repeated over and over again. All young people knew was class struggle. We were told stories – how bad the landlords were. We had meetings to recall the sorrows of the past and savour the joy of the present. We had lots of such meetings. People came to the meeting to tell their stories in tears. But all were lies. But we were young. We weren't experienced. We believed in them. In these ways, young people were poisoned by these lies.

A few politics teachers took out the personal records of every other teacher and told students what their family background and misdeeds were. They made up lots of it and posted 'big-character posters' about the teachers everywhere. They were all lies. For example, my father had six siblings. Altogether they owned about a dozen acres of land. But in the poster, they said our family was the biggest landlord of our village. It's all nonsense. Then the persecution against our family started. [They] wrote more than 200 big-character posters. A number of them mentioned my father. I remember it clearly. [It] said that our family owned more than 500 acres of land. That is not possible. The whole village only owned 500 acres of land. Many families shared them.

Cheng Zhang Rang

The posters were full of lies and rumours. They denounced people for different things based on nothing. They criticised people out of nothing. I remember my father once told me this movement seemed different from before. It's really different. Before, after every movement, there would come a correction process. If anyone was wrongly criticised or denounced, that would be corrected. There were lots of movements like Three-Antis and Five-Antis, or Four Clean-ups Movement, or the Anti-Rightists in 1957. After all these movements, there was a process to examine if you are what you are accused of.

[The Cultural Revolution] turned out to be really different. They could accuse you of anything. You can have doubts on anything. Yes, you can doubt anything, but you can't accuse people of things out of nothing, without any basis. My father graduated from Tsinghua University. He always talked about facts. Since we were kids, he told us to speak on the basis of facts.

Students at the No. 1 Middle School of Tongxian County saw Beijing had founded the Red Guards, and said we should follow suit and found a Red Guard group too, because it was backed up by the supreme leader of the country. Then they just messed around and made trouble. They didn't know what is right and what is wrong. As soon as they denounced you as a class enemy, landlord, capitalist, capitalist roader or cow demon and snake spirit, they could arrest you, criticise you and persecute you. They hit you, cursed you, put you into a labour camp. They even set up a labour camp unit in the school. A school was turned into a labour camp.

Cheng Zhang Gong

There were very few Red Guards at the very beginning. There were only two at my class who were qualified to be Red Guards. Later on, there were more and more. They listened to a temporary Revolutionary Committee. They were the people who controlled all activities at the school. By the end of July, they had put many teachers into confinement. They denounced those teachers as crime-gang members.

Anyway, all these 50-odd teachers were denounced as criminal gang members by them. They forced them to do physical labour. Starting from the end of July, they asked all those teachers and school directors to do physical labour. By early August, it was getting worse and worse.

[On 6 August 1966] at 3 or 4am, they woke them up and physically pushed them to the school. Each of them held a stick. They were forced to do pipe ramming under the hot sun. Everyone knows early August are the hottest days in Beijing. They made them work. It was quite cruel. They were not allowed to drink water. They were not allowed to rest. They tortured them. If you refused to work, they would use a stick to hit you, to poke you. It was quite cruel. I started to feel nervous. But I didn't think it was really a big deal. I felt it was a mass movement. My father said that too. It was a mass movement.

Around noon, my father didn't feel well. A friend of his told me that my father fell to the ground and I should go and find him. I rushed out to look for my father at the school. I was told he was by the swimming pool, doing some repair work. I went there and saw my father was sitting on the ground under the hot sun. A member of the Revolutionary Committee was with my father. My father told him, 'You were wrong to do this. You shouldn't just hit people and curse people. You shouldn't do that.' The member of the Revolutionary Committee said to my father, 'Stop talking like this. You are talking poisonous nonsense.' He cursed a lot. I was standing at a distance from them, so I didn't hear every word they said.

At that moment, I desperately wanted to get my father back home. But I didn't dare to get close. Because there were a few Red Guards and the member of the Revolutionary Committee and they were cursing my father the whole time. Then I followed my father to walk home. Halfway there, we saw my younger brother, and we both followed my father home. He was already in a very bad and weak condition. He couldn't stand straight when he walked. If we walked past a tree, he would lean on the tree to rest a bit. Slowly, we walked to the gate of the school. Only at that time, I dared to get close to him and held his arms.

We took him home. I was saying that we should take him to hospital to have a check. I went to somewhere near Luhe Hospital and rented a tricycle to take him. At the hospital, a doctor said that he didn't have any big problem – he was just dehydrated and had sunstroke. The doctor suggested my father have a glucose drip. So I paid the fee, got the medicine and he had a drip. Then my father felt better. The doctor said that you can't stay here, you can just go home. We felt it was not a big problem. So I asked the doctor to write my father a sick-leave permit.

When I was near home, I saw a big crowd outside our house, and inside. They were threatening my father, saying he had to go back to work. They said, 'You can't pretend to be sick to avoid work.' I told them that the hospital just gave my father a sick-leave permit, and gave it to them, but still they insisted my father go back to work. A few of my classmates were there ... Because they were my classmates, they acted more proactively. They forcefully took my father back to school. [One of them] was shouting at my father, 'Will you go with us? If you don't go, we will hit you.' He used his stick to hit the floor, to threaten to hit us. My father looked at them and knew we couldn't do anything. I couldn't have any influence. There were so many of them.

So I saw my father leave with them. I had no choice. I was extremely worried. We were so worried at home, every second seemed really long. In the afternoon, I went into the school. My classmate […] saw me and said to me, 'Look, your father was sweeping the floor. You said he couldn't work.' I said to him, 'He is sick.' I said we have a sick-leave permit. 'He is pretending to be sick,' he said.

I didn't dare to argue with him and went to sit in my classroom. After sitting there anxiously for a while, I went back home, but didn't see my father. I was thinking about what was going on, why they still don't let him come home. To be honest, I was worried, but I didn't know what to do. So I waited. I waited till around 10pm, nearly 11pm, when I heard something from the gate of the school entrance. We lived very close to the school, about 200 metres away. I heard some noise. And then I heard people shouting: 'You are pretending to be sick!'

We were really nervous and looked out – we couldn't see anything. After a little while, my father came home with dirt all over his head and body. He actually fell into a coma. He said to us, 'How can I have been sleeping till now?' Even at this situation, we tried to not worry. My elder sister said to my father that this is just a mass movement, don't be too nervous. Then my mother said to let my father rest: 'Don't talk any more.' So my father washed his feet and went to bed with clothes on. That night, my mother said that there was blood in my father's urine.

They came to my home again next morning at 4am with sticks and forced my father to go back to do physical work. They said he had to go. I asked him not go to. But those people forced him to go. My father didn't have a choice and went with them. He never came back again.

At around eight, I felt really worried and really anxious. So I went to the school. There was a sandpit outside my classroom, and my father was lying between the sandpit and the building, breathing heavily. I tried to hold him up and asked him what was wrong. My father didn't respond.

He was actually in a coma. I wanted to help him stand up, but my classmates all came to me and pushed me and hit me. They didn't allow me to save him. I said to them that I wanted to take him home. But they didn't allow it. They kicked me. They asked me what political stance I was taking.

I didn't have a choice, so I went home. I saw my mother, and told her that my father was lying on the ground. He couldn't move. They didn't allow me to get close to him. My mother was worried and went to the school with me. But there was nothing we could do. My classmates surrounded me, pushed me and kicked me.

I tried hard to get close to my father; I couldn't. My mother wanted to get close to him; she couldn't. They asked us, 'Who do you think this person is?' They said he is pretending to be dead. They didn't allow my mother to hold my father's arms. After a while, my mother still couldn't even get close to my father, so she said, 'Do what you want to.' She left for home. I was pushed and kicked and couldn't get close. So, I went home as well.

I told my sister they hadn't let me take my father. Then we remembered that Beijing had just formed a new Party Committee. We were thinking maybe we should complain to the new committee to see if they could save him. So my sister and I took bus to the committee. An official [...] said he would phone the school for us to find out about what was going on. We felt hopeful again, so we went home. When we were near home, we heard that everyone was crying. My father was dead. That's how my father was tortured to death by them. Later, when we had an autopsy, he had bruises and scars all over his body. They didn't even let us save him. He could have been saved when I went there, if they allowed me to take him to hospital. But they didn't. That's how they killed my father. After that, they wrote a note on my father's body: 'Landlord and capitalist, class dissident'. Those people didn't have a heart. They were so cruel to us.

Cheng Zhang Rang

People were not allowed to speak. They denounced you for a crime and they persecuted you. They even killed you. At that time, there was no law. They denounced my father for various crimes. I had nowhere to go to appeal. If there had been a procedure, I would have had a chance to defend my father. Then he wouldn't have been attacked by the students. The students didn't know anything. They strongly believed my father was a class enemy, was a bad person. But he wasn't a bad person. He was a very good man. So the root of the disastrous Cultural Revolution was that it was lawless.

Cheng Zhang Gong

We lost the family income – my family had mostly relied on my father. My elder sister was a primary-school teacher. We felt that we don't know how to live our life any more. We didn't know what could happen. We were always worried and scared. We didn't know when somebody would come in and do something to us. Then they ransacked my house and partly shaved my mother's head. It was a sign of being a 'class enemy'. They also shaved one of my elder sisters, who was disabled. They poured ink all over their bodies. They made them stand there and punished them. They ransacked the house and took away anything they wanted. My mother slowly shipped all our stuff to the school under their force. They used sticks to threaten her. Among them, there were Zhang Rang's classmates, my classmates and classmates of our youngest brother. They were the main people that persecuted my family. They ransacked everything and threw the stuff they didn't need everywhere. They didn't leave us any rice or food. So we couldn't live there any more. They also had big-character posters everywhere and asked us to go back to our hometown. They said that we had to leave before a certain time. So we were kicked out and went back to hometown in Shanxi, where we had relatives who could help us. When we left, we had nothing but the summer clothes we were wearing.

Meanwhile, **John Weston** *was a young British diplomat living with a Chinese family in Hong Kong and studying Chinese at Hong Kong University, in preparation for taking up his post as a Second Secretary at the British Mission in China. In January 1967 he and his wife landed in Peking. He was 26.*

Mao had been going through a difficult few years as a result of the Great Leap Forward, so-called – there had been mass famine throughout the country imposing very, very heavy losses and suffering on Chinese people as a whole. That had got out of hand. Liu Shaoqi, the President, had begun to realise what a gigantic mistake it had been. Therefore Mao took against him and effectively realised also that in Russia after Stalin, a phenomenon was taking place that he was frightened about – namely that Soviet Communism was becoming more reasonable. He was afraid that that was going to happen in China – so a short way through to doing something about that was to launch the Cultural Revolution, which was a gigantic purge, but in this case largely a purge of the official classes. So, at the point when we arrived in Peking [now Beijing], this was in train and getting worse.

We knew that the whole underlying strategy of what Mao was doing was to set young people against their parents' generation and the whole of the official class in

Communist China. The whole appeal of that was that the young people should get up and exercise their energies in destroying what was portrayed as being the initiation of a bourgeois replacement for true Communism. So, it followed from that that one was seeing all the time large numbers of boys and girls being grouped together and following along a road with red flags flying, shouting out stuff at the top of their voices. [They were] being encouraged by the placement on every street corner of loudspeakers – there was an absolutely constant torrent of stuff coming out of that. So the whole atmosphere daily and much of the night was being whipped up into a frenzy, and very often the expressions of violence directed by one Chinese person against another, and particularly against older people, [were] of course the natural consequence of that.

Our job was to go out into the streets, to comb the streets for Red Guard newspapers, to read the big-character posters on walls all over the place for the latest news about what was going on. We were trying as hard as we could to find out and report accurately to London the inner stories about the rivalries that were going on at the top. And indeed, in so doing, we were seeing in real life a lot of the troubles going on. There was an influx of young men and women from schools and universities from other parts of China. Often their battles between themselves were carried out on the streets of Peking and it was not altogether unusual to see dead bodies.

As it got worse, there were mass demonstrations – very noisy young people. Then sometimes you'd see a lorry come down the road with some unfortunate middle-aged man or woman on top of it, held in the so-called jet-plane position, while he or she was carried off to whatever their fate was to be. On more than one occasion, we had to take care of ourselves and plead diplomatic immunity, or get on a bicycle and ride away very fast. It was a very heated – overheated – atmosphere.

Among the other diplomatic missions there who we relied on and exchanged information with – the Russians were certainly one of those. They were on the receiving end of some Red Guard attention; as I recall, some kind of minor siege was laid to the Soviet Embassy. We had a couple of good contacts there. I used to see them every week: we'd exchange materials with them. We all felt – the Russians, the other East Europeans, the Czechs, the Poles, the Hungarians, even the Mongolians, the Indians, the French – those were all foreign diplomatic missions in Peking with whom we had regular contact, and with whom we exchanged information the whole time – we were all in the same game. What was going on in this country? Where is it leading and what does it point to at the top?

By 22 August, after the Indonesian Embassy had been burned down and tensions had risen over Hong Kong, the British Mission was becoming a target.

John Weston

It began like any other day. There were a number of the wives with us, who would come and go in the normal scheme of things. Around the middle of the day, we saw that the Public Security Bureau guards on the gate of our mission, who were there ostensibly for our protection, were becoming quite nervous and when we tried to go out, to walk along to where the diplomatic flats were or whatever, they said, 'No, no, you can't come out.' We said, 'Why not?' They said, 'Look, look, it's for your own safety, you can't come out.' By this time there were smallish numbers of Red Guard crowds who were coming – which wasn't that unusual, we had all this in June at the time of the Six-Day War, we knew big demonstrations outside the British Embassy happened all the time. However, in this case it was unusual to be told by the Public Security Bureau guards that we couldn't leave, so we thought maybe this is the kind of siege stuff like the Russians had. So we settled down. We had plenty of food in the office building. Those like my wife who were there and couldn't get out made themselves useful in the library or whatever. As the day went on, the crowds got bigger. They got bigger and bigger and bigger. Moreover, when we phoned out, we found out the telephone line had been cut. That seemed to be a little bit … there's something special was going on here. We just sat it out; we thought if we have to sleep in all night, it's not the end of the world. Donald Hopson, the head of our mission, who was a very phlegmatic ex-military man, with a Military Cross to his name, was playing some bridge upstairs with one or two colleagues. The rest of us were getting on with life, preparing an evening meal, and making sure we had covered all the angles if this got nasty. But we didn't really expect it to.

Darkness began to fall. I remember going out after dark just to take a peep. The building was surrounded by a wall – I remember going out under the cover of darkness and just taking a good look at what was happening outside. It was very unusual. A huge crowd, all very quiet – not shouting at us, all sitting quietly, occasionally being lectured by whoever the major domo was out there. Nothing else. So, I came back in and reported that.

Nothing changed until the absolute minute of 10pm, at which point, as we subsequently learned from some colleagues in the Polish Embassy, a Very light was fired into the sky and that turned out to be the signal. At that point, the entire crowd outside – who the New China News Agency told us later had been at least 10,000 – got to their feet, swarmed over the walls of the embassy's premises and came at the building. At that moment, Donald Hopson's voice could be heard throughout the mission from upstairs at his bridge table, shouting, 'They're coming in!' and we realised we had to do something quick. We quickly barricaded or locked all the outside doors and went to the part of the mission which had iron bars protecting it, where the Registry was and [the] Communication Centre. Getting all the lights out, hunkering down quietly, as we hoped, until it was over.

It wasn't over: we realised very quickly they were setting fire to the building. They came armed with lots of stuff, including cans full of petrol, which had been spotted by our friends down the road at the Polish and the Czech embassies – but they couldn't reach us because, of course, the phones had been cut – and the building in no time was on fire. We just kept quiet, we didn't want to attract too much attention to where exactly we were inside the building. We had to do some fast thinking. Windows were broken; stuff was brought up.

The building was getting hot and smoky inside. It's not fun being inside a burning building. After about 30 or 40 minutes hoping this would all somehow blow over, we realised it wouldn't. At this point, some of the groups outside were actually demolishing the brickwork of the building in order to force their way in – it turned out they had battering rams. We had an escape door at the ground level, which wasn't entirely visible from the outside and was never used, but it was reinforced inside and it was the escape if we were ever caught in a situation like this. The order was given to get that door open from the inside and, on the word from Donald Hopson, we all went out into the forecourt of the mission, into the hands of a very, very angry mob. That was the most difficult part of it all, because the gap between exiting the emergency door and reaching the outside of the circumference wall seemed like an eternity, and the whole of that space was filled by these enraged young men and women who were out to do us – and they did do us. It was very unpleasant being beaten up in that way.

We were carried on the flow of those people. I was holding on to my wife with one hand and another female, a secretary, with the other, and it became very nasty. All one's primal instincts come to the fore at that point. My wife had her long hair pulled back by one of these people; someone else put their hand under her skirt. I remember thinking, 'The only way I'm going to get this guy to let go of my wife is to physically bite him', and I was just going down on to his arm with my teeth – and we gradually, gradually, forced our way through this mob, raining blows on us, to the point where I suddenly saw a member of the People's Liberation Army and grabbed him and said in Chinese, 'Do something, you're a soldier, you're supposed to protect us!'

They were there to do that, but they were told they couldn't go into the compound because that's diplomatic immunity – never mind the fact the Red Guards were all there. But once we got out of the wall, then they could go through the motions of attempting to protect us. Gradually, it all simmered down. We were eventually evacuated in a large lorry where all the soldiers stood up round the outside of the lorry, so it looked as if it was full of soldiers. We were told to lie down so we were not visible and we were evacuated. By this point, the building was a seething mass of flame. The British Mission building was completely burnt out. Donald Hopson's residence, which was 20 yards down the road, the next building, had also been sacked, but not burned. We went away to lick our wounds.

The physical impact primarily, which we all shared, was intense shock. We all had superficial wounds of one sort or another. Our head guard, who was a man near retirement age, died within a year of this, and he was laid out for quite some time after the event. Another member of our staff had severe concussion from blows around the head. He was looked after by a doctor in the Czechoslovak Embassy as I recall, and he couldn't move. He was absolutely supine in his bed for a couple of weeks. Someone else was badly mentally affected and had a serious breakdown. We were in a position where we couldn't get out at will because, at this time, even British diplomats were not allowed to leave the country – we were basically hostages. All that took some time to weather the storm, but we collected ourselves and 'made do and mended' as much as one could, and reported it all to London.

'They didn't want to live in the dark any more'

The Prague Spring (1968)

The Prague Spring was a brief burst of reform in Czechoslovakia, which reached its peak during the government of Alexander Dubček in 1968. It was brought to an abrupt end in August of that year, when a Kremlin-led invasion of tanks and troops moved in to crush it.

The de-Stalinisation process begun by the Soviet leader Nikita Khrushchev in the mid-1950s had raised hopes that the Kremlin would also allow political reform in its satellite states in Eastern Europe. While Khrushchev's 'thaw' had ended with his ousting by conservatives in 1964, however, the reform process in Czechoslovakia had a different trajectory. The course of liberalisation began more slowly, continued for longer and intended to go further, to build on the democratic traditions the country had enjoyed before Klement Gottwald and other Communists seized power in 1948.

For some, an early hint of a new easing of controls came in May 1963, when the Czechoslovak Communist Party reluctantly sanctioned a writers' conference devoted to the prominent Prague writer Franz Kafka, a figure who until then had been shunned as too 'bourgeois'. Another impetus came in the mid-1960s, when the failing economy forced the government into reforms that empowered local managers and gave greater priority to goods wanted by consumers. In June 1967 the political waters were tested again when members of the Union of Czechoslovak Writers suggested that literature should be independent of party doctrine and argued the case for democratic government.

By the end of 1967, Czechoslovakia's hard-line Communist leader, President Antonín Novotný, was in trouble. He was being blamed for half-hearted reforms that had failed to stem economic decline, and he was facing a possible mutiny from reformers within his own party. Hoping to bolster his position, he invited the Soviet leader, Leonid Brezhnev, to visit Prague. But when Brezhnev saw the extent of dissatisfaction among the top echelons of the party, he refrained from endorsing the Czech President, paving the way for Novotný's removal in January 1968. He was replaced as head of the Czechoslovak Communist Party by a bold reformer from Slovakia called Alexander Dubček.

With Dubček at the helm, the 'Prague Spring' began in earnest. Unlike Hungary in 1956, it was not intended to be a rebellion against Soviet rule. The push for reform came not from anti-Communists but from leading intellectuals inside the Communist Party apparatus. Their vision was to replace the repressive Stalinist model with a more moderate version of a socialist state, still under Communist Party oversight, but with more political diversity and freedom of expression. It became known as 'socialism with a human face'.

In April 1968, Dubček and his reformist colleagues launched an Action Programme, which called for the easing of censorship, a curb on the powers of the secret police, a ten-year transition to democratic elections, and for Czechoslovakia to be turned into a federation of two equal Czech and Slovak nations. It also proposed that close ties to the Soviet Union and other Eastern Bloc countries should be balanced by better relations with Western countries.

Between April and August, the appetite for change gathered momentum. The abolition of censorship opened the door to a more critical look at how Communists had ruled Czechoslovakia since the war. A commission began to investigate those who had been purged, imprisoned and executed, including a re-examination of the infamous show trials of Rudolf Slánský and 13 other leading Communists in 1952, most of whom were forced to confess imaginary crimes and then hanged as traitors. The playwright Václav Havel (later a prominent dissident and the first post-Communist Czech President) became spokesman for a group of non-Communist writers clamouring for human rights redresses. Anti-Soviet voices became louder, and some activists began to organise themselves into alternative political clubs and parties.

In June, writers and scholars endorsed a manifesto known as 'The Two Thousand Words', or, to give it its full title, 'The Two Thousand Words that Belong to Workers, Farmers, Officials, Scientists, Artists and Everybody'. This called for citizens to take action to hold to account those Communists promising change. The snowballing pace of the debate alarmed hard-liners in the country's Communist Party. But though they urged Dubček to rein in the radicals, he refused to resort to repressive measures.

Dubček was also coming under increasing pressure from other Eastern Bloc Communist leaders, including Władysław Gomułka in Poland and Walter Ulbricht in East Germany, and also from the Soviet leadership in Moscow. At a series of meetings, he tried to reassure them that the reforms were an internal matter, he had events under control and Czechoslovakia remained a faithful Soviet ally. But his position was becoming increasingly untenable and the Moscow leadership was unconvinced.

From the point of view of the Kremlin, what was happening in Prague looked increasingly like a blatant challenge to its authority and a dangerous experiment, which might prove contagious. The fear was that if the Prague Spring took hold, the whole Communist system in Eastern Europe might begin to dissolve. Besides, Czechoslovakia was a key frontline state with borders to both Austria and West Germany. Even the slightest prospect that a reformist Czechoslovak government might lift the Iron Curtain by easing border restrictions with the West was intolerable to Moscow. It was a potentially dangerous breach in its Cold War defences against the NATO enemy. At no point did Dubček suggest that he wanted to abandon one-party rule or take Czechoslovakia out of the Warsaw Pact, but the suspicion remained in Moscow that his loyalty could no longer be counted on.

In mid-August the Soviet Politburo met in emergency session. Contingency plans for a possible military intervention had been on the cards for months and recent military exercises meant that large numbers of Warsaw Pact troops were poised conveniently close to the border. But a final decision was needed. Among those most in favour of an invasion was the KGB chairman (and later Kremlin leader) Yuri Andropov, who, as a Soviet diplomat in Budapest in 1956, had witnessed the Hungarian Revolution at first hand.

In the end, the Politburo took the decision to send in troops. A formal pretext was provided by a message from members of the hard-line faction within the Czechoslovak Communist Party, warning that right-wing elements had whipped up an 'anti-Communist and anti-Soviet psychosis' and urging the Politburo to 'use all means at your disposal' to save the country 'from the imminent danger of a counter-revolution'. The decision to invade would later be justified according to the so-called Brezhnev Doctrine, which stated that the Soviet Union and its client states reserved the right to intervene in any part of the Eastern Bloc where socialism was under threat.

On the night between 20 and 21 August 1968, Prague airport was seized by Soviet paratroopers, and 250,000 soldiers and 2,000 tanks poured into the country. The total number of invading troops would rise to half a million. Besides the Soviet Union, other Eastern Bloc nations taking part were Poland, Hungary and Bulgaria. East Germany was also involved but asked not to send troops in case it exacerbated local tensions, given memories of Germany's wartime occupation. Romania's Nicolae Ceauşescu, who had sided with Dubček, refused to participate – a reluctance to fall into line that marked Romania's detachment from the Soviet Bloc for the next two decades. In Albania, Enver Hoxha also refused to join in and later withdrew from the Warsaw Pact entirely.

The invasion caught the Western world by surprise. It provoked rifts in and resignations from some Communist parties in Europe, but at a government level there was no formal attempt by the West to counter it. In 1968, the United States was still reeling from the assassinations of Martin Luther King Jr and Bobby Kennedy. Distracted by the growing anti-Vietnam War movement and keen to pursue the possibility of an arms control treaty with Moscow, President Lyndon B. Johnson was reluctant to step in. And so, as with Hungary 12 years earlier, although the United States and its NATO allies condemned the invasion there was no appetite for a potential clash with the Soviet Union over Czechoslovakia.

Inside the country, unlike in Hungary in 1956, the invasion did not lead to a national uprising. In order to minimise bloodshed, Czechoslovak troops were confined to barracks. The local population also refrained from fighting back. Dubček's government urged them to stay calm. The response was a largely peaceful resistance on a massive scale, as citizens took to the streets to engage and challenge the occupying soldiers, and also to confuse them. Road signs were removed or painted over and some small villages renamed themselves to disorientate the invaders further.

Almost immediately after the invasion, Dubček, along with several other leading reformers, was arrested and flown to Moscow, where he was held and interrogated for several days before being forced to sign what became known as the Moscow Protocol to reverse reforms. His broadcast to that effect signalled to the people of Czechoslovakia that the Prague Spring experiment to humanise the Communist system had come to an end. A year later he was expelled from the Communist Party in disgrace.

In January 1969, a student called Jan Palach set fire to himself in Wenceslas Square in the centre of Prague and died from his burns several days later in hospital. His act of suicidal protest caused widespread dismay and his funeral turned into a major demonstration against the occupation. For many it signalled a grim end to the brief blossoming of hope that the Communist system could be transformed and Czechoslovakia could go its own way. Across the entire Eastern Bloc, the possibility of reform from within had been set back, as it turned out, for two decades.

Those who could – some 300,000 in all – fled into emigration. Those who remained in Czechoslovakia battened down the hatches. Most of them gave up political activity, resigning themselves to a dreary and restrictive life under an oppressive Communist government, which annulled almost all the

Prague Spring reforms and kept a firm grip on power for the next 20 years, until the fall of the Berlin Wall in 1989 and the collapse of Soviet rule in Eastern Europe.

Despite her family's poverty, Prague-born **Zdena Tomin** *was a true believer in Communism from a very young age. This changed during her teens.*

By the time I was 14, 15, Hungary happened, 1956, and I woke up and realised what it was that I had been ecstatic about. It was just a shock. I never became a violent anti-Communist, I just realised that what I was living was a religion. People were not meant to live in a dark, Communist, Stalinist society. People were not meant to live in the dark. I think that's what it was, really. There was a younger generation, of my age, who didn't have that utopian enchantment, when war ended, of socialism and never having another war and everything's going to be equal. But even those people were realising this was an illusion, this was a mistake and we're not meant to live like that. People started to talk about the horrible crimes that had happened, the many people executed, the many people put in jail for life, the horrible gulags, all that was coming out. And people just wanted to live differently. They wanted toilet paper as well, and a better car, the possibility to go to the Riviera if they wanted to. But mainly they just didn't want to live in the dark any more. Or I didn't.

It was a broad movement, a broad awakening, everybody was involved. Don't tell me this was just a silly power game within the Communist Party Committee. It was not. And it did not start in '68, it started in '63 with the Kafka conference. There were more and more books being written, theatres especially were going around the censorship, lectures happened, but the Kafka conference in 1963 – that for me was the beginning of the Prague Spring.

At the time of the Soviet invasion 18-year-old **Hana Laing** *was about to begin her first year at university in Prague. She had enjoyed the relative liberation of the preceding years.*

There were a lot of theatres, small experimental theatres. I remember seeing all the Pinter there was at that stage, and there were literary magazines one could read. There were suddenly translations from more risqué authors from the West, there were political discussions. It was much freer, yes, a new wave of films, new wave of plays, writing, [Václav] Havel part of it. But yes, it was very exciting, it had a different feel to it altogether. You could travel, you could make your own opinions of what you wanted to do, you weren't in this sort of cage. You suddenly had a hope that things are changing and perhaps we would be able to escape the clutch of our 'friends'.

Julius Tomin *was born in 1938. He had been imprisoned twice before the age of 20, once for refusing military service and later for trying to escape the country. At the time of the Prague Spring, he was a writer and a researcher at the Philosophy department of Charles University in Prague.*

The march towards the Prague Spring culminated, in 1967, in summer with the Seven Days War in Israel. The Czech intelligentsia was always very pro-Israel. And the writers wrote a letter to Novotný, the President, asking for a positive attitude towards Israel. And that was the end; then the writers' congress was finished, the literary weekly completely changed editorial board. There was a period of darkness, which then ended on the 17th of November. The students made a big demonstration and went with candles, asking for light. For God's sake, students that were Communist Party members. Here started the change.

Zdena Tomin *remembers how Dubček was installed in January 1968, after Novotný was deposed.*
Before then, nobody knew who [Dubček] was, some sort of under-secretary or something. He looked incredibly boring. And then suddenly, some meeting or other, he began to feel very flattered by the attention he was getting and young pop singers were flocking round him. And in March or April he suddenly smiled. None of us forget that. There is this absolutely boring, unremarkable chap and he had this funny face and he smiled, and he smiled literally from ear to ear. This unbelievably charming, slightly ridiculous smile. And we've never seen party secretaries smile. Certainly not like that. Imagine Brezhnev smiling, just imagine it. Try. Dubček was terribly pleased with where things were going, pleased that he was suddenly this adored leader. But he wasn't spearheading anything, he really was just a weak Communist functionary who played an enormously important role, because he was somebody people could internalise. He was the human face of socialism, he really was. He was the face. But he was a weak man. He was carried on the wave of the time. And when the Russians came that was it for him.

Hana Laing
It felt like a huge change because until then the socialism didn't have a human face. And I don't think any of us particularly wanted to become a capitalist country. Whatever the disadvantages were in living in the socialist country, there were huge advantages as well. You were not allowed to be unemployed, they would find you a job, so you could work. You would always be supported by the

state. It was relative poverty but safety. And you also didn't have responsibility for your actions; the state pretty much dictated what you would do and how you would do it, so if you were happy with that you could lead quite a happy life, not thinking about things much […] So the human face of socialism became very attractive, because we didn't necessarily want to change the system, but we wanted definitely to be more human, whatever that meant.

Julius Tomin

After 'The Two Thousand Words', things became more heated. The streets were full of people. They were just criticising the regime from every possible aspect, from their own experience. People were on the streets day and night. I remember a meeting in the night in front of Prague Radio and [people were saying] 'Communists worse than fascists!' Next day, there was a big meeting in the Old Town Square and there were people giving talks and again: 'Communists worse than fascists!' So I just thought, 'For God's sake, I must try to do something.' So, I went there and started to talk. I said, 'Look, I never was in the Communist Party, I was in prison, I am very critical about the regime. But I know one thing: if we have any chance to survive then it is through the Communist Party. No de Gaulle will come to our help, no Johnson will come to our help.'

Hana Laing

Of course, we were always scared of the Soviet Union, but we had several months when nothing seemed to be happening, so we were emboldened by that and were hoping that it would last and we would get away with it. Of course, we were always afraid that something would happen, but we also hoped – we thought that the times have changed and maybe they wouldn't dare to do such a thing – and surely the West will come to our rescue, and they wouldn't dare even think about invasion. But the atmosphere was totally intoxicating and you didn't particularly want to think about it.

On the morning of 21 August 1968, **Zdena Tomin** *woke to discover that Warsaw Pact troops had entered Czechoslovakia during the night.*

It was early in the morning, just dawn, and I was woken up by this weird noise, so I looked out of the window and there were coming big-bellied military planes carrying tanks, big-bellied beasts, one after another, a row of them going to the airport. That was a horrible sight. I went into the streets and people did as people do: they went to grab as much food as they could, so there were queues in every shop. I thought, I'm not queueing, so I went home again and phoned around. Then Julius and I made posters, as many people did, in Czech and in Russian. In the night, we would go to the centre of Prague and hang them up. You should have seen the centre of Prague. Most of them were very funny. 'Lenin wake up, Brezhnev's gone mad', that was the most famous one, but there were lots of them. 'Ivan go home'. They were not hateful.

Hana Laing

I wasn't actually there when they invaded. I was in Germany, staying with various friends. I learned about the invasion in a rather dramatic way, because I was staying at the university hall of residence, and not one friend but two came to pick me up in the morning and take me to breakfast. And I said, 'How come you're both here?' I thought something must have happened. I said, 'Has anything happened to my parents?' And he said, 'No, no, let's go and have breakfast and we'll tell you.' As soon as we got out I saw crowds of people in front of shop windows. They tried to steer me away from this display in the window but … there was a newspaper spread out in the window and it said, 'Soviet Troops Invade Czechoslovakia'. And I just couldn't move, I was completely stricken. It was the end, I knew it was completely the end of any hope we might have had.

I didn't know quite what to do. My parents were not in Prague; they were travelling with my brother. I was supposed to fly on the 26th back home, but of course nothing was flying, there were no aeroplanes, so I bought a ticket from Frankfurt and got on the first train that was going to Prague. Nobody wanted to return at that stage, but I knew I had to go back. I had the university to go to, I had a boyfriend there, so I simply wanted to go. I was waiting for the train, buying bread and things because we had reports that there was no food. And as I was waiting, about ten minutes before the train was due to go, suddenly I hear from the tannoy saying my name and that I should go to office number 4, first floor. I thought, 'What? How? What's happening?' So I ran there and I was given a telegram, which was following me all over Germany and caught up with me there. It was from my parents and it said, 'Stay where you are, don't go back until we have a chance to speak.' But I just couldn't do that. And so I telephoned my boyfriend and said, 'Look, I'm coming back tonight. I'll be there at about half past eight.' He said, 'You can't do that because there is a curfew from seven o'clock.' I said, 'I can't stay here,' and he said, 'Okay, well, don't go to the main station. Get off at the smaller one on the outskirts and we'll try and come and get you.' He had an English friend staying and so they took his elderly Saab, put a Union Jack on it and went to fetch me from this railway station, where I was scared to death. But he did it – good man – and drove me to the house. Luckily nothing happened. The following day I went out. I just wanted to see what was happening in Prague. So that was on the 24th of August. And it was unimaginable.

Julius Tomin

I was on the streets. Students had tables with big papers and marker pens so that anybody could write anything, so I took the opportunity and I wrote: 'Soldiers of the occupation army, try to think for yourselves – we welcomed your fathers with love and flowers, but nowadays nobody gives you even a piece of bread or a glass of water.' I took it to the Old Town Square and stuck it to the wall near the Old Town Hall, facing the Jan Hus monument. There were two Russian soldiers who wanted to see what was happening and they were called back, so I turned back and read it aloud, and as I finished reading it the two Russian soldiers grabbed me and took me behind the circle of soldiers and stepped on me and broke my glasses. Then they stood me facing the armoured car with a gun in my back. And then there came a Russian officer shouting, 'What's happening here?' I said, 'Well, they beat me up and they don't even allow me to sit down.' He shouted, 'Sit down! Tell me what's happening.' I didn't answer, so he commanded a soldier to bring me a bottle of water and said, 'Drink!' And I didn't drink. So he said to the soldier, 'Drink it, show him that it's not poisoned.' So I said, 'I'm not afraid that it's poisoned. I won't talk to you before you apologise for what you did.' So he apologised. I drank from the water and started a long discussion with him.

With another soldier, I talked. I asked, 'Why did you come here?' 'Because of the counter-revolution.' I said, 'Did you see any counter-revolution here, anywhere? Did

Julius Tomin, 1968.

you see any Czech fighting?' 'Well, they were throwing stones on our tanks.' I said, 'But you are an occupation army! Have you seen any Czechs fighting Czechs?' He said, 'It's all our propaganda.' I said, 'Yes, it's propaganda. If they told you there is a monkey on this tree you would say yes, yes, there is a monkey on the tree.' And he said, 'Yes, but we drank this propaganda from our childhood.'

Hana Laing

The first tank I saw was on the embankment, which was rolling down from the National Theatre to the Charles Bridge, destroying basically the paving. It was totally surreal. You had tanks rolling through the streets, with the soldiers standing up. You had people writing graffiti on the walls and singing songs like 'Ivan go back, Natasha is waiting'. But you look at these soldiers – they were no Ivans. They were somewhere from the far east of the Soviet Union, they were sort of Mongol, Chinese, I don't know what … I think they simply had no idea where they were, what was happening. They were told that there was counter-revolution, if they knew what it meant, and they were stone-faced, completely stone-faced. People tried to talk to them, to discuss, to persuade them, this is no counter-revolution, to tell them what it is, and they were just looking ahead, not moving a muscle in their face. And then when they had enough they would just turn with the Kalashnikov towards you and aimed. And I can tell you that we stopped trying to discuss things with them soon because it was not possible.

Zdena Tomin

It was one of the best weeks in my life. I have never been so proud of being Czech, seeing so many people being helpful to each other. People flocking around a huge tank that could kill you all and arguing. With a tank. It was only after a week, when they changed the troops, we were told by our still-functioning media to stop it because they were the elite troops. They were no longer the confused youngsters and they were prepared to shoot. And so, after a week it did stop, the celebration – it was a celebration of unarmed resistance. Not peaceful resistance because we weren't peaceful, we were taunting them, but unarmed, proud resistance, not to the soldiers themselves, but to the machinery of it. I don't think there are many examples of that in history.

I liberated a bridge! I was crossing a bridge to my part of the river and suddenly [...] a big truck full of Russian soldiers came in. The captain said, 'Close the bridge,' so they stood in a big line and said, 'Bridge closed, go away people.' And I got terribly mad because I had a child at home and I wanted to go home and why should I go and look for another bridge? So I said, 'No, no, no' – in Russian – 'this is my bridge, this is my river, in my town, there is my child, I'm not going anywhere.' A bunch of other people who wanted to cross were standing just behind me. The captain ordered the line of soldiers to move and put on bayonets. I had this young soldier – I remember him, red hair, blue eyes – and he came to me in order to march forward, and his bayonet touched my stomach. I knew he was not going to go through me, I knew that, I wasn't afraid. He dropped it on to the floor, the captain ordered the soldiers back on to the truck and they went. Not to illustrate my heroism, because it was more silly than heroic. I was just mad. This is our country, we're not giving up to a few rusty bloody tanks. Go home. There is no counter-revolution here. I don't often agree with Milan Kundera but I agree with him on that one. It was a beautiful week.

Hana Laing

It was a whirlwind of things and we were all getting together discussing, waiting for new developments. A terrible despair came over us: we really thought the world had ended. And then it was the first time that we realised – I'm talking about young people, 18, 19 years old and younger – that we can't expect any help from the West, that they would not come to our rescue. They probably couldn't even because of the consequences of this action, but still you feel completely betrayed. I realised that certain things are possible and certain things are not …

After Dubček was taken into custody in Moscow and returned to Prague, **Zdena Tomin** *remembers hearing his radio broadcast.*

A week after the occupation, Dubček was on the radio. I heard it and the Russian soldiers were making noise and I shouted at them to shut up, which was a bit foolish of me, but they did. And there he was, sobbing. Every word was a sob, you could hear the sobs coming through his words. He was sobbing, he was giving up. And I knew that was the end of Dubček and very probably the real end of the whole Prague Spring. And it was. I mean, it went on for a few more desperate months, but that was really it. That was really it.

The Communist Party of Czechoslovakia in 1968 probably had historically the biggest trust of the population of any Communist Party anywhere. They had an almost absolute trust. When the Dubček smile first appeared, the media became free, censorship went, everything was moving, people were debating on the streets, every square was a debating chamber, everything was moving. We were told everything that happened, it was just wonderful. And because it was Dubček, the Communist Party leader, people suddenly trusted them. Never did before. And never did after. And that's why when Dubček sobbed and gave it all up, that's why people absolutely went home, shut the doors, didn't want to hear any more. From now on we don't want to know anything about any party, anything about any movement, anything about anything. Shut the door. They began to live this complete dual morality: when at home you can say everybody's a bastard; when you're at your place of work you just agree with anything they want you to agree with. Make sure you grab as much material goods as you can, get your children to school, and absolutely shut yourself away from any involvement with society, any involvement with any movement, with any effort. Just don't. We've been there, we trusted them. People risked their lives during the occupation. I did, several times. People were willing to risk their lives for a few Communist leaders who were kidnapped to Moscow. And then they come and do a few sobs and say sorry and that's it. And that was the real reason. It wasn't the Soviet power in the end, it was the absolutely broken trust of people in any possibility that a society within the Soviet empire would move anywhere and do anything, and everybody's better trying to live a small life. And it still makes me mad.

Hana Laing

We were furious. We were desperate. We wanted to talk to somebody, to negotiate, to tell them that this was not necessary, but you feel totally powerless against, not only a tank, but the power which generated all this. And I'll tell you what I found the most dispiriting: that it wasn't only the Soviet Union, but it was the Warsaw Pact. I couldn't believe that the Hungarians and the Poles – I'm leaving the Germans aside – that they didn't feel that it was a good opportunity to join in with us. They were in the same situation. They also had their own Prague Springs happening there. The Hungarians had their own experience of 1956, and it was such an opening to my mind that I just couldn't forgive them for joining in. So, I think we were bewildered and totally in despair. I couldn't see the future [...] because it was quite evident that the few years where life was easier, well, they would turn on the screws again and it will go back to the fifties. And it did.

Suddenly all these things started shrinking, shrinking, shrinking, and that was the normalisation. Your life started shrinking in the same way. You were not allowed to do this, that and the other. The writers who had this wonderful freedom to speak freely, to write freely, the filmmakers who had the same, that was very swiftly stopped, and we went back to the old, very dusty socialist regime with those terrible films and series on television, about ordinary people leading ordinary lives being blessed by the Communist Party. I mean, it was just dire. So, at that stage a lot of people left as well. Prague was emptied of people after the invasion. I can't tell you how dreadful that was. I lived by the National Theatre, which is right in the centre, and I could walk to the Philosophical faculty, which is on the river as well. Before, I used to meet friends, acquaintances. It took quite a long time to get somewhere because you stopped and had a chat ... [but after the invasion] there was nobody, nobody. I think what saved me was that I made new friends at university.

Zdena Tomin
I suppose it was heart-breaking from the very beginning. It must have been. You don't get this courageous, to flock around tanks and argue with Kalashnikovs, if your heart's

not breaking. But the fact that we were able to withstand it somehow, even for a week … the heart-break must have been there, even from the beginning. And then Dubček sobbed on the radio and that was slowly it. The last time we went on to the streets and still felt like a nation, or like a group of citizens, fellow citizens, was Jan Palach's funeral.

Hana Laing

Jan Palach was also a student at the Philosophical faculty, although I didn't know him personally. And the faculty was boiling with debates, discussions, plans, what to do, how to do it, trying to somehow change the whole terrible thing that has happened. The whole thing was absolutely feverish. And Jan Palach was there as well, listening to all this.

Zdena Tomin

He saw what I described as people going home and locking the doors, locking the windows and all that. And to his young soul that was probably something he couldn't cope with, and he just wanted to say to people, 'I'm going to burn so you realise that you have to go out into the streets again.' It didn't work. It was too late. It was too unimaginable what he'd done. The only thing that it did was we went out once more in hundreds of thousands and marched through Prague. Never achieved that again until 1989.

Julius Tomin

I remember an enormous funeral procession from the Philosophical faculty. That was the moment of great unity. At the same time, I realised soon that it had its negative side. For all students, the attitude was this: 'If I really had the courage and stamina I would do what Palach did. But then I can't do what Palach did. Well, then I can just prostitute myself. And why not get some benefits from being a prostitute.' This normalisation and consolidation could succeed only because the young people were ready to step into the shoes of all those who were expelled from the party and from their places.

Hana Laing
And after that, I think it was the final proof that we can't change anything, whatever we do. It's also the fear of powerlessness and your own insignificance, not only personal, but of the country as well. That people didn't think that this was important enough, that we were important enough people, to come to our rescue.

'I can't wash that stain away'

America's Vietnam War (1965–73)

America's embroilment in Vietnam began modestly enough. The team of American 'military advisers' sent into South Vietnam in 1954 consisted of just a handful of men: intelligence liaison officers whose job it was to train the South Vietnamese army and spread the word not to support the Communist North. President Dwight Eisenhower had been careful to limit the extent and nature of any US presence. He knew that after US losses in the Korean War (1950–3) there was little appetite among the American people to send their boys back so soon to fight another war in Asia.

Nonetheless, the significance of what was going on in Indochina, as Laos, Cambodia and Vietnam were called, was clear to Washington. In 1954, following a settlement known as the Geneva Accord, France – the former colonial power in Indochina – evacuated its last forces from Vietnam and French Indochina came to an end. Vietnam was divided into the Communist North, under the formidable and determined leader of the Vietnamese independence movement, Ho Chi Minh, and a weak and corrupt US-backed anti-Communist regime in the South.

Viewed through the lens of the Cold War, this had Washington worried. In less than a decade since the end of the Second World War, Communists had taken over in Eastern Europe and China, had acquired the atom bomb and had invaded South Korea. At one point, even France and Italy had looked in danger of a 'Red' takeover. Geopolitically inclined intellectuals warned darkly that this trend could well continue; 'information' films were made showing Communist colours seeping across world maps. Washington's worry was that with China and North Korea already in Communist hands, there was a real danger that the Vietnamese Communists, led by Ho Chi Minh, might take over South Vietnam too. And what then would stop all of South-east Asia following suit, in what would be a gigantic enlargement of the Communist world?

Eisenhower did not stop to consider that perhaps each country in the region might want to forge its own path, and that the Vietnamese nationalists who followed Ho Chi Minh's vigorous lead and flocked to join the fight against French colonial rule may have been driven more by a desire for Vietnamese independence than by a wish to promote world Communism. Instead, as he put it when he expounded the now famous 'domino theory' in 1954: 'You have a row of dominoes set up, you knock over the first one, and what will happen to the last one is the certainty that it will go over very quickly.' In other words, one by one they would come tumbling down: 'the loss of Indochina, of Burma, of Thailand, of the Peninsula, and Indonesia'.

Pursuing a containment policy for South-east Asia, as dictated by this domino theory, was one piece of the advice President Eisenhower gave his successor, John F.

Kennedy, when he handed over to him in 1961. The new President took heed. Eisenhower had already steadily and stealthily increased the number of American military advisers in South Vietnam to help tackle the Communist insurgents, dubbed the 'Vietcong', operating in the South. President Kennedy doubled and then tripled the numbers while maintaining in public that the USA was not militarily involved. By 1963, there were roughly 11,500 US military personnel in South Vietnam, officially 'advisers' and 'trainers' not combat troops, but soon there was talk of an 'undeclared war'.

After Kennedy's assassination in November 1963, the next US President, Lyndon B. Johnson, was forthright in private, while denying in public any plans to escalate US involvement. 'I am not going to lose Vietnam. I am not going to be the President who saw Southeast Asia go the way China went,' he told the US Ambassador to South Vietnam, who had warned him that Vietnam might 'go under any day if we don't do something'. By the end of 1963, there were 20,000 Americans stationed in South Vietnam, where unrest was beginning to spread due to the corruption and incompetence of the South Vietnamese government.

On 2 August 1964, the situation escalated. In the Gulf of Tonkin, off the coast of North Vietnam, a US naval destroyer, the USS *Maddox*, came under attack from North Vietnamese patrol boats. Two days afterwards there were reports, later shown to be groundless, of more attacks, and Johnson for the first time ordered North Vietnamese bases to be bombed in retaliation. He went on prime-time television to explain his action to the American people, and sought approval from the US Congress. On 7 August, Congress passed the Gulf of Tonkin Resolution, which gave the President authorisation to take any measures he believed necessary to retaliate and secure South-east

Asia. In essence, it was a mandate to expand US military action in Vietnam as he saw fit.

Meanwhile in the North, Ho Chi Minh was successfully playing off Moscow against Beijing to secure large amounts of aid for his Vietcong guerrillas. By late 1964, some 170,000 fighters had infiltrated the South and were launching attacks not just on South Vietnamese targets but American bases.

The final straw that brought the Americans definitively into the war was a Vietcong assault on an American barracks at Pleiku in the Central Highlands in February 1965, which killed eight Americans and wounded over 100 more. President Johnson ordered a sustained bombing campaign in response, and a month later the first American combat troops waded ashore.

By April, there were 33,500 American troops in Vietnam. By the end of June the number had doubled, and the soldiers were now going out on patrol, no longer just defending bases. By the end of 1965, the number had gone up again to 183,000 US troops. America's war in Vietnam had begun in earnest.

Two years later, the United States was spending what was, by the standards of the time, a staggering $20 billion a year on the war, and had nearly half a million US troops in Vietnam. Over the course of the war, more explosives were to be detonated than during the whole of the Second World War. Yet the impact of all this weaponry and manpower was questionable. In 1968, a war-weary Lyndon Johnson announced he would not be standing for re-election, leaving it for the next American President, Richard Nixon, finally to extricate the United States from the conflict five years later.

Few Americans would have anticipated when the US committed itself to sending in combat troops in 1965 that eight years on it would be pulling out in failure. In more recent times, the bitter pill the United States had to swallow would become common medicine for big powers taking on small and agile insurgencies, whether in Iraq, Afghanistan or Syria. Nowadays, we are more aware that sophisticated weaponry, air power and greater financial resources do not necessarily win out on the battlefield when fighting far from home against an enemy guerrilla force that knows the terrain well, with well-motivated fighters and a dogged refusal to give up. But when the last US diplomats were airlifted off the embassy rooftop in Saigon in August 1975, the symbolism was shocking: a global superpower, armed with nuclear weapons and the biggest military arsenal and budget in the world, was unable to do anything except flee in haste from a home-grown band of rebels.

The original reason for the American intervention had been to contain Communism and stand up for the principle of liberty. But for many of the young soldiers who enlisted to serve their country because they believed the war to be a noble cause, the reality of the conflict was a profound shock. Many expected to be welcomed by the Vietnamese, but found instead that they were treated as the enemy. As US casualties grew, so did American mistrust towards locals. Killing Vietnamese, whether guerrillas or civilians, came to be seen as a necessary part of staying alive. For some, the crusade against Communism degenerated into a racist and murderous spree.

Back home, as the war wore on, more and more Americans began to wonder what they were fighting for. The damage done by the Vietnam War was not just to the United States's global prestige, but to the fabric of American society – it was a nation rocked by anti-war protests and no longer so sure of its core values.

Initially, most Americans supported President Johnson's intervention. But by 1967, opinion polls suggested the mood was turning, and a majority were starting to think it was a mistake. Some were opposed to the draft call-up because it put young men at risk of being sent off to war without a choice. Some objected on moral, legal and practical grounds, arguing that who ruled Vietnam was none of the United States' business and the idea of a Communist threat had been overblown, and anyway the mission lacked clear objectives and looked increasingly unwinnable. And some were shocked by the television pictures, broadcast in Americans' living rooms for the first time in a war of this kind, revealing in graphic terms the impact of American bombing on Vietnamese civilians. Some argued that the violence used by US troops and its South Vietnamese allies was clearly illegal and justified the idea of breaking the law at home in order to oppose the war.

Reports from the front line also conveyed a sense of just how far the United States was from victory. By the beginning of 1968, hundreds of American troops were being killed weekly. When, at the beginning of that year, North Vietnam launched its Tet Offensive and the US Embassy in Saigon was attacked, viewers back home saw American weakness. Even though in military terms the offensive turned out to be a tactical defeat for the North Vietnamese and their insurgent comrades in the South, the National Liberation Front, it further fed the anti-war mood in the United States.

By 1969, hundreds of thousands of people were joining anti-war movements across the United States. The ceremonial burning of draft call-up cards and public invitations for people to hand in their draft cards to signify their opposition to conscription and the war turned into a mass disobedience campaign. By the late 1960s, some 25 per cent of all the cases going through the US courts were about draft dodging. Students, feminist groups, African Americans and Asian Americans all joined the anti-war movement.

For the hundreds of thousands of returning soldiers, many of whom were psychologically and physically battered by what they had been through, this opposition to the war was often hard to take. Unlike their fathers, welcomed as heroes on their return from the Second World War, these young men were sometimes greeted with opprobrium. Some were so horrified by what they had seen and so mistrustful of their own government that they became powerful voices in the anti-war movement, making a point of speaking out about the atrocities they had witnessed or taken part in, and in Detroit in 1971 some delivered powerful testimonies at a public event known as the 'Winter Soldier Investigation'. Others found it impossible to talk about what they had experienced and internalised their trauma for years, never really adjusting back to American life.

They were just some of a whole generation of young Americans whose lives were turned upside down by the war. More broadly, many felt their illusions had been shattered and their own government was no longer to be trusted. In 1971 excerpts of a secret Department of Defense study, which became known as the Pentagon Papers, were leaked to the press. Its exposure of the previously hidden extent of US involvement in South-east Asia fed mounting public suspicion that the war had not been politically or morally justified, and that the government had misled the American people. Instead of the anti-Communist near-hysteria of the 1950s McCarthy era, the enemy was no longer external – Russia or China – but internal: a government at home that had taken the nation to war without due thought or cause.

In time, after Nixon negotiated the United States' exit, the anti-war movement subsided, but the experience of Vietnam had polarised and traumatised the nation. A political innocence had gone. And when over the following two years the Watergate scandal engulfed the Nixon presidency, American confidence was undermined again. In the Cold War context, the world had got greyer. No longer could it so confidently be claimed that the West was always morally right and the other side always wrong.

John Ketwig *graduated from high school in 1965, in western New York State.*

We were brought up to believe that Communism was the great evil, that it was on a par with fascism or Nazism, and we were engaged in a struggle to take over the world – that if we didn't stop them and draw a line and say, 'This is the limit of your influence,' one country after another after another would topple and become Communist, and we couldn't allow that to happen. Khrushchev I remember very clearly thumping on the desk at the United Nations and saying, 'We will bury you.' It was very aggressive and very scary. The Russians were the first to put a satellite into space. I remember going out on a summer night and looking up and here went this light travelling across the sky, that was Sputnik – 'Oh my God, they were ahead of us in the space race.' The next thing that came along, and it's hugely important to the story, was when Fidel Castro and his people took over Cuba, 90 miles off our shore. We're going to have a Communist country that close and everyone was scared of that.

Along came news of something going on in some place called Vietnam – I had no idea where it was or what it was all about. It was us versus Communism – the Cold War theme we were brought up under. The next thing I knew, very much against my will, it was obvious I was going to be drafted, so it was a very stressful, difficult time.

Scott Camil was born in Brooklyn but grew up largely in Florida, with his mother and step-father, a policeman and a member of the extreme anti-Communist John Birch Society.

I grew up in a right-wing household – we had an American flag flying from our house. We were taught that it was our duty to stop Communism before it got to our country. No one in my family had ever been to college. I was raised to believe I should finish high school, and that after high school I owed a debt to my country, and I would repay that debt by going into the military to serve my country and help stop Communism. In high school they had military recruiters, and the recruiters told us we were going to get drafted when we graduated, but if we signed up now, we would have better benefits. So I signed up. Three days after I graduated high school, I was at Parris Island, South Carolina, for my Marine Corps training.

Paul Sutton grew up in a military family; he served in Vietnam in 1965, and then returned for a further tour in 1968.

My dad was a student of history, and he convinced me that the domino theory was real. President Eisenhower had developed the idea that if we didn't support [the] South Vietnam government created [in] 1954, next it would be Thailand or Laos. If we don't face those folks we'll have fewer friends, as more countries [will be] run by Communist regimes. I was opposed to Communism in the fifties and sixties and am right up to now – it's an evil we cannot allow to take hold anywhere.

In September 1967 **John Ketwig** *arrived in Vietnam.*
They loaded us on buses to take us to the camp where they would assign us and there was wire mesh on the windows of the buses. Someone yelled to the driver, 'What's this all about?' and he said, 'That's so the people won't throw a grenade in.' And it was like, 'Excuse me, wait a minute, I thought we were here to help them?' I was very confused because I thought it was going to be like the pictures we'd seen where the Americans came into Paris and chased out the Nazis and all the girls stood along the street and tossed flowers. I thought the Vietnamese would be very happy we were there to help them and it was very sobering to find out that wasn't the case.

Scott Camil

Right after training, I volunteered to go to Vietnam. Three weeks after I got there, on the night of April 18, 1966, the unit I was part of, that I was on guard duty for, was attacked by Vietcong sappers and overrun. Out of 90 of us, we had five men killed and 28 wounded. The enemy penetrated the base and destroyed artillery pieces. That was the first time I killed anyone; that was the first time I saw anyone killed.

The next morning, after reinforcements came to help us, I went and against a bunker there were five dead Marines with ponchos over them. I pulled the ponchos off their faces to see who they were, and one of them was my first friend, Maine. I was devastated. A light bulb went off in my head. I realised I was in a place where it was people's job to kill me. I felt that we had gone to Vietnam to protect the South Vietnamese; they wanted freedom, and the

John Ketwig with a Vietnamese child during his year in Vietnam.

Paul Sutton outside Danang, early
September 1965.

North Vietnamese were trying to take their freedom away. But the people who attacked us were South Vietnamese – they were Vietcong sappers. So, it made me angry that I had gone to help South Vietnamese, but they attacked my camp and killed my first friend. I decided that day I was going to be ruthless and get them back for what they did.

Paul Sutton
In 1965, we were there to fight the enemy and get the job done. When I went back in 1968, it was like I was in a whole different environment, because by that time our people were just getting ramrodded by pretty much everybody, including the high command. Nobody seemed to have a clear picture of what we were doing from day to day. The weaponry that the enemy had had vastly improved.

We came to learn quickly that the decisions were not being made by the colonels and the generals, [but] back in the States – [probably] in the White House, and certainly by the Secretary of Defense. A mistrust began to grow that the civilians who are technically running this war haven't a clue.

John Ketwig was increasingly troubled by the mindset he saw developing among some in the American military in Vietnam.
They had a philosophy – kind of jokingly referred to as the 'MGR' or 'Mere Gook Rule' – that the Vietnamese people really didn't matter. If one of them walked in front of your truck, 'don't go out of your way to miss them. It's so important that you get up the road in a supply convoy, or whatever, just run over them.' It's amazing how easy it was to fall into that state of mind so you're running up the road and guys would take canned food from rations and kids would be along the road begging – they'd try to throw the can to hit the kid in the head or hurt them in some

Scott Camil in Vietnam, 17 February 1967. He was wounded for the first time the next day.

way. That kind of influence was everywhere. The thinking was – and our training was – we were taught continuously, 'the only good gook is a dead gook: kill 'em all. Let God sort them out.' There was no thought of what was good for them as a people, trying to establish why democracy was better than Communism, or capitalism better – none of that mattered. They were all considered a threat: the thinking was kill them before they kill you.

Paul Sutton served in a mortar unit supporting the infantry. When he returned to Vietnam in 1968 for his second tour, he found tensions had risen markedly.

Before I got back in country, at the base camp where I was stationed, the [Vietnamese] guy who was the barber – his body turned up outside the wire one night, because he was a civilian barber working for the US military during the day and he was a Vietcong at night! Those kind of things happened pretty frequently. We rapidly came to distrust any of the Vietnamese civilians that were around.

Scott Camil

We measured our success by body count. We were told if we killed ten Vietnamese for every American that died, we would win. I wanted to kill as many Vietnamese as I could. That's what I did for the next 20 months. I killed my prisoners, I killed women and children, I burned villages – it didn't matter to me. To me, the life of one Marine was worth more than all of the Vietnamese in the whole country. If I had been in charge, it would have been okay to nuke the place. I had no empathy for the Vietnamese; I only cared about our side and because we were judged by how many people we killed, I wanted to kill as many people as I could so I would be looked at as a good Marine.

In a guerrilla war, it's not Marines in uniforms fighting the other side in uniforms. We're fighting against the public. And some are supportive, some not. If you run into a Vietnamese in the jungle, if they're shooting at you, you know they don't like you, but if they don't have weapons, you don't really know. The rationalisation I used was: 'We go by, and these people can report to the Vietcong how many we were, what direction we were going in, how long ago we left, what arms we were carrying, but if we killed them they couldn't tell anybody anything.' So, I just killed everyone, and in my mind I was just erring on the side of safety. If they're dead, they can't hurt us. Fuck 'em.

At one point, on a mission with a comrade to an isolated base camp in the jungle, **John Ketwig** *witnessed a particularly horrific killing, committed by a combination of American Green Berets and South Vietnamese soldiers.*

They had captured three young Vietnamese women, and we watched a certain 'ceremony' where everybody circled around and they tortured these women with lit cigarettes. In this little base camp, there was an American fire truck in the mud, kind of leaning a little bit, but parked. There came a point with these three young ladies where they were trying to get information – one of their buddies had been killed downtown. They were trying to get information, but it was also a revenge type of thing: hate against the Vietnamese, the 'gooks', who had killed their friend. There came a point where the one girl, they held her down and put the hose from the fire truck between her legs and turned on the water and exploded her. And the explosion of body fluids splashed across our faces. And I tell people that in 47 years or however long it is – it's been a long time – I've washed my face countless times and I can't wash that stain away.

The day came when it was time to come home. You had to fly in your uniform to get the low rate. When I got to the airport at Rochester, New York, Mum and Dad were there, and my brother, and they threw [their] arms around me. I excused myself and went into the men's room, got my luggage, got a pair of jeans and a T-shirt and threw my uniform away, stomped the hat flat, put it in the trash and said, 'I will never wear that uniform ever again.'

Access to news in Vietnam was limited, but American soldiers had some sense of the opposition to the war building back home. **Paul Sutton** *came back from Vietnam in 1968 under the saddest of circumstances: the death of his young son.*

When I came back in 1968 to bury my son, we landed at a Marine Corps airbase in California at 2.30 in the morning, and we were told before we got off the aircraft we were to walk down off the aircraft and go into this hangar next to which our airplane had parked, and we were to exchange our uniforms for civilian clothes. We were not to go off the air station in uniform. This was November 21, 1968. I thought, 'What the devil?' They actually took our uniforms away from us. One of the guys we got talking to, who was running a shuttle from the hangar after we got our civilian clothes, said there were people hanging around the gate of this airbase 24 hours a day, and if you came out in uniform, they were stoning people, throwing eggs at them, spitting on them. He took us two blocks off the base and dropped us off at a bus station so we could catch a civilian bus into Los Angeles and make our connection home.

There was such a mistrust of everything that was related to the government, including those of us who served in uniform, which I firmly believe impacted many of us who came home – who had served honourably, who did what we were trained and told to do, and came home and were unwelcome in their own homes. The people in the community – there was a different attitude when you put a uniform on and walked down the street than if you just walked down the street in a pair of slacks and a shirt, and that attitude persisted for a long time. I know guys who were literally shunted to the side by their families because 'this clown had served in Vietnam' – that was the attitude.

*Once **Scott Camil** arrived back in the United States, with an array of decorations including two Purple Hearts, he enrolled at the University of Florida. This would lead to him deciding to testify at the Winter Soldier event organised by Vietnam Veterans Against the War.*

When I came home, I was very hostile to the anti-war movement. When I started college, people would wear black armbands to protest the war and I would wear my Marine Corps tropical shirt and I would bump into them and try to pick fights. Then I read a book [*Vietnam: The Logic of Withdrawal* by Howard Zinn (1967)], and when I learned the true history of Vietnam, about how we broke our word, it made me really angry, like, my country broke its word – I couldn't believe it. They lied to us – I was really angry about that. Then the Pentagon Papers came out and I got to read that, about how much more lying the government did to us. Those things made me angry. Watching TV and reading the newspaper – what the news was saying was different from what I knew to be the truth, so I was also upset about that.

Jane Fonda came and spoke at the University of Florida. I went to see what she looked like because she was a movie star and I wasn't thinking about her politics at all. Something she said grabbed my attention: she said that we live in a democracy, and in order for a democracy to function the public has to have access to the truth. And that the public was being lied to by the government about what we were doing in Vietnam. She said it was the duty of patriotic Vietnam vets to tell the public the truth. And when she said that, I felt like she was speaking to me. I understand duty, I am a patriotic Vietnam veteran, I believe in democracy, I think the public has the right to know the truth. That's pretty simple. They said, 'If there are any Vietnam vets who are willing to talk about Vietnam, come forward.' So I went forward and gave her my name and phone number and all they knew was that I was a Marine who served in Vietnam. A couple of days later, I got a phone call inviting me to come to Detroit and testify at Winter Soldier. I really went because I felt like I didn't get proper recognition when I got home. I wanted to come home and be a hero and have parades and have people be proud of what we did, but I came home and it wasn't like that.

Until that time, I only knew about what we did in my unit – I didn't know what people in other units were doing. But after three days of the testimony, hearing everybody else, I could see on what a large scale our conduct against the Vietnamese was. So, at the end of the testimony there was a meeting of all of the veterans that testified, and we talked about how we had been moved by what we had heard everyone else say; not only that, but there were some Vietnamese who testified about how they were treated. All of a sudden, I was struck with empathy.

We decided that the public had a right to know the truth, and we decided to take Vietnam Veterans Against the War, which was a small organisation in six states in the north-east, and make it a national organisation. That was in January [1971]. In February we met, we wrote the constitution, we wrote the bylaws, we divided the country into 28 sections. I became a regional coordinator for Florida, Alabama and Georgia, and I started organising veterans to do activities to make the public aware about the truth of the war.

And all of a sudden I started getting arrested. The freedom of information papers came years later, so at the time I didn't realise this was how the government was operating; all I knew was they just kept arresting me. In a six-month period, I was arrested on 18 different charges: I was facing death plus 120 years in prison. I'm a Marine sergeant, a combat Marine sergeant – I'm not the kind of person you can intimidate and if I believe that I am doing something right and you're trying to stop me, I'm going to give that 100 per cent I gave in Vietnam, and that's what I did.

One of our meetings decided we would march on Washington and throw our medals away. That was really extremely hard for me to do because the medals were all that I had to show for the sacrifices I had made. I went to Vietnam with the intention to win medals so I could prove to my family that I was patriotic, that I was a man. I came home and those medals were in a box on top of the fireplace for everyone to see. So we discussed this demo, we planned it; it was a majority vote, we decided to do that. But I didn't know if I was going to be able to do it or not. I was in line with all of the guys throwing their medals away, and it wasn't until it was my turn that I made the decision to do it. It was hard for me to do but, once I did it, all of a sudden I felt this kind of freedom. Throwing those medals away was like cutting the umbilical cord between me and the government. I was now free to say what I wanted to say, and do what I wanted to do.

People who haven't experienced war have a different view from people who have. Americans have no idea of what it's like to be occupied and what occupying soldiers do. We wanted to help the American public understand what these things were we were talking about. The home-coming parade is a parade the University of Florida has every year – a long march with floats and bands that goes from the university to the middle of downtown. So, the theme of the parade was 'the Impossible Dream'.

We practised 'guerrilla theatre'. Along the parade route we had these people that we had worked with. A lot of them were old, and there were mothers carrying children and underneath their clothes they had packets of pig's blood. In our part of the parade, we had three people carrying a banner saying, 'VIETNAM VETERANS AGAINST THE WAR, GAINESVILLE, FLORIDA'. Then we had four people carrying a casket, which had a flag draped over it, and on the front was a sign that said, 'The Impossible Dream: No More War'. Behind the casket were guys dressed in their military clothes, carrying toy M16s, real fighting knives and bayonets. As we would pass the group of civilians that were watching the parade, and that were working with us, I would light a little smoke bomb and throw it into the crowd. As soon as that happened, the first squad broke out of the parade and 'attacked' the citizens watching the parade, 'shooting' them and 'stabbing' them. People started falling on the ground, screaming and 'bleeding'. The police didn't know this was guerrilla theatre; the citizens didn't know. Just as fast as that first squad went out and did this, they came back into the parade, and the second squad fanned out to both sides of the street and handed out leaflets. The leaflets said 'An American Infantry Company has just come through your village. If you had been Vietnamese, these are the things we would have done to you.' And it listed all of the different things we were doing to people in Vietnam.

Before we started Vietnam Veterans Against the War, there were anti-war demos, but the government would say, 'These people are unpatriotic, these people aren't willing to serve their country. These people don't know what they're talking about: they're just draft-dodgers and Communist sympathisers.' When we started Vietnam Veterans Against the War, it gave a lot of credibility to the anti-war movement. It raised the issue about the conduct of the war and how we felt about it, so I think that in the end it was a really good thing to do.

John Ketwig, meanwhile, was to keep his feelings about the Vietnam War inside for over a decade.
In January 1982, I happened upon the CBS documentary *The Uncounted Enemy*, which purported to say that General Westmoreland [commander of US forces in Vietnam, 1964–8] had lied about the number of enemy troops opposing us in preparation for the Tet Offensive. I went crazy that night. I went and got a big bottle of Scotch and started drinking like crazy. I was just going to numb this thing down. I put myself back together: on Monday morning I went to work, and nobody had a clue but my wife. She had seen this big explosion, this big emotional upset, and didn't know what to make of it and began to wonder, 'Is my husband going to go off the deep end?'

We'd been hearing about what is today known as PTSD. She was home during the day and watched a Baltimore local TV interview show. They had a lady who had been a nurse in Vietnam and had done a book. My wife said, 'I want to read her book,' and we went to the mall to get that book. I couldn't imagine with something as big and powerful and important as Vietnam someone writing a book about it. There was a shelf of books about Vietnam. I was shocked. I bought every one and went home and started reading one after the other. Every one of them was valid, but they didn't say what I needed to say, what I wanted my kids to know about this reality. So one day I started making notes about what I would want my kids to know. Within a few days this became an obsession. I had a small manual typewriter and I started trying to tap it out in a more readable form, and it just became an explosion. Every night, I would sit in the living room and put on the old sixties music and try to relive and bring back what had happened and how I felt about it. I'd work until two or three or four in the morning, grab a couple of hours sleep and get up and go to work, and nobody ever noticed. In the morning, if I'd done two or three or four pages, I'd hand them to my wife and when I came home from work, she'd give me a bit of feedback. I had no idea about writing a book. It was something that I could communicate with her, and then we'd put it on the shelf and, when the kids got older, someday they could look at it.

Through a strange set of circumstances it became a book. It came out in 1985. I'm proud of it. I've had letters from people all around the world, particularly a lot of Vietnam veterans who said, 'Man, you got it. You got it right.' I've had a number of correspondences with people who said, 'My brother came back from Vietnam and wouldn't talk to us' – some of them went off and built a log cabin in the woods and lived on their own, 'and I read your book and I tried to understand, and I gave it to my brother, and he came to Thanksgiving dinner.' It broke down barriers.

'Everything that you thought is not true any more'

The Coup in Chile (1973)

Throughout the Cold War, one of Washington's key concerns was to keep countries in Latin America and the Caribbean from moving into the Soviet camp. Whether a government declared itself to be Communist, like Castro's Cuba, or was merely a left-wing administration that Washington feared could be infiltrated by Soviet sympathisers, the assumption was that it represented a potential threat. It was a new take on an old mindset, a rewriting of the so-called Monroe Doctrine, according to which the United States would not tolerate outside powers interfering in Central and Latin America, which it claimed as its sphere of influence.

Thus, in 1954, the CIA sponsored a coup in Guatemala to depose a left-wing government. Eleven years later, in 1965, Washington sent US Marines to counter what it feared was a left-wing takeover of the Dominican Republic. It was the reason why there was such alarm in US government circles when Fidel Castro took over Cuba in 1959. It was also why, from the mid-1960s onwards, there was such an American focus on Chile, a major South American power with a long tradition of stability and democracy, where the US had extensive interests in the copper and silver mines.

In Chile's election of 1964, the CIA spent millions of dollars quietly shoring up the campaign of Eduardo Frei Montalva, the Christian Democrats' candidate for President, and trying to scare voters away from his Socialist opponent, a former doctor and senator called Salvador Allende, who was heading a coalition of Communists and Socialists. Allende lost, but when the next presidential election came around in September 1970 he stood again, and this time in the first round of voting he came top, although without an outright majority.

The Americans had been distracted by the war in Vietnam and were caught unawares. President Richard Nixon was furious and blamed the CIA and the State Department for neglecting to exert influence on the vote, creating the danger that Chile might 'go Communist'. He called on his Secretary of State, Henry Kissinger, and his CIA chief, Richard Helms, to do something. A twin-track plan was devised to try to make sure that the second run-off vote to be decided by the country's Congress would deny Allende an outright victory.

The hastily concocted mission did not go well. The first part of the plan was to try to persuade Congress to opt for the conservative candidate who had been the runner-up. An onslaught of CIA-inspired propaganda in the local and international media blasted out messages aimed at undermining Allende's chances.

The second element was a plot to kidnap the commander-in-chief of the Chilean armed forces, as the first step towards staging a military coup. But the abduction plan went wrong, the victim was mortally wounded and the renegade Chilean general who had been hired by the CIA to lead the coup was arrested. With the botched operation a failure, there was no fall-back plan to stop most members of Congress voting for Allende. As a result, on 24 October 1970, he won the second round – the first Marxist leader to come to power in democratic elections, and the first to become a Latin American president.

Once in office, Allende wasted little time in restructuring the economy according to what he called 'the Chilean path to Socialism'. The copper mines and other large-scale industries were taken out of private ownership and nationalised, as were the banks. Large landed estates were expropriated and converted into farm cooperatives. A government healthcare and education system was established. More rights were granted to workers, and there was greater welfare provision for the low-paid. Diplomatic relations were established with Castro's Cuba.

In Washington, this was just what President Nixon's administration had feared, and the Americans set about doing what they could to weaken and destabilise the Allende government. According to Helms's notes from a meeting with Nixon and Kissinger in September 1970, their aim was to 'make the economy scream'. Loans from the World Bank failed to materialise, US aid to Chile was withdrawn, and millions of dollars were allocated to opposition groups.

Faced with a shortage of funding, President Allende turned instead to the Soviet Union and its allies for alternative support. The Cuban leader, Fidel Castro, visited Chile and urged Allende to move further to the left. Moscow provided some assistance, but it was disappointingly limited and the Soviet Union failed to deliver on credit loans. Possibly the Kremlin did not want to antagonise Washington and spoil chances of détente, given that

Brezhnev and Nixon had just exchanged visits. Possibly Moscow took a hard-headed decision that the unstable Allende government might not survive, so expending capital on supporting it was not a good option.

In time, the strain on the Chilean economy began to take effect, because of both external factors and the strains resulting from Allende's socialist reforms. Export income for copper fell drastically. The population began to feel the pinch from rising inflation and unemployment. Strikes called by truck drivers, teachers and doctors all contributed to undermining the economy and the country's stability still further. Some of the unrest was fuelled by covert CIA operations. Right-wing Christian Democrats who dominated the country's Congress accused Allende of leading the country towards a Cuban-style Communist dictatorship.

Throughout the summer of 1973, political tensions mounted and the country became increasingly polarised. In June, the colonel of a tank regiment surrounded the presidential palace (known as La Moneda) in another failed coup attempt, this time sponsored by right-wing paramilitaries. At the end of July, workers in the country's copper mines went on strike. In August, Allende faced a series of constitutional challenges, including a charge by some Congress members that he was seeking 'absolute power' with the 'goal of establishing a totalitarian system' and was heading for a confrontation with the armed forces.

Then, on 22 August 1973, the commander-in-chief of the army, who had been loyal to Allende and resistant to any idea of the army assuming control to restore order, submitted his resignation after concluding that he had lost the support of the Chilean military. The next day, his place was taken by his deputy-in-command, General Augusto Pinochet – a man whom Allende mistakenly judged was someone he could count on. Less than a month later, on the morning of 11 September, General Pinochet and his top commanders set in motion a military coup against the Allende government.

The coup was well-organised. Within hours, most television and radio stations in the capital had been seized or disabled, telephone services were cut, and the combined branches of the armed forces were able to declare that they now controlled most of the country. President Allende retreated to the presidential palace with his bodyguards and refused to accept defeat in return for safe passage out of the country, despite a threat from the coup leaders that they would bomb the palace. In an emotional final speech from inside the palace, he warned the people of Chile that a *coup d'état* was under way and declared that he would rather die than agree to surrender.

General Pinochet ordered armoured and infantry troops protected by helicopter gunships to open fire on the presidential palace. Then he gave orders for the Chilean Air Force to start bombing. It took several hours for the junta's soldiers to fight their way in because of resistance from Allende's defenders. First reports suggested that Allende was killed amid the fighting, but a later autopsy concluded that he had taken his own life, shooting himself with an AK-47 rifle.

The military junta moved fast to suspend the constitution, impose strict censorship, declare a curfew, halt political activities and dissolve Congress. Chile was now in the hands of a military dictatorship, with General Pinochet at the helm, along with two other generals and an admiral, representing between them the three branches of the armed forces and the military police.

Once its grip on the country had been secured, the junta set about ruthlessly rounding up and eliminating the opposition. Allende's cabinet was arrested and his widow and family fled to Mexico. Many of those detained in the wake of the coup were held in the country's National Stadium. Over the next few years, tens of thousands of Allende supporters were tortured. Some were executed and others simply disappeared without trace so that their families never knew what had happened to them.

On the economic front, the socialist policies of Allende were sharply reversed. Factories, land and banks were returned to private ownership, and Chile was transformed into a liberal free-market economy on an American model.

The United States could now rest assured that Chile's socialist government had not ended up in the Soviet orbit, but the outcome came at a cost, not least to the United States' own reputation. Pinochet's military coup brought to an end nearly 50 years of democratic government in Chile. The brutal crackdown against the opposition was widely denounced as a flagrant violation of human rights.

There was sufficient public unease about the CIA's possible role in the coup and its aftermath for the US Senate to launch hearings in 1975, overseen by the Church Committee. It looked into the range of CIA covert activities in Chile to ascertain whether it had a hand in the overthrow and death of Allende. The Church Committee's final conclusion was that there was no hard evidence of direct US covert involvement in the coup of 1973, but that nonetheless it had given the impression it was not against it.

Subsequently, the CIA admitted its covert role in trying to stage the earlier failed coup to prevent Salvador Allende from becoming President in 1970 and its support for the opposition once he was elected, but insisted that it did not try to instigate the Pinochet coup of 1973. It claimed that it was not involved in bombing La Moneda Palace and had only learned of it just before it took place.

Whatever the full extent of CIA involvement in Allende's downfall, the US government and the CIA did actively support Pinochet's military junta afterwards, and the damage in the court of public opinion was done. The military coup in Chile in 1973 and the litany of human rights abuses and violence attached to it are often cited by critics as an example of why the United States cannot claim the moral upper hand during the Cold War.

While the Soviet takeovers and crackdowns to cement Communist rule in Eastern Europe may have been more extensive and shocking, the fate of Allende's government in Chile underscored the stark fact that, when it came to a fear of Communists in its own backyard, the US government was also prepared to foment unrest and engage in subversive activities to make sure its own sphere of influence remained intact.

Osvaldo Puccio was a 20-year-old student at the time of the coup. His father was President Salvador Allende's private secretary.

We had two cats in our house: one was called Agrarian Reform and the other Proletarian Revolution. That shows how ideological the country was. A large contingent of my generation thought that Allende was not revolutionary enough, that he was a reformer. At that time being reformist was an insult. Nowadays being a reformist is almost a word of encouragement. Allende was seen by the youth community as a very moderate person. Besides, they said that he was an old man, wearing a suit and tie, a parliamentarian. He wasn't Che Guevara! He wasn't a revolutionary.

Jack Devine in Chile, 1971.

*In September 1973 **Jack Devine** was a clandestine CIA officer based in Santiago.*

After the [1970] coup failed, there was a directive that the CIA would cease and desist from coup plotting. You certainly were expected to develop sources that could report on the military, report on what was going on in the country. And there was authorisation to support the opposition, in other words the political parties, the media, who were under tremendous pressure to be able to resist the encroachment of what was perceived to be a leftist and potentially Communist government. In my particular case, my brief consisted of paying close attention to the political parties and being supportive and at the same time working with the media to resist the Allende leftward movement.

The context of Chile was the view that the Russians and the Cubans were going to use Allende as a pathway to creating another Cuba. I think Kissinger referred to it as a 'Red sandwich'. I don't believe Allende was a Soviet agent, but you had the Communist Party in his coalition. So, it wasn't just Allende, it was a question of the external forces, so that eventually the Communists would come to power and that we would have a Red Cuba and a Red Chile. Now, that was the view not just of Nixon, but I think it was broadly shared in the power structures in Washington at the time, and certainly Dr Kissinger was of that view as well.

__Steven Volk__ was a graduate student at Columbia University when he arrived in Chile in July 1972.

I knew there was really only one place I wanted to be at that time, which was Chile. This was a world historical experiment, the first time that a socialist government was democratically elected, and so I selected a topic that would take me to Chile.

Steven Volk in Chile, 1973.

As well as his academic research, **Steven Volk** *worked on a progressive print news bulletin called* FIN (Fuente de Información Norteamericana).

We decided at the end of 1972, why don't we get an office? And so using personal names, not with the name of the organisation, we rented an office, which we shared with a lawyer, about two blocks from the Chilean Congress. And when we arrived, two very strange things: there waiting for us on our doorstep was the complete works of Enver Hoxha of Albania – and we had no idea how he knew we were there! And we moved into the office and there was a phone installed and almost as soon as we were in the office we picked up the phone to make a call out and before dialling or anything somebody on the other end said, 'US Embassy, can I help you?' So, we were already connected to the US Embassy in Santiago at the time. It was very clear to us that the embassy had its eye on us.

I lived in a building close to the centre of town. Kitty-corner to my apartment was a construction site. One day in October of 1972, I saw all of the workers gathered in front of this construction site. I stopped and said, 'What's going on?' And they said that somebody had come by and offered the workers at this site a full month's pay if they would stop working. And this was at the moment of the 1972 economic boycott that the opposition to Allende called on. And I said where was the money coming from, you know, who's going to pay you for not working for a month? They told me the CIA. Now, I had no way of knowing whether that was true or not. As it turns out, it was true. But it was clear that they were being paid money to join the boycott against Allende. I said, 'What are you going to do?' and they said, 'We're going to continue to work. This is our job. We're going to get paid for working and that's what we should do.'

Osvaldo Puccio

There's a short story by García Márquez called 'Chronicle of a Death Foretold', the story of a crime that's going to be carried out, everyone knows it's going to be carried out. Everyone acts as if in a Greek tragedy so that finally it comes about, even though most people want to avoid it. I think this story is key to understanding Chile's situation in the last months before the coup.

After the last election in March 1973, the radical right wing, which was already very large, realised that there was no democratic way to unseat Allende. So, they concentrated on the conspiracy. At same time, the government was getting more and more radical and the moderates within government were being marginalised.

Jack Devine

Late in August and September [1973] you had strikes and demonstrations and you could feel the instability and the fact that the government was losing its power base. But I think the important note – and I have direct first-hand knowledge of this – [was that] the CIA did not find out about the coup plot until 72 hours before the coup, and that report came from an asset that I had. The message was very brief, and it's contained in a declassified cable that I drafted, and it reads something like: 'On September 11th the military will move against the President. It will start in Valparaiso and it'll be announced on Radio Agricultura at … ' They said 7am and it turned out it was 8am or so. I sent the cable and then later that night I met another source who basically repeated the same thing. So, I was feeling comfortable that the reporting was accurate. A third report, which was very detailed, came from an active duty military officer, but I think he was authorised by the command: go tell the Americans what's going to happen so they're not surprised, but tell them so late that it doesn't change anything. And that's precisely what happened. So, Washington found that the 9th September cable was the first notice.

The assumption was you would have a bloodless coup and that there would be an election.

Osvaldo Puccio

On the night of September 10, I finished at the university late at night. I went to the Moneda Palace to meet my father and then go to the house together. My father was Allende's private secretary. He was in charge of the presidential cabinet. When I saw my father, he told me that the police had reported the illegal entry into Chile of the head of an extreme right-wing terrorist group, responsible for organising the attempted coup in June.

We went to the house and had dinner. Very early in the morning, about 5.30am, we received a phone call from a very good friend of the family, who was married to an air force officer. I answered the call and she said, 'Tell your dad that the thing is on.' I went to my father's room to tell him what our friend had said, and at that moment we received another call, this time from the house of President Allende, asking my father to go immediately to the Moneda.

That day I had a law exam in college, and I put on my most elegant clothes because I thought that after going to the Moneda, I would go to college to take the exam. Regardless of my illusions, it shows that the crisis was a state of normality at that time. I thought it was not so extraordinary, a coup having begun, that the university would cancel the exam.

We received very contradictory news. Then conversations began with the military command. Pinochet sends a message through my father asking the President to go to the Ministry of Defence. And Allende answers him also through my father, telling Pinochet not to be a coward, that the President of Chile only receives people in the Moneda and the one who must move is him.

Around 10.30am, Allende got all the people who were in the Moneda together and gave a little speech. It was extraordinary, offering a moral justification to those people who wanted to leave the palace. He also thanked those people who stayed, without any obligation or pressure on people to stay. The President asked me to leave, and I told him that I wanted to stay. Then he hugged me and said, 'Well, I won't ask again, because the President of Chile cannot oblige any man to be where he doesn't want to be.' So I stayed.

In retrospect, I see Allende now as a very distant man, who had an attitude that projected an immense inner peace. I have no doubt that he knew what the consequences would be for him. He knew it. He acted as if he already knew this was his last day and he was going to die. He was calm and aware of what was going to happen.

Steven Volk

I was living about eight blocks from the Moneda. I would usually get up at about six-thirty, seven in the morning and go off to work at the library by about nine o'clock. [On the day of the coup] I went to my front windows which faced out on the Alamada, which was the main street that runs through the heart of downtown Santiago, and saw that the traffic was running the wrong way, that the cars were all headed out of the city as opposed to into the city. So, I immediately turned on the radio and there was nothing there, and I flipped around and finally found a station and it reported that there was a coup going on at the time, that the navy had revolted in Valparaiso and that the army had rebelled against Allende. At that moment, it became clear also that the government stations were going off the air and as I listened in on one of them I could literally hear the doors being battered down, shouting, gunfire and then the station went off the air.

I listened to the military reports saying that Allende was given a certain amount of time to give up the presidency and that he would be flown out of the country. And I was listening to what turned out to be Allende's last speech on the radio in which – I can't really explain, I still get emotional thinking about it, hearing him talk about the hope that he had had for the Chilean people and for this process, the betrayal he felt over these officers that he had appointed and that he would remain as President of Chile, he was elected to do his job and he wasn't about to leave.

Osvaldo Puccio

I was right next to him, physically next to him, when he made his last speech. At that moment, I did not realise the significance of the speech. I heard it again after everything happened and I returned from having been in prison. It was then that I realised its meaning: it had been a speech to make an assessment and to say goodbye. It was spontaneous, he didn't have any paper – a completely improvised speech. And if you listen to it you know it's the speech of a man who's going to die.

A battle had already started. The *carabineros* [national police force] distributed arms to each one of those who were in the palace. Also, they distributed helmets and some masks because gas was being fired at us. As soon as the first group of people left, they started firing on the palace. There was an exchange of shots.

I was on the second floor of the palace and President Allende told me: 'Young comrade' – that's what he called me since I was a little boy – 'go check the posts to find out how many of the *carabineros* we have left.' And I walked unconsciously from the office to a wide corridor where the busts of the Chilean former Presidents were and somebody shouted to me, 'Get down, they're firing!' When you're in a situation like that you don't think about being brave, you think that the bullets are aimed at everyone but you.

There were many shots fired before they started bombing. The pipes had been broken and water flowed through the palace. The floor was half flooded. There was a conversation between my father and the military about when they were going to start the bombardment. First the bombing was set at 11am, and then finally it was announced for 12pm.

We tried to protect ourselves. We had to sit on the floor, but the floor was flooded. I was thinking, 'I'm going to mess up my good trousers that I wore to take the exam at university.' President Allende had given me a watch a few days before. It must have been the most modern watch available at the time. It had a button on it and, when you pressed it, it lit up to show you the time – in 1973! A digital watch! And when the first bomb dropped I immediately looked at the watch to see if the military was on time. The clock ticked 12.00. The first of the bombs hit us at 12.00 on the dot.

Steven Volk

There we see up in the sky these two jets and they're coming in. They circle around behind the building where I am and then you see them coming down the other way and heading on what would look like a bombing run towards the centre of the city. Then I could see the jets pull up on the other side. And nothing happens. We think, 'Absolutely, they can't do this, the idea of bombing your own White House is just incredible.' So, we feel a moment of elation and then there the jets are again behind us and they circle once more and they go down on a bombing run and they come up on the other side and this time there's a huge black cloud of smoke and it's clear that they had bombed the Moneda. At that moment, everything sort of snapped into focus, that this is not what we had talked about as a *golpe blando*, which is a sort of mild coup in which Allende would be escorted out of the country. This was a way of saying, 'Everything that you thought is not true any more. We are now in charge, this is our country and we will stop at nothing to stay in power.' From that moment, it just became absolutely clear that there was nothing ahead of Chile except dark days.

Osvaldo Puccio

After the bombing, there was a new dialogue with the military and they agreed that a delegation would go out to negotiate. This delegation consisted of a minister, the deputy interior minister, my father and myself. We had gone to negotiate but they arrested us immediately, and the talks didn't last five minutes.

We were imprisoned in the basement of the Ministry of Defence when they brought in a group of comrades who had been with us in La Moneda, including Carlos Jorquera, a journalist who was Allende's press chief. And he told us only with the movement of his lips: 'The Doctor is dead.' The people closest to Allende called him 'the Doctor'. That's how we found out.

I had a very bad night because I was tortured, and the next day it was the same. Then they took me to the National Stadium – some very difficult days. They burned my body with cigarettes. I had a beard like all the leftist students at that time, and they got a soldier to take off my beard and made me eat it. A fellow next to me was literally kicked to death. I felt very scared, because you feel a lot of impotence. It was totally arbitrary. Well, that's how dictatorships work. Dictatorships that are not arbitrary serve little purpose. Fear is produced by arbitrariness, not by order. Then they took me to the Military School, where I met with my father. After that, they took us all to Dawson Island, which is an island at the south of the Strait of Magellan, located in the south part of the country which goes down to the Pole.

Jack Devine
Once the government had been suppressed, they put a curfew in. It was lifted for a few hours and a number of people returned home. The curfew continued for weeks. You were allowed on to the streets, but after five or six o'clock (I don't remember the exact hour) there was no movement on the streets. We did have people reporting eventually about what was taking place in the stadium and that was pretty gruesome. So, you still didn't have a sense of how many people were wrapped up. You knew there was violence, people were killed, but there probably wasn't a good reading of it for several days.

Steven Volk
I didn't have a telephone in my flat and I had no idea where anyone was or what's going on. By Saturday, the curfew was only an evening curfew, so we started to get in touch with each other again. And it's over the next few days that we learn for the first time, this is about September 18th or 19th, that one of our colleagues, Charlie Horman, has been disappeared from his house. His wife and a

colleague who was with Charlie come to visit me in my apartment and basically detail to me the story that would later be broadcast in the Costa-Gavras film *Missing*, about what he had heard in the Viña del Mar, the port city, about his return to Santiago in a military car and what had happened after that time. So at that point, that was the first time, about ten days after the coup, in which a North American had been missing. We had no idea where he was, and in fact the Horman family would not find out until the middle of October that he had been killed and buried in an unmarked grave in the wall of the Santiago cemetery.

My second colleague Frank Teruggi had been arrested with his roommate David Hathaway when soldiers had come to their house. It later appeared that they had been denounced by neighbours. So they were taken down to the National Stadium. I went to the morgue, which was a horrifying sight, with hundreds of bodies stacked along the floor in double rows, with rows above and below, and unfortunately that's where I found Frank's body.

When I saw him, the clothes were taken off the bodies and they were lying there, and Frank's throat had been slashed. There was a cut from the chin-level down to the right and he had two bullet holes in his chest. When the official autopsy report would come out of the government, the arguments the Chilean military was making was that he had been released from the National Stadium, was out after curfew and had been shot 17 times by a passing patrol. I'm a young college student, this was a very traumatic time, but you can't mistake 17 bullet holes for a slashed throat and 2 bullet holes. By the time his body was returned to the US, there was no ability to make another autopsy, so that's how it stood. It was quite clear that these were all victims of military violence, and you would see bodies on the street. I saw a number of them as I walked around. I joined with the other crowds as we stood on a bridge over the Mapocho river and bodies would be floating by on it.

In terms of my own safety, I figured my best approach would be to become very public to the US Press Corp that was down at the time. I would meet with them fairly regularly and say, 'Look, today I'm going to go here, and tomorrow I'm going to go there.' And so at least they would know if I wasn't around. My own apartment was searched two different times by the military, as part of a larger sweep of the building. There's a fairly famous photograph taken by David Burnett of soldiers burning books on the streets in Santiago. Quite literally those were my books that they took out of my apartment.

Jack Devine

I think Washington was initially pleased to see the coalition and the Communists and Socialists had failed in their efforts, and I think there was satisfaction with it. As the reality set in, I think the Pinochet government had increasingly difficult relations with the US. I can tell you from the intelligence side from the earliest days there was cautioning that we would not be providing help if there were any human rights violations in anything we were working on. The human rights issue was joined fairly early in the aftermath.

Osvaldo Puccio

We were imprisoned on Dawson Island for a full year. After that, they took us to Santiago. On the island, we'd been separated into four groups, according to each branch of the armed forces. I was in the police group, so when we were taken to the city they left me at one of their facilities. In that place, I spent 73 days in a solitary cell. I was eventually expelled thanks to the mediation of the CIME, which was the United Nations agency to coordinate migration. I ended up living in Romania and then East Germany. I returned to Chile in 1984.

Jack Devine

Remember the basic premise here, which is the CIA was not orchestrating that military attack. I believe in the CIA; I thought it performed a unique mission in the Cold War. It stopped us from getting into fighting wars. The Russians actually believed that this was a pathway forward and we blocked them. We made an effort to block them there and it failed, whether it was the military that took the initiative or not. It was the last time that the Russians tried through the ballot box, certainly in Latin America, but I believe worldwide, to try and bring about change. So that was a contribution and I think it was the last hurrah for the Cubans as well. They had pretty well spent their energies after that. So, the combination of all the things we did in Latin America I believe stemmed the tide of the Communists. It's so long ago that most people have forgotten just how real the Cold War was.

'These were just ordinary men marching in the street'

The Fall of Saigon and the Aftermath of the Vietnam War (1975–9)

Before dawn on 30 April 1975, American Marines hurriedly ushered the US Ambassador to South Vietnam into a helicopter on the US Embassy roof in Saigon and whisked him away to safety. A few remaining Marines checked that all equipment and paperwork had been destroyed and then secured the building. The final helicopter with the last lucky evacuees lifted off some three hours later, while below, outside the embassy gates, a crowd of desperate locals watched in anguish as their only hope of getting out before the South Vietnamese capital fell into enemy hands disappeared. The same day, North Vietnamese troops and members of the NLF – the National Liberation Front of South Vietnam, otherwise known as the Vietcong – overran the city.

Since it was first formed in 1960, the driving aim of the NLF had been to bring down the South Vietnamese government and reunite North and South Vietnam under

Communist rule. Since the early 1960s, a steady stream of their Vietcong guerrilla troops, weapons and supplies from the Communist North had made its way south along the so-called Ho Chi Minh Trail cut through thick jungle and treacherous mountain terrain, on a mission to fuel the insurgency and spearhead the North's offensives against the South Vietnamese and their American backers.

But by the early 1970s, the Americans were on the way out. Most US troops had been withdrawn by the end of 1973, and US aid to the South was steadily diminishing. A North Vietnamese offensive in the spring of 1975 pushed southwards through the central highlands towards the South's capital, Saigon. There was a final two weeks of fierce fighting as Southern troops, heavily outnumbered, made a last-ditch attempt to block the advance. By 21 April 1975, that Southern resistance had crumbled and the way lay open for the North to take the city.

Now, on 30 April, the NLF was on the point of victory, its troops capturing key buildings as they made their way into Saigon. Several fighters set their sights on the presidential palace to raise their flag over the building – a symbolic declaration of their triumph. Duong Van Minh, the general who had been President for a mere three days, had already announced the unconditional surrender of the South Vietnamese government in a radio broadcast that morning. President Minh pleaded for reconciliation between 'brother combatants' on both sides, and said his administration was waiting to transfer power, in order to avert pointless bloodshed. The Vietnam War was over, the Americans had gone and a new phase had begun.

Within months, North and South Vietnam merged into a single Socialist Republic of Vietnam. For all the near-hysteria of those in the South who had feared what might come next, there was at first little evidence of vengeful bloodletting or mass executions by the Communists now in charge, although hostility and suspicion simmered. Those who had worked for the Saigon government and the American military kept their heads down in trepidation. Hundreds of thousands of South Vietnamese earmarked as collaborators ended up in re-education camps to be subjected to hard labour and even torture amid appalling conditions.

As for the Communist victors, they might have sent the Americans packing, but now they had to tackle the poverty and disarray the war left in its wake. After decades of conflict, the country was in ruins and its economy barely functioning. Nearly a decade of war with the Americans had left more than two million Vietnamese civilians dead and millions more wounded, and hundreds of thousands of children orphaned. Carpet-bombing by the Americans had devastated whole areas of the North. The countryside was littered with unexploded ordnance and landmines, and the residue of the poisonous American herbicide and defoliant Agent Orange. The cities were crowded with jobless refugees. To restart farming and boost rice production, the government encouraged and coerced city 'volunteers' to relocate to 'New Economic Zones' in rural areas.

Yet Vietnam's challenge of rebuilding and uniting a divided, war-torn country was soon put into stark perspective by the monstrous horrors unfolding next door in Cambodia, as the after-effects of the Vietnam War continued to ripple out through the region. Cambodia's fragile political balance had already been jolted by the Vietnam War in 1969 when President Richard Nixon ordered US bombing raids on North Vietnamese sanctuaries in Cambodia, followed in May 1970 by American and South Vietnamese troops invading the country. More

American bombing followed in the early 1970s as the US government began to wind down its involvement in Vietnam. Nixon claimed that destroying North Vietnamese supply bases in Cambodia would help speed up the US withdrawal.

At the same time, the Cambodian government was under mounting pressure inside the country from an extremist Maoist movement called the Khmer Rouge. In the first half of the 1970s, the Khmer Rouge, backed by China, gradually extended its control over the country and in 1975, just as the Vietnam War next door was coming to a close, it captured the Cambodian capital, Phnom Penh, and seized power. The fanatical, ruthless leader, Pol Pot, declared he was restarting the clock at 'Year Zero' and the country would henceforth be called 'Kampuchea'. Then he unleashed a reign of terror; over the next four years probably close to a quarter of the population would be murdered, starved and hounded to death in a genocide that became known as Cambodia's 'Killing Fields'.

The aim of Pol Pot's nightmarish social experiment was an anti-intellectual, anti-industrial, strictly agrarian society. Money, banks and private property were abolished. All religions were forbidden and all foreign influence banned. Cities were cleared at gunpoint and urban evacuees marched into the countryside to become forced labour on collective farms. Anyone with any learning or who just owned a pair of spectacles was pulled aside and taken off to be executed.

The Vietnamese Communists had, in the 1960s, supported the Khmer Rouge but, as the diplomatic chill deepened between their respective patrons – the Soviet Union for the Vietnamese and China for the Khmer Rouge – their local relations also deteriorated. Vietnam looked askance at the Khmer Rouge's barbaric excesses. They in turn feared that the Vietnamese were aiming to establish themselves as the dominant power in the region. The paranoid Khmer Rouge leader ordered a purge of Vietnamese and Soviet agents he believed had infiltrated his government.

In 1978, fearing an imminent Vietnamese attack, Pol Pot ordered a series of pre-emptive incursions across the border into Vietnam and killed hundreds of Vietnamese villagers. Vietnam ordered its troops to invade, and in January 1979 Vietnamese troops captured Phnom Penh and drove the Khmer Rouge out into the countryside, occupying Cambodia and installing a puppet government.

Vietnam's invasion brought Pol Pot's murderous rule to an end, but it also brought to a head another problem: the continued rivalry between the two Communist giants, Chinese and Soviet, who both saw the region as territory where they could and should have a decisive influence. Like the Khmer Rouge, China suspected that Vietnam – with Moscow scheming behind it – had evicted Pol Pot as part of a wider plan to extend its dominance over this part of South-east Asia. So, the Chinese leader, Deng Xiaoping, decided to teach the Vietnamese a lesson and launch China's own border war on Vietnam. To reinforce the point, he also warned Moscow that he was putting Chinese troops stationed along the Sino-Soviet border on full alert.

China's invasion of Vietnam in February 1979 caught the rest of the world by surprise. With the United States now gone from the region, the assumption in the West was that Indochina had succumbed to Communism – that the domino theory had been proved right and that was the end of it. Now, suddenly, it was once again a battleground, and the world's two biggest Communist powers were on opposing sides for the second time in a decade (the first being the Sino-Soviet border war in the late

1960s). The two armies – Chinese and Vietnamese – were soon engaged in fierce battles that were causing heavy casualties.

That said, though the Soviet Union provided weaponry, intelligence and logistical support and sent thousands of Soviet military advisers to Vietnam, beyond that Moscow chose not to intervene to fight the Chinese directly. Perhaps they calculated that the conflict would not last. If so, they were right: after a few weeks of fighting, the Chinese withdrew their forces and a wider war was averted.

But the clash showed that while the Vietnam War was over, the region remained a tinderbox, even if now the United States could look on as a detached observer. Having taken office in January 1977, President Jimmy Carter made it clear that this time the United States had no intention of getting involved in a conflict 'between Asian Communist nations'. No longer was the United States ensnared in South-east Asia's turmoil.

The Vietnam–Cambodia and Vietnam–China wars both caused a sharp increase in the exodus of refugees from the region. Many were Hoa, the ethnic Chinese in Vietnam, who had already been discriminated against by official policy and persecuted from mid-1976, on the basis that, as China–Vietnam tension increased, they were a security risk. In 1978 and 1979, a steady stream of them took to small, overcrowded boats to make the hazardous sea trip from Vietnam to seek sanctuary in Hong Kong, Thailand, Indonesia and Malaysia. They became known as the Vietnamese Boat People. Tens of thousands were put into refugee camps to await resettlement, amid complaints from countries in the region that they had 'reached the limit of endurance' and could not accept any new arrivals. The Boat People refugee crisis is now largely forgotten, but it serves as a timely reminder that large influxes of refugees from conflict zones, as recently in Europe, are nothing new in the world.

Eventually, the United Nations stepped in and many refugees were resettled in other countries, including in the United States and Canada, to start a new life, literally half a world away from the mayhem and madness of South-east Asia in the 1970s.

Nguyen Huu Thai, a Vietnamese man who had been the President of the Saigon Student Association in 1963, eventually became an undercover member of the Vietnamese National Liberation Front (the Vietcong). In the 1960s and 1970s, his opposition activity landed him in prison more than once.

Prison became like school for us young people in South Vietnam. I was three times in jail. In prison I learned much, not only about anti-war activities, but I learned my architecture. I could learn Chinese and my English. I became a teacher in prison.

We didn't know much about the regular war in the countryside, but prison got me close to Vietcong fighters. I recall one very strange lesson. When I taught one guerrilla, I asked him: 'Why do you study English?' He said, 'To become an interrogator of American prisoners later.' The Vietnamese fighting spirit is strong.

That same year, Dr Minh-Hoa Ta was born into an upper-middle-class ethnic Chinese family in Saigon, and found herself growing up in a country at war. In the early hours of 31 January 1968, the NLF launched a lightning attack against the South Vietnamese government: the Tet Offensive.

I remember the Tet Offensive in 1968; the fighting was right in my neighbourhood. We lived one block away from the security forces [building], and it also served as a prison for political prisoners. There was a conflict there because

Minh-Hoa Ta in front of her family's home in Saigon – and her father's precious Volkswagen – in the early 1970s.

the Communist troops were trying to rescue some of the political prisoners. The houses across my neighbourhood were completely burned down. My house was full of bullet holes. I remember I got dragged from the second floor down to the first floor. For the whole evening, we were caught inside this house, listening to grenade explosions, machine guns, people screaming outside the house. We couldn't get out. We didn't know what would happen. Everyone was terrified. I was crying. My mother kept asking me to lower my voice. I remember listening to the helicopters circling on top of the rooftops, and we had to just sit there and wait for the gunfire to cease. I remember feeling like a bomb could have dropped on top of me any moment. That was a really terrifying evening – an ordeal for at least four or five hours. In the morning, we were all allowed to get out of the house. There were casualties in the neighbourhood. There were lots of military men surrounding the entire neighbourhood. Houses were burned down across the street.

My mum sent me away with some of the neighbours to the countryside because there was a fear that there would be another gun battle. So, I was separated from my family for the next month. That was my very first time in my life that I was separated from my parents, and living in the countryside with friends of the family, with my sister. I remember every evening around 4pm, when the sun was beginning to set, my sister and I would be walking to the riverside and beginning to cry because we were missing our family so much. The family did not know how to deal with us because every day we repeated the same ritual: at four o'clock, we would walk to the riverbank and we would sit there and start to cry. After a month, they had to bring us back to the city and return us to our family.

In 1974 **Nguyen Huu Thai** *was released from his third stint in prison, though he still had to avoid police round-ups of opposition activists. By April 1975, he had joined up with a group of militant students. He was working for the overthrow of the South Vietnamese government in Saigon, hoping they could be persuaded to surrender, but expecting a prolonged battle and planning to set up refugee centres.*

We students gathered – there were also many former soldiers, even officers. They deserted from the South Vietnam army. We had many weapons, too – small weapons. We organised many committees. We asked ourselves, if the war lasts, what can we do? We must use pagodas as centres for civilian [refugees] to hide in, if the fighting continues. We organised many pagodas because we foresaw a very long war if Saigon wanted to resist.

It's a strange thing. Saigon, at the time, they had three million people only. At the last moment of the war, Saigon had five million people because people were fleeing from surrounding provinces, mostly soldiers. And Saigon began to have many disturbances from South Vietnamese army soldiers. The problem was how to keep them quiet. At the last moment, there were many people looting and doing many very bad things.

Minh-Hoa Ta

There was martial law imposed on all the people in the city. We were not allowed to leave our house. There were lots of rumours that many cities had fallen under the control of the Communists. There were lots of people frantically trying to get out of the city. We had two plane tickets to get out. However, we had ten family members and no one wanted to leave because no one believed Saigon would fall.

About three days before the fall of Saigon, there was artillery coming in to Tan Son Nhat Airport. We would be sitting inside the house, and you could feel the house was vibrated, shaken when the artillery attacked. But we had to stay put inside the house. There was no electricity. BBC Radio was the only radio station we were able to listen to – but since our English was so limited, I had to depend on my second elder brother, who was a university student, to interpret what was said in terms of what was going on with the war at that moment. We heard that there were lots of refugees beginning to pour into the capital, the US troops were being evacuated, Saigon would be captured by the North Vietnamese pretty soon. They were saying there would probably be a treaty between the US and the North Vietnamese Communists to make South Vietnam a neutral country. Even though we were afraid, at the same time there was a feeling of hope that maybe this was the end of war, that there would be some sort of peace treaty and then we'd be safe.

On 29 April 1975, as the North Vietnamese and Vietcong approached Saigon, **Minh-Hoa Ta**'s *family were increasingly anxious about her older brother – a former volunteer in the South Vietnamese army, now in the National Guard – and her two uncles in the military.*

I remember my brother was still at his National Guard station. He didn't get home. One by one, his friends arrived at my family home on April 29, telling us that he escaped from his military station, telling us that there were lots of gunfights and lots of people who got killed, and the military just abandoned their posts. He was one of the military men who deserted his post. It was complete chaos. We were so worried. We would just wait and wait for my brother and my uncles to come home.

Nguyen Huu Thai

On the night of the 29th, we heard about the shelling of Tan Son Nhat Airport, and we said, 'Maybe this is the last moment.' We organised people ready for a long resistance from South Vietnamese soldiers. We foresaw [the fight] lasting at least until the birthday of Ho Chi Minh on 19 May. But on the night of April 29, the shelling was very intense. We thought maybe this was the last moment coming. That night – I lived near the American Embassy – we saw many helicopters going back and forth and the last Americans evacuating from Saigon. We said maybe it's the last day of Saigon. For a long time, there had been very bad propaganda from America and South Vietnam that said that if the Vietcong come, maybe there would be a bloodbath, and that at least a million people would die through Vietcong atrocities.

Minh-Hoa Ta

On April 30, that morning, I saw my brother and my uncle come home, and also that morning there was a helicopter that was shot down by the military men who deserted their posts. They were angry that some people were able to get on the helicopters but they were not. That helicopter that was shot down was just two blocks from our house, and body parts were all over. We could see that from our balcony.

Nguyen Huu Thai

Early in the morning of April 30, you saw people continuing to loot everything. The last American evacuation was at about 7am, but at 9am the government declared on the Saigon Radio that they would like to hand power to the other side, and they were waiting for them to come. Saigon was so deserted – people were afraid about the situation.

We students, one group of us went directly to the radio station and television station, because we recalled about the Tet Offensive in 1968 that we could not capture the radio station, and there was no declaration from the NLF side.

I decided to go to the President's palace to make contact directly with the Minister of Information, my friend Ly Quy Chung. One month before, I hid in Ly Quy Chung's home. I said to him, 'Why don't you take a government car and we'll go directly to the radio station?' At the radio station, there were many South Vietnamese soldiers on guard and they could fire on us. But the [official] drivers refused, because they said there was shooting and they were afraid. We were discussing with them and I saw in front of me, on Thong Nhat Boulevard, an NLF tank coming. The first revolutionary tank entered the presidential palace.

*Then the commander of that first tank took the antenna off his vehicle, complete with a small red and blue NLF flag, and ran towards the palace, keen to raise the victors' colours from the palace flagpole. On the steps, **Nguyen Huu Thai**, wearing an NLF armband in the same colours, offered to show him the way up to the roof.*

I met the commander of the tank that crashed into the President's palace, Bui Quang Than, coming with the flag in his hand. The palace was bombed 20 days before, so we had to use the side elevator to come to the roof. But Commander Bui Quang Than refused to enter – it was the first time he had seen an elevator. And he says, 'If we enter in it – it looks like a coffin, very dangerous – if you enter in it and you could not get out, how do you do it?' We climbed to the roof of the palace. We had to climb a wooden ladder to reach the flagpole but the South Vietnamese flag was so big it took at least five minutes to get it down and raise the very small NLF flag. But looking at the ground before the palace, we saw many cars, many tanks and soldiers with weapons, waiting for us to get the flag up. They were waiting for a long time, at least five minutes. When we got that small NLF flag up instead of the South Vietnam flag, all the guns were firing.

When we got the flag on to the President's palace, a strange thing happened. There were three of us – myself from Danang in central Vietnam, Professor Huynh Van Tong from South Vietnam and tank commander Bui Quang Than from North Vietnam. We were three young people from three parts of Vietnam present there. I was very proud. Vietnam had become independent and unified.

Meanwhile, North Vietnamese forces were spreading across the city, including the street where **Minh-Hoa Ta** *and her family lived.*

As a child growing up in South Vietnam, we were educated to believe that Communism was evil, that the North was our enemy. At that time, I could not actually visualise a Communist person. In my mind, they were probably alien or non-human because I had never seen one. There were so many evil things said about the North Vietnamese, so my imagination of the people of the North was that they represented the force of evil and they were not really human.

By noon on 30 April – peeking out from the window because we were not allowed to leave the house – I saw trucks and trucks of South Vietnamese military men. They would get off their trucks and strip off their uniforms and were running all over in different directions. As an 11- or 12-year-old, I was shocked, in disbelief, and very confused because I didn't know what was happening.

It seemed the military had deserted their posts, and the security police one block from my house, but they left behind lots of machine guns. So, people went inside and picked up those guns and shot up into the sky. There were so many machine-gun sounds that you had to cover your ears. People were running all over the place. We just had to stay put inside the house.

Then, finally, we saw the Communist tanks pass by the street. The Communist troops, the North Vietnamese troops, drove by. Some of them were waving at us. People were beginning to pour out to the street, waving at them. I remember looking at them and I didn't know what to say. It was a chaotic scene. As I recall, there was more fear than happiness.

[This was] the first time I saw a real Communist military man: I remember looking at them in their banana-leaf green uniform, and they were smiling at us and they were quite friendly. They didn't exhibit mean or angry expressions because they were happy that they were finally taking over South Vietnam. They were sitting on top of the tank, many of them were in the back of the military trucks, some of them were marching on the streets. They were waving at the people pouring out on to the street. My impression of them was: 'Oh, so they're actually not much different than any one of us!' The only difference was that they were all in that green uniform and their sandals. Their uniforms were so different compared to the South Vietnamese military – high boots, heavy machine guns. These were just ordinary men marching on the street.

*Back at the presidential palace, with the NLF flag triumphantly aloft, **Nguyen Huu Thai**'s focus returned to the urgent question of getting the now former President, General Duong Van Minh, to the radio station, and broadcasting the message that the revolutionaries – like the President – supported reconciliation.*

Our students and soldiers were already there. The students went to find a technician and we got the radio running again. I announced first that two hours ago we raised the revolutionary flag on the President's palace, and now we brought the last President of the South Vietnam government to make a speech. Commissar Bui Van Tung accepted the surrender speech by General Minh. It was the first transmission of the revolutionary force.

When we got back from the radio station we saw in [the] street people appeared everywhere, and even entered freely to the President's palace. Before, it was very deserted. A Western journalist there said they could not imagine the ending of a war being so peaceful.

*For **Minh-Hoa Ta**'s family, life changed only by degrees – at first.* The first two months after the fall of Saigon was more like a honeymoon period, because the North Vietnamese troops were trying to understand who we are and we were trying to understand who are these people, even though we know they are North Vietnamese Communists. Our school was beginning to open again, but with a different kind of instruction; the curriculum was mostly about Ho Chi Minh, Lenin, Russia and China.

There would be one guard in charge of every five blocks of the neighbourhood, and every fourteen blocks there would be a supervisor, a security head person. If we wanted to go from one city to another we would have to ask permission. There were more restrictions that applied to the family – that you no longer own a business, or the business is no longer able to continue, and they were beginning to have food rationing. You can only have however many kilos of rice to purchase, and then we had to stand in line to receive one kilo of pork or fish for that week.

My brother, who was in the military, got a call to report to the headquarters of the supervisor of the 14th block and then he would disappear. He got sent to a re-education camp. First, my brother and then my uncle and all my brother's friends were also sent to re-education camps. My father was called to the security headquarters and got interrogated for being a landowner, and [they] questioned him [about] how he made his money, whether he had harassed his employees, the labourers that worked for him. He was put in front of a group of interrogators, who were mostly made up of some South Vietnamese – underground Communists who finally surfaced to claim themselves as Communist agents. Some of them were our neighbours, and we didn't know that they were Communist agents underground before 1975. Then, with some of the security force from the North, they began to question all the people who owned businesses. My mother would be constantly worried – what will come next?

After my older brother and my uncles were sent to re-education camp, my older brother was actually released after three months because his rank was so low, so he was not considered a significant threat. He was sent home with the requirement that he had to report to the security force. I had to go to school every morning. My former school, a Catholic school, was closed; all the papers and books were burned. I had to attend a new school, about half a mile from where I lived. My old school was just across the street.

Every morning I had to join the youth groups to ask people to sweep their front door, to keep the city clean. I had to learn how to march like a young military cadet, salute the new flag, learn the North Vietnamese propaganda, sing the song of Ho Chi Minh. No one trusted each other. The government decided to change the currency.

They wanted every household to give up all their currency, but you have to put all the $5 bills together, $20 bills together, and then you would bring it to the security head-quarters and turn over all your currency. If you had coins, those coins were still acceptable, you can use them on the market, but if you had paper currency, you had to turn [it] over. And no matter how much you turned over, each household would be given $200 in the new currency.

The evening before the announcement of the changing of the new currency, my mother gave me lots of money and then I would go out to the market with my sister. And I would just buy anything – but as a 12-year-old girl, I didn't know what to buy, I just spent the money. People say one kilo of rice is 2,000, I would give them 20,000 because we knew that tomorrow the money would become useless. That morning, my sister and I went to this black market. People were selling all kinds of stuff. I remember buying chilli pepper, buying something that, as a child, I think will be useful for me: cookies, candies, anything I want to buy. Then suddenly the security force arrived, and we threw everything behind us and left because we didn't want to get arrested, and ran home.

After the change of the currency, people no longer had money to buy things they usually had access to. I think that was a way to control how much we could eat. And because of the way the blocks [were] divided, the neighbours became suspicious of one another, and people were asked to go to the security force to testify against one another: who was a bad landlord in the past, who was a bad employer. Some people who had done bad things in the past were afraid that they would be brought up to interrogation. They would tell the Communist secu-rity force who was a bad guy before 1975, with the hope that the more people they could report, they would face a reduced sentence if they ever got brought up for the crimes that they had done.

The whole climate had changed. We no longer got in touch with our neighbours. I was told by my parents: 'Do not open your mouth. Don't tell people what we eat at home. Don't tell people where we hide the money.' My mother would hide her gold bar inside a vase, or she would have it melted and sewn on to my clothes. I had a gold belt I would put on every night before I went to sleep, and she would give me a small bag: my clothes, some medication, a bag of rice. She would tell me, 'If something happens tonight, what you need to do is take your bag and run. Remember that you have this gold belt and you can use that to survive.' So, every night I would sleep next to that bag and I would always remember to put on my gold belt.

We were living under lots of fear. On top of that, my family was ethnic Chinese, and there was conflict between China and Vietnam, so the anti-Chinese sentiment was really, really high. Many of my neighbours were being deported to the countryside to the New Economic Zone. At night, we'd hear screaming noise from the neighbours because they only came to take people away in the evening, so the evening was always the most fearful moment. Everything happened in the evening: people disappeared in the evening; the security troops would knock on your door in the evenings.

Finally, in 1978, **Minh-Hoa Ta***'s ethnic Chinese family decided to flee their Vietnamese homeland.*

My uncle was in a re-education camp. We knew that my family would be next to be sent to a re-education camp or to a New Economic Zone. My mother began to plot the escape for the whole family. But before my escape with my mother and the rest of my siblings, there was a failed escape; four of my siblings were captured and were sent to jail.

The second attempt, my mother and the rest of her children were put on a boat. My mother and a few of her friends got together and planned this escape. She had to pay a lot of gold bars to get us on the boat. I didn't know about the planning until the night before. I was told that tomorrow my brother would come and pick me up and I needed to get ready. So, that evening my mother sent me with one of my cousins to this address. I followed her directions, and I and my cousin went to the marketplace where we got instructions from a stranger passing a note to me and saying, 'This is the address where you need to go next.' When I got into this alley and into this house, I saw lots of strangers. I was reunited with my sister; I saw my mother. I remember seeing other people coming in. There were about 40 of us. We stayed in that house until 3am; I was asked to go out in a group of two and just follow the flashlight. The flashlight led me to a small fishing boat that was docked at the riverbank. When I got down to the engine room, it was already packed with so many women. Later on, I saw my sister come down; my mother came down. We were hiding inside the engine room.

I heard some commotion on the upper deck. We just had to sit there very quiet. Then I noticed the engine beginning to start. The boat started to move, and after four or five hours the fumes from the gasoline were so unbearable – I felt suffocated. I remember starting to throw up. The women started to bang on the doors – 'We need to get out!' – but we were not allowed to get out until a day later.

I don't have a good recollection of how I got to the upper deck. For the next two days, I know I was unconscious. When I woke up, we were in the middle of the ocean. There was nothing else, just the sky and this tiny little boat in this vast ocean. People were lying on the deck, on top of one another; there was not enough space for you to lay down. We were packed together like cows in a cage. I saw my brother and some of the men working on the boat – they would give us some water, but if we drank or ate, we would start throwing up again. It was my first experience of sea sickness. It took three days to overcome that. I kept telling my mother, 'Mom, I'm going to die, I'm going to die.'

Three days later, I was beginning to get used to the motion sickness, but the fear – I never realised the ocean is so huge, and I was so tiny in the middle of nowhere, and we only had each other for comfort. In four days, I heard someone say, 'It seems like we see some land.' Everyone was pouring to the front of the boat, and we saw this dark spot, like a black bean, far, far away. And then that small dot got bigger and bigger and bigger. It was land.

*Even then, the ordeal was not over: the Indonesian police pulled the boat back out into open water. Only after another three days were **Minh-Hoa Ta** and her fellow refugees finally able to reach another island – and begin again.*

I was happy that the boat journey ended there. We did not have water, we no longer had any food, and the boat was leaning to one side so there was lots of water inside the boat. I finally had a sense of hope that we were not going to die in the middle of the ocean, that we'd finally get rescued, and I knew that I would survive. The dangerous part was over. I was very happy that we had made the journey and had finally arrived in a safe place, and everyone on that boat had made it. What kept me going was a sense of hope that I had finally left Vietnam and had arrived in a new country with a new beginning.

'We fell into each other's arms'

The Cold Peace and Ostpolitik (1969–79)

As the Cold War wore on through the 1960s and 1970s, positions on both sides became entrenched, but at the same time governments in both East and West were keen to avoid unnecessary escalations. Neither Moscow nor Washington wanted to repeat the experience of the Cuban Missile Crisis in 1962, when the world had teetered on the brink of nuclear destruction. The implication of the West's passive response to the Soviet-led invasion of Czechoslovakia in 1968 was that while the United States and its allies might not like what had happened, they were reluctantly prepared to live with a divided Europe. It seemed that on all sides a consensus had emerged that 'normalising' relations, so that they became more predictable, was the safest course of action.

In the early 1960s the Soviet Union and the United States signed a Partial Test Ban Treaty to end all but underground nuclear testing. This was followed in the late 1960s by the Outer Space Treaty (to limit the use of weapons in space) and the Nuclear Non-Proliferation Treaty, and in the

1970s by the Biological Weapons Convention (to ban the production of biological weapons), the Anti-Ballistic Missile Treaty (to reduce the risk of a pre-emptive strike by limiting missile defence systems) and two agreements known as SALT (Strategic Arms Limitation Talks) I and SALT II. Alongside each treaty, summit meetings brought Cold War adversaries face to face, providing new opportunities for them to sound each other out and reduce the risk of dangerous misunderstandings, even if mutual mistrust and suspicion persisted.

Thus, in a triangular bid to warm up relations with Beijing and unsettle the Kremlin, President Richard Nixon paid a historic visit to China in 1972, the door having been opened by a ground-breaking Chinese–American ping-pong tournament and a top-secret trip to Beijing by Nixon's Secretary of State, Henry Kissinger.

Nixon then buttressed his Cold War diplomacy by making a visit to Moscow in 1972 to sign the SALT I Treaty – the first serving American President to set foot inside the Kremlin. The following year, the Soviet leader Leonid Brezhnev paid his first visit to Washington, where he and Nixon signed a series of bilateral trade agreements and a declaration that they would both do what they could to prevent nuclear war.

But it was not only the spectre of nuclear war that drove this new era of détente: it was also political expediency. For the Americans, Nixon and Kissinger, fruitful superpower diplomacy helped offset the domestic fallout from the Vietnam War disaster. For Brezhnev and his Politburo colleagues, the aim was to gain greater international acceptance of the Soviet Union while retaining a free hand to keep an authoritarian grip at home. They also wanted greater recognition and greater security for their client states in Eastern Europe. The first steps towards realising that ambition came in 1969, in a drive to improve relations between the two Germanies, inspired by the first Social Democrat to lead West Germany, newly elected Chancellor Willy Brandt.

Throughout the 1960s, East Germany had been in lockdown, ruled by Walter Ulbricht's hard-line Stalinist dictatorship, which was deeply suspicious of the capitalist West. The conservative Christian Democrats in power in West Germany maintained a similarly hostile stance. They insisted that their neighbour to the east was an illegal obstacle to the ultimate goal of German reunification, and were even prepared to break off diplomatic relations with countries such as Cuba and Yugoslavia that recognised the East German state.

But Willy Brandt had been Mayor of West Berlin when the Berlin Wall went up in 1961 and was committed to pursuing reconciliation, well aware that relieving tensions would make life easier for people on both sides of the divided city and improve cross-border commerce. His advisers also argued that closer contact with the East was a better way to undermine Communist rule in the long run than maintaining a hostile distance. So, he launched a fresh approach towards East Germany called the New Eastern Policy or *Neue Ostpolitik*.

Willy Brandt's Ostpolitik, as it was known, aimed to normalise relations between West Germany and Eastern Europe. Erich Honecker, the new East German Communist leader who replaced the recalcitrant Ulbricht on Moscow's instructions, responded positively. Brandt signed treaties with the Soviet Union and its satellite states, recognising East Germany's existing borders with both Poland and West Germany, and in 1970 he travelled to East Germany for the first ever summit between a West German Chancellor and his East German counterpart. His Ostpolitik also underpinned the Quadripartite Agreement on Berlin signed by the Occupying Powers in 1971, which confirmed the city's post-war status and expanded cross-border ties.

Most controversially, in December 1972 Brandt's government signed a 'Basic Treaty' with East Germany an implicit acknowledgement by both sides of the other's existence, thereby, paving the way for broader recognition. Before this, West Germany had insisted that it alone repre-sented the entire German nation. Now East Germany had acquired a new legitimacy. Some West Germans welcomed it as a way to promote 'change through rapprochement' and break down East Germany's siege mentality. Others – especially refugees who had escaped from the Communist East – saw it as a betrayal.

The practical impact of all this on German citizens was considerable. Since 1963, brief visits to East Berlin had at times been possible with *Passierscheine* (day passes), but Ostpolitik substantially opened up access for West German citizens, including West Berliners, to travel to the East, as permits became easier to obtain and more crossing points were established along the border. The East German government saw it as a chance to prove to Western visitors that their socialist state worked and they invested heavily in making East Berlin into a show-case. But Ostpolitik also meant that West Germans could travel throughout East Germany and see the country as it really was.

Another result of the greater contact and easing of restrictions was the impact on the East. It was possible to make direct phone calls between East and West Berlin again, though only a lucky few in the East had private tele-phones. Families were reunited; East Germany even 'sold' some of its political prisoners to the West. Their departure to freedom made a handsome profit to East Germany's stricken coffers. And a degree of dissent was able to creep

Soldiers of the People's Liberation Army reading the *Words of Mao Zedong*, often known as the 'little red book', 1971.

Cultural Revolution poster from the People's Republic of China, c. 1968. The text at the bottom says, 'The Many accomplish great things.'

Demonstrators climb on board trucks in the centre of Prague on the first day of the occupation, 21 August 1968.

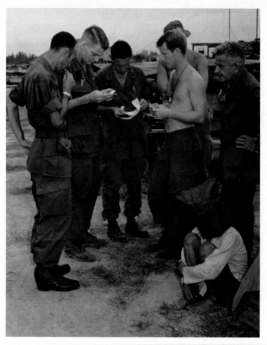

US soldiers with a suspected Vietcong fighter captured during an attack on an American outpost near the Cambodian border, 20 December 1968.

US troops waiting at the Bien Hoa Air Terminal for a National Airlines flight home after finishing their tours of duty, 15 February 1968.

Anti-Vietnam War demonstration outside the United Nations Building in New York City, 15 April 1967.

Crowds surround the train carrying Chilean Presidential candidate Salvador Allende on a whistle-stop campaign tour, 1964.

A convoy of South African Defence Force vehicles crosses a pontoon bridge over the Kavango River, upon the withdrawal from southern Angola, 30 August 1988.

Residents of Khost inspect foreign weapons seized during a military operation in the area of Jawhara, Afghanistan, 9 June 1986.

Strike leader Lech Wałęsa stands on a platform at the gates of the Lenin Shipyard in Gdańsk, Poland, telling the shipyard workers that the strike was now over, 9 September 1980.

Berliners celebrate the border opening at the Berlin Wall near the Brandenburg Gate, 10 November 1989.

People from all over Germany celebrate with sparklers on the Berlin Wall, 11 November 1989.

A huge crowd celebrates German Reunification under the Brandenburg Gate in Berlin, 3 October 1990.

Thousands of people form a human chain from Tallinn, Estonia, to Vilnius, Lithuania, 23 August 1989.

Tanks on the streets in Moscow during the *coup d'état*, August 1991.

People decorate tanks with flowers in downtown Moscow, 20 August 1991.

in to the East. Greater freedoms were given to Protestant churches – places that in the 1980s would develop into centres of opposition debate. Comedy became more daring and rock music became popular among the East German youth – perhaps more potent symbols of disaffection than the Communist authorities realised.

But if the point of Ostpolitik had been to break the old stalemate at the heart of Europe, ironically it also created a new one. By easing contacts between East and West Germany, a new status quo emerged that soon pushed the idea of eventual German reunification off into a realm that began to seem unimaginable.

This was underscored by another diplomatic breakthrough, seen as the high point of détente: the broader international acceptance of the political divisions of postwar Europe, which came in the summer of 1975 with the signing of the Helsinki Accords. Thirty-five nations from East and West agreed to respect one another's sovereignty and the inviolability of their borders, refrain from the threat or use of force, and – in theory at least – respect human rights and the self-determination of peoples.

What the Soviet Union wanted from the treaty was an acknowledgement from the West that Europe's post-war division was there to stay and that the boundaries of the Communist countries of the Eastern Bloc would not be challenged. The Soviet leader Leonid Brezhnev hailed it as a triumph.

But his KGB chief, Yuri Andropov, was more circumspect – and with good reason. In time, the West would fasten on the clause that called for human rights to be respected and use it as a new means to hold the Soviet Union to account. And a vocal band of dissidents across the Eastern Bloc would use the Helsinki Accords as a yardstick to attack their governments' approach to human rights and individual freedoms, an insubordination that would have momentous consequences.

Nonetheless, in the short term neither Ostpolitik nor the Helsinki Accords and the process of détente it signified could change the fact that, in the late 1970s, the Soviet Union and its allies were still police states under rigid Communist control. In East Germany, the fundamentals of the dictatorship, symbolised by the omnipresence of the Stasi secret police, remained firmly in place.

And détente did not last. It had already stalled by the time the Soviets intervened in Afghanistan in 1979. A year later, the chill in relations worsened when the United States responded by boycotting the Moscow Olympics. The boycott was initiated by President Carter; Ronald Reagan's election as US President later in 1980 returned the world to heightened tensions and new fears of war.

So, did the 'Cold Peace' of the 1970s lay some of the groundwork for the transformations of the 1980s that would reunify Europe and end the Cold War? Or did it only bring a semblance of dialogue and better relations, solidifying a status quo that made change less likely?

On balance, it probably did both, sowing some seeds that would later bear fruit, but also reinforcing a sense that the world was now permanently frozen into rival ideological blocs that had accommodated each other's existence and cemented the division of Germany.

*Cousins **Eva Eberbeck** and **Ingrid Bartel** had been separated by the post-war division of occupied Germany: Ingrid lived in West Berlin, and Eva lived in Falkensee, a town in East Germany to the north-west of Berlin. This meant they could see each other only with difficulty.*

Eva Eberbeck

My father wanted to go and live in Falkensee, so we ended up in the East. Then he left us in 1951 and my mother was left in this unloved house, alone with us children. Then we were really cut off.

My cousin could visit us because she had my Pioneer [Communist youth organisation] ID card. There was no photo. She had to learn my name and my birthday by heart. She wasn't allowed to slip up had she been checked. The card was valid until I was 14 years old.

Ingrid Bartel

I mainly went in the summer holidays with my cousin Eva's card and spent several days in Falkensee. Back then, only from the age of 15 did one get a proper passport. At that age, we both looked very childlike, very slim, and I knew all the school information for my cousin, so if the People's Police had not let me out of the railway station at Falkensee, I would have been very knowledgeable. But I was always scared and when I went back on Sundays, my father was always standing at the S-Bahn train station Beusselstrasse [in Moabit, West Berlin] to pick me up, so I always had to take a certain train at a certain time so that my father could be sure he had his daughter back.

With the construction of the Berlin Wall in August 1961, even these meetings became impossible – and further separations were in store.

Eva Eberbeck

The evening before, I was out dancing and the next morning I had been sleeping for a very long time when my mum came into my room and said, 'Eva, the border is closed.'

My brother was away on holiday with his girlfriend. A few days later, he returned from the holidays and, five days after that, he fled across the border to the West, across the barbed wire.

The family was torn apart. My brother was gone, and later I realised that we had grown apart. That, of course, was a sad experience. In the end, my brother became a proper West German. He didn't understand us properly any more. He adopted a completely different mentality. I also have to say, in his defence, that he was just 20 years old when he left.

*Having fled the country in 1953, **Annemarie Knecht** had already seen enough of East Germany to make a rapid decision when she heard the Wall was going up.*

I married in 1961. My husband and I were in East Berlin with my parents-in-law. They had a summerhouse in Rahnsdorf. And in the night, we heard tanks and a colleague of my husband came by and said: 'You have to make sure you get back home again. They're raising fences and closing the border!' We packed our things and drove home. There was also a pretty strict control at the border.

In East Germany, everything was grey on grey. First, there were always strict controls at the border. We always had to show everything – for instance, when we brought presents, as one did, like coffee or chocolate, and all the things that did not exist as such in the GDR. You had to open everything, unpack everything. It was an economy of scarcity over there. Although those in East Berlin were always better off than the people who lived in the 'Zone' [the GDR]. They were even worse off than those who lived in Berlin.

The introduction of day passes in 1963 allowed West Berliners to visit relatives in East Berlin.

Eva Eberbeck
For the first time, in 1966, we met at my cousin's friends' house in East Berlin. We hadn't seen each other for five years.

Ingrid Bartel
We fell into each other's arms. We were certainly a bit taller. She had married in the meantime, her hairdo had changed, but we had remained close through our letters. And in the meantime, packages were always sent across in response to their requests. So, there was still a constant correspondence – we shared our thoughts. There was no alienation.

Annemarie Knecht
In 1970 my grandmother died in Barby, at the river Elbe near Magdeburg. It's a small town. No one from my family, not even my mother, could go to the funeral. I was the only one who had a West German passport, and could travel via Braunschweig [West Germany]. First, I travelled to my cousin in Braunschweig, and from there I went by train to Magdeburg to the funeral. That was an event. That was a great excitement. At the border at Braunschweig, shortly before Magdeburg, where the border station was, I had to get off, and I had to unpack all my things and had to display them on the table. It took half an hour – all my hygiene articles, and I was a young woman – and I had to unpack everything, then pack everything back in, and then they asked where I wanted to go. I said I would like to go to my grandmother's funeral. Then I was allowed to go back on the train and continue my journey. In Magdeburg, my aunt picked me up. Then we drove home and met up with my mother's family. It was a nice episode, although a bit sad because my grandmother had died and then the funeral. I was only there for two days and then back home.

Eva Eberbeck.

Ingrid Bartel.

She brought me back to Magdeburg. My mother loved onion sausage, and my aunt gave me a small piece of 100 or 125g. I was supposed to give this to my mum as a surprise. And I boarded the train and I reached the border again. Once more, I had to get off and show everything – and I had this little package with the sausage. He said, 'You are not allowed to take that with you.' Then I had to get off, pack a parcel and had to pack the sausage into a box and return it by post to my aunt in Barby. That was my highlight. That was terrible. That was an excitement. The train had to wait until I had finished. Then I could board again and continue the journey. I will never forget the way they had taken me apart. And I was alone. No one from the family was there because no one could be.

The bigger changes as a result of Ostpolitik, which opened up access to East Germany from the West, allowed **Peter Pragal**, *a West German journalist, to take up one of the new openings that had begun to appear.*

In 1972, under the social democratic-liberal government in Bonn, there were negotiations which resulted in the Grundlagenvertrag (the Basic Treaty), in which the relationship between the two German states was defined. In the wake of this there was an additional agreement, regarding the exchange of journalists.

Of course, it was clear that through this Ostpolitik possibilities had opened up, so, even when I did not have correspondent status any more, I could visit my friends in East Berlin.

My friends, including the ones in the West, approved of Ostpolitik. But I also knew people who said that it was a concession to the GDR and you can't make any pacts with a dictatorship. They considered the fact that the GDR had been recognised as a state as a wrong decision.

*In 1971, **Annemarie Knecht** and her husband moved to Steinstücken, where their son **Lorenz** was born in 1974. Steinstücken was a tiny enclave of West German territory to the south-west of West Berlin, enclosed by East Germany. So for her, Ostpolitik made a big difference.*

Annemarie Knecht

In 1972 Willy Brandt was in government and they bought this corridor of the GDR and then a free access was built. They started to build it at the beginning of 1972, and it was finished in September 1972. Then also the bus could enter it. Everybody could come through.

I remember that at the beginning we still had to go via Friedrichstrasse. At that time, we did not go that often. Maybe four times a year. And Friedrichstrasse was terrible. I can still remember this big station there, and we had to get through and the people were all afraid and trembling. And it was always done with fright and sweat. It was strenuous. Afterwards in 1972, when things became easier, we could simply drive by car directly via Dreilinden to Caputh and to Potsdam to our friends, and that was considerably better.

In the sixties, you could only cross with *Passierscheine* at certain times of the year; in the seventies it became easier. In the seventies we went once a month.

We saved hours. With waiting at the border, it sometimes took one or two hours, but otherwise, it would only have been half an hour from where we lived. Before that it took longer because we first had to drive into Berlin and go via Bornholmer Strasse [a crossing point in the district of Wedding]. It took at least three or four hours until we could see each other.

Lorenz Knecht

I can vividly remember the visits to the Forum Steglitz. It was a highlight for me as a child because it was a shopping centre, and I can still see the clerks in my mind's eye as they sat there in a row in their sad grey uniforms. It was basically always the usual procedure: queuing, waiting. The room was also completely furnished with GDR articles. As a child, that was always a stark contrast to what one knew from the West, flooded in consumer goods. From then on, it was actually rather uncomplicated: you applied and could then travel pretty comfortably via the Dreilinden crossing point in West Berlin to Caputh in East Germany.

I spent many weeks there as a child with friends and family. We rowed in the boat a lot, along the Havel. It was a great childhood. I did not know anything different. In that sense, it is difficult to draw a comparison to children who grew up in West Germany, perhaps. That was my lived normality. I did not feel I was lacking anything. And as I saw it as a child, the friends and acquaintances in Caputh were not lacking anything either, apart from that one could not visit the same Western places as we could.

Ostpolitik meant **Ingrid Bartel** *and* **Eva Eberbeck** *could see each other much more easily too.*

Ingrid Bartel

We got the permission to visit relatively quickly – that is, within one week. Of course, we had to agree on dates first, always through letters. There were always the bank holidays, Easter, Whitsun, Christmas. My cousin has her birthday before Christmas, so we went in December to Falkensee.

Lorenz and Annemarie Knecht.

These were the usual days, but you mustn't forget we were all working. [We] saw each other four or five times a year, but one could not go every month because the effort was very big: applying for *Passierscheine*, collecting them, buying things to take, getting through the border controls.

And you never knew whether or not your car would be pulled aside – that is, getting out of the car, opening the boot, unpacking things, lifting the seat in the back. They checked the car with a mirror from below. You were always glad when you had got this procedure behind you and had not been asked to go to an extra little house, where the whole car would have been taken apart. Luckily, I never experienced that personally.

One aspect of Ostpolitik was that it became slightly less risky to watch West German TV in the East – if, that is, you could afford a TV – which brought access to Western pop culture.

Eva Eberbeck

We never watched East German television, we only watched West German television. We went to the theatre a few times but we had to leave early to get the last train home. That was not fun for us any more. We were a bit cut off in Falkensee.

We also only listened to hits from the West; we did not listen to Eastern music – the music from the East we found daft. We were not oppositional, but we did not take part either. We were really orientated to the West. Since the broadcast antennae were nearby, we could watch Western television, listen to Western radio. The East did not interest us at all. Only what you needed to know for school.

Peter Pragal

There was a rock scene that was embraced by the youth. They had certain liberties. 'Kabarett' – political cabarets – had to submit their programmes. Some lines, some scenes, were censored. But people understood what was meant anyway. The skill of reading between the lines was well developed. In the theatre, too. For example, when there was a line by Schiller saying, 'Sire, give us freedom of thought', then they all applauded. This was not associated with the conditions back then but with the present day. For artists, there was always a very grateful audience. Clearly a more appreciative and attentive audience than was common in the West.

Another impact of Ostpolitik was a huge rise in the volume of phone calls between West and East. But for most people in the East, phone contact was still difficult.

Eva Eberbeck

We did not have a telephone. Only after the fall of the Wall were we allowed to apply for a telephone. In the GDR there were no telephones, only for particular people like doctors, or for the privileged, or in houses where there had always been a telephone. There were only very few telephone connections in Falkensee. We had to go to the post office to register a phone call, but not to the West because the connection only came at night, when the post office was closed. That was utopian for us – we could not telephone.

I know in a distant neighbourhood there was a telephone, but we would never have dared to go there and ask because the people in that house had Communist leanings. And in Berlin there were telephone boxes with coins. When I wanted to speak with my relatives in West Berlin, I first had to go to East Berlin in order to arrange a meeting or say other important things.

Peter Pragal

At the beginning, I made phone calls from my flat. There was a telephone that was sometimes out of order. There were still construction works nearby and sometimes a cable was cut, and then the telephone was not working again. In addition, it was a so-called double line. This means the line was also used by someone else and when the other person, who remained unknown to me, made a call, my telephone did not work. Then I had to go to West Berlin because the *Süddeutsche Zeitung* [the newspaper for which Peter wrote] also had a West Berlin correspondent bureau and filed my articles from there. At some point, I finally got an office. It was in the district of Mitte, the former Clara-Zetkin-Strasse that is now the Dorotheenstrasse, with a view of the Reichstag and the Wall. But I wasn't always reachable there, so I applied for an answering machine at my publishers. They granted it immediately and it was delivered, but I had to register it in the GDR.

Then a few people came and said they had to take it with them, it had to be examined. That took a while and at some point I got it back. And later, from my Stasi files, it emerged that they thought that this apparatus had a remote retrieval function, a mechanism which they weren't familiar with back then, where you could listen to these recorded messages remotely. But that was not the case. I could only listen to the received messages in my office. They even asked for money for that examination, but I protested and said: 'No, that is out of the question!' And then the matter was finished.

Annemarie Knecht

When we came for a visit, my friend said, 'Now, we need to go for a walk in the woods,' so that we could talk freely with one another. Because they were watched everywhere, even on the telephone. When we spoke on the phone it always clicked. Then we knew they were listening.

Ostpolitik may have made crossing the border to East Germany easier, but the East German secret police – the Stasi – kept a close eye on incomers from the capitalist West.

Peter Pragal

The Stasi was set on us without a gap. There were surveillance reports ... so when we brought the children to the kindergarten, they followed us by car. They watched everything. But there was one thing I was surprised they had not picked up on. I had a friend in the neighbourhood and nearby there was a swimming pool with a sauna. And he said, 'I will take you with me one day.' And then we went there. You had to fix a date and time weeks in advance and there were other people sitting there. By then, I had already developed a discerning eye. And when I looked at them, they had strange haircuts. They had this uniform cut, which they had in the army as well as in the People's Police, probably at the Stasi, too, which was common there. When I looked at them more closely, I thought, they must be from the security forces, and they had no inkling that the class enemy was sitting among them in the sauna. They were chatting about things from day-to-day life which did not appear in the newspaper. That was a nice source of information. I was surprised because otherwise they always picked up everything. But that seemed somehow to have slipped their notice.

Annemarie Knecht

The Stasi always knew exactly when we were there. The cars always parked there at a certain distance. You could always see them right away and we knew they were watching us.

Peter Pragal and his family on the East side of the Brandenburg Gate, 1970s.

The surveillance was creepy, it was really bad. My friend's husband was a manager in a big company of rose cultivators, and the Stasi came and urged him to work as a spy to pump us for information. He was supposed to write things down and always watch us. He refused. Then they asked my friend's mother, and even the children at school were urged to work for the Stasi. It was really severe. Even my daughter was stopped at the border. She studied physics back then, and they would have liked to have her work for the Stasi too.

*Dissidents began to be in public view after the Helsinki Accords in 1975 but – as **Peter Pragal** saw – dissent still had strict limits.*

The climate was actually not that bad. You had hopes that there could be a change towards more liberalism. The first backlash was the expulsion of [the singer and poet] Wolf Biermann, and the protests against it. And intellectuals, writers, artists who protested against this expulsion were also put under pressure. And in cultural politics, stricter criteria were applied.

There was this Riesaer Petition. A doctor called Karl-Heinz Nitschke [...] formulated a petition demanding the freedom of movement. He collected signatures among friends and acquaintances in this little town of Riesa. Then he came to East Berlin and wanted to get in contact with correspondents in order to make the petition public, because we had a special function. These Western journalists differed from Western correspondents who were based in Moscow: when you were in Moscow, you just reported for your audience from Moscow, but we did not only report from East Berlin for the viewers and readers in West Germany, but also for the citizens of the GDR. Our reports always fed back into the East via TV and radio.

Then the people who initiated that petition came to me, and I reported about it. I also took it to West Berlin, where it reached the right places. These people then got into deep trouble. I went to Riesa myself and spoke to the people who had initiated it and who had been charged and imprisoned. Later they were sold to the Federal Republic.

Ostpolitik had helped to normalise the division of Germany, but that made the idea of a radical change seem all the more distant.

Peter Pragal

Revolution was not foreseeable. Even in the middle of the eighties I didn't expect that the GDR would end the way it did end.

Ingrid Bartel

We believed that the Cold War would certainly last our whole lives.

Annemarie Knecht

We believed that it would not go that fast. We thought it would take longer. The Cold War – we believed it would last forever, although we quietly hoped 'Well, maybe one day it will be different,' but we did not believe it.

'The country was left with no protection at all'

The Angolan Civil War (1975–2002)

By the mid-1970s, the Cold War had moved into a new phase. Europe's division was now a fact of life. Further afield, and complicating the new 'Great Game', a nuclear-armed China had joined the fray. Skirmishes on the Soviet–China border had been alarming but had not turned into a full-scale war and, given the stockpiles of missiles building up, all sides seemed to want to keep it that way. The deadly logic of the doctrine of 'Mutually Assured Destruction' had also delivered détente between the United States and the Soviet Union, yielding not just the SALT 1 arms-control deal, but also an agreement between Washington and Moscow that they would not – in theory at least – take advantage of each other by upsetting the equilibrium in the 'Third World'.

Yet precisely because it was too dangerous for the major powers to go to war with each other, the temptation to do it through intermediaries was becoming greater. The United States' experience in Vietnam had been a salutary lesson in what could go wrong, but – despite détente – each side continued to look for ways to secure strategic advantage and anchor influence, and on occasion swoop in to prop up smaller allies under threat. Wars through surrogates were becoming part of the new playbook across the world.

Nowhere was this truer than in Africa, where the old European colonial powers had for the previous two decades been in the process of pulling out. For the Soviet Union, always keen to couch its arguments in terms of an anti-imperialist struggle and international solidarity with the oppressed, this was fertile territory for enlisting new Marxist converts. The Americans, too, were on the lookout for new friends. Over the course of the 1950s and 1960s, more than 30 African countries had gained their independence and some were inevitably eager for big-power political patronage and economic aid, plus the military arms and training needed to fight local wars.

From 1975 onwards, one country in south-west Africa where a Cold War proxy conflict would unfold with quite extraordinary complexity was oil- and mineral-rich Angola. Until the mid-1970s, Angola, like Mozambique and Guinea-Bissau, was still under Portuguese rule. Portugal was one of the last European powers to relinquish its hold on its colonial subjects. The Portuguese government at the time was a right-wing authoritarian dictatorship. It was tolerated as a member of the NATO alliance because of its anti-Communist stance, even though its attempts to keep the lid on in its colonies involved rigid military control. But at home the cost of the counter-insurgency campaigns against colonial rebellions was unpopular.

On 25 April 1974 a group of military officers staged a coup to depose the Portuguese government in the 'Carnation Revolution', so called because of the carnations reportedly stuffed in the muzzles of soldiers' rifles and in the buttonholes on their uniforms by the many in Lisbon who celebrated the end of the dictatorship. Portugal's new leaders declared they would return the country to democratic rule, introduce economic reforms and rid the country of its burdensome, troublesome colonies. A loosening of colonial ties began without delay.

At this point, the conflict in Angola was already multi-layered. The insurgency fighting for independence from Portugal was divided into three separate guerrilla factions, each with a different tribal allegiance and their own constellation of international backers – a three-way battle for power, and the basis, once the Portuguese withdrew, for a protracted civil war.

The MPLA (Movimento Popular de Libertação de Angola/Popular Movement for the Liberation of Angola), led by Agostinho Neto, had grown out of the Angolan Communist Party and was socialist in orientation, with strong support from the educated urban elite in the capital, Luanda. Before independence, it was already receiving aid and training from the Soviet Union and from Fidel Castro's regime in Cuba. This dramatically increased as the civil war got underway.

The FNLA (Frente Nacional de Libertação de Angola/ National Front for the Liberation of Angola) had started as a separatist movement in the north, and had strong ties to its anti-Communist leader Holden Roberto's brother-in-law, Mobutu Sese Seko, the US-backed dictator in neighbouring Zaire (as the former Belgian Congo was then called). The FNLA was receiving covert backing from the US and Israel, among other countries, via Zaire. It also received some support from the Chinese.

The third group, UNITA (União Nacional para a Independência Total de Angola/National Union for the Total Independence of Angola) emerged in 1966 when its flamboyant leader, 'Dr' Jonas Savimbi, broke away from the FNLA to create his own liberation movement, supported by the country's largest tribal group. Among several flirtations with left-wing movements, Savimbi had established ties with China, and at one point early on UNITA presented itself as a Maoist-schooled alternative to the pro-Soviet MPLA. But by 1974 Savimbi had moved to the right to become a resolute anti-Communist, and his main backers became South Africa and the Americans.

At first, it looked as though the three rebel movements were prepared to share power. A joint settlement, brokered by the Organisation of African Unity, was signed by all parties in January 1975, with an agreement to hold elections and fix a deadline for the Portuguese withdrawal to coincide with the start of Angola's independence on 11 November 1975. But almost immediately trust between the three separate liberation movements broke down and, as each side vied for the upper hand, egged on by rival outside powers, the country slid into civil war.

The self-serving jockeying between the superpowers and others with a stake in the conflict had begun before the January 1975 agreement was signed. Once it had collapsed, new injections of outside military aid raised the stakes. What might have appeared a nasty little civil war tucked away in a corner of south-west Africa turned into a crucial Cold War subplot.

The Soviet Union, believing the United States was weakened by its experience in Vietnam, saw a chance to extend its footprint in southern Africa, where it already had important ties to the partly Communist anti-apartheid movement in South Africa. The Chinese wanted to counter Moscow's assertiveness. The United States likewise wanted to keep the Soviets at bay, both to stop Angola's mineral resources from falling into Soviet hands and to forestall any risk of Moscow furthering a bigger ambition to extend its influence all the way down to the tip of South Africa, where it would be able to control the strategic sea routes around the Cape. The United States was also keen to re-establish its global reach after the failure of Vietnam, although attempts by the US government to ramp up military aid were blocked by Congress, which had experienced enough of involvement in distant foreign adventures. Other countries pitching into the fracas to back their preferred sides included Romania and North Korea.

The two most important interventions came from Castro in Cuba and the apartheid government of South Africa. Castro – no puppet of Moscow – saw the conflict as a chance to spearhead the spread of Communist revolution across Africa. Cuba's eagerness to assist the MPLA goaded the Soviet Union into increasing its own involvement. South Africa – which likewise had its own agenda beyond Washington's – entered the war as a backer of Savimbi's UNITA, primarily to stop the MPLA from turning Angola into a launching pad for attacks either on its client state of Namibia or on South Africa itself.

On one side, Fidel Castro poured in thousands of Cuban troops and shiploads of arms to help the Marxist MPLA. On the other side, the South Africans, collaborating covertly with the CIA, sent in thousands of their soldiers – both members of the South African Defence Force and mercenaries – to fight alongside FNLA and UNITA rebels. The two sides dramatically clashed head-on in fierce fighting in November 1975. The Cubans stopped the South African advance in its tracks at Ebo, in what was a decisive victory. This left the way open for the MPLA to take decisive control of the capital, Luanda. On 11 November 1975, the date set for Angolan independence, the MPLA leader, Agostinho Neto, declared a new socialist People's Republic of Angola with himself as Angola's first President.

It was a setback for both South Africa and, hovering in the background, the United States, and it proved to be a turning point. Both in Washington and in Moscow, the assessment was that the Americans, having failed in Vietnam, had now 'lost' Angola. It would embolden the Soviet Union to get involved in other African wars, most notably between Ethiopia and Somalia, and subsequently in Central America, later episodes in the Cold War saga of Third World entanglements.

But the tussle for power in Angola was by no means over. By early 1976 the MPLA was in control not just of Luanda but the oil-rich Atlantic coastline. Its People's Republic of Angola was swiftly recognised by the Soviet Union, and a year later by the Organisation of African Unity, though an application for UN membership was vetoed by the United States. In 1977 the ruling MPLA adopted Marxism–Leninism as its official ideology, turning Angola into a fully fledged Soviet client state. But the civil war did not end there; it would go on for years, until well after the demise of the Soviet Bloc.

Fidel Castro continued to supply the MPLA government with a steady stream of military aid. Over a 15-year period, some 300,000 Cuban troops rotated through the country. In the 1980s the Reagan administration increased support to UNITA as part of its mission not just in Africa, but in Afghanistan and Central America, to push back the tide of Communism. Savimbi, dressed in his signature red beret and army fatigues, was invited to meet President Reagan in the White House, where he was feted as an important bulwark against Communism in Southern Africa.

Finally, an Angolan peace accord was signed in 1988, part of a wider pattern of regional conflicts winding down as the Cold War petered out. But even then, in Angola the violence did not stop. Jonas Savimbi was still fighting from his hideouts in the bush, on and off, until he was killed by government troops in 2002. By this time, the rest of the world had moved on, and the Cold War was long gone. But in Angola it left a grim legacy: the 27-year civil war left an estimated 500,000 people dead, one-third of the population displaced, and the country littered with 15 million landmines. After Korea, Vietnam and Afghanistan, it would be remembered as one of the deadliest of the Cold War's surrogate conflicts.

Osvaldo Leitão was born into an Angolan family with a tradition of fighting for the country's liberation from colonial rule.

My father belonged to the Movimento para a Independencia da Angola [Movement for the Independence of Angola] in the early fifties, along with my uncles and other nationalists. When I was two years old in 1959, the PIDE [Polícia Internacional e de Defesa do Estado/International and State Defence Police, the secret police of the Salazar regime in Portugal] arrested a group of nationalists, people that were fighting for the independence of Angola, and my father was part of that group. The PIDE said that the grounds for arrest were belonging to a secret and subversive group.

So, after the trial my dad and his group spent two years under arrest in Luanda, in a prison called Casa de Reclusão. In 1961, after 4 February [when the first armed attack on the Portuguese by pro-independence groups was made], they were sent to Tarrafal in Cape Verde [a town in the northern part of the island], and my dad stayed there for another eight years. So, my dad was under arrest for some ten years; imagine how it was for me: I was four years old when he went to Cape Verde. I recall perfectly going with my mother there, and the images are indelibly printed on my mind. Time passed, we grew older; we gained political consciousness from what we heard around us and the unjust imprisonments; the discussions of the students in high school; and this was necessary for us to dedicate our lives to the independence of our country.

In April 1974, **Willem van der Waals** *of the South African Defence Force was in Rundu, on the border between Portugal's colony, Angola, and South African-controlled South West Africa (now Namibia), as some of the companies of his battalion were to be deployed there later in the year on counter-insurgency operations.*

In the officers' mess in Rundu, on 25 April, in the early evening, over a beer, I heard rumours of a *coup d'état* in Portugal, and some of my colleagues asked me as an old Angola hand what I said about it. I said, 'This is serious – as far as I'm concerned this is even more serious than a change in government in South Africa. This means war.' There were three liberation movements in Angola and they would tackle each other and it would be a civil war – and in the process South Africa would surely become involved some way or another.

By 1974 **Osvaldo Leitão** *was 17 and a high-school student.*
When we heard what was happening in Portugal, of course we were surprised and at the same time we thought there would be a possibility of finally getting independence for Angola. For sure they're going to meet and sit with us, we thought, [...] and see how the process is going to develop.

Osvaldo Leitão in the 1970s.

After a few weeks, I became part of the MPLA officially. I ran away to the bush, to better contribute to the liberation of my country.

I received my first training in fighting at the same time as training in political consciousness, over a few months, because it was very important that the two were done together, so that we learned about the [reason] behind the fight of the MPLA. After a few months of training in the tactics of fighting, there came agreements with the Portuguese authorities [Accordos de 1974, after the Carnation Revolution], and of course the MPLA at that time had to transform itself from a guerrilla force into an organised army, an army that would be suitable for a newly independent country, to promote the national interest. So, I was lucky to belong to the first group of young people from the city to go abroad to the USSR to receive training in Simferopol in Ukraine, by the Black Sea – a very intensive period of training with Russian military people for six months. We received very intense training from morning to night, and we watched propaganda films from the Second World War.

*In September 1975 **Willem van der Waals** was secretly deployed into Angola by South Africa.*
I followed in newspapers the start of the civil war and the fact that the MPLA was strongly supported by Russia, with a lot of military supplies from Russia and with Cuban military training missions. Then at one stage – I was then a lecturer at our Defence College – Major-General Viljoen [Director General Operations of the South African Defence Force General Staff], whom I knew personally very well – asked me as an old Angola hand what I thought. I said, 'Well, General, given the

Russian and Cuban support for the MPLA, we should have been involved already on the side of the pro-Western movements.' He asked me whether I would be prepared to go in.

I said I would like to become involved on the side of UNITA. Within a week, I was tasked to go into Angola to Savimbi and to assist him. My orders were: number one, [...] the MPLA advance on Angola's second biggest city Novo Lisboa [Huambo since 1975], which was for all purposes UNITA's capital – the MPLA advance must be stopped. We knew the MPLA were making use of armoured vehicles, possibly even tanks. Secondly, hold the city of Nova Lisboa at all costs until 11 November, Independence Day, because we would have been out of Angola by the 11th. Furthermore, to train two brigades – 3,000–4,000 people – of UNITA, one defensively, the other one offensively, within 50 days. That was a virtually impossible task. And then to serve Dr Savimbi with strategic advice.

On 23 September, I landed in Silva Porto [now Kuito] and met Savimbi, who was very surprised to find out that I spoke Portuguese. I informed him that I had served with the Portuguese for about three years as the camouflaged South African Military Attaché. I also informed Savimbi that the Portuguese had a six-figure grid reference of his position, and said to Savimbi: 'Knowing that, I asked the Portuguese, "But why don't you go out and kill him?"' And he said, 'Oh you did, did you!' And that's when our friendship started.

*In the bush south of Silva Porto [Kuito], **Willem van der Waals** was busy training UNITA battalion, when he had an encounter that underlined the way the Angolan conflict had become a square on the global chessboard.*

I noticed periodically from a distance that there was a young white man in the presence of Savimbi, and there were no white people left in Silva Porto or that area – they'd all left. I said to Savimbi, 'Look, our involvement here is top secret – who is that person?' He said, 'Don't worry, he's a friend.' I didn't see the friend for a long time until the war really started getting hot. One day, he walked into my operations room and asked, 'How's the military situation?' I asked him who he was, to which he replied, 'Never mind – I want to know what's happening.' I said I wasn't going to tell him until he identified himself. He said his name was Skip and he was from the CIA.

Osvaldo Leitão remembers military materiel had been arriving from the USSR since August, including BRDMs – Soviet armoured vehicles – and mortars. His section of the MPLA was charged with trying to stop UNITA and the South Africans taking the western cities of Lobito and Benguela, by pushing them eastwards, back towards their de facto capital, Nova Lisboa (now Huambo). In early October 1975, as independence drew closer, he and his MPLA comrades found themselves fighting UNITA at Balombo, halfway between the two sides' strongholds.

We surprised the enemy. I was the one who commanded that battle. It was just us, the Angolan people. First, we bombarded them with artillery, and then we advanced with tanks and assault cars. This was between 23 September and 5 October. In this battle, there was a South African commander who had to be evacuated because of his injuries. He had to go back to South Africa. Four hours of battle, more than four hours. The enemy [UNITA] were young and inexperienced, and they ran away leaving the South Africans to fight alone.

Willem van der Waals

On our side, we had a few armoured cars that had been donated to UNITA by [Zairean leader] Mobutu and three ENTAC anti-tank missile vehicles with missiles. And then there was a UNITA company. So, it was a rag-tag force. We drove into a very well-prepared ambush. We were fired on by what our people said were tanks, but later I was informed by the Angolans there were no tanks – only BRDMs and other armoured vehicles. When the real fighting started, the UNITA company of 150 fled and left us to our own devices. We used our ENTAC missiles and two of the armoured cars and managed to extricate ourselves. But, the point is, there and then the MPLA advance on Nova Lisboa stopped.

We withdrew, and I immediately informed Pretoria that this was serious and suggested that we either go in properly or get out – but not to do things in half measures. Once again, I requested a number of armoured cars. I knew how sensitive our involvement was – I would have been happy with six. Our State Security Council decided that armoured cars could be employed in Angola and, without my being informed properly about this, the next moment I found C130s landing at Silva Porto and disgorging armoured cars, two at a time. And when I saw I had 22 armoured cars with crews – I didn't have any food, or decent ammunition, or sufficient fuel; that all had to be flown in – but then we started forming what we called a battle group.

Osvaldo Leitão

From Balombo, our intention was to arrive at Huambo, and we took Londuimbale on our way. We could surprise the enemy, because UNITA were not organised enough. They didn't even know we'd taken Londuimbale; it was

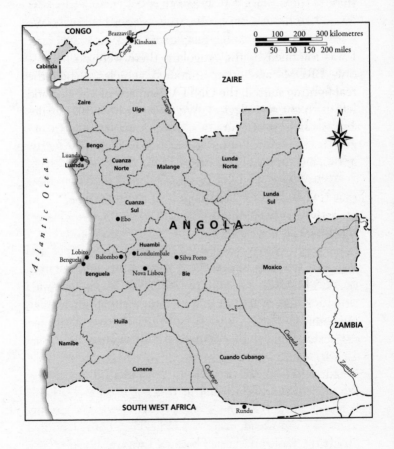

lack of communication between them. After two weeks, there a little plane showed up with the flag of the MPLA. We were having breakfast and I told my colleagues, 'This is not possible – we don't have any planes.' The plane went around three times and started to shoot at us. Right after, we started to hear the South African bombs falling behind us. 'Let's retreat,' I said, 'otherwise we're going to die.'

To our amazement, the South Africans came at us with ten 'Panhards' [armoured cars]. Also, the geography of the field was not in our favour; the ones coming downhill have an advantage, but because of the trees and the bushes, the tanks could not pass. There we fought three hours, but it was hard, because the road was 10 metres wide, and then you had fields. There the South Africans had an advantage over us, and we had to retreat, and that's when the South African invasion started.

I think we destroyed two or three of their tanks and they destroyed all our tanks; they all burned inside and died. I was the only survivor. I opened the hatch and jumped and hid in a tree just to breathe. I came down and I started to crawl. After ten minutes, the tree was bombarded and blown up. I managed to find our artillery at the rear, so I said to them, 'This is bad. This is the worst-case scenario. The South Africans are all over us. We need to retreat.'

I was in deep shock. I was 17 years old; I joined to the MPLA when I was 15, but at this point I was 17. I was a leader at 17 years old. I was crying, crying because my comrades were dead, inside the tank. They burned, burned inside the tank, and I cried because I was in shock.

As **Willem van der Waals** sees it, South Africa got involved to thwart the grim prospect of a Soviet-backed group taking power in Angola.

The threat perception at that stage in South Africa was of an aggressive Soviet Union with eyes on the Cape – strategic Cape sea route, minerals, etc. Typical Cold War scene. Maybe it was overrated, but that was the threat perception at that stage.

We didn't have any territorial ambitions – we went in to support UNITA and the FNLA in order to enable them to regain their traditional areas of influence, so that if free elections should take place then obviously the two pro-Western movements would do well, and we would have a peaceful Angola on our border, and most probably a government well-disposed to the West. It was important that Angola should not be a launching platform for the South West African People's Organization, SWAPO, who were then involved in a revolutionary struggle for the independence of Namibia. We had to prevent that.

To South Africa [the threat of a Soviet-backed group taking power in Angola] was very serious, not only because of the defence of Namibia: in general strategic terms. At one stage, for instance, speaking to one of my colleagues in Rundu, I said to him what we were going to do in Angola. He was then training the FNLA in southern Angola, and he said, 'What the hell do you think the Russians are going to do about it?'

I replied, 'The Russians are interfering in our Western sphere of influence, the south Atlantic Ocean. And surely this will not be tolerated by the United States. And the Russians will come to realise they are interfering especially when they meet up with us.'

But South Africa's intervention had to be deniable. **Willem van der Waals** *and his fellow soldiers had to be ready to pretend to be mercenaries.*

In terms of our then Defence Act, the deployment of the South African Defence Force outside the borders of South Africa needed parliamentary approval. Obviously, there was no time for that. We didn't want a debate in Parliament about this because everything had to be top secret. Imagine – if it had become known earlier that apartheid South Africa was supporting UNITA and the FNLA, it would hang them, it would crucify them.

We didn't take any South African articles in, nothing. The first group that went in [was] myself and two signallers. Only later came our armoured cars. But then the sensitivity of the operation was a little bit less, we were involved on a bigger scale – it was virtually impossible to keep it all secret. We didn't even use our names – we had book numbers. I was 'Book number 101', being the first one in.

I turned up at the airport and journalists were speaking to some of our troops, national servicemen, asking them who they were. 'We're mercenaries.' 'Where are you from?' 'Ing-ur-land.' The South African accent was so obvious, everybody at that stage should have known we were involved, but to a very large extent we managed to keep it secret for a very long time.

*As Angola's Independence Day, 11 November 1975, approached, Cuban instructors were already busy training Angolan soldiers. **René Hernández Gatorno** was a military officer, and was told he would now be taking part in a military intervention on the other side of the Atlantic.*

During the first days of November of 1975, they called me to explain to me what had happened with the instructors that were sent to Angola to prepare the future Angolan security forces, because after the departure of the Portuguese, the country was left with no protection at all. So, when the South African troops entered the country from the south, and the ones from the Congo entered from the north, Angola's government asked Cuba to send support to stop this invasion, and Cuba decided to do it. It was then that they asked me to be part of a special unit that was going to Angola.

We entered through the capital and it looked very messy. You could see a lot of support from the people for President Neto. The only weird thing was that you could hear many shots, but it was because one of the characteristics of the Africans is that when they are happy, they shoot into the air.

I thought UNITA were being helped by a big power, South Africa, that the Americans were supporting them too, and that the biggest purpose they had was to defend their system, apartheid, and not to have a nation as economically strong as Angola on their border, since Namibia was theirs.

In early November, **Willem van der Waals** *learned that the South Africans were planning to leave after Angola's Independence Day.*

General Viljoen – who was the man who liaised regularly from Pretoria with Savimbi – informed Savimbi in my presence that we would be out by 11 November. A very downhearted Savimbi then spoke to me and said [we] couldn't leave as [they] would lose everything that has been gained over the last 50 days. He said he wanted to speak to our Prime Minister about us leaving: 'If your Prime Minister Vorster wouldn't speak to me then I'll go to Kenneth Kaunda [President of Zambia] and ask him to speak to the Prime Minister.'

So, we remained until around 25 January, when it was finally decided that we would withdraw, because from around 4 November there was a massive inflow of Cuban troops into Angola: by 11 November, 4,000; by the end something like 12,000. They were flown into Brazzaville in Congo, then straight into Luanda. And our Prime Minister at one stage said, 'We are not going to fight the free-world battle alone, without any support from the free world.'

We said we would stay as long as we could handle the situation without international support. It was obvious that, given Operation Carlotta, the Cuban operation, with that massive influx of Cuban troops – that we would have had to mobilise in South Africa, and at that stage our involvement was still kept secret from the South African population. It was an impossible situation, politically speaking.

René Hernández Gatorno

We always had a force from the MPLA operating with us. That's how we did the offensive up to Namibia: together. They did very well. You have to take into account that the majority of them were young, untrained civilians from the countryside. In many cases, they didn't even know the modern armaments that the South Africans had. We had to explain to them that they were vulnerable. They started realising it through combat. During the offensive, they learned that the South Africans could also lose, run and die.

Osvaldo Leitão

I was in the battle of 11th November. Angola was being invaded in the north by the Zairean army [of Mobutu]; we were together with the Chinese, to defend Angola. President Agostinho Neto was concerned with our ability to respond. The Zairean army was very organised, with a lot of equipment, with several cannons, and this explains President Neto's insistence with the government of Cuba to send troops. They helped us to defend the independence of Angola.

I knew as an Angolan person that there were people on the other side that would do everything to fight us; I knew that there were other countries supporting these people. Those opposition forces would do everything to strangle our fight and ensure the fall of the new state. I went to become part of the MPLA, but I'm not a socialist or a Communist. I'm a defender of people's rights. I'm a defender of people's right to fight for their country. What I want is the wellbeing of people; I want the state to be faithful to their role, to improve the life of the common citizen. During the fight, of course, a group of guerrillas would knock on every door to try and gain support for their fight, independent of their ideology. Of course, inside the MPLA there were some who had a Communist ideology or a more conservative ideology. But I can say for sure that not all the leaders of the MPLA were Communist or socialist.

In late November 1975, South African, Angolan and Cuban forces clashed near the town of Ebo.

Osvaldo Leitão
I was only there for two days. At that point our troops were disorganised, and in that area, before the Cubans arrived to stop the advance of the South Africans, the South Africans were using small groups of people to reconnoitre. There were a series of ambushes and they captured a lot of MPLA fighters. Only when the Cubans arrived did we organise ourselves with a safe rearguard, with trenches and mortars and a secure back line, to stop the advance of the South African troops. It was then that the South Africans started to retreat. They could not advance from Ebo, so they decided to retreat. I don't know if they received orders to retreat or if they saw that they were losing, but

the fact is they retreated. At this point, there was a series of deaths on all sides, ourselves, the Cubans and also the South Africans.

René Hernández Gatorno
I directed that battle. We were able to take ten tanks and all their logistics from them. They had a large amount of casualties, and it was the first time that the South Africans ran and broke bridges themselves. It was a battle in which they lost a lot of strength; they were totally disintegrated. They lost a lieutenant-colonel who was the tank commander whose name was Niel Lombaro. He died there, and they were unable to recover his body.

It was a very hard battle, a battle with some irregular characteristics. For the first time, we used a BM [rocket launcher], that was our reactive artillery, and it lasted from seven in the morning until seven in the afternoon, when they started retreating. At the moment they retreated, they crossed the Keve river; they retreated very fast. It was their first big loss in Angola and that was one of their large units.

When the combat ended, I was exhausted. But, at the same time, it felt good to see that we had just one man killed and four injured. Comparing that with the amount of casualties and the material losses that the South Africans had, it was a very good battle, a battle with phenomenal results. And there were five of them for each of us.

Willem van der Waals left Angola on 15 November 1975, but not before he had been spotted by a journalist, who broke the story on 23 November. South African forces formally withdrew from Angola two months later.
Fred Bridgland – then correspondent of the *Washington Post* – identified South African armoured cars, identified me in person, and made it known to the world that South

Willem van der Waals immediately after his return from Angola.

Africa was involved. Then it went off very badly for the FNLA and UNITA.

The invincibility of the South African Defence Force had really taken a knock: the fact the so-called mighty Boers could be defeated militarily. We pulled out in late January 1976, not having been defeated militarily but because we lost the political fight. Our prestige had also been severely dented, and the perception took root in Africa that the Boers could be beaten on the battlefield.

The opposing sides in the conflict in Angola were mortal enemies. But looking back today, **Osvaldo Leitão** *emphasises unity.*

All of us were happy that things ended up the way that they did. The comrades from several sides got together and hugged each other. Some generals from UNITA, when they arrived in Luanda, didn't have their financial lives organised, and I personally helped them to organise themselves. We are friends, we are brothers. The past is finished, it's history, it's part of our history. It's a reality that UNITA has its own history, the MPLA has its own history. They all participated in the liberation of the country. We respect everyone and, God willing, we continue that way.

'The newcomer holding a weapon is the enemy'

The Soviet Invasion of Afghanistan (1979–89)

On the night of 24 December 1979, large numbers of Soviet Airborne troops landed in Kabul, followed soon after by columns of armoured tanks rolling across the Soviet border in the north, accompanied by tens of thousands of ground troops. In less than three days, Soviet commandos had taken over strategic installations in the capital Kabul and stormed the presidential palace, where they killed the Afghan leader in order to install a new surrogate deemed to be more loyal to Moscow. It was the start of a full-scale Soviet invasion of Afghanistan.

The reaction in the West was unmitigated alarm. In Washington, President Jimmy Carter instantly sent a sharply worded message to the Soviet leader, Leonid Brezhnev, warning that the invasion was a clear threat that 'could mark a fundamental and long-lasting turning point in our relations'. Weeks later, Carter followed that up in his annual State of the Union Address by calling the

Soviet invasion 'the most serious threat to peace since the Second World War'. A US trade embargo was announced and US sanctions imposed, defence spending was ratcheted up, and a US naval presence was stationed in the Indian Ocean for fear that oil interests in the Persian Gulf might also be targeted. The next year, the United States further signalled its displeasure by boycotting Moscow's 1980 Olympics. To help repel the Soviet occupiers, the CIA stepped up its covert supply of weapons to Afghan rebels, funded by the United States and Saudi Arabia and delivered with the help of Pakistani intelligence. It marked the end of the era of détente, and the start of one of the Cold War's most far-reaching proxy wars, whose consequences are still reverberating nearly 40 years later.

Moscow's interest in Afghanistan as a strategic prize went back to the nineteenth century and the battle for territorial influence between the Russian and British empires known as the 'Great Game'. By the 1970s, the Soviet Union saw Afghanistan as a strategically useful pawn on the geopolitical Cold War chessboard. In 1978, in an attempt to maintain it as a Soviet foothold, Moscow threw its support behind a Marxist government, which had ousted and executed the previous pro-American regime in Kabul, and signed a friendship treaty pledging Soviet economic and military support to Afghanistan.

The new government, led by Nur Mohammad Taraki, instigated a radical programme of modernisation to eradicate illiteracy, uphold women's rights and promote secularism over Islam. Many conservative Afghans were deeply hostile, especially in rural areas, and Islamic clerics saw the policies as offensive and sacrilegious. With little regard for the likely consequences, Taraki responded brutally to put down their resistance.

In March 1979 a violent uprising erupted in the western city of Herat, in which many Afghans and some Soviet advisers were killed. Herat was situated near the border with Iran, which, months earlier, had toppled the Shah in an Islamic revolution. In panic, Taraki appealed to Moscow to help quell what he now feared was an Islamic insurgency, possibly with Iranian involvement.

The Politburo was reluctant to send in troops. There was suspicion that the Kabul government was weak and fractured. There was a worry that what was left of détente with the United States could evaporate. There was concern that Soviet troops might be cast as the aggressor, fuelling Islamic fervour and extending tensions to Muslims in Soviet Central Asia. In short, there was a fear that to intervene would only make matters worse.

Over the summer of 1979, infighting inside the Kabul government and further rebellions elsewhere in the country made it look as though Afghanistan was on a slide towards civil war. Then, in September 1979, Taraki was brutally murdered by a deputy whose allegiance to Moscow looked less certain. Realising that Afghanistan was slipping from its grasp, the Soviet Union decided the only option was to intervene and reassert control.

The decision to invade, framed as coming to the aid of a Soviet ally according to the friendship treaty obligations, was taken by the Politburo on 12 December 1979. The main backers were the Soviet Defence Minister, Dmitri Ustinov, the KGB Chief, Yuri Andropov, and the hard-line Politburo member in charge of ideology, Mikhail Suslov. The Foreign Minister, Andrei Gromyko, also endorsed the move. The ailing Soviet leader, Leonid Brezhnev, gave his signoff after being told by advisers that it would all be over in three or four weeks. In fact, the invasion was to turn into a quagmire that would bog down the Soviet army for nearly ten years and end in a humiliating withdrawal.

At first, the Soviet troops considered their role was to provide backup to the Afghan army. But low morale and high desertion rates among the Afghan forces meant that it soon became apparent that Soviet soldiers would have to do the fighting. By the end of 1980 there were more than 125,000 Soviet military personnel in Afghanistan.

The Soviet army controlled the cities, larger towns and main communication routes. The mujahidin or 'dushmans', as the Afghan resistance fighters were known, held sway in the countryside. And though the Soviet forces had the advantage of air power and military hardware, which they used in large-scale offensives against rebel strong-holds, their cumbersome equipment also made them easy targets for their Afghan enemies.

As the military campaign dragged on, it became abundantly clear that the Soviet Union might be a global superpower with nuclear weapons, tanks and airpower, but it was no match for the ambushes and sabotage traps of the mountain tribesmen of Afghanistan, especially since the mujahidin was being supplied with weaponry and military training by the United States and its allies. Not for the first time – or the last – the dogged persis-tence of local Afghan fighters, determined to drive out the foreign invaders, would take on and defeat a major outside power.

For the many ill-prepared teenage soldiers drafted into the Soviet army as conscripts, active service in Afghanistan was a reality shock. Some persisted in seeing it as a roman-tic adventure and part of their patriotic duty. For others, it was a nightmare.

Back in the Soviet Union, the reaction of the popula-tion was at first muted. Official reports, heavily coloured by propaganda, painted a picture of a heroic endeavour and gave little indication of what was really going on. But as more and more families in towns and villages across the country found their precious boys – often only sons – were arriving home as corpses in sealed zinc coffins, which could not even be prised open to bid a proper farewell, rumours began to spread and a simmering undercurrent of resentment and growing lack of confidence in the Soviet government gathered force.

Those soldiers who did come home alive were often battle-scarred and traumatised. Some returned as hardened drug addicts and alcoholics. Some were men who had gone out as fit young conscripts and came back as limbless invalids, eligible for only limited welfare from the Soviet state. Like the American Vietnam vets who failed to adjust to civilian life in the United States, the Soviet 'Afgantsy' became a cohort of disaffected former warriors, often disenchanted with their own government and unable to shake off the horrors of the war they had witnessed and taken part in. Their plight became known as 'the Afghan Syndrome'.

The grim experience of the Afghan War also became a factor in the internal debates that led to Mikhail Gorbachev's perestroika reforms when he took over as Kremlin leader in 1985. It reinforced the view of those in the reformist wing of the Communist Party that the old guard of Leonid Brezhnev and his ageing colleagues were no longer competent to rule. It also strengthened Gorbachev's argument that it was time for a major rethink in foreign policy, to end costly interventions aimed at propping up pro-Soviet regimes in the Third World and to replace these proxy conflicts and a crippling nuclear arms race with a new engagement with the United States.

In 1986, the United States took the decision to supply the mujahidin rebels with handheld Stinger missiles, which could target Soviet planes and helicopter gunships more effectively. Some in the West saw this as a crucial factor that turned the tide of the war against the Soviets. But by then, Gorbachev was in charge in the Kremlin and was already intent on an exit strategy in any case.

Finally, in 1988, a settlement was signed in Geneva. The Soviet Union pledged to withdraw its troops and the pull-out was completed the following year. By this time, the human cost had been substantial. The Soviet Union had lost 15,000 soldiers; 50,000 more were wounded and 10,000 left disabled. In Afghanistan, probably over a million were killed, with millions more left homeless. Both superpowers had spent billions on their military operations. And once the Soviet pull-out was complete, Afghanistan descended into full-blown civil war.

In the West, the Soviet withdrawal was initially seen as a defeat for Moscow and therefore a triumph for Western policy. The United States, in particular, had pumped huge sums into covert aid to the Afghan mujahidin, seen by the Reagan administration as 'freedom fighters' taking on 'Communist aggression'. But, in time, Washington's policy of fostering jihadist resistance fighters was to boomerang back on to the United States. Among those who benefited from American largesse were Osama bin Laden and his al-Qaeda terrorist organisation. In 2001, it was from his base in Afghanistan that bin Laden masterminded the 11 September attacks on the United States. From then on it was the turn of first the United States and then NATO to be drawn into their own Afghan quagmire.

In Russia, the memory of the Afghan War continues to colour attitudes. It left many people with a deep-seated aversion to the prospect of mass casualties among Russian troops, a point to which successive Russian governments remain highly sensitive, whether in Chechnya, Ukraine, Syria or any other conflict.

Dmitri Fedorov was born in 1963 in Kolomna, near Moscow. He was drafted into the army in 1983 and served in the 860th Independent Motor-rifle Regiment, stationed in Faizabad, north-east Afghanistan.

I volunteered to go to Afghanistan as soon as my training was over. I wanted to prove myself. I was drawn to the unknown.

There was very little information. For the most part I relied on rumours spread by my acquaintances. The only available official information in the USSR was about the international duty our soldiers performed in Afghanistan. But what exactly was happening there I did not know. You could learn something only through some people who returned from Afghanistan. In addition, zinc coffins arrived regularly. So one could deduce something. We only began talking about losses after the Soviet army left Afghanistan in 1989.

Aleksandr Gergel was born in Moscow in 1961. He arrived in Afghanistan in late October 1983 as a member of the 860th Independent Motor-rifle Regiment, based in the town of Baharak in the north-east of the country.

When I was still at school, I dated a girl. Of course, I really wanted to impress her. Once, after compulsory attendance at the enlistment office, I told her jokingly that I was going to be sent to Afghanistan. It was 1978 or 1979. You can almost say that I doomed myself.

In 1979 I was admitted into the Institute of Transport Engineers. I was studying there for less than four years. It turned out that this whole sphere was not my cup of tea and I dropped out. Six months later, I had to go to the army.

The training unit was such a stressful situation that we were happy to escape anywhere. Therefore, at first, we were very upbeat. But as we were approaching Afghanistan we became more sour. But everything was so different: it was different nature – exotic way of life compared to the European part of Russia. And the situation in the army also differed greatly from the strict and repressed atmosphere in the training unit. As they say, the closer to the front lines you get, the freer you become. Relationships among soldiers tended to be more humane.

The journalist **Vladimir Snegirev** *was born in 1947 in Siberia. In 1981 he began an extended assignment as the Afghan War correspondent for the newspaper* Komsomolskaya Pravda.

The editor-in-chief told us: 'We have received a directive from the Central Committee of the Communist Party to send someone for a long-term trip to Afghanistan. Are there any volunteers?'

Everybody lowered their eyes and was silent. Afghanistan then was a black hole. No one could understand what was going on, but everyone knew that there was a war. The corpses were already coming from there. But it was all covered in the full veil of silence. A day passed, and again: 'Colleagues, we've got to react to this directive and send someone. Who would like to go?' Again everybody was silent.

A third day. The editor-in-chief started panicking. 'Who would go to Afghanistan?' And I raised my hand. I wasn't brave. I didn't know anything about Afghanistan then. It seemed to me that I was getting a bit bored, I wanted to experience something new.

But I had, thank God, two months before the trip, and I started then learning Dari, one of the Afghan languages. I started reading books about Afghanistan and started understanding something. And on 21 March 1981, I arrived in Afghanistan.

Dmitri Fedorov

We crossed the border by road and eventually we were deployed to our bases by helicopters. It was very hot. I found myself in the mountains, which I had never visited before. There were armed soldiers all around me.

We lived in tents during summer and winter, and the winters were harsh. The temperature sometimes fell to minus 20°C, and you need to take into account strong winds, heavy rains and snows. In the mountains, the snow easily reached waist level. We conducted military operations regardless of the season.

There was a huge and very effective propaganda machine in the USSR. It strengthened our resolve. But our morale was high, regardless. We were raised on the examples of our fathers and grandfathers who had fought in the Great Patriotic War [as the Second World War is known in Russia].

Aleksandr Gergel

I was just amazed by the routine of this service. I thought about war through the images of the Great Patriotic War, but in Afghanistan everything was completely different. I was surprised, above all, by the conditions in which I had to live. The battalion was placed in the ancient fortress near the village of Baharak. It was surrounded by walls. There were rooms inside; we called them cockpits. Each cockpit had a place for a platoon of 15 to 20 soldiers.

Aleksandr Gergel (right) and Dmitri Fedorov after local fighting near Ardar Village, Badakshan, 7 January 1985.

We had normal beds, pillows, blankets. Nobody was covered with greatcoats. There was a brick stove; we needed it for the winter. There were small windows in the wall; we covered them with cellophane tape. As it was supposed to be in the Soviet army, everything was pretty clean.

The routine was approximately the same: morning rise, physical exercises, breakfast. Then there was an assignment for the services; somebody was sent to the posts. It was ordinary routine, as in the other parts of the Soviet army.

Dmitri Fedorov

We got up and started with the physical exercises. More experienced soldiers did their best to avoid it. Afterwards, there was breakfast and daily assignments. Part of the battalion trained in shooting; part was ordered to do maintenance work. Then we had lunch and prepared for either guard duty or what else officers needed us to do. We had dinner in the evening. Sometimes we watched films.

Plus the political officers regularly tried to brainwash us and gave us mandatory 'Lenin's lessons'. We tried to skip them, of course. They asked us to copy some [of] Lenin's works and all such nonsense. Also, we were told that, if not for us, the Americans would be in Afghanistan. I never believed the Communist Party, although I was a member of Komsomol [the party's youth division]. I was raised in a family which was very sceptical about the party.

It was difficult for me to communicate with the political officers. I could not understand why they tried to brainwash me. The war was all around us: 'Don't play mind games with me, let me fight.' They even tried to interfere in the daily routine and military preparations, even though they understood nothing in these fields.

Vladimir Snegirev

I was so naive that I wrote what I saw, and when I got the newspapers, I read there absolutely different things. Everything was ruthlessly edited. Military action became 'manoeuvres'; killed and wounded turned into 'sick with diphtheria or dysentery'. It was all so repulsive and humiliating. The war was hidden, and there was no exception for anyone. Censorship edited out everything that related to military action. Yes, the Soviet soldiers are present in Afghanistan, but what are they doing there? They're planting trees, handing out flour to the local peasants, treating these poor Afghans' various diseases, teaching them to be literate. But they are not at war, not at all. This, of course, was horrible.

You couldn't go anywhere. There were checkpoints, and without passwords, papers and orders you couldn't get anywhere. The army controlled everything there, in Kabul and the provinces: the roads and the skies, everything. Therefore, whether you wanted to or not, you better be friends with the military.

The first years it was very difficult, because they thought that we would get in, defeat the dushman mobs and – with great honour, with the flags raised and the orchestras playing – would get back out, and would report to the party and the government that everything was great. And we got stuck there almost for ten years.

Aleksandr Gergel

Our task was formulated very clearly: 'We fulfil our military duty and guard the southern borders of our homeland. It so happens that we do it here, in Afghanistan, because this friendly state turned to us for help.' It was constantly stressed that Afghanistan is a friendly state. Therefore, commanding officers very closely monitored the behaviour of the soldiers. Marauding was strictly prohibited and discouraged. Nothing that was shown later in films like massacres or robbery was even close to reality.

Vladimir Snegirev

This whole thing turned into a war that got more and more intensive: they shoot, we shoot. One attacks with missiles, another responds with grenades. Step by step, eye for eye, tooth for tooth, deeper and deeper into the conflict. When we [first] entered, there were only local clashes but in two years' time it was already a full-scale, brutal war. The cities were under control only in daytime, but at night all of them, including Kabul, were totally in the hands of mujahidin.

Dmitri Fedorov

My battalion was a raid battalion. We had the highest number of military operations in the regiment. Once or twice a week, we went out into the mountains. And we had multi-day operations; sometimes they lasted for a week or even 20 days. I was wounded several times. We were ambushed several times. Two times it happened in the exact same place and time [15 February] with a year difference. There were losses. The first time, it was a support platoon. One guy was taken prisoner. His name was Sergei Korshenko. Much later, we discovered that he took part in the prisoner uprising in Badaber in 1985, where he was killed. But it was a war, after all.

[The second time] we had a week-long operation to destroy their outpost. It was spring in the valley, but we were deployed in the mountains – more than 2,700 metres above the sea level. It was still winter there. We had only minimum provisions, because we were promised supplies later through helicopters. We froze in the snow. It was extraordinarily harsh. Soviet soldiers and officers rarely surrendered. Only weak or seriously depressed soldiers wilfully surrendered. Death was [the] preferable option. Soviet troops preferred to commit suicide or blow themselves up with the dushmans to avoid being captured.

Aleksandr Gergel

The main type of operations was a night ambush. In our case, the battalion consisted of two companies and a mortar battery. One of the companies was in turn assigned to conduct military operations. The ambushes were arranged in summer, because in winter everything is covered with snow and it was impossible to do pretty much anything. But in the summer almost every night one of the companies went on combat duty. The unit formed a fighting group, which consisted of 20 to 30 soldiers. They went into the night [and] advanced to the place of ambush, which had been chosen by the command in advance. I do not know how these places were selected – most likely on intelligence, I suspect. As a rule, it was the dominant height in order to eliminate the possibility of attack from above. We sat until the morning and watched. Basically, most of the time nothing happened. The dushmans did not show up. Either the data turned out to be incorrect or we were detected. The notification among the local population was well developed. They saw the group and immediately signalled. But sometimes dushmans did come across – and then there was a fight.

The first time you shoot in combat, it turned out not to be scary – rather, unexpected and surprising. Then you get used to it, and in time you even start to have some perverse fun. You want to show off.

Vladimir Snegirev

Afghans are very friendly, open, hospitable and mostly unselfish people. If you communicate with them in a good, kind way, they will also turn to you with all their souls. The most mysterious ones for us for a long time were the mujahidin. We were strongly accustomed to [the] thought that they are the beast, and God forbid getting in their hands. Why were we given pistols? Not to fire back. So that you could kill yourself. It's impossible to defeat someone with [a] Makarov pistol. But you could shoot yourself in the forehead if there was a danger of capture. God forbid becoming their captive – they'll cut you into pieces, rape you, kill you, torture you to death. Such myths and legends were very popular for a long time. To some extent perhaps it was justifiable. It was a very brutal war and there were mujahidin detachments, such as the one under the command of Gulbuddin, that would right away kill any Russian or put him in a pit. Many of the Afghans I met in Kabul truly believed that they [were fighting] for the good cause; they were very naive leftist revolutionists. Most of them, or maybe even all of them, had connections with the Soviet Union [or] went to study there.

Aleksandr Gergel

The area we lived in was very small. Every day you see the same faces, you know everybody, you talked to everyone about everything, you sang all the songs. Every day was painfully similar to the previous one. It came to the point that we asked for extraordinary combat tasks to interrupt the routine. The officers invented entertainment for us. For example, in summer we took a car and asked for volunteers. We found abandoned gardens and picked apples, apricots there. The main thing was to leave the territory, just not to sit still inside the fortress.

Dmitri Fedorov

The interrogations were very harsh; there were cases of beatings. But for the most part we did not ask about their reasoning for war with the USSR. We were interested in the location of bases, mines, gang leaders and their relatives. It was a war. But we did not push needles under their fingers.

One of my fellow soldiers was taken prisoner in early May 1984 in the region of Argu Pass. He was part of the company which were returning from an ambush. He fell asleep because he was exhausted, and he was caught by [a] surprise dushmans' attack. He fought to the best of his abilities, but was captured nonetheless. He was seriously injured during the fight. Rebels tried to help him, but did not succeed. He died. The location of his grave is still unknown. Nobody could show the exact place where he was buried.

Aleksandr Gergel

In 1984 the war had already [been going on] for five years. I was horrified that during the Great Patriotic War we were able to drive the Germans back to Berlin, but here we were stuck for five years and there was no end in sight. More and more militants poured into Afghanistan from the neighbouring Pakistan. Even I – a young and inexperienced soldier – understood that we could not close the entire border. It was impossible to put a guarded frontier in the mountains physically. Without external assistance, the militants would have quickly lost. Later, I learned that the Soviet military contingent accounted for 100,000 soldiers, but there were at least three [times more] dushmans.

Jack Devine became Director of the CIA's Afghan Task Force in 1986. He remembers the United States' increasing involvement in the war.

When the Russians invaded, the Carter administration started supporting at a very modest level. They formed an Afghan Task Force and in the early eighties you were looking at a programme of around $100 million. But by '85, '86, the White House and the American people were getting tired of the war and there was a push in '86 to give it one more big try to see if we can't turn the tide here. The budget by late 1986 was $1 billion.

There is a game changer in the deployment of the Stinger missiles. There were about 125,000 fighters in Afghanistan at the time, so it's quite a logistical task to supply them with AK-47s and trucks and mules and everything you need, RPG-7s [rocket-propelled grenade launchers], mortar – it's just a huge logistical task. But even though there was a big push, most of the materiel was suppressed by a combination of the *Spetsnaz*, which was the [Soviet] special forces – and the Hind helicopter. So, nothing was moving on the ground. And we were frustrated because we'd only used Soviet-made weapons or Soviet-style weapons; we didn't want to rub it in their faces by using American weapons. Then, in spring of '86 we became aware of the Stinger missile, which was a heat-seeking missile, so if you fired it and the helicopter was generating heat, if you fired it in the opposite direction, it would self-redirect towards the heat and hit its target. An awesome weapon when you see it for the first time.

Those that were managing the programme had a White House meeting and there was a mock video, a test done. You saw this missile fired and the sense in the room was, 'Look, we're going to recommend to the President that we deploy this.' Until then the CIA did not want to put the weapons in, didn't want to provoke the Russians unduly and provoke World War Three, and they didn't want to change the policy of strictly non-US weapons. Now, my view was that it wasn't going to provoke that – that the Russians understood perfectly well what was going on. We would try something, they would try something else, and this was within the parameters. But at that meeting, when you saw the results of the test it was hard to pass on it. So, it went to the President and once the President signed it, it's just a logistical job: how do you get those weapons from the US military to the agencies? Being responsible for the Afghan Task Force, it was my job to go over and talk to the three-star general, who was a very solid and highly respected general. He said, 'Well, Jack, our own frontline troops don't have these. You're not getting anything out of me.' And I said, 'Look, I'm just telling you what the President of the United States has authorised.' He said, 'Well, it's been a lovely discussion with you. I wish you Godspeed.' I went back and reported to the White House that we'd run into a brick wall. I was instructed to stand down for 24 hours and then call him back. Basically, I went to see him again and we had a discussion about how many I needed. He was probably biting into his tongue talking to me.

Aleksandr Gergel
We knew that the dushmans had Western advisers. Our command was keen to capture such a specialist. Once our regiment took part in a large military operation near Faizabad. We were briefed by the counter-intelligence officers and showed photos of the leaders of bandit formations and even of some defectors. They also told us that we could possibly meet English-speaking men. We were aware that the dushmans were receiving American weapons.

Dmitri Fyodorov

They benefited from Stingers and English anti-aircraft Blowpipe [missiles]. They forced the Soviet aviation to operate from higher altitudes, where these missiles could not get planes and helicopters. It slightly decreased the effectiveness of the Soviet war effort, but it was compensated by the number of bomb strikes. All the same, the Soviet army achieved the desirable results.

Jack Devine

The Stinger changed history, not because it shot down so many Hind helicopters – it shot down a fair number. But on September 26 of '86, when it was deployed to the field, General Dynamics who made it were estimating that it would have a 25 per cent success rate. It turned out it was on the other side of 75 per cent. There's a video that was taken of the first attack and you'll see the first shot of a helicopter and it hits it square on, and then two others were shot out of the sky. Why it's so important is that the next day the Russians started flying out of its range, which then allowed all that weaponry that I talked about to roll over the border. The Russians sitting back in the Kremlin were already uncomfortable. They were bogged down, quagmired, so to speak; it was going nowhere from their perspective. And when they had to pull back their air power, I believe a decision was made shortly thereafter to pack it in, even though they hung in there until 1989.

Vladimir Snegirev

Everybody felt a great relief [when Soviet troops were withdrawn]. People were tired of this war – the military men, the politicians, everyone. Also the war was standing in the way of perestroika. Gorbachev has announced the era of a new way of thinking and renewed relations with the West. People thought, 'Now we'll start living. We'll be friends with everyone.' Afghanistan was like a splinter – painful and irritating. So, it was a relief. But it was not so easy to pull the troops back.

For the Soviet Union it was, of course, a very dramatic tragedy because it speeded up the collapse of [the] Soviet empire. It's not even a subject for discussion; it is an absolute fact. It also pushed the Communist system to its end. Everyday life in the Soviet Union was also affected because Afghanistan has flooded Russia with drugs and weapons. The problems that we can't solve even today have their roots in Afghanistan.

Dmitri Fedorov

I think that too much was promised to the soldiers in Afghanistan in order to boost their morale. The Council of Ministers of the USSR and the Central Committee passed a whole package of privileges for [returning] servicemen. However, upon return, few were able to receive these benefits. That is how this 'Afghan Syndrome' started: 20-year-old boys with war experience considered themselves isolated in the society. Many men became drug addicts. People were offended – the country did not give them what they were promised. There was no rehabilitation. And the farther from the capital you were, the worse the situation was. You could achieve something in the Moscow region, but there was little you could do in the provinces. Many were left without apartments and strips of land promised to them. But the USSR is long gone, and there is nothing you can complain to.

Vladimir Snegirev

Afghanistan and the tragic story of the Russian troops invading it and getting stuck there for ten years is mostly the result of the Cold War paranoia, from both sides – Moscow and the West, the US. Our elders from the Politburo were afraid that they will be attacked with missiles. And really the short- and medium-range missiles were located in Europe very close to our borders. They were afraid that if we lose Afghanistan, the missiles will be placed even closer in the south.

It was a tragic mistake because they based their expectations on experience with Hungary and Czechoslovakia, especially Czechoslovakia. It was very close in time – Czechoslovakia in 1968 and Afghanistan in 1979. Tanks have entered Czechoslovakia, there was no resistance, no bloodshed; some students have protested a bit, and order was restored very quickly. The country remained in the socialist camp, in the Soviet orbit. They thought here will be the same: the guys with long beards wearing galoshes are running around, we'll crack down on them with our tanks and missiles in no time. But it turned out differently. A giant proud country with no infrastructure at all, no communications, guerrilla war. Afghans are not Czechs. Afghans love foreigners who come with money, but they don't like foreigners who come with weapons. Foreigners who come with weapons automatically become the enemy. It was this way when [the] Brits were there, then the Soviets, then the Americans. For any Afghan of any ethnic origin, the newcomer holding a weapon is the enemy. The same happened when the Russian troops came. At first, the locals did not quite understand what is happening. During first few days, they were even holding meetings proclaiming that 'the Soviet Union is our brother'. But then they saw that 'the brother' is shooting, throwing grenades and behaves as heavily armed people usually behave.

Dmitri Fedorov

You can destroy [a] village with bombs, but the Afghans have a long history of fighting for their freedom. No conqueror succeeded in enslaving them. The Afghans protest against everything. They can invite you for a cup of tea. You can accept the invitation and become a guest. If the enemy suddenly attacks, the host will protect you to his last breath. But never come to Afghanistan with weapons. In comparison to the United States, the Soviet military actions were several times more intensive. You can destroy the Afghans. But you cannot win over them.

'We came out victorious'

The Birth of Solidarity in Poland (1980)

On 16 October 1978, scarlet-clad cardinals in Rome announced a new Pope. Their choice was Karol Wojtyła, the first ever Polish pontiff. Nowhere was there more excitement at the news than in Poland, a country that had been under Communist rule since 1947 but remained staunchly Catholic. That one of their own was now the worldwide leader of the Catholic Church gave Poles new confidence to believe that anything was possible, even political change in their country.

A year later, John Paul II paid his first papal visit to his homeland and ecstatic Poles flocked to hear him speak. Preaching more than 30 sermons in 9 days, he urged them not to be afraid, as though tacitly encouraging them to take action. It did not take long for that action to surface through a nationwide movement that was to transform political and social life in Poland. It was called Solidarity.

The antecedents to Solidarity went back some time. Perhaps more than any other country in Eastern Europe, Poland was a problem for the Soviet authorities. Not only was it Catholic and therefore not particularly receptive to Soviet atheist ideology, it was also a country where workers retained real clout. Their protests had forced a change in the country's leadership in 1956, and in 1970 they had once again pushed the country's Communist leader to resign after workers' rebellions against price increases turned into riots in Gdańsk and other places. These were put down by the army and the police, leaving dozens of people dead and hundreds wounded.

In time, a pattern began to emerge: the Polish government, faced with a crippling foreign debt and an economy in disarray, would periodically announce steep price rises; incensed Polish workers would stage strikes and other disruptions, including on one occasion the torching of a party headquarters; then the authorities would back down, but the troublemakers causing the unrest would be arrested.

In response to this, in 1976 a group of Polish intellectuals set up the Workers' Defence Committee, Komitet Obrony Robotników (KOR), to provide legal and financial aid to the arrested workers. KOR developed into a network of opposition activists across the country who helped forge links between free trade unions and the Church, and whose underground publications, such as their newspaper *Robotnik* ('The Worker'), helped educate workers to put their individual concerns in the context of a wider debate about the viability of a Communist state.

In July 1980, just over a year after John Paul II's visit, the Polish government once again announced a steep hike in food prices. In response, Polish workers announced new strike action and the work stoppages began to spread.

At the Lenin Shipyard in Gdańsk, an added grievance caused events to escalate. On 7 August 1980 a popular activist and elderly crane operator called Anna Walentynowicz was fired by the management for her unofficial union work. It was just months before she was due to retire, so the dismissal meant she would lose her pension benefits. On 14 August

1980, some 17,000 workers at the shipyards put down their tools in protest at the unfair dismissal. The initial agitation for the strike came not from a shipyard employee, but from an experienced political activist called Bogdan Borusewicz from KOR. He recruited three younger workers to distribute leaflets and spread the word to get the strike going.

Support was also enlisted from a charismatic free trade union activist and born troublemaker called Lech Wałęsa, who had been dismissed from the shipyard for his part in earlier strikes. Although Wałęsa was later to become an iconic leader, that first strike at the shipyards started without him. He arrived late and, as he had no pass to get past the guards, he had to clamber in over a wall to bypass security. Once inside, he leapt up on to a piece of machinery to deliver an inspiring speech to the assembled workers. With that, he established himself as the man to head the strike committee's negotiations with the authorities. The initial demands were that both Anna Walentynowicz and he should be reinstated, that workers should get increased pay, and that a monument should be erected for the Gdańsk workers killed in the protests in 1970.

On 16 August the management offered the shipyard workers a pay increase. Wałęsa was ready to call off the strike, and it almost collapsed. But others, including Anna Walentynowicz, argued that bigger political issues were at stake and solidarity needed to be shown with other striking workers who had not had their demands met. Sensing a change of mood, Wałęsa changed tack and declared the strike should go on.

As a result, the walkout became a solidarity action with striking workers at other factories, mines and shipyards. The strike committees clubbed together to compile a much longer list of 21 demands, which were pinned to the gates, alongside a picture of the Pope. These demands ranged from the legalisation of strikes and free trade unions to the right of Catholic worship, more respect for freedom of speech, the freeing of political prisoners, as well as better pay and welfare benefits. But the list steered clear of more radical political demands that could have been interpreted as a challenge to Communist rule.

On behalf of the Strike Coordinating Committee, Wałęsa led the negotiations with the Polish government. On 31 August 1980 both sides signed the so-called Gdańsk agreement, a ground-breaking social contract for an Eastern Bloc country, which accepted many of the demands, including the right to strike.

By November, the group of strike committees that had emerged out of the Lenin Shipyard strike had officially registered as a nationwide organisation of free trade unions under the name Solidarity or, in Polish, *Solidarność* – the first officially recognised independent labour union in a Soviet-bloc country. Wałęsa was its leader, and before long he was the de facto spokesman for a significant proportion of the Polish people.

Over the next year, Solidarity transformed itself from a trade union into a social movement with a political reform agenda. Between 9 and 10 million Poles joined its ranks – about a quarter of the country's population. Its aim was to force a change in government policies. 'Not only bread, butter and sausages, but also justice, democracy, truth, legality, human dignity, freedom of convictions, and the repair of the republic', stated the Solidarity programme.

In March 1981 the movement called a strike involving 12 million people, which paralysed the country – the largest ever strike in the Eastern Bloc. It was an indication that the ruling Polish United Workers' Party (as the Polish Communist Party was called) had lost control of events and its political authority was fast being hollowed out by a powerful national opposition movement. Throughout the summer of 1981 the atmosphere in Poland became increasingly tense, as the country's economy continued to deteriorate, amid wildcat work stoppages, hunger strikes and street protests.

In Moscow, Kremlin leaders had been watching with mounting alarm what was beginning to look like a nation-wide revolt against Communism – the worst threat to the cohesion of the Eastern Bloc since the Prague Spring of 1968 in Czechoslovakia. As early as August 1980, the Politburo had begun discussing top-secret plans for a possible invasion of Poland. Other Warsaw Pact leaders issued urgent calls for collective action to save Poland from 'the threat of counter-revolution'. As an exercise in sabre-rattling, Warsaw Pact troop manoeuvres were organised on the border.

But when it came to it, the Soviet leadership decided against an invasion. Already bogged down in a war in Afghanistan, Moscow may not have wanted to shoulder the military and economic burden of another intervention – or the pain of further Western sanctions. And Poland was a special case where the Brezhnev doctrine, it seems, did not apply. Unlike Czechoslovakia in 1968, any Soviet troops who went in would be facing a national resistance movement led not just by intellectuals, but by the nation's working class, in a Catholic country where support for Communist rule had always been problematic.

At a Politburo meeting on 10 December 1981, even the hard-line chief ideologist Mikhail Suslov agreed that it was too risky. 'If troops are introduced, that would mean a catastrophe,' he said, adding, 'There can be no consideration at all of introducing troops.'

But that was not the message conveyed to Poland's Communist leader. Installed months earlier to take a grip of the crisis after the former leader Edward Gierek was removed from power, General Wojciech Jaruzelski was a Soviet-trained military man who was also combining the posts of Prime Minister and Defence Minister. From the outset, he had been instructed to prepare the country for martial law if he wanted to avoid an invasion.

On 13 December 1981 Jaruzelski finally made his move, in his mind to save Poland from a Soviet military takeover. In the early hours of the morning, he abruptly declared that Poland was now under martial law. A strict curfew was introduced, strikes were banned, key industries were put under the control of the military and media freedoms were curtailed. Soldiers and tanks appeared on the streets to maintain order. Most importantly, Solidarity was banned and thousands of Solidarity activists were arrested; Wałęsa was imprisoned for 11 months. As a military operation, it was extremely effective. Solidarity supporters mounted a series of strikes, but the crackdown successfully dampened down any sustained resistance.

Martial law was not officially terminated until July 1983, but Solidarity as an opposition movement did not disappear. It went underground, strengthened its links with the Church, and remained a simmering political force until 1988, when Poland's Communist government offered to open talks with Wałęsa and his fellow opposition activists about legalising Solidarity. A year later Solidarity candidates swept to victory in parliamentary elections, delivering a humiliating defeat to the Polish Communist Party. Lech Wałęsa, once an unemployed electrician, became Poland's first post-Communist President.

Although not originally from the city, **Jerzy Borowczak** *was a young worker at the Gdańsk shipyard at the time of the strike in August 1980.*

When the riots erupted in 1970 in Gdańsk, they didn't show much on TV but it was spoken of a lot. And every year people would lay flowers at the shipyard gate. My father listened to Radio Free Europe, so I knew that there was an opposition at work. I hadn't heard the name Lech Wałęsa yet, but there was Bogdan Borusewicz, who was a Workers' Defence Committee activist.

I arrived in Gdańsk in 1979. I had just left the army and I walked into the recruitment office at the shipyard and said that I'd like to ask about work. And the man said, 'Give me your ID.' He put a stamp on it, and said that I've just become an employee of the shipyard. I made a connection to the free labour unions, meaning with Bogdan Borusewicz, very quickly.

In 1979, **Bogdan Borusewicz** *was working with KOR, the Workers' Defence Committee. He was a seasoned activist by the time of the strike.*

When I was growing up, my mother would keep telling me not to get involved [in demonstrations]. 'If you want to do something, stay at the back. Why elbow your way to the front line all the time?' To which I would answer: 'Mother, if there will be no one at the front, then there'll be no volunteers for the back. So I have to be at the front.'

I was arrested because I wrote and distributed pamphlets after the student demonstrations in 1969. I was betrayed by my favourite teacher, who turned out to be an agent of the Security Service, and was sentenced to three years in prison. My friend had handed out three pamphlets and was arrested for ten months. It was an ordeal. That was the time when I became determined about what I was going to do.

You know, prison either breaks you or else it reaffirms you in your views.

While being moved to the prison, I escaped from a Security Service transport and they issued an arrest warrant for me. I was shown in the press and TV, and the warrant had stipulated that I was a 'dangerous criminal'. So they used lies. And it was clear to me that it was lies that were at the base of that government, as well as violence, because if you throw a young boy, a 19-year-old, into prison, then it's that other element of executing authority: violence. Lies and violence.

When I came back to Gdańsk after my studies, I started organising a group of workers within the structures of the Workers' Defence Committee, and of the illegal *Worker* journal, and I conducted self-education workshops. We managed to create a workers' intelligentsia. They founded little libraries. They read the same books I did, smuggled in from the West. It was a group of very intelligent young workers. I did discuss with them about the strike in 1970, but I wasn't telling them that I was preparing them for a similar such event.

*A young freelance journalist from Dublin, **Jacqueline Hayden**, found herself drawn to Poland after the papal visit in 1979.*
I was 21, 22, very idealistic. I got into a dispute with a friend of mine who said that Irish journalists were complete lefties, they had no open minds, they had no interest in the truth, that nothing critical of a leftist or a Communist regime would be covered or broadcast. And I just said that's ridiculous, fund me and I'll go.

I was very taken at the time with the impact of the Pope's visit, so I said to myself, that's the place I'll go. So, I got myself organised and I spoke to a number of newspaper editors and I was given a commission to do a series on the impact of the return to Poland of a new Polish Pope and to write about what it was like in Communist Poland. I set out at the end of July 1980 and got myself to Warsaw.

When I arrived, the first thing was this incredible sense of how helpful people were. My first plan was to go and speak to an influential member of KOR [...] I literally got off the plane, got a taxi, got myself over to his apartment and he wasn't there. 'Oh, you're a foreign journalist, no problem,' said this young man who was there. 'What you really need, though, is we have these really good friends Jan and Krystyna Lityński, and they speak English and they'll be able to help you.' It was all a bit surreal. On one level, here was I thinking I was doing something terribly secretive, but there was just this very open attitude and in that, in retrospect, I understood a core part of the philosophy of those that were connected with KOR, which was to act as if you were free, behave as if everything was normal.

The Lityńskis' apartment was simply a hub of activity. There were people coming and going, meetings going on. Jan was the editor of *Robotnik*, the underground newspaper, and so suddenly I'm in this place which is literally a hive of political activity and it's the tiniest little apartment. Sitting there was Jan's mother and she was typing furiously on this old Remington, a prized tool of dissent. She was smoking away on this Gauloise cigarette and head down typing away, and she was typing whatever Jan's latest article was. It was very, very exciting, dynamic. I was struck at the time by a sense of a deep, passionate, but really resolute sense of knowing what they were doing and what their goals and aims were.

You could set out a list of the goals in intellectual terms, but I just remember talking to Krystyna and when you talked to her about what it is they wanted she would simply say, 'We just want to live a normal life.' And there was nothing normal about the conditions in which they were living.

Jerzy Borowczak

[In the shipyard at Gdańsk] I quickly learned how things worked on the job, and it annoyed me. They would delegate us to assistant posts, and then at the end of the month the foreman covered himself by assessing my work at 30 per cent and his at 300 per cent. And we were doing his work! He was sly. I thought, 'I'm getting 1,800 złoty for this work,' and in early 1980 there was nothing you could actually buy for that kind of money. So that's what interested me, this kind of injustice. Not an intention to topple the system, because I would have had to be mad to imagine – given their tanks and nukes and all that – that we could bring them down. It was about making Poland more just, to point those out who are being unfair.

I would visit Anna Walentynowicz every now and again because her house was on my way home and I'd drop by. She treated us like a mother. And when we found that she had been fired from the shipyard, I myself had decided that I must protest. I don't know, perhaps some posters, or maybe a banner on a building. But Lech Wałęsa announced that we would be launching a strike.

Bogdan Borusewicz

When they fired Anna Walentynowicz, I decided that the time had come to react, that we must organise a strike in her defence because, otherwise, my two years of work will have been a waste of time. They will fire all of them, and not many were left, just a few of the young ones. That was the basis of that decision. I couldn't allow them to cut me off from the workers, nor let them be fired just like that. Blacklisted and discarded from work. It wasn't the first time for me, so I wasn't worried. I was a professional revolutionary. When they fired Anna Walentynowicz in

August, it was a sign that they were going to fire every last one of them.

Jacqueline Hayden

This was not Anna Walentynowicz's first fight, and people knew that. People knew who she was in Gdańsk. She was a very iconic figure. If you think about the imagery of Communism, the strong woman carved almost from rock – Anna was that. She was a crane driver and so the very fact that she had been one of these heroines of socialism and had in her early days been a very committed Communist, that in itself is quintessentially part of the danger that these people were to Communism, because if Communist ideology put the worker as the central plank of their ideology and this woman who was a hero of socialism and who believed in it enthusiastically is suddenly herself leading opposition on the basis of the defence of workers, it poses this really problematic threat to the whole idea of what Communism is about.

Bogdan Borusewicz

I wrote a pamphlet about Anna Walentynowicz. I printed about 8,000 of those pamphlets, in an underground printing facility. There were only three young shipyard workers in the know: Bogdan Felski, at whose house we would meet, Jerzy Borowczak and Ludwik Prądzński. And, while I was preparing the technical side of the strike, I was meeting with them and had to convince them to do it. Wałęsa found out about it at the last moment, at a general meeting. A few of our colleagues had just left jail. We called a meeting, and I took Wałęsa aside and told him, in front of them, that we're planning a strike and that he has to be part of it. The others had been coming to me with this request, saying that someone older simply must get involved because they're too young. I did it in front of them because I knew that Wałęsa was very ambitious: if I told him

487

to be part of the strike then he would not refuse in front of them. Just in case, I asked Ludwik Prądzński to go to his house every day and remind him, in case he forgot, that the strike's in three days, the strike's in two days, etc.

Jerzy Borowczak

We decided that we would do the strike on the 13th [of August]. Ludwik Prądzyński went to Lech, and we got this magnetic drawing screen. Kids have them these days, you pull it and erase it. Ludwik had one like that and so he went to him on the 12th in the evening and wrote to him: 'Lechu, 13th, 5 a.m., Gdańsk Shipyard, Gate number 2, be there.'

Lech said: 'No way, I can't tomorrow, I have to go register my child' – because I think that's when his daughter Ania was born – 'Danka would kill me, no way, I can't tomorrow!' So, I asked him, 'How about Thursday? The 14th?' 'Ah! The 14th is fine! I can do it.' So, I rushed over to Bogdan Borusewicz and said, 'Bogdan, unfortunately Wałęsa can't make it. He can only make it on the Thursday.' Bogdan said, 'Okay, I'll pass it on to the printers to print some additional flyers. So, let's make it the 14th, at 5am, meeting point by the gate of the shipyard.' All five of us, including Borusewicz.

Then, on the 14th, I was the only one to turn up. It was twenty to six, which is when Ludwik goes to work, and I see him emerge with a colleague who was not included in any of the strike plotting. I said, 'Ludwik, damn, what's happening?' And Ludwik said, 'Well, I don't know! I don't know!' I said, 'Okay, let's just go for it, let's proceed as planned. I'll start at K5, I'll take some people along and let's go.' But he goes, 'I don't have any flyers.' I said, 'What? There's 7,000 of them, so where are they?' 'Felski has them.' Goddamn it! I thought I was going to lose it.

So, we made a run for it to my department, and I gave him maybe 1,500 flyers and three posters, and I said, 'Go on, scram to your department.' It was two or three minutes to six. People were in the locker rooms already. And that's how I got it rolling.

I ended up walking out of my sector with 100 people, walking across the shipyard as planned. We entered the different departments, distributing the flyers and telling them that they had fired Anna Walentynowicz, that the shipyard in Gdynia is on strike, that Remontowa [a Gdańsk shipyard] halted, that everyone's on strike. Of course, we were lying, no one had stopped. And it was a coincidence that I saw a tractor, and I climbed on top of it. I called for people to make up a strike committee and for strike demands. And people brought them to me, on scraps of cigarette packets, and there were many different things: that [...] the meals were cold, the milk hadn't been delivered, there's no hot water, a whole load. The director of the shipyard came over. He climbed up to us and said: 'Since you have your strike committee picked out now, get back to work! I'll negotiate with them!'

Frankly, I started looking around, wondering how I should flee, because I could see the crowds starting to disperse. And Borusewicz isn't here, Wałęsa isn't here. I didn't know what to do! I wouldn't go to negotiate because I would be put away immediately, so I was looking around, and all of a sudden I noticed Lech Wałęsa. He was running in from the direction of the gate and he was pulled up on the roof [of the tractor] at once, completely pumped up, out of breath, and he goes: 'Director, do you recognise me? I worked here, I received a mandate for earning the trust of my team. You fired me!' And that sucked the people back in. I gave him the paper and he read the first few names [of the strike committee] and then he said: 'My name should be on here too, do you all agree to that?' Bravo! And that's how Lech became the leader of the strike.

Jacqueline Hayden

I remember someone trying to explain what happened: that Wałęsa simply jumped up on to a piece of equipment, seized the microphone, jumped on to the gates and made that famous speech of exhortation and inspired the workers. But I suppose the big thing was that by this stage there was a media presence and the impact of that particular moment and because he was able to seize the moment, because he had the charisma, that was really his great gift and his great contribution. But there were faults, there were problems.

Jerzy Borowczak

On the Saturday, the director came by himself and accepted all the demands. Borusewicz caught Wałęsa by the sleeve and we went out of the room. 'What will we do? Damn it! What now?' And the workers came along and I remember one of them screaming, 'What the fuck are you doing! The director's giving us the money, what are you plotting here? You're playing this out politically! We're not interested in that!' So, what was Lech to do? He went back in and grabbed the mic, and he said, 'I'm a democrat. We're going to vote. Who's for ending the strike, and who's for continuing it with other factories?' We counted the votes up: 25 for and 120-plus against. And he took the mic back and said: 'Since it's a democracy, we have voted. I consider the strike to have come to an end.' And that's how it unfolded. But it was because of the committee's vote, not because Wałęsa had said: 'I'm ending the strike, go home.' That was the democracy.

When Wałęsa announced that he considers the strike to have come to end, they switched off the mics, and just the director ended with: 'Whoever doesn't leave the shipyard by 6pm will not receive their 2,000-złoty raise.' Can you imagine what was going on? I feel ashamed. I called out to one colleague. He goes, 'No way, Jurek! I never ever earned 2,000 złoty. You heard what the director said! If I don't leave, I won't get it!' So they all ran ... I was just scared. We closed the gates and people were jumping over the fences. I was so disappointed that people would let themselves be bought for 2,000 złoty. It was terrible. Even today, when I close my eyes I can see them throwing their canvas bags over the fence, clambering up there. Damn, you can't imagine the scene ... Incredible.

Jacqueline Hayden

The immediate cause of the strike being called was the sacking of Anna, and so the immediate goals purely related to the issue of the sacking and of course then the background of conditions and payment, etc. But in a sense, the genesis of what would later fracture Solidarity can be seen in the different personalities because, even then, you could see [Lech Wałęsa] was a pragmatic person. There was a charisma about him, I mean he was somebody who could engage. At a certain point he took the decision that the grounds of their complaints had been dealt with by the authorities and he actually called the strike off, and it was other people, most importantly Anna Walentynowicz herself, but Alina Pienkowska, a nurse who many would have thought [of] as a more quiet and thoughtful person, it was her who actually stood up and found her voice and demanded that the strikers not prevent any further activity, that they would remain on strike, because of the fact that workers in other enterprises had so far not had resolution. It could've all collapsed. And it was the fact of Wałęsa initially being prepared to stop the strike at an early stage, that was held against him and really was one of the earliest reasons for the turning of some members of the group against Wałęsa and the development of this story about Wałęsa being a Communist agent. And the biggest piece of evidence that is put forward is that

Jacqueline Hayden with Lech Wałęsa.

Wałęsa wanted to stop the strike. He was quick enough to catch the atmosphere and therefore was quick enough to know that he had to basically change his mind and do so publicly and he did so, but it was because of the actions of a number of women, including Alina Pienkowska.

Bogdan Borusewicz

I put the '21 Demands' together. There was even a 22nd demand, which my colleague had added, for free elections. I told him to cross it out immediately because a demand for free elections means a stipulation to the regime: 'Give us our power back immediately.' And, of course, we couldn't do that. The demand for free labour unions was already on the edge of being accepted.

The whole time I was aware that we were playing not only with Warsaw, and the party in Warsaw or [Edward] Gierek, but also with Moscow. And the whole time I was careful not to breach a certain line, and that's why, when the strike unfolded, I did not call for a general strike. Because I was worried that if a general strike would take place, if the railways came to a halt, and the Russian armies became cut off from their railway routes and bases, there could be an intervention. Either they would pressure our authorities to use force or they would do it themselves. So that of course, at the moment, was also a game with Russia. But three days into the strike, it had become nationwide.

Jacqueline Hayden

It was physically hard to get close to the gates. The place was absolutely jammed with people, but you could see the '21 Demands' there. But I think the important thing to remember is that an awful lot of Polish people saw it because it was televised and it was that issue of the decision

Jerzy Borowczak (left) carrying Lech Wałęsa on his shoulders.

to allow the cameras to remain that became the real problem for the Communists. I often think back to when people talk about when regimes are weak, and regimes become weak of course when they begin to change or democratise in some shape or form. And so perhaps the first moment of real weakness for the Communist negotiators was allowing the imagery of the gates, the imagery of Wałęsa, the imagery of negotiation, the '21 Demands' – for that to be so visible. That was the crucial thing. The whole of Poland saw it and the whole of the world saw it and that was an absolutely new image.

Bogdan Borusewicz

After that strike, when we came out victorious, when we won the strike, I knew that Poland would have to change. But I also knew that I would never surpass this achievement in my life. It was depressing for me, because I was 31 at the time. A man of 31 knows, or believes, that his whole life is ahead of him, there are many successes ahead of him. He can change a lot, he can still achieve a lot. And I knew that I couldn't, that this strike that I organised was the biggest thing that I would achieve in my life.

Jerzy Borowczak

Lech Wałęsa had that something. He knew how to react in every single moment. That's why I keep saying that people loved him because it was obvious. I myself would lift him up with my hands. We're walking around and people would start yelling, 'Lechu up! Lechu up!' And so I would lift him.'

'A threat to our mutual humanity'

The Nuclear Arms Race and CND (1981–7)

On 1 September 1983, a South Korean civilian airliner on its way from the United States to Seoul was shot out of the sky and plummeted into the Sea of Japan, killing all 269 passengers and crew on board, including 22 children. The plane, Korean Air Lines Flight 007, had mistakenly veered off course into Soviet airspace and failed to respond to warning signals. The Soviet Air Defence Command classified it as a military target, probably an intruding American spy plane, and gave the orders to fire air-to-air missiles to bring it down.

It was a moment of dangerous, tragic drama at a point when tensions between Moscow and Washington were already climbing to new heights. President Ronald Reagan called it an 'act of barbarism' and a 'crime against humanity which must never be forgotten'. The Kremlin leader, Yuri Andropov, apologised for the loss of life but claimed it was the result of a deliberate American provocation and blamed Washington for a 'criminal act'.

Two months later, there was another Cold War scare. A NATO war game so alarmed the Soviet Union that it put some of its forces on alert, this time seemingly bringing the world to within a hair trigger of nuclear disaster. The annual NATO Able Archer exercise, involving 40,000 troops throughout Western Europe, was to practise the escalation of conflict from conventional to chemical and nuclear weapons. In November 1983, the way the scenario was played out included new elements that made it more realistic than in previous years. The Kremlin was already so fearful of the Americans' capacity to mount a surprise nuclear strike that for a brief moment it looked as though they believed the American commands they were eavesdropping on were genuine and a real nuclear attack could be imminent.

The two incidents revealed how perilous the world had become. Relations between the Cold War rivals were back in the deep freeze. Détente had evaporated. Belligerent rhetoric on both sides was ratcheting up the pressure. Russian, European and American citizens all began to wonder, as they had during the Cuban Missile Crisis in 1962, if war between the superpowers really could be around the corner.

Several factors led to the deterioration in relations and this new fear of nuclear war. From the point of view of Western powers, Moscow no longer looked like a viable partner. They pointed to increasing Soviet meddling in Third World conflicts, the direct intervention in 1979 in Afghanistan and the imposition of martial law in 1981 to crush Solidarity in Poland. From Moscow's perspective, the arrival of President Ronald Reagan in the White House in 1981 meant they were now dealing with an unapologetic Cold Warrior whose mission was to undermine and ultimately destroy Soviet Communism.

Reagan made no secret of the fact that his conservative Republican presidency was a world away from the previous presidency of the Democrat Jimmy Carter. In a speech to the British Parliament in June 1982, which laid out what later would be called the 'Reagan Doctrine', he announced 'a plan and a hope for the long term – the march of freedom and democracy which will leave Marxism–Leninism on the ash heap of history'. A year later, he went one step further. Soviet Communism, he said, was 'totalitarian darkness', 'the focus of evil in the modern world' and – the phrase which would reverberate worldwide – 'an evil empire'. Reagan's position was clear cut. He believed that the Soviet Union was not as strong as it appeared, and he wanted to weaken it further. He had no time for détente, dismissing it as 'a one-way street that the Soviet Union has used to pursue its own aims … world revolution and a one-world Communist or socialist state'.

To push back against Soviet influence, Reagan boosted funding for anti-Communist groups around the world, like the mujahidin in Afghanistan, UNITA in Angola and the Contras fighting a left-wing government in Nicaragua. He sharply increased American defence spending to make it harder for the Soviet Union to match it. And instead of the nuclear arms deals of his predecessors, he ordered a massive American military build-up, embellished with new weapons and systems, including research into an experimental missile defence shield, dubbed 'Star Wars'. He also pushed for the deployment of a new generation of medium-range Pershing II and cruise missiles in Western Europe to counter the SS-20 Saber missiles being installed in Eastern Europe by the Soviets.

The idea that a new class of faster and more accurate intermediate-range nuclear missiles should be placed in Europe was a matter of considerable controversy. In the first place, it looked as though, by placing them on European soil, both the Cold War superpowers were now prepared to contemplate a scenario where Europe could become the theatre for a limited nuclear war. In the second place, some saw the first strike capability of the missiles as especially dangerous and aggressive, and a feature that could further escalate the nuclear arms race.

The Pershing II ballistic missiles were intended for West Germany. Most of the mobile, land-based cruise missiles were to be sited in Britain, a decision that caused heated debates in a deeply divided House of Commons. Opposition Labour MPs accused the Conservative government of Margaret Thatcher of 'reckless cynicism' in agreeing to host them. When the first shipment of the American-made cruise missiles arrived in Britain in November 1983, there was an outcry from anti-war protestors.

On the ground in Western Europe, not everyone shared Ronald Reagan's anti-Communist views. Some even saw his belligerence as downright hazardous, far more of a menace than any Soviet threat. They argued his policies were turning places like Britain and West Germany into targets, especially in the village communities close to the American bases where the new US nuclear missiles were to be stationed, because these would be the first places to be struck by Soviet weapons if ever there were to be a nuclear war in Europe.

The debate revitalised anti-nuclear movements such as Britain's Campaign for Nuclear Disarmament (CND), which had been somewhat in decline since the first wave of anti-nuclear protests in the late 1950s and early 1960s. Its rallies grew in size and so did its membership. A huge demonstration in London to protest against the deployment of US cruise missiles in October 1983 was mirrored by other equally large rallies in cities across Europe.

The Soviet Union saw the European peace movement as a highly effective means to try to harness public opinion, not just against missile deployments, but also to counter what at first had been a formidable anti-Soviet information campaign by the incoming Reagan administration. It was a tactic that was in some ways self-defeating as it risked the peace campaigners involved in the protests being tarnished by association with Moscow, although allegations of Soviet funding being channelled to groups like CND were vigorously contested and never substantiated.

At the local level, anti-nuclear civil disobedience campaigns in the UK were a world away from Cold War geopolitics. One campaign network tracked down and tried to block trucks carrying cruise missiles on public roads. In the end, to avoid them, orders were given for the missiles to be moved around only at night and under police escort. Campaigners focused on the two bases where US cruise missiles were sited. In Berkshire, women's camps were set up outside RAF Greenham Common; green, religious and political protestors established them-selves outside RAF Molesworth in Cambridgeshire. And side by side with the Cold War fear that nuclear holo-caust might be just over the horizon were the pressures and personal interactions of village life in small English country parishes.

In the end, it was big-power politics rather than small-town protests that caused the next and final Cold War shift. In time, President Reagan came to realise that the fact that the Soviets also saw the Americans as potential aggressors was in itself a threat, and something had to be done to rebuild trust. In 1984, he declared in a speech that he was prepared to 'meet the Soviets halfway'. The following year Gorbachev, intent on reform for his own reasons, took the helm in Moscow. The two leaders agreed to meet for an ice-breaking summit in December 1985 in Geneva. By

1987, they had transformed US–Soviet relations and built up enough understanding to conclude a ground-breaking deal to eliminate a whole class of nuclear missiles.

In 1982 **Guy Bower** *was an American fighter pilot stationed at airbases across Europe.*

If you were in a frontline war fighting unit like I was in at [Spanish airbase] Torrejón, you were always concerned about what might evolve that could lead up to some kind of nuclear exchange. Flying the F4 at Torrejón, I sat Active Nuclear Alert at İncirlik [in Turkey] and at Aviano airbase in northern Italy. My F4 had a single B61 nuclear weapon attached to it; you were living in there in a bunker and at any moment you could be launched, and that's as close as you can get. You get more used to the idea it could happen, as opposed to the local citizenry off the base who know there's nuclear weapons there and airplanes sitting alert – and that could make them considerably more nervous than we were as the active players who would launch and carry this thing into a war zone if that was what transpired.

In the early 1980s, **Jeanne Steinhardt** *was a Quaker and eventually a member of the Fellowship of Reconciliation, a group she describes as a Christian-based ecumenical charity concerned with pacifism. She was bringing up her children in Wellingborough in Northamptonshire, when she heard that US cruise missiles were going to be arriving at RAF Molesworth.*

The shock for me was that it was going to be 17 miles from where I lived with my children – that was a real shock. And I thought, 'I don't want my children to grow up to be part of this way of living.' The stuff about nuclear weapons suggests there is this terrible threat out there, that there is this great machine that's about to be involved in attacking us and we therefore have to respond in like fashion. Because of my children I wanted to say, 'It's not like that – there can be a different way of living, and it's wrong to think about attacking some other woman's child.' I believe there is something unique in every person and that every person is a 'child of God', and that is how we should be trying to approach each other. We should try to approach each other in such a way that it diminishes the risk of threat, of attack – trying to seek common ground without giving way on matters that seem of crucial importance, such as killing.

I saw the real threat as a threat to our mutual humanity, rather than a threat from Russia to Britain. I think the process of the Cold War was just what happens in any situation where people are different. People become pigeon-holed; one gets a back-against-the-wall mentality where striking out seems the only answer. The Cold War was just that human activity on a bigger scale.

*Thirteen miles from RAF Molesworth there was another base, RAF Alconbury, which also saw anti-nuclear protests. **Terry Pinner** farmed land on the edge of the base, and at the time he was chair of the local parish council.*

I was born here. My grandfather farmed Alconbury up to the start of the Second World War, when it was commandeered for the American Air Force to come here. Immediately after the war, my father had the land back as a tenant to the Air Ministry. We carried on farming it till around 1955, and the farm was taken back again. My father had 250 acres of winter wheat nearly ready to harvest and the whole lot had to be ploughed in. The Americans have been here ever since. They've been very good neighbours to us, easy to get on with. The one thing

RAF Alconbury did was to create an awful lot of employment in the area – land maintenance, building maintenance, properties they've rented, the local women used to babysit – it was the main source of employment up until recent days.

I remember the cruise missiles arriving. It was no great shock to us. We were already used to a high military presence here, with the U-2 spy planes and the other bombers and strike aircraft that were here, so we just accepted it as a military operation.

The Americans were here to protect us, and it was only right we should support them.

*Later in 1982, **Guy Bower** was assigned to RAF Alconbury. His job was to role-play a Soviet pilot in military exercises.*
I landed at Heathrow and my sponsor met me and we got on the train north to Huntingdon. Two days of debauchery and fun, because our squadron was a bunch of very talented air-to-air fighter pilots and they were enthusiastic partiers as well. One of the ways we did that was to welcome new guys with several different traditional forms of celebration. It started from the minute I got on base. At about four o'clock that afternoon a very long and fun night began.

I found a great house in a little village south-southwest of the base in Great Staughton. It was a gorgeous little estate and everybody was so friendly. I moved in as a single guy; everyone there was families with little kids. I bought a left-hand drive local automobile, but I also had a fairly high-end motorcycle that drew a lot of attention. When I moved in, I was overwhelmed by the welcoming committee – two neighbours across the street coming over separately. They even had a little gathering at the church recreation centre to welcome the 'Yank' into the village.

When I first moved in, I pulled [my motorbike] into my driveway, and one of the neighbours I had not yet met across the street, a young guy who went to and from work on his Honda 250, a small motorcycle – he came over and was admiring my bike. We got to talking and I got through cleaning and inspecting it and said, 'Here, here's the key – go for a ride.' It was a Kawasaki KZ1000 Mark II – as big and as powerful a bike as you could buy – and he looked at me … and came back an hour later and we were fast friends from that day forward.

On base, the Cold War was something that was always there in the background. The reconnaissance squadron flying RF4s trained and had missions. They would be an integral part of any hostilities that broke out. But when I first got there, there was little or no conversation. There was interest in Americans being based there but it wasn't new. The older the individuals I met, the more open, accepting and actually welcoming, [more so] than some of the younger ones … Knowing how things transpired during World War Two, they thought having us around was not so bad. The younger folks weren't less welcoming, but the older folks seemed to have a better appreciation that we were not there to take over England, or to be anything other than good neighbours and help defend our allies in Europe. That held true pretty much the whole time we were there. There were periods of tension – when the Falklands became an issue and it was decided the Harriers were going to go and be the main air arm of that conflict, and the 527th Aggressor Squadron played an integral role in their preparation.

Jeanne Steinhardt

The first thing I did was that I was involved in visiting the camp [at RAF Molesworth]. Initially, there was quite a small group who took a position outside the base, and that grew and grew and grew, particularly in 1984 when there was a 'Green Gathering'. People stayed. Then there was this huge village known as the 'Rainbow Village'. People were there for all sorts of different reasons – not necessarily spiritual – maybe for green reasons, or maybe just wanting to have a different way of life, a sort of freedom.

I was involved in daily vigils outside the fence, especially once we had the Peace Chapel partly underway. I was involved in dialogue, usually with the police. There was this fear, this threat of this alien body – the Communists out there. There were rumours that CND were really Communists – it wasn't true, although perhaps there were some, a small amount – but that's not what it was about. So, it was interesting to be able to talk to people and find out what there was in common, to find some really nice people the other side of the fence.

A lot of what went on at the camp at Molesworth [was] attempts to make connections between people and to try to demonstrate a more constructive way of being. There were things like, just part of the normal discussions, where you might say, 'Can we be allowed in to witness?' And they had to say no. We'd explain why we wanted to do that. I remember a policeman telling me he'd started reading up on Quaker history because he found it interesting.

I remember an incident where the police had been told by the church, I believe, to remove all constructions from what was known as Peace Lane. There was a tent named as a 'Tabernacle'; a local minister – known as 'Mick the Vic' – used to come once a week and carry out some sort of communion service in there. Some of the people camping were Buddhist or into serious meditation. It was said this tent known as the Tabernacle had to be removed. A few of us were there when the police came and told us to take it down, and we refused. We said it was a place of worship and quiet, and a safe place for people. We asked, 'Surely you can contact the church and say, "Do they really want to demolish this?"' That policeman tried to contact the church but couldn't. We were all sitting down, and the policeman took it down.

In one act of protest, **Jeanne Steinhardt** *and her fellow campaigners tried to stop building contractors accessing the base to – they thought – help create facilities for the cruise missiles.* On that particular vigil, we held a sort of communion as we were fastened in chains to each other across the road. Included in the maybe seven or eight people were a couple of anarchists – who would be atheists – a couple of Quakers, a monk, and 'Mick the Vic' serving orange juice and brown bread. We had a notice asking people to stop; there was another member of the Fellowship of Reconciliation a little bit down the road, stopping vehicles as they approached to say this was happening. It was a very peaceful atmosphere. Of course, the police came out and separated everyone and cut the chains. It was all very amiable, in a way. It was interesting the way the police would regard us. It was once said we were not 'proper criminals'.

Within the Rainbow Village, there would be some people who really had a resentment that here were Americans coming to our country to try to control us. It's not something I would feel strongly myself at all, but there were people that would think that – not along Peace Lane where the camp ended up, but for some within the Rainbow Village.

Terry Pinner
I had no objections at all to the cruise missiles; we did have a problem with the CND. They came into villages

and tried to set up a peace camp inside our parish. The Bishop of Huntingdon was going to come and bless it. I was chairman of the parish council and I asked him not to. I told him that we had a perfectly good Church of England church inside the village, and the peace campers were more than welcome to attend our church. I didn't want to see this camp being blessed by the local bishop.

Our church hadn't got a vicar and I asked the Bishop if he could find a vicar for us, which fell on deaf ears, so while he was coming to bless the peace camp, my wife and I wrote a big placard – 'PLEASE CAN WE HAVE A VICAR FOR OUR CHURCH FIRST?'

A retired American serviceman who was on the airfield had been ordained as an Anglican priest. He saw what was printed in one of the international newspapers and he approached us, and we had many happy years with him as our vicar.

Jeanne Steinhardt's campaigning was focused on RAF Molesworth, but she remembers one hostile encounter near RAF Alconbury.

I remember some sort of demo where we were involved in walking all round the base, and going through Alconbury. There was a woman came out and shouted at me and told me to get a job, and said, 'We pay rates here!' I said, 'Yeah, I have a job and I pay rates too!' I think she was struck dumb by that.

[At Molesworth] I can recall some local people who would get involved in creating the Peace Garden at the corner of Peace Lane. Equally, I believe there was a pub that banned anybody from the camp. The only hostility I encountered was the woman shouting at me to get a job.

Terry Pinner
It wasn't just here that we had problems. There was a peace camp at Molesworth as well, and these people would park their caravans or tents at the side of the road, on private property. It was just this one element that was not only slightly vulgar, but very much left-wing. The local councillors from Molesworth and from here discussed things, but they had their own problems over there.

When the CND moved in, it was the way they acted and carried on – they tried to bully people. There was definitely a rent-a-mob element inside the CND. They came and pitched up camp inside our parish. I nearly got locked up one night because I went up on my horse and asked them to move, and they accused me of harassing them, but that went by the by. As time went on, we decided they ought to be moved; they decided they weren't going to be moved.

There was a lovely couple who used to sit outside the gates. They were in their sixties, and it was a cold, wet morning when they sat there, all huddled up. As I rode by on my horse, I asked them how they were. I said, 'Have you had any breakfast this morning?' They said no. I said, 'You do realise that [the Catholic priest and CND General Secretary] Monsignor Kent has just got out of bed, just had a shower, he's just got dressed, he's just had his breakfast laid out – he's in a nice comfortable house and you're here getting wet through.' They said, 'You're absolutely correct,' and packed their stuff up and went home.

I farmed quite an area of land which the airbase surrounds so the boundary of my land was the security fence. What we objected to was the way an element of the CND ran all over our fields trying to get on to the airbase, coming through our farmyards. It wasn't the bulk of them – it was a small element of the objectors. I've no objection to doing it peacefully, but I do object when they do it violently.

There were an awful lot of people in the CND who believed in what they were saying and doing. One night after coming home from the pub, there were several of them outside the base gates, and I said to them, 'Listen here, it's not on, we shouldn't be doing this. We should be doing this in a different way. Why don't you pop down to the farm and we'll have a cup of coffee and discuss it?' Probably half a dozen of them came down here, with one of my friends, and we had a discussion about what was right and what was wrong. They didn't change their point of view; I didn't change mine. We didn't fall out. They left quite happily. There were a lot of good people in the CND, as well as a lot of bad people.

Jeanne Steinhardt

I climbed the fence [at RAF Molesworth] just outside the Peace Chapel. It was terrifying. It was after we'd been told we could not go and witness at the Peace Chapel. I think the fence was 15 foot high. I fell off the top of it because the person behind me climbing made everything vibrate. I was picked up by a policeman. We walked away and he was hanging on to my arm. I said, 'I'm not going to run away.' He said, 'I can see that, but it's my job.' We had candles, and lit them in the holding room in the base, where they hold you to decide what to do with you. It was an act of witness.

There was a protest at Burghfield [Atomic Weapons Establishment], on Holy Innocents' Day. Most people were planting little crosses inside the base, with pictures of children. Myself and a couple of friends from Molesworth had planned to go as far as we could inside the base, as near as we could get to the final assembly point. On the

Jeanne Steinhardt and comrades holding a vigil to try to prevent construction at RAF Molesworth to accommodate US cruise missiles.

way into the base – we crawled under the fence – two of us fell into the ditch. We got sopping wet; it was December. We got fairly well into the base, and then we were spotted. I stood there waiting for this man to come up to me. He was presumably army, as he had a gun, and another, I think, policeman held me with my arms in a half-nelson behind my back, and this man pointed the gun at me. I looked at them and I said to the man with the gun, 'Do your children know what you do?'

I felt so sorry. He was stunned and as we walked back to the holding room he had tears running down his cheeks. I thought this is just a man trying to do a job, trying to look after his family. To me, it would be an awful thing to confess to my children that I was involved in the machinery of war, but this man believed he was doing the right thing and was looking after his family, and I shouldn't have said that.

While protestors were entering the airbases as an act of protest, other British people were invited in as the guests of the Americans.

Guy Bower

The experience of having British nationals come on to Alconbury was one of the highlights. We did a joint 'dining out' with the base next door. Their squadron officers came over to our Officers' Club; some of them brought their wives, and there was a lot of local leadership, government officials from Huntingdon and the surrounding area. It was a formal night of nice, relaxed conversation, great food and beverages. As the night progressed it got a bit rowdy, as events like this would do with fighter pilots in the auditorium. At the end, there was a lot of handshaking and hugging.

Mary, the bartender at the Alconbury Officers' Club, [and I] became great friends. When I came back to the States, I was involved in the F-117, the Stealth fighter, when it was still top secret. We flew our A7s over to Europe because we had to exercise where we might deploy in the F-117, and I made it my purpose to cross country to Alconbury not only to see some of my buds who might still be around the neighbourhood, but so I could go to the Officers' Club and give Mary a hug. We used to entertain boy scouts and girl scouts. We'd give them a tour of our squadron building and show them a film about what we did and why, and let them crawl around an airplane – all good memories.

Terry Pinner
The Americans used to invite us on the airbase to different celebrations they have through the year. For people living in the country, it was a bit strange because, when you got on to the airbase, they had their clubs and their bowling alleys, and it was just like being in the centre of a big city. They were self-contained inside there.

We used to be invited to Thanksgiving, where they used to have their pumpkin pies, and they would pair an English with an American couple. The Americans looked after us all through the proceedings. The great entertainment we had was on the Fourth of July celebrations, where they had their fairgrounds, with their hot-dog stalls, their burger stalls and their candy-floss stalls. At the end of the evening, when it got dark, they'd have a massive firework display, and that would go on for three-quarters of an hour – as good a firework display as you've seen anywhere. They sent a personal invitation to each person inside the parishes of Great and Little Stukeley to attend these functions. The other thing they had on the airbase was three marvellous clubs – their NCOs' Club, Officers' Club and an Airmen's Club. Being chairman of the parish council, I was invited quite regularly.

The thing people complained about was the noise of the aircraft, more than the thought of a nuclear war. The American Air Force paid for a lot of the houses in the village to be double-glazed , which made an awful lot of difference. But being brought up with the airbase here, a lot of us took no notice of it.

They would have exercises on a regular basis. They would generally let me know when something was happening because they didn't want the parishioners to think that this was for real. So, we knew when there was a base lockdown. They secured the base as if it was on a war footing.

Newcomers would come and live inside the parish and they would object to the Americans flying at night. The only thing we old locals used to say to them was 'You chose to live here. We went through the Second World War. We've always been here with the Americans. They've always been our neighbours, and we're going to support them.' Some of them didn't like that very much!

One day they were having a military exercise. They were flying sorties with aircraft of all sorts and practising their exercises. It went on through the day, and was going on through the night. The noise of the aircraft was absolutely awful. Being chairman of the parish council, half the parishioners were phoning me through the night, and asking me if I could stop the aeroplanes from flying. I'd got a very good repartee with the base commander, so at two o'clock in the morning, I phoned him up and I said, 'I'm awfully sorry but my parishioners are going to lynch me if these aircraft keep flying.' He said, 'I can't sleep either – we're going to call it off!'

Guy Bower

[During the 1983 NATO exercise Able Archer], as active duty Air-Force guys in Europe, we had some briefings about what went on, but they were mostly after the fact. We had some insight into the beginnings of this potential problem, but we got the brunt of our news after the fact from the news, and from our intelligence folks on base at Alconbury.

A command-and-control exercise has to be as realistic as possible. In this case, this exercise had some new aspects of command and control, and had high-level government agencies involved, and of course it involved NATO headquarters in Western Europe, in Belgium, and their communications are monitored. To me, that was the downfall: we did different things and it showed a different approach to exercises than had been previously viewed by the Soviet Union. I can see where they would mistake it for something other than what it was. In this case, the fault in my opinion was adding new types of communication and new players in the communication protocol. We really telegraphed that we were on the verge of upgrading to Def Con One; that would imply a coordinated first-strike nuclear attack. We learned from that.

How we felt about this debacle, Able Archer, after the fact, was probably less than what the average British citizen would think. It sounds cavalier but because we knew how things worked, we weren't overly concerned – very concerned but not to the point of being nervous of all-out nuclear war. But that is one time when some of my British neighbours questioned me.

Finally, on 6 February 1985, some 1,500 police officers and soldiers were deployed to remove the Rainbow Village camp outside RAF Molesworth.

Jeanne Steinhardt

I got a phone call in the early hours of the morning, maybe midnight, to say that the village was being surrounded by police and that everyone was being told to get off-site. One of my friends who lived in the Rainbow Village asked, if there was any problem and her children were taken away, would I be prepared to have her children? It was that bad. I said yes. So we did try, first thing in the early hours of morning, to get there, but the roads were closed all around.

The police lined up and formed barriers to close roads, so people were being channelled along particular routes.

It was a horrible situation and I can't remember what time we finally managed to get on-site. By then, I didn't know where my friend was. We didn't know what was happening. There were fires everywhere – some of the travellers set fire to their caravans. Some who were travellers in origin did that in the way one would signify a death. It was very heart-rending, very traumatic. People were trying to get cleared off as much as they could. The army standing guard, the fence going up and the razor wire – it was all pretty awful.

It was some time before we managed to get a message that my friends, with some other trucks, were being held in a layby and the police were not allowing them to move. There were little children there. We went there with water and food. A policeman tried to arrest me. I asked why. He said, 'This is a public layby.' I said, 'Precisely. Because it's a public layby, you are not going to arrest me. I am bringing water and food.' So, we delivered the water and food.

Guy Bower

The protests that went on at some of the bases that were getting new capabilities – on one hand, you felt empathy with those who were willing to put their life on hold and camp out and protest and paint signs. Then on the other hand, the rule of law is something that, as a conservative fighter pilot, you were glad to see it brought to an end. Maybe not in the best diplomatic way, but it did settle things down. As a well-received, welcomed American in the UK during that time, you didn't want to breed controversy and express your opinion with your neighbours even if you knew they were like-minded.

A smaller protest presence remained. But finally, in the wake of the 1987 Intermediate Range Nuclear Forces Treaty between the US and the USSR, the cruise missiles were withdrawn from RAF Molesworth.

Jeanne Steinhardt
When the missiles left, that was a great day. I seem to remember huge transporters moving out, and quite a small number of people just standing there watching, with a sense of release.

'Everyone wanted change'

Gorbachev's Perestroika (1985–91)

In the early hours of 11 March 1985, Mikhail Gorbachev and his wife, Raisa, stepped out into the grounds of their dacha or country house outside Moscow and went for a walk. It was a frequent habit of theirs, to get some air and exercise, but also to be able to talk frankly without fear of being monitored by the Soviet KGB, whose listening devices eavesdropped even on members of the Politburo. The previous day, the ailing Soviet leader Konstantin Chernenko had died, and Politburo members were due to gather to choose his successor.

It was the third time the country had said goodbye to a sick and ageing Kremlin leader in as many years. First, Leonid Brezhnev – a figure of conservative continuity but also a symbol of the country's stagnation – had died in 1982, having been in power for nearly two decades. Then in 1984, Yuri Andropov, the former powerful KGB chief and Gorbachev's patron, had succumbed to the kidney disease that had plagued his final years, after only 15 months at the helm. And now Chernenko had gone, yet another member of the Soviet gerontocracy, whose feeble and bumbling leadership had continued to undermine the country's standing in the world.

Gorbachev knew there was now an appetite for a new broom, someone to reinvigorate the Communist Party and re-establish the Soviet Union in the eyes of the world as a superpower on a par with its American Cold War rival. He also knew that he was the obvious choice and had done what he could to secure his chances by seeking the support, among others, of the veteran Soviet Foreign Minister, Andrei Gromyko.

This chat with his wife was the last chance to take stock and brace himself for the challenge ahead. 'We can't go on living like this,' he told her, in what would later become a catchphrase to explain what drove the impetus for change. He was referring both to the Soviet economy – so moribund that the state could not even feed itself, let alone keep up with the United States in a newly intensified arms race or maintain the Soviet Union's costly interventions abroad in such places as Afghanistan – and also to the dysfunctional and corrupt Communist bureaucracy, which had for years stifled the possibility of reform.

Later that day, Gorbachev was indeed chosen as the new Kremlin leader, proposed by the ruling Politburo and endorsed by the larger Central Committee of top party members. He lost little time in starting to implement his programme of reforms. To begin with, the changes ushered in by perestroika, as his reform programme was called, were deliberately limited. In Russian, '*perestroika*' means 'restructuring', and its initial purpose was to refresh the Soviet Communist system, not to do away with it. One new slogan merely called for '*uskorenie*', or the speeding up of economic production. Another set of new laws sanctioned small-scale cooperatives and joint ventures, while still banning private business. State ownership remained sacrosanct, and any political reforms that might challenge the Communist Party seemed a long way off.

Within a year, though, Gorbachev and his fellow reformers launched a new policy of 'glasnost' or 'openness'. This signal from above, giving a green light to free expression, had a dramatic impact on Soviet society. Political prisoners, including the Soviet Union's most famous dissident, Andrei Sakharov, were released from prison or brought back from exile. Censorship was lifted, generating an explosion of activity in journalism and the arts. Subjects once taboo could now be aired. Books previously circulated only in underground hand-typed samizdat copies were now available in print, including Aleksandr Solzhenitsyn's mammoth chronicle of the Soviet forced labour camp system, The Gulag Archipelago. New investigations into the repressions of the Stalin era began. No longer afraid to speak out, people began to gather in public for the first time in decades to debate, challenge and argue. It was an extraordinarily heady atmosphere and exactly the sort of grassroots political engagement that Gorbachev believed would secure his reform programme from below and fend off the objections from more conservative Politburo colleagues.

Abroad, Gorbachev's enlightened approach brought equally dramatic results. A tentative 'getting to know you' summit with President Ronald Reagan in Geneva at the end of 1985 was followed by a more ambitious meeting in Reykjavik in Iceland at the end of 1986. Though this produced no breakthroughs, it forged a new understanding between the two Cold War protagonists, resulting in an arms control agreement to slash nuclear arsenals in 1987. An historic visit by President Reagan to Moscow followed in 1988. The conservative US President, who just a few years before had denounced the Soviet Union as an 'evil empire', was now on first-name terms with the Kremlin leader, and amiably chatting to Soviet citizens on walkabout in Red Square.

By now, the pace of perestroika was quickening. Inevitably, this alarmed prominent conservatives in the Communist Party. They began to coalesce into an anti-reform camp, led by Politburo member Yegor Ligachev, and started to speak out, warning that the reforms were going too far and yielding too much ground both abroad and at home. But at the other end of the spectrum there were impatient demands for a more radical agenda. Some groups wanted to challenge the Communist Party's monopoly on power. Others wanted a more complete economic overhaul to abolish central planning, reintro-duce private property and transform the country into a proper market economy. And voices from other Soviet republics were calling for a serious discussion about the 'Nationalities Problem' and the relationship of the constit-uent republics to the centre, something that for decades the Soviet Communist Party leadership had considered too dangerous to be aired.

Gorbachev's way of handling these competing pres-sures was to play them off against each other. For a while, his masterful manipulation worked. In June 1988, he summoned top Communists from around the coun-try for a special meeting in Moscow known as the '19th Party Conference'. It was a pivotal event, which not only exposed the deep split in the party between radicals and hard-liners, but was also used by Gorbachev to push through an astonishing political reform: the creation of a new legislative body called the Congress of People's Deputies, whose members were both hand-picked top Communists and elected representatives from around the country. When its sessions began in May 1989, the often-fiery debates were broadcast live on Soviet television and the entire country was gripped.

But by 1990, as demands from different groups grew more radical, Gorbachev's deft juggling act was becoming hard to sustain, and it began to look as though the process he had initiated was no longer under his control. Where once he had been able to play off hard-liners in the party and KGB against radical reformers seeking faster change, thereby enhancing his own role as final arbiter and ultimate leader, now the two sides were pulling so hard in different directions that he risked looking hesitant and unsure of what to do.

Nationalists from the Baltics and from Ukraine, outspoken academics, former prominent political prisoners, plus former Moscow party chief Boris Yeltsin, who had allied himself with Russian liberals, were all beginning to demand a deeper political transformation incompatible with traditional Soviet Communist rule. Gorbachev's gamble had rested on the assumption that he could exploit his status as General Secretary of the Soviet Communist Party to dictate policy from above and expect others to follow suit. It was becoming clear that this was no longer the case. The reforms he had unleashed had encouraged plain speaking, in the media, in Parliament and on the streets. Famously, he had declared that 'no one, not even the General Secretary of the Communist Party, is above criticism.' But an increasingly pluralistic press was now taking him at his word and regularly criticising his leadership. No longer was it so clear that where he led, others would follow without question.

In March 1990 Gorbachev created a new post of executive Soviet President – a move designed to augment his authority. But he decided not to risk a ballot where the Soviet people would be asked to vote for him directly.

Instead, he staged an indirect election by the Congress of People's Deputies and made himself the sole candidate on the ballot. The election gave him the extra title of Soviet President as well as head of the Soviet Communist Party, but it did little to enhance his domestic prestige. His political power was ebbing away.

All the while, the crumbling and chaotic Soviet economy was slowly grinding to a halt. Across the country, a sense of crisis intensified as shop shelves emptied and queues for basic goods lengthened. No longer were all Soviet citizens enamoured of perestroika. Many were beginning to tire of the turmoil it was causing and the strain it placed on their daily lives.

Ironically, the more Gorbachev came under pressure at home, the more his star rose abroad. In the United States and Western Europe, he was applauded for the transformations he had brought about, which looked as though they would bring the Cold War to a close. In particular, they cheered his willingness to engage in meaningful international arms control deals and to withdraw Soviet troops from the long-running war in Afghanistan.

Meanwhile, Gorbachev's policy of disengagement from client states in the developing world was mirrored by his instruction to Communist leaders in Eastern Europe that he was no longer prepared to use force to keep them in power, and that instead of relying on Moscow they should look for local solutions to their problems. It soon became evident that without the threat of a possible Soviet intervention to back them up, local Communist parties in the Eastern Bloc were extremely exposed, as they commanded little or no public support. With that realisation, there was little to hold the Soviet Bloc together. First, the Berlin Wall came down in November 1989, the demolition of a potent symbol of Europe's division, then one by one Eastern

Europe's Communist governments lost power. Most of them eased out peacefully, although in Romania President Nicolae Ceauşescu was overthrown more violently. All the while, their populations applauded Gorbachev in Moscow for giving them the opportunity to break free.

But inside the Soviet Union, exhilaration was giving way to a darker mood. At the end of 1990 one of Gorbachev's closest allies, his Foreign Minister Eduard Shevardnadze, abruptly submitted his resignation, delivering a dramatic warning that reformers were in retreat and 'a dictatorship is coming.'

Gorbachev remained in power, but to consolidate his hold, he filled his government with a mix of bureaucratic nonentities and die-hard Communists who were openly hostile to reform. At the start of 1991, it looked as though perestroika was in trouble and the old guard were intent on taking back control. Few could imagine that by the end of the year, the whole Soviet edifice would have come crumbling down.

Pavel Palazhchenko was born in 1949 near Moscow. He was the chief English interpreter for Mikhail Gorbachev between 1985 and 1991.

After three General Secretaries – Brezhnev, Andropov and Chernenko – died in succession, it was obvious that someone younger was to be elected. Everyone expected Gorbachev to be elected because he was, under Chernenko, the number-two person in the country. And everyone expected him to undertake some kind of change. No one really had any idea what kind of change that could be. People were considering different possibilities – change that could be similar to what was happening under Andropov for example, putting the house in order, greater discipline in all areas, more responsibility, etc. Some people, however, were expecting a different kind of change, but there was no consensus about what kind of change it could be. But everyone wanted change, there was a consensus on that.

The journalist and editor **Vitali Tretyakov** *began writing for Moscow News in 1988. He describes the newspaper during these years as 'the pulpit of glasnost'. One of his early articles was an exposé of the privileges of Communist Party officials.*

This article played a big role in my professional career. It was my idea. But Yegor Yakovlev [editor of *Moscow News*] didn't print everything. They say that he was the bravest editor, but that's not quite right. Still, it came out on the first or second day of the 19th Party Conference [in June 1988]. And Yegor Ligachev criticised this article directly from the podium of the conference. After that Yegor Yakovlev was proud! The *Moscow News* was directly criticised by a member of the Politburo, from the podium of the 19th Party Conference – Yegor was happy! After that he made me a political columnist for the *Moscow News*.

Lev Ponomarev *is a physicist and political activist. He was born in 1941 and grew up during Khrushchev's thaw. In 1987, he was one of the founders of Memorial, which began as a campaign for a monument to the victims of Stalin's terror.*

I was lucky because the Institute of Experimental Physics was a sort of oasis. We all spoke freely about everything and discussed any topics with our colleagues. I understood that everything's bad in the country, but didn't understand what I could do. I was waiting for a calling. That calling came when I found out that Gorbachev had called Andrei Sakharov and suggested he leave his exile. Initially, I observed Gorbachev. He says a lot, and maybe says a lot of the right things, but I could see that he's inconsistent and I didn't see any real change. But when he started talking about the release of political prisoners I understood and I began believing him. I realised that my time had come and I started to think about what I could do. I understood that any public service should first of all begin with commemorating the millions of people who perished in Stalin's camps.

In January or February of 1987, I read about a group that had proclaimed the same aim as me. And so, for two months we were debating with each other, creating a document about the founding [of Memorial] and the necessity of memorialising the memory of a million of those who died. And when we wrote it, we decided to collect signatures under this call, to demand of Gorbachev that he create a permanent memorial and archive. So, the aim was narrow to begin with.

How can we build a democratic state without having told the truth about the monstrous repressions? Many millions died, and we're the descendants of those people. Some people's parents survived, some people's didn't. In order to build democracy, we need to understand why it happened, so as not to make a mistake the next time. All this remains true today – we're still saying the same things.

*One of **Pavel Palazhchenko**'s first international summits was Mikhail Gorbachev's initial meeting with President Ronald Reagan, in Geneva in November 1985.*

The negotiations were difficult because they happened after a six-year break in the normal routine of summits, so a number of problems had piled up. At that time, President Reagan was seen in the Soviet Union as a very conservative, very right-wing, very anti-Communist politician, and many Soviet experts and diplomats believed that nothing could change while Reagan was President because he was so ideologically minded. And, indeed he was. Nevertheless, he and Gorbachev were able to develop a rapport and that started there in Geneva.

They started with a general overview. They committed to trying to improve the relationship, but both outlined in very strong terms their differences on the various issues, in particular Afghanistan, arms controls, INF [Intermediate-Range Nuclear Forces] missiles, and the various regional issues that at that time were quite acute. Another thing they discussed was whether it was possible to work out some joint statement. Before the summit, the Americans told us they were not happy with the practice of issuing long joint statements that were, as they said, long on rhetoric but short on substance. We thought that it would be a good idea to try to put on paper the areas of agreement and the areas that needed work. Despite what they had been saying before, Reagan surprisingly said that he would consider a joint statement. They instructed their diplomats to work on that joint statement, and ultimately it was adopted the next day. That was a big step forward. It was in that statement that Reagan and Gorbachev proclaimed that a nuclear war cannot be won and must never be fought and that they would not seek military superiority. That was a very important statement that set the tone for the relationship. But it was a difficult discussion, because [in] most of the areas that were discussed, the positions of the two leaders were very much apart.

There was initially a lot of mistrust on the part of Reagan. But also, surprisingly, mistrust on the part of Bush, who became President in 1988. One would've expected that, given the fact that he had been the Vice President under Reagan and he was very much in the loop on all of the things that were happening in the negotiations and at the previous summits, he would just pick up where Reagan had left off and they would start interacting and moving forward. But apparently there was some mistrust even then and it took Bush and his administration some time to restart the relationship. You shouldn't think that this was an easy prospect. At all times, it was a combination of the legacy of the Cold War and the new thinking, the new relationship, the new approaches to problems. But it was difficult.

The first real arms-reduction agreement was signed in December 1987. So, it took more than two years to develop that first, ultimately rather modest, step in the arms-control area. Then it took another three and a half years to sign the START [Strategic Arms Reduction Treaty], which was a huge reduction in the amount of nuclear weapons, but that took rather a long time to prepare. Those were difficult times. It was not a totally smooth relationship. It was interrupted by things that unfortunately happen from time to time, such as spy scandals, misunderstandings at various levels. But I think the great merit of the leaders of the Soviet Union and the US was that they did not allow themselves to be distracted from the main goal – that is normalising and improving the relationship, moving towards cooperation – by those obstacles and difficulties and even scandals that happened from time to time.

After the proposed monument to the victims of repression was half-heartedly endorsed by Gorbachev in 1988, Memorial broadened and transformed into a nationwide movement that saw **Lev Ponomarev** *campaigning for democracy and civil rights.*

It was clear that an alternative to the Communist Party was unprecedented and needed some preparation. We decided that the founders of the national movement should be creative unions. They should become the founders, not us individuals, but specifically already registered creative unions. And with the creative unions it was clear that many were already heading that way, through their publications. The first creative union I approached was the union of cinematographers of the USSR. Then I went to the Union of Artists, then the Union of Architects of the USSR, then the Union of Designers.

We started preparing a founding congress. We were told, 'Yes, yes, everyone is coming.' But suddenly the other founders [of the initial incarnation of Memorial] told us that they're not ready, they won't support it. They're the founders! And here we'd already made an agreement with the Dom Kino [House of Cinema, the venue for the congress]. So, I went to Andrei Sakharov and I told him the situation. Then he in front of me said, 'Well, I've got the phone number, I'll call the Central Committee.' He wasn't a party member or anything. So, he phoned up the Central Committee and said, 'We know it's the Central Committee forbidding our founding congress. People are already coming for it. Keep in mind, we are going to hold it whatever happens, either on the street or at my home, but the congress will be held.' And we were given permission.

*In 1990, a new law was passed, stating that 'the press and other forms of mass information are free.' At this time, **Vitali Tretyakov** left* Moscow News *in order to establish his own newspaper. Called* Nezavisimaya Gazeta *(Independent Newspaper), it would be one of the first truly independent newspapers in the Soviet Union.*

Firstly, I asked my friends who were journalists whether they wanted to [write for *Nezavisimaya Gazeta*], and none of them accepted my offer. Everybody was discussing freedom of speech, democracy, new possibilities for publishing, but everybody was sitting still. For example, I invited people from *Izvestia* [a long-running daily newspaper]. But what did *Izvestia* look like at that time? They had special phones for dialling the government buildings in downtown Moscow. The employees had country houses and cars. And all those democratic journalists who had nice workplaces did not accept our offer 'for some reason'.

I was stating openly that we were creating a newspaper guided by Western norms. I already knew which qualities distinguish good publishing from the one existent in the Soviet Union at that time. I took Western newspapers as a model. I thought the text should be organised differently – a certain type of headline should be used, a summary has to be added, describing the main theme of the story. This all was non-existent in the newspapers by that time. We initiated a lot of changes. However, I always appreciated Russian journalism was always more literary; we did not aim to get rid of this trait. Another thing was that our journalists love discussions, which are not always preferable. I tried to fix this by giving rules: 'First describe the facts, later provide your thoughts.' Nobody was interfering with the *Nezavisimaya*'s affairs, a daily quality newspaper distributed nationwide. And we were criticising Gorbachev hard.

Pavel Palazhchenko

Initially, there was very little opposition [to perestroika], because people in the Communist Party bureaucracy, people in the Politburo at that time, understood the need for change but they did not realise how far Gorbachev was prepared to go in that change, so they initially supported him. It was after Gorbachev moved toward more than just glasnost, towards the democratisation of the system, it was after he moved to relatively free elections, that the real differences of opinion began to emerge, and that the real opposition began to emerge. They felt that what was happening was moving toward a system where they, the Communist Party bureaucracy in particular, would become irrelevant, and they did not like that. They disagreed with many aspects of the foreign policy as well. When Gorbachev decided that he would not use force to stop change in Eastern Europe, they disagreed with that. When he took a similar position on German reunification, there were quite a few people that disagreed with that. They believed that by agreeing to German unification we were losing the fruit of victory in the Second World War. There were real differences, but they emerged as perestroika progressed and evolved and as Gorbachev's thinking evolved, and as the problems and the difficulties that were part of perestroika began to emerge and became more evident. They were real differences but they did not manifest themselves during the first couple of years of perestroika.

Vitali Tretyakov

I was writing in my articles that Gorbachev is destroying the Soviet Union. The demise began in 1989, when the First Congress of People's Deputies took place, and it was streamed live on TV. Gorbachev thought: 'I put [the Congress] together and they will support me.' But later everybody started to criticise him, denounce him effectively. I wrote that May 24th 1989, the first day of the Congress, was the beginning of the end of the Soviet Union. One could still have changed things, had Gorbachev conducted clever politics, but it was not so, therefore everything crashed.

Pavel Palazhchenko

Glasnost and freedom of speech, the publication of *The Gulag Archipelago* by Aleksandr Solzhenitsyn, the publication of previously banned or restricted Soviet and

Russian literature, that was a big change with the pre-Gorbachev era. But there was more than that. There was criticism of Gorbachev. Political competition and political struggles became a norm. As soon as the first free elections were held and the First Congress of People's Deputies was broadcast live on television, it became obvious that this is no longer the same country. I wasn't uncomfortable with the fact that Gorbachev was being criticised. I felt that a lot of that criticism was unfair, but I think it was normal that people were allowed to express their opinion and give their views about anyone, including the leader of the country.

Vitali Tretyakov

I got to know Gorbachev in person only in December 1991 when the Belovezhskaya Pushcha [the location in Belarus where the signing of the 'Belavezha Accords' established the Commonwealth of Independent States on 8 December 1991, effectively dissolving the Soviet Union] took place. He gave me an interview and he was talking as if we had been acquainted for a long time. I don't know what he believed in: his genius or his luck. For sure, he lost his luck and, regarding genius, we are all arrogant. I also think of myself as a smart person, but to claim that I am a genius, to think that I am going to outwit everybody in this world, this is idiocy. At that time, we started to criticise Yeltsin and his politics, and a lot of readers abandoned us. Later, some scandals happened but we maintained our publishing tradition. Yeltsin or Gorbachev, it didn't matter, one minister or another. I tried to uphold this attitude, and on one hand this was the basis of our authority, but on the other we lost a lot of readers because it was clear what the big bosses and bureaucrats wanted from our newspaper.

Lev Ponomarev

Gorbachev was isolated, essentially saying some things all on his own, but he didn't have many concrete actions. The release of political prisoners is a concrete action, he did that. And later endless discussions, the fracturing of the party. There was a ferocious battle in the Central Committee and Politburo, and he drowned in that battle. The only thing that was a great achievement was the freedom of speech, freedom of the press: *Ogoniok*, the *Moscow News*, and many other newspapers and books began to be published. Gorbachev gave people the opportunity to talk about the past and discuss the future. That is his huge achievement. But the Central Committee was cracking and it was obvious that he was not winning there, which effectively was demonstrated by the later events of 1991.

Pavel Palazhchenko

Gorbachev was doing something that was necessary but it was his persistence in moving along that path rather than going back, rather than backtracking on the main promises of democracy and change. That was a possibility. The coup in August 1991 was precisely about that and the fact that Gorbachev said, 'No,' to the coup organisers who came to him and basically asked him to declare an emergency and to put a stop to the entire process of democratisation. That fact, I think, says it all. It was Gorbachev, it was his determination to continue to move along the path of change that made all the difference.

Vitali Tretyakov

At some point, when I started to heavily criticise the government in my articles, to criticise Yeltsin and everything happening around him, people started to ask me:

'You seemed to be supporting Yeltsin, Gorbachev and democracy, but now you are apparently against democracy!' My personal life is something different from the life of my country. As for me personally, I benefited from glasnost and perestroika. But ask a regular person whether they benefited from those events! Also, where is my country now? The Soviet Union was not an empire of evil for me. I regret that my homeland does not exist any more. I am saying this taking into account all the drawbacks which we had then.

My attitude to Gorbachev changed gradually. We maintained a friendship for some time, at conferences in the Gorbachev Foundation and trips, celebrations. Once we flew together for a celebration of the tenth anniversary of perestroika. Nobody celebrated here [in Russia]. It was celebrated in Italy and I flew there, together with the Gorbachevs. Then I saw that he absolutely lacks self-criticism. We had a quarrel and I said, 'You lost everything. You lost your personal power as a USSR President, and transferred the power to a person who you thought to be below yourself, worthless. Socialism with a human face? There is no socialism with a human face. We lost the Soviet Union. Just please don't say you are a winner in this situation, that you saved the world from threats. You lost everything and you are a loser.' He continued to argue with me. But there were people who were maybe more cynical and had more experience, who said almost right away that this person is a complete failure and will harm the country. A lot of people were saying that, but their voices were ignored.

Pavel Palazhchenko
As Gorbachev said in his farewell address, the changes that had happened under him were so enormous that they really transformed the country for decades to come,

and we're still digesting the changes that happened under Gorbachev.

Vitali Tretyakov

Gorbachev used glasnost and perestroika to lead the country to a dead end. I cannot admire glasnost and perestroika, despite the fact that I personally benefited from it. Yeltsin was absolutely indifferent to the country's destiny; he bought power at the expense of a country. He needed power and didn't care what would happen to the Soviet Union and the people living there. When Gorbachev issued the book *Perestroika: New Thinking for Our Country and the World* [in 1987], I was really horrified. Everything was collapsing at once. I even thought to write an answer to this book: 'Where is your conscience? What right do you have to make such global and ungrounded statements? Your country is suffering because of this new way of thinking, and you want to address it to the whole world!' A failed, catastrophic politics for tens of millions of people, the majority of the citizens of the Soviet Union. Could things have been done otherwise? Yes, they could. We could have reformed our country, to promote democracy differently. Nobody says that the monopoly of the Communist Party was a great thing. But a lot of people just don't care about the Communist Party: they simply lived better then than they do now. Knowing everything that I know now, having analysed, having read and having lived through this, I can confidently say that a completely different politics could have been carried out, achieving better democracy, and a better glasnost, without demolishing the country and the lives of people. This is the only way I can assess it.

'They are not so different from us'

The Fall of the Berlin Wall and German Reunification (1989–90)

In the autumn of 1989 the East German authorities were facing mounting civil unrest and insistent calls for the lifting of controls on emigration to the West. Over the summer, tens of thousands of East German holiday-makers took advantage of Hungary's decision to dismantle its border fence with Austria and poured into Western Europe. It was the largest exodus of East Germans west-wards since the Berlin Wall went up in 1961, and it set in motion a dramatic chain of events that no one was expecting, not in Moscow nor East Berlin nor indeed in the Western world.

When East Germany eventually closed its border with Hungary, East Germans wanting to leave trekked across the open border into Czechoslovakia instead and either slipped into Hungary from there or sought sanctuary in the West German Embassy in Prague. Eventually, the East German government gave its consent for those holed up in the embassy to leave for West Germany in special sealed trains, stripping them of their right to East German citizenship. But then, in early October 1989, it shut off all escape routes out to the West via East European countries. East Germany was now effectively sealed off. Disaffected East Germans had no other option than to join the rallies that were spreading throughout the country, as citizens took to the streets to vent their frustration.

On successive Mondays, the numbers attending the weekly mass protest rallies in the East German city of Leipzig, which had begun in September 1989, continued to escalate. By Monday, 16 October, the crowd numbered tens of thousands of people. Two days later, Erich Honecker, the hard-line East German leader who in 1961 had supervised the building of the Berlin Wall, was forced to resign and was replaced by his deputy.

Honecker's resignation signalled a dramatic shift. It came only ten days after celebrations in East Berlin to mark the 40th anniversary of the East German republic. In his trademark homburg hat and raincoat, Honecker stood rigidly next to his guest of honour, the Soviet leader Mikhail Gorbachev, as they reviewed a night-time military parade and declared that the socialist accomplishments of East Germany had endured for 40 years and would still be there beyond the year 2000. But Gorbachev and his aides had already made clear in private that Moscow would no longer intervene militarily in Eastern Europe. He used his trip to Berlin to warn Honecker that he must cooperate with all sections of society or 'life punishes those who come too late.'

With Honecker gone, the protest movement continued to grow. Despite attempts by the government to clamp down, people refused to be intimidated by threats of arrest from the East German police and plainclothes agents of the Stasi state security. On 4 November hundreds of thousands of East German citizens gathered in Alexanderplatz in East Berlin to demand political change, the largest demonstration there had ever been in the country.

On 9 November the East German Communist authorities decided there was no option but to cave in and ease up on exit restrictions for those wanting to travel to, or leave for, the West. The idea was to allow a more orderly exodus into West Berlin and West Germany via existing crossing points from East Germany. The plan was for new regulations to take effect the following day. But not all the details were fully communicated either to East Germany's border guards or to the East German Politburo spokesman, Günter Schabowski. At a chaotic press briefing that evening, he told assembled journalists that, as far as he knew, the new regulations were to come in 'immediately without delay', including in Berlin.

Journalists rushed to report the historic news that the border restrictions were being lifted and 'the gates in the Wall stand wide open', as one West German correspondent put it. The news reports were beamed straight back into East Germany. Almost immediately that night, East German citizens headed for the checkpoints between East and West Berlin and demanded to be allowed through.

The bewildered border guards had no instructions and did not know what to do. They were unable to clarify with the East German authorities whether they were supposed to block the exodus using force. Vastly outnumbered and without clear orders, they decided to give way. Soon, eager East Germans were swarming past the checkpoints into West Berlin, the border guards giving only a cursory look at their documents. Before long, young people from both sides were leaping up on top of the Berlin Wall to celebrate. Souvenir hunters attacked the Wall with hammers and chisels, demolishing parts of it and creating several unofficial openings.

It was a momentous event. The most potent symbol of a divided Europe was literally being torn down by the very citizens who had been oppressed by it. Official demolition of the Berlin Wall would not start until June 1990 and was completed only in 1992, but it was the beginning of the end of the Soviet hold on Eastern Europe.

It was also the start of frenzied, breathless negotiations over what would happen next to East and West Germany. On 28 November 1989, the West German Chancellor, Helmut Kohl, startled Western powers and the Soviet Union by presenting a ten-point plan for eventual German unity, starting with closer cooperation between the two states. By the summer of 1990, the deal for reunification was all but done.

In March 1990, the ruling East German Socialist Unity Party – which had hurriedly changed its name to the Party of Democratic Socialism, to no avail – was trounced in East Germany's first free elections. The coalition government that replaced it called for reunification as fast as possible. The country's economy was near collapse and in May a new treaty set the stage for legal, economic and social union between the two states. In July, the West German Deutschmark was introduced to replace the worthless East German currency, creating a monetary union, and West German laws came into force in the East.

In the international arena, the idea of German reunification initially dismayed many West European powers. Britain's Margaret Thatcher, in particular, worried that Germany would once again become an expansionist power and a destabilising force in Europe. But European concerns were overcome by the United States, which threw its weight behind the idea, so long as the new enlarged German state stayed within NATO.

The Soviet Union at first called for a new united Germany to be made a neutral power, outside NATO and with no nuclear weapons stationed on its territory. Eventually, Gorbachev shifted his position to say that 'the Germans must decide for themselves what path they choose', provided that no foreign NATO troops or nuclear missiles were deployed in former East Germany.

In later decades, Gorbachev was to complain that NATO's subsequent expansion into Eastern Europe 'violated the spirit of assurances' he was offered at the time, though he made it clear that no promises were given. The Russian President, Vladimir Putin, went further to claim the West had lied to Russia by failing to keep to a pledge not to expand eastwards. This complaint was to become a major source of his subsequent hostility towards NATO. In 2015 the Russian Federal Assembly even contemplated passing a motion to condemn what it called the undemocratic 'annexation' of East Germany by West Germany. But West German and US negotiators involved at the time have since insisted that any assurances given to Moscow in 1990 only referred to former East Germany, and the question of possible further NATO expansion eastwards was never raised.

Moscow's acquiescence to the deal was also coloured by an agreement reached between Gorbachev and Kohl, whereby West Germany agreed to ease the Soviet Union's spiralling economic problems by paying billions of dollars to shoulder the momentous task of withdrawing and rehousing the hundreds of thousands of Soviet troops who were stationed in East Germany.

In September 1990 the four post-war occupying powers – the United States, the United Kingdom, France and the Soviet Union – signed an agreement to confirm a settlement for Germany. The final step came on 3 October 1990, when the five states of East Germany were absorbed into the West German federal state and the black, red and gold flag of what was now a new united Germany was raised over the Brandenburg Gate in Berlin.

For all Germans, *die Wende* – the period of sweeping change that was triggered by the fall of the Berlin Wall – was a complex process of rehabilitation. For the government, there was the costly business of reconfiguring the two German political structures and the enormous sums to be poured by West Germany into the East to rebuild and reshape its economy. For ordinary people, the vast differences between East and West meant walls had to be broken down socially and psychologically.

For some in the East, the *Wende* marked a positive turning point in their life, a chance to travel, speak freely, start a business for the first time, or otherwise change their profession or place of residence. For other '*Ossis*', as citizens from the East were called, it was a turn for the worse, their lifelong employment terminated when a workplace closed down, leaving them redundant and disorientated, with no savings or property to fall back on. Especially for older people, who found it harder to find another job, there was a sense of loss, their identity as East German citizens snatched away and replaced by a disquieting feeling that they had become second-class citizens.

For '*Wessis*' too, as those from the West were labelled, there was a price to pay, as the country absorbed the cost of reunification and acclimatised to the huge influx of new citizens from the East, some of them with a markedly different outlook on life.

And for citizens in West Berlin there was both loss and gain. On the one hand, no longer were they hemmed in. For the first time, they could get out easily into the East German countryside. But on the other hand, West Berlin had been a unique Cold War community, cossetted and protected, overseen by the Allied occupying powers. When the Wall came down, its citizens were deprived of their special status and the reunified city, now the capital of the reunified country, had to carve out for itself a new distinctive character.

On both sides of the now demolished Cold War divide, everyone had to make an adjustment to a tumultuous, historic change which, even months before, few of them could have foreseen would turn their world upside down.

In 1989 **Gisela Hoffmann** *was teaching English in a secondary school in Röbel, a small in town in Mecklenburg-Hither Pomerania, to the north of Berlin.*

We saw that there were changes in the Soviet Union. There were changes everywhere and I thought, 'If nothing is going to change here, I have to change myself' – and the change for me was to stop working as a teacher and to do something else. But I didn't stop teaching because the changes began here. The demonstrations began, in Leipzig first and then they began in our region too. We met every Monday and we had discussions, and I saw who came to these meetings and who didn't.

We met in our marketplace. Sometimes there were 50 people, sometimes 100. We discussed, for example, with our mayor what had to change in the town; we discussed how we did not want to be observed by everybody and we did not want to send all our boys to the army or the Stasi ... They asked us as teachers to send the boys to the Stasi but I said no.

Elisabeth Heller *was in her early forties, a single parent with a son in East Berlin, and working as a music producer with Radio DDR 1, one of the East German state broadcaster's stations.*

We were only allowed to play 40 per cent of music from the so-called non-socialist countries and 60 per cent from our country and the socialist countries. These were the guidelines and then the singers and composers needed to adhere [to] the party line or at least appear to do so. For example, when a composer had left for the West, we were suddenly not allowed to play singers he had composed for any more. And that was the problem – since 1989, more and more artists had defected to the West. At the end, we didn't know who to play any more because they were taken out of the card index.

Everybody had the feeling, during that time, that something had to change or was going to change. But no one had an inkling that the Wall would actually fall, and certainly not so fast.

*That summer, **Katharina Herrmann** had just graduated with a degree in sociology, and took one last long holiday, in Bulgaria, before taking up her first job, in East Berlin. On her way home, she passed through Hungary, which had recently opened its border to the West.*

I went to Budapest for a bit of sightseeing, and shopping for records which were not available in my home country. I was actually actively avoiding the groups of people who seemed to gather in these areas – I was on my way home, I had finished university, I had a job going. I absolutely didn't want to get mixed up in that sort of thing. I did not want leave my country. I didn't really want to associate with the people who did because I didn't think that was the right way to go. Being young and idealistic, I always thought it would be better to work on what we had and make it work better and improve it. I always thought leaving was a bit of a cop-out. There was the question of what would happen in the long run, but we all assumed that some sort of order would be re-established, though how was not clear. This had positive outcomes for the people who stayed behind. For example, I was desperately trying to find a flat in Berlin – because so many people had left at the time, it was easier for me to find one, which was quite unusual.

I never sensed the Wall would fall soon – I was assuming that some sort of order would be re-established. I didn't assume the Wall would fall until the day it happened.

Elisabeth Heller

I experienced the fall of the Wall, like thousands of people, as something really unbelievable: joy, pure happiness, euphoria all the way. We all wanted to test if it was really possible as a Berliner to go from the eastern part into the western part.

I had a visitor from Thüringen and the reaction was: 'We have to go there immediately!' But as dutiful as I was, because I was on leave looking after my ill son, I said, 'That's impossible, if someone sees me, I am on sick leave and haven't gone to work.' Even in that moment you were intimidated and you couldn't believe it, but, of course, the wish was there, to test this as soon as possible.

After an exciting night, on the next day, 10 November in the morning, we went to the Wall. The first thing we saw was people, people, people, and more people who moved in clusters in the direction of potential crossing points. I only needed to have my ID card stamped. We should have got a permit first, but we were allowed through anyway: a stamp and then across the bridge.

*On the other side of the Berlin Wall, **Otfried Laur**, manager of a club for West Berlin theatregoers, was also filled with joy on the evening of 9 November.*

That was one of the greatest and most beautiful days of my whole life. We were invited to a birthday party for Ulrich Schamoni, the famous theatre person. And suddenly a murmur spread through the hall, and artists from East Berlin, like Helga Hahnemann and many others I knew, came in. We were celebrating, but then we stormed out to the Wall to experience that for ourselves: how the East Berliners came to West Berlin and we could welcome them. Of course, we also had relatives in East Berlin. We telephoned them at once and arranged to meet the next day and with a big bottle of champers we then celebrated by the Wall. It was, of course, wonderful.

For me personally, work started straight away. I immediately grabbed the chance: two days later, a bicycle courier cycled over to the artistic directors of the East Berlin theatres with our brochures to introduce us as the Berlin Theatre Club. We said: 'We would very much like to include the productions of the East Berlin theatres in our brochure for our West Berlin members.' Crucially, we offered to pay the theatres in the East the same amount in western Deutschmarks as we paid to the theatres in the West.

We were pushing at an open door. After just two months, from January 1990 onwards, we already had all Berlin's theatres and we could release a brochure for the whole of the city. I sat at my typewriter, with tears in my eyes when I could write for the first time 'Staatsoper' and 'Friedrichstadt-Palast' and 'Metropol-Theater' and 'Deutsches Theater'. That was, for me, very emotional.

Andreas Austilat, *a 32-year-old journalist in West Berlin, was otherwise engaged.*
We'd packed all our things because we planned to move the next day with all our furniture to another apartment.

So our TV was packed, but we had a radio, and I noticed that something was happening at the border and I told my girlfriend, 'Well, it sounds as if they will open the border.'

The next morning, when we tried to get to our new apartment, which was in the centre of West Berlin, the streets were crowded with people from East Berlin. I think even the subway station was closed. That was the moment when we noticed, 'Wow, the borders are really open and they are all coming to us,' which was very strange at first.

It was a big surprise. The happiness lasted several hours because we had friends in East Berlin. They called us and came to visit us. That was so amazing because, you have to imagine, up to this point we could visit them but it wasn't possible for them to visit us. So, it was always an artificial relationship because we couldn't show them how we lived.

In the first few days, things weren't really clear. Is it stable? Can we cross the border without our documents? Could they close the Wall again? Because it was so new and so surprising, we actually didn't really know what was happening.

Elisabeth Heller

It was finally possible to travel in all directions without any restrictions. Without having scissors in your head [censoring yourself] and speaking freely without being afraid of things, to be able to vote freely and to enjoy tropical fruit, because that was a desire we all had.

The effect it had on my work as a music radio producer was positive in every way. We finally could make programmes with the music we always wanted. It was also significant for producers in the other departments. And we did everything to make a fresh start in the [East German] media.

I felt wonderful and free as never before. I had enjoyed doing the work before, but this was a feeling that I expe-

Otfried Laur with his wife, Reni.

rienced only at this time. Not before and not after. You finally had the feeling you were recognised, you were taken seriously. You did not have the feeling any more of being a second-class person, and constantly being pushed around or having to adhere to regulations. It was like a dream.

Katharina Herrmann

Once we realised it was probably a permanent feature, there obviously was a sense of adventure. But also the question – what now? Is everyone going to go? Are lots of my friends going to leave? And if so, where to? It was incredibly exciting to think about travels that might be possible in future. But it was also very worrying to think about my professional future because I was quite aware of unemployment rates for people of my professional background – I was a trained sociologist. In Germany, you are quite linked to your professional qualifications, so it's quite difficult to switch from your chosen subject to another without retraining.

I was quite taken aback when very soon there was talk about unification. I was born a very long time after the war and the building of the Wall. I didn't really consider myself as part of a larger Germany; I didn't have much in common with a lot of the West Germans I met because of the different ideology. I had a lot more in common with a lot of Czech and Polish people I knew at the time in my way of thinking and how I saw my future. Being reunited was an alien idea to me. I would have thought and hoped that there would be a getting-closer process as part of being in the European Community – that was the process I would have liked much better.

Gisela Hoffmann

I wanted to be part of this new time. They asked me to become headmistress of the school. I helped to change my

Elisabeth Heller with her son in West Berlin, 1989.

school into a grammar school. Before that, there was no grammar school in my town. All the students who wanted to take the *Abitur* [advanced level school exam, taken at 18] had to go to the neighbouring town, which meant travelling 20 kilometres every day by bus. We wanted to have that in our town, too, and we wanted to give more students the opportunity to take the *Abitur*. Before, only pupils who were chosen could take it, and the parents had to be in the party. The really good students were not chosen to take the *Abitur*, but rather students who had the 'right' family.

*For **Andreas Austilat**, the fall of the Berlin Wall meant he could now visit the countryside outside Berlin.*

We went to the south-west of West Berlin, the former border. The border was still there, of course, but it had holes in it. We noticed two young soldiers with their car, a military vehicle. My girlfriend told me that she would like to have a souvenir. So, I came to the former Wall, with its holes, and asked a soldier. First I called: 'Would you please come over here?' And he said, 'Yes, what's happening?' Which was a strange situation because several weeks before he would have shot me. I asked him, 'We would like to have a buckle from the belt from the National People Army, the East German Army.'

And he wasn't as astonished as I thought he would be. He said to me, 'Okay, no problem,' turned back to his vehicle, and took out a couple of belts. And he asked me: 'What do you want? Fabric or leather?' And I was so surprised that meanwhile he changed from soldier to a kind of merchant.

Well, I bought the belt, the buckle, a medal and his cap. It was a funny situation. It showed how much had changed. Because these soldiers – before, they were very strict, and kept their distance and were very cold – and now you could talk to them easily and buy their belt buckles. That was new.

Andreas Austilat, 1989.

Katharina Herrmann, 1990.

From the perspective of some East Germans, reunification with the West was a mixed blessing.

Katharina Herrmann

I was not entirely happy or excited. I really resented the idea of success being measured in money – which would become part of our future lifestyle. I very much resented the West German body of law being implemented as part of a reunification process – that was about things that affected me as a woman. For instance, the law on abortion would change, and as far as I was concerned, it would go backwards 30 years. Generally, the perception of women working in the West of Germany was very different than the East, where over 90 per cent worked, and that was what they expected to do once they left education regardless of whether they had a family or not. Also the whole image of women in the media was very different from what I was used to and what I liked.

I had to totally re-evaluate what I wanted to do with my professional life. It totally changed the range of options available to me. I had grown up being quite concerned about potential unemployment, and I did become unemployed soon after the Wall [came] down – but I had underestimated my own ability to deal with that. I was able to go much further, not just in terms of moving country but also professionally, than I had ever expected myself to be able to before I found myself in that situation. A lot of the things I worried about at the time didn't come to pass, but other things I hadn't prepared for did. I have made the most of it.

The unification of Germany involved bringing together many institutions from West and East – or, in some cases, the closure of the East German version, such as the state radio broadcaster to which **Elisabeth Heller** *had dedicated her career. So, just under a year after the fall of the Berlin Wall, things began to change.*

For the first station, Radio Berlin International, the fun was already over. For me, working for Radio DDR 1, which was renamed Radio Aktuell, the end came a year later. I personally had the feeling of someone cutting my throat. Consternation, bewilderment, deep sadness, lack of understanding, because no one could understand that. You did your best, you'd invested everything, you were happy – and suddenly it was over.

There were measures by which they thought they could redeploy people but, as it turned out, that was an illusion. I had to go to the job centre, where I was told: 'At the age of 42 and with a child, you will never get a job again – you better marry a rich man.' I was left to my fate – no one helped me because everybody was busy with him or herself. We were almost like a family, and suddenly everything was gone. Nothing was like yesterday.

Katharina Herrmann

People probably expect big sweeping statements about feeling free, about the wonders of democracy. I didn't really feel as unfree as I probably should have felt in the eyes of a Westerner in East Germany. The main thing I was unhappy with was not being able to travel. I didn't rail against the system. I liked this type of egalitarian society. I actually quite liked the idea that there were no extremely rich people. At the same time, there was free healthcare for everyone. I could see the good sides there.

Sometime after the fall of the Wall and the whole unification process, I started to develop a feeling as if I was a second-class citizen. I didn't really think of myself as a German at the time – I thought of myself as an East

German, but that wasn't really the accepted opinion any more. I was very unhappy and upset about the way the whole unification process went because I think the word 'unification' is a bit of a misnomer – it was a takeover. There was actually very little that was positive about Eastern laws, regulations, life circumstances that was adopted into the unified Germany, so it felt a bit like being colonised. There was the assumption that if you were in or from the East and you weren't an active dissident, you were automatically a Stasi member, or somebody who had totally wrong and undemocratic ideas. There was the assumption that you would immediately accept West was good, East was bad. There was a lot of deliberate misinterpretation about what had been going on in East Germany. There was a lot of very negative propaganda about people like my parents, for instance, who had spent their lives trying to build on something very worthwhile and positive – an egalitarian social experiment, no matter how flawed. That did not make them bad people who had supported the wrong thing. But the assumption was that if you were not against the system you were automatically a Stalinist, and that was really wrong and very upsetting.

There was also the assumption that if you'd trained or gone to university in the former East, it automatically would be worse. The education process was quite comprehensive – you had to learn several languages even to be admitted to university.

I found there was a lot more emphasis on appearance than there had been among my friends, at least in the East. Clothes were hugely important to a lot of people I met from West Germany. I was far more interested in substance over style, I was never particularly interested in fashion. I had some very strange experiences trying to go shopping in big department stores and asking for something like plain black trousers. I was told by the shop assistant this wasn't fashionable at the moment so this would not be available. I remember finding that quite weird. This was partly to do with being brought up on the propaganda that everything was there for sale in the West, if only you had the money to pay for it. There were quite big differences in the shopping culture, but a lot of it was really quite disappointing. You were told by advertising that the customer is king; I found a lot of people, when I went shopping, quite dismissive of me.

Elisabeth Heller

I suddenly found myself in a strange country, although I hadn't changed location, and in that strange country, whose laws weren't clear to me, I became unemployed – a situation I hadn't known in the country I had grown up in, where everything, from the cradle to the grave, was taken care of. You had the feeling of being a nothing. You always had the feeling of having to justify yourself to other people who didn't understand why you were unemployed and had no job. It was an exasperating state, which lasted until I reached pensionable age.

During that time I did all sorts of things, always in the area of media and education, but it was always short-term, such as three weeks covering someone's leave at a broadcasting station here, or a several-week or month-long retraining course there. Or a so-called job-creation measure, where people came together who had no clue what to do with one another, because they came from all walks of life. As far as I can remember, the people were just frustrated – in despair and frustrated. In the end, it was just a fight for survival, in which one didn't know what best to do and one practically did not have any support. Nobody supported me except for one so-called case manager, who recognised what a desperate state I was in. He enabled me to do a distance-learning course and to get a digital recording machine. Apart from that, I was always treated like a second-class person. Humiliations without end – and that has consequences. Your self-esteem disappears.

It was so difficult to get a foothold because I was not the only one. There were many others who were looking for work. I was always told: 'You are overqualified and too old.' It was difficult to convey to your own child that education would be of use, because I did several further training courses in the area of media education and multimedia. I did a long-distance course in the care of the elderly, in the hope that I could teach students of that subject. They were all delighted with my work, but said: 'No, but we are not able to pay you.'

Gisela Hoffmann

I became more open to the world. I found out that it is normal to go to other places because you find normal people there. They are not so different from us. When you are friendly to them, they are also friendly to you. And when you show interest in them, they also show interest in you. And for me it was also very interesting when we went to London for the first time, to see all the people coming from all over the world. We hadn't seen any people from India or from Jamaica, or from anywhere else. It was very, very strange for us, but they behaved so normally and they were normal people of England. And that was also a very interesting idea for us.

Before, I could never speak more than three or four sentences in [English]. I never taught an English lesson entirely in English. We spoke a lot of German in our English lessons because we only had the vocabulary and the grammar, and we explained everything in German.

Later, with a colleague, also an English teacher, I organised a 14-day trip to England every summer holiday. The students who came with us wanted to learn English. They were very interested. They took all the opportunities to speak English and we asked them to do everything that was necessary. We let them do the check-in in the hotels, we sent them to buy things we needed for our meals or we sent them to get tickets at a theatre or for a musical and so on. We let them organise a meal at a restaurant for a whole group. And they did it, and they did it very well.

Katharina Herrmann, *fed up with feeling like a second-class citizen in the new, unified Germany, moved to London.*
Moving from East Berlin to London has made me a lot more confident than I ever thought I would be, a lot more outgoing. When I was young I was the kind of person who sits in a corner and reads a book, who doesn't particularly talk to other people unless they are spoken to, quite cerebral, quite shy. Because of the way my life has developed, I absolutely had to come out of that shell to a much, much larger extent than I ever thought I could or would. There have been moments when I missed my quiet life and when I found it very onerous to do this, but in the long run I have lived far more up to my potential than I would have otherwise.

For me, [the big thing that was not possible before] was the ability to go and see places I had never imagined I would see – and that was something I was systemically working on to make that possible. After I had moved to London, got a job here, I spent a lot of effort trying to save my money and use my annual leave to go to places like China, India, Japan – places I'd always looked at with some sort of mystical aura – 'I'd love to see that, it's so different, but it's not likely to happen.' I had a huge collection of books on India and China, for instance, while I was still a student in East Germany, but I never at the time imagined, reading all that stuff, that I would be able to go and see that. That really is one of the great outcomes.

'The greatest value of mankind is their freedom'

The Baltic Republics Leave the Soviet Union (1988–91)

Perched on the western edge of the Soviet Union, the three tiny Baltic republics – Estonia, Latvia and Lithuania – had for decades been a thorn in the Kremlin's side. When Gorbachev's reforms of the 1980s signalled that Soviet repression was being relaxed, they seized the chance to push for independence, clearing a path for other republics to follow, a process that would ultimately lead to the Soviet Union's demise.

Etched in the memories of most Baltic citizens was the horrific experience of occupation and repression, which began in the Second World War when their previously independent countries were seized first by Stalin's army and then by Hitler's troops. After the Nazi retreat from Estonia in 1944, they were recaptured by Soviet forces and incorporated into the Soviet Union. Moscow insisted it was an entirely legitimate process, on the basis of pre-war treaties and the result of popular referendums. Much of the Western world and many Baltic citizens saw it as illegal: a forcible brutal annexation, with the installation of puppet Communist governments and harsh treatment for any 'traitors' and 'Nazi collaborators' who resisted.

Well aware of how unpopular Soviet rule was, Moscow kept a tight political grip on the Baltic region, cracking down hard on any troublemakers. It is estimated that upwards of half a million people from the Baltics were deported to Soviet labour camps between 1944 and 1955, a huge figure considering that in 1950 the combined population of Estonia, Latvia and Lithuania was less than 6 million. Later, a systematic policy was introduced to change the demographic balance through 'Russification'. Much to the alarm of many locals, large numbers of ethnic Russians and other nationalities were brought in from other parts of the Soviet Union to fill political and managerial posts and provide manpower in factories. Especially in Estonia and Latvia, there were fears that in time, if the influx continued, non-Baltic Russian speakers could become the majority.

In the 1980s Mikhail Gorbachev's perestroika policies changed everything. When his policy of glasnost, or openness, was introduced in 1986, it lifted the lid on controversial subjects that had previously been taboo. In the Baltic republics, it was seen as a chance to start talking about national identity and the explosive issue of a nation's right to self-determination.

The campaign for independence was not just political, but born from a desire to protect and promote nationhood through language, culture and music. Estonia, like the other Baltic States, had a long history of song festivals and large open-air concerts, which brought the nation together. In May 1988 an open-air rock concert in the university town of Tartu became the first place where the blue, black and white colours of the previously banned Estonian national flag were waved. Soon, national singing competitions were occasions for spontaneous mass singing of patriotic songs. Concert venues became indistinguishable from political rallies. It was described as the Baltic 'singing revolution'.

At the same time, new organisations in all three Baltic republics sprang up to pursue a more political agenda. In Estonia, the Popular Front, which helped launch the singing revolution, initially backed Gorbachev's perestroika reforms but later favoured breaking away from the Soviet Union altogether. The more radical Estonian Citizens Committees argued that Estonia could not secede when it had been annexed illegally, and instead the country should insist on the legal continuity of its pre-war statehood and establish a parallel set of Estonian institutions and elections, outside Soviet control or influence. As the mood in Estonia became more radical, their ideas took hold.

They also set about compiling a new electoral register of citizens from before 1940, plus their descendants. This pointedly excluded more recent Soviet immigrants, which hardly enamoured them to the prospect of Estonian independence. After 1991, this distinction was written into Estonia's post-Soviet laws, and similar laws were passed in Latvia (but not Lithuania), denying an automatic right to citizenship for those who had settled during the Soviet period, which would lead Moscow to complain that Estonian and Latvian nationalists were infringing the human rights of local Russian speakers.

By 1989 the singing revolution had become a clear call for Baltic independence. On 23 August 1989, the three countries came together to form the Baltic Chain, a human chain stretching from the Estonian capital, Tallinn, in the north, via Latvia's capital, Riga, to Lithuania's capital, Vilnius, in the south. All along the 600-kilometre highway, people linked hands to demonstrate their wish for freedom from Soviet rule.

The date was significant. It marked the 50-year anniversary of 23 August 1939, when the foreign ministers of Hitler and Stalin signed the Nazi–Soviet Non-Aggression Pact (the so-called Molotov–Ribbentrop Pact), whose secret clauses had carved up the borderlands between German and Soviet territory into spheres of influence, laying the groundwork for Hitler to invade Poland in September 1939 and for Stalin's occupation of the Baltics in June 1940.

At the end of 1989, the Berlin Wall came down and, in a major shift in Kremlin policy, Gorbachev signalled that he was prepared to let Eastern Europe leave the Soviet bloc. The Baltic republics immediately made moves to follow suit. But it turned out that this was a red line for Gorbachev and he was not prepared to give them the same freedom. He warned that it would fuel an upsurge in ethnic tensions. He no doubt also feared – rightly, as it turned out – that the secession of one set of Soviet republics could start a rush for the door by others.

All through 1990 and 1991 tensions with Moscow escalated. At the start of 1991, Soviet troops based in the Baltics, under orders from Kremlin hardliners and on the pretext of putting a stop to public unrest, moved in to try to seize control. The Estonians managed to avoid bloodshed, but in Lithuania and Latvia the Soviet troops shot dead a number of civilians and caused an international outcry. The troops quickly backed down and returned to barracks.

By the summer of 1991 all three Baltic republics had declared their intention to restore independence and repudiate Soviet laws, and were in the process of trying to persuade the outside world to recognise them as independent entities.

Meanwhile, the Kremlin was becoming increasingly alarmed by moves in other Soviet republics to seek more autonomy from the centre. In some places, such as the Caucasian republics of Georgia, Azerbaijan and Armenia, the process was being driven both by populist politicians and by fledgling democratic movements at the grassroots level. In other places, such as Central Asia, there was a more pragmatic calculation by local political elites who had little interest in democracy, but reckoned that ridding themselves of Moscow would increase their own power.

Most importantly, Boris Yeltsin – Gorbachev's nemesis – had become Russia's first popularly elected President and was demanding that the Russian Federation, likewise a Soviet republic, should also be given more rights to rule itself, a direct challenge to the authority of Gorbachev as Soviet President and his central Soviet government.

It was this danger of a fracturing union that prompted the Soviet KGB chief, Vladimir Kryuchkov, and other Communist hardliners to try to roll back the clock through an attempted military coup against Gorbachev on 19 August 1991. In Tallinn, as in Moscow, news that Soviet troops were advancing on strategic locations prompted locals to take to the streets to try to stop them. Alarmed at this new attempt at a crackdown from the centre, Estonia and Latvia lost no time in following Lithuania's example and declaring that they no longer considered themselves part of the Soviet Union.

Within three days, the coup leaders in Moscow had lost their nerve, and the coup collapsed. Over the next few months the entire Soviet system would unravel. By the end of 1991 the Union of Soviet Socialist Republics was no more, and Estonian, Latvia and Lithuanian independence, which only a few years before had seemed a distant pipe-dream, had become reality.

Marju Lauristin was born in Tallinn in 1940, just two months before Estonia lost its independence as Stalin occupied the Baltic states.

I was born in independent Estonia, a citizen of independent Estonia. But it ended very soon. Immediately after the war, there was a short period when it was not very clear what would happen. Estonians still hoped that they would gain their independence back, but those hopes were cruelly ended with the Yalta agreement [in February 1945], signed by Winston Churchill. Then the situation became more and more and more awful because it was a time of Stalin's power. My step-father was arrested in 1950, and that was a fate of many, many families in Estonia. [At the time of] Stalin's death in 1953, I was in sixth grade. For Estonians, this was really a happy day. Russians in Estonia were all in tears; Estonians all were smiling. And then after Stalin's death came Khrushchev's time and when I was graduating from secondary school it was 1957. Then already it was the first year that people started to come back from Siberia, from gulags, from camps. My step-father returned also in 1956.

It was a feeling that we were imprisoned. If you were at university, you felt every day this kind of mental imprisonment because, for example, we couldn't read the books we would like to read. We didn't have access to international journals, we couldn't publish anything outside, even in so-called socialist countries. Happily, we could teach in the Estonian language, which really meant that our controllers from Moscow didn't have a clue what we were talking about in our classrooms. But we still had to be cautious because we knew that among the students in our classrooms, there may be in a group of 20 at least one who was reporting to the KGB, so we had to be quite conscious about what we could say and in what way. All those people who have read Orwell's *Nineteen Eighty-Four* and who think it's a kind of dystopia, they have to understand that life in the Soviet Union was very much like that. The Orwellian world is quite a realistic picture.

Me and my friends, we joined the Communist Party in 1968. I was a rank-and-file member; I was never in any active position. In this time, many young activists joined the Communist Party with the hope that through the Communist Party we could help to change the situation. That was a sincere belief. Unfortunately, after the tanks on the streets of Prague, our hopes and dreams came to an end. The Communist Party wasn't just the group of people who were adamant and ideologically convinced, but for many, many people in Estonia, and other countries, the Communist Party was also a kind of practical organisation through which you got information. You got opportunities to make things, to manage life – I'm not talking about private life, I'm talking about life around you.

Brezhnev's time is called now a time of stagnation. You could call it a rotting time. Everyone was feeling this system is rotten, that it's coming to an end, and many people were just thinking *how* will the end come? And when? Nobody had any kind of seriousness concerning Soviet ideology any more. It was a time of an almost absolute cynical attitude. Then among that cynical environment there were people, mostly cultural people, artists, writers, film directors and academics in universities and so on, who really kept a kind of active attitude, trying to prepare for different times and work for that. One part was teaching students, another part was publishing books and poems, which really created the spirit of protest and the expectation of changes.

Artur Talvik was also born in Tallinn, in 1964, by which time Estonia was firmly part of the USSR.

In those days, we didn't even have a ferry line to Finland. Later, the ferry line to Finland started, so it was one of our bridges to the Western world. What was different in northern Estonia was that we saw Finnish television, and Finnish television was really our link to the Western world. Through this television station we knew about new bands, Western bands, and I became familiar with punk rock. I was one of the first punks in Tallinn. And for sure I was one of the first who did a Mohawk haircut in Tallinn, me and my friend actually. This was something unbelievable during the Soviet years. We were very soon arrested by the KGB and they said that we can't have such a haircut, that it's not a Soviet haircut, you show Soviet life in not a proper way. So, we had these haircuts for maybe five days and after serious pressure by the KGB we got the hair cut off.

We spoke Estonian. The schools were in Estonian. The language is one of the most powerful things which has kept us alive as a nation. Estonia is very small: there are only one million Estonians in Estonia, and the language for us is very important. The schools were in Estonian, although we began to learn Russian from the very beginning.

In the late seventies and early eighties, new waves of Russification started in Estonia: a lot of Russian workers were brought to Estonia and the power that we had in Estonia was very Russian-minded. That worried everyone. At the end of 1980, there were some youngsters' riots in Tallinn. I was 16 years old, and a lot of things were happening. After that, a kind of pressure started again. This was the situation shortly before perestroika. In the mid-eighties, Gorbachev came to power and everything started to change.

Marju Lauristin

The first open demonstrations were concerning phosphorite mines. Then, in 1987, there were open demonstrations concerning demand for [the] abolition of [the] Hitler–Stalin pact and the end of occupation already open in the streets, and certainly Gorbachev opened these doors because, like all Communists of this era, Gorbachev didn't have a clue about what people were really thinking about the Soviet system. When he called people to glasnost, he didn't expect what these words and thoughts might be, what people really wanted to express. One part of them concerned the system, which most people in Estonia really hated, and the other thing was about the lies, lies told about life before the war for Estonians, then about the occupation, about the real nature of the Soviet system, then about the arrests and the repressions and deportations and purges – and even in Russian people were saying we want now to live without these lies, we need real truth. Gorbachev was really in an uncomfortable position: he expected people to come to him and discuss how to make Communism better, but people were not interested in that.

Andrus Öövel was born in Tallinn in 1957. As a young sportsman he competed as part of the Soviet canoeing team between 1979 and 1983.
When I was a child, we didn't dream about [the] political independence of Estonia. The parents of my generation

didn't believe any more that it could be possible. And therefore memories about the first republic [were] nice to have but we didn't prepare our life in a way that we could devote it towards a struggle for the re-establishment of independence. I was involved in sport. I saw my future life as a leader of Estonian sport movement. But life is full of surprises.

I graduated university in law and worked [for the] first four years in [the] criminal police. Before being promoted to chief of [the] human resource department in the sports society, I got the opportunity to conduct the security during the first open-air rock festival in Tartu. It was an event when for the first time in modern Estonian history our national flags came out, meaning 10,000 visitors to the rock concert brought with them the first national flags and waved them during the concert. I think that this was the moment when we first started seriously to think about this, and I think that from there a movement started very rapidly.

Marju Lauristin
We have in Estonia very old traditions, since the middle of the nineteenth century, of the national song festival. That means that those that can sing are participating in choirs, local choirs, school choirs, in the municipalities, and the choirs gather every five years in Tallinn in a very big arena, which is called the Song Festival Arena, Song Fest Field. That means that about 30,000 will be there sing-ing, and about 300,000 will be there listening and singing along. And that is a ritual.

Andrus Öövel
Estonians are a singing nation. We are extraordinarily proud about the history of our singing festivals. It's more

than 120 years of them, and most probably without the singing festivals we could have lost our identity and not been able to re-establish independence so easily. Singing festivals started in 1869, and even in the hardest Soviet period the singing festival took place. Of course, political power could dictate repertoire, meaning that in many singing festivals choirs sang so-called Soviet songs, but what is really interesting is that not one singing festival in Estonia ended before people and choirs sang together 'My Fatherland Is My Love'. There were many attempts to avoid it. Soviet propaganda and Soviet organisational power did everything to avoid this moment, but they didn't manage because when the festival was over the crowd stayed in the stadium or the singing square. Choirs stayed on stage – they didn't move. Doesn't matter what kind of measures had been taken, they didn't move until we could sing this song. And after it was done everybody quietly went away. It kept alive our identity, it kept alive an idea about the future where we by ourselves can decide what is right and what is wrong and make arrangements according to our own wish and will.

Marju Lauristin
These big first political rallies at the end of the eighties, they were going on in the same song-fest arena – and there are smaller song-fest arenas that we have around Estonia … [These] formative song fests and the formative political rallies, they were put together in a very peculiar way, and at the same time this meant that this political revolution was *cultured*. It was going on in this kind of cultural form. And one part of that was that there was no idea of violence. There was this idea of spiritual strength, keeping us together and fighting together against Moscow, against the Soviet system, having a strong spirit. But

having a strong spirit wasn't just about songs and slogans. It was real work.

There were other movements across Estonia also. There was another movement dealing with Estonian national heritage protection; then there was the network which was dealing with creating grounds for Estonian economic independence. There were a lot of different networks, and the Popular Front was the network of networks. It wasn't an organisation like a party, so it didn't have any kind of list of members. It had the list of groups who really wanted to join this network, and it had the organising centre, the elected board. At the Congress in October 1988, a programme was passed and this programme was really a programme of restoration of Estonian independence. The most important goal for all movements in Estonia was the same: to get freedom back. In the end, the restoration of independence went through this scenario of ending occupation, restoring independence, without achieving the dissolution of the Soviet Union. The dissolution of the Soviet Union came afterwards following the logic created by Yeltsin, because Yeltsin wanted to have a free and independent Russia and that was really the engine which really brought the dissolution of the Soviet Union.

Andrus Öövel was asked to manage the security at live events organised by the newly formed Popular Front.
Our task was to guarantee that everybody who came to the meetings could go back home similarly well like he came. The first event, on 17 June 1988, was a meeting where we hoped that around 50–60,000 people would gather. In the very beginning, I didn't want to take this responsibility, but [I agreed after] having spoken in this time with the Minister of the Interior of Soviet Estonia who invited me

and said, 'Andrus, you should understand that the police force in Tallinn consists mostly of Russian-speaking officers and if we will task them with security for the upcoming meeting we will get conflict. Doesn't matter how it will happen but conflict will happen and it is exactly this that we don't need. If you will take responsibility and organise by yourself the security, it can be that this meeting will end successfully.' And we organised the security service of the Popular Front. It was 400 men strong, based on [the] wish and will of each individual member. We announced in the Popular Front that every member who feels he would like to be part of the security service should announce about it and can join and we really managed to put together [a] 400-men-strong unit. I think that in everybody's family [there] has been someone who has had the opportunity to spend 20, 25 years in excursion to Siberia, meaning that these men who came and announced that they will take care of security of this first meeting have been sons and grandsons or fathers or grandfathers who have suffered from the Soviet order and who knew very well what can happen next. But it was their opportunity and they demonstrated iron inside of themselves. [...] We took care about the security of this meeting. And we succeeded. The meeting succeeded and we succeeded. From this moment until the re-establishment of our independence, this security service took care of our organisational side of all big events that happened during our singing revolution.

Artur Talvik

We had a big concert in the middle of town and suddenly this concert moved to the song festival place, which is a bit out of the centre, and there I saw our blue, black and white flag for the first time. A motorcycle guy had this flag and was driving around and around. It was a good feeling. It's hard to describe, it's very powerful emotionally. Although I'm not a fan of these signs, but in those days our flag was really, really emotional to see. I have to say that during the Soviet years all kinds of combinations of blue, black and white were forbidden, even stupid combinations. If you had a white shirt, black tie and blue jacket or something like that, everyone immediately recognised it that you have this bad combination of colours. So, this flag was extremely important and [it was] extremely emotional to see it.

Marju Lauristin
We were expecting a couple of thousand, maybe 10,000. And then we saw how people started to come and come and come and come, and in the end there was 150,000 people. It was unbelievable. This feeling, the first time in my life, to be in this kind of arena, 150,000 people there, with slogans, with national flags, chanting 'Estonia! Estonia!' And then to tell them something about what we want and where we're going and so on, that was really this kind of feeling. It was once in a life.

Andrus Öövel
People who brought the flags were the brave ones, and I think that it is always brave to do something for the first time. We didn't know what the next step will be. We still didn't dream that Estonian independence would be established in the next three years only. But I think that it was our possibility to proclaim who we are, what we would like to do and how we will achieve it.

And when these first flags had been brought out and waved over the crowd, I think everybody felt proud. It was our manifestation to say that we are Estonians, we don't think that it is possible and it is necessary to try to create a new Soviet nation. We like our identity and we could show and declare through the flags our identity. But even at this moment I don't believe there were many people who could believe that this gesture would lead to anything else than simply to emotional highlight.

When the idea arose for the Baltic Chain in August 1989, **Marju Lauristin** *was in the leadership of the Popular Front.*
The chain started in Estonia at a big tower where now is our Parliament building and there is an ancient medieval tower. I was with the Chairman of the Estonian Supreme Soviet, Arnold Rüütel, who later was elected as the real President of the Estonian republic, and some other people. We were there at this tower and we had microphones and through these microphones we really started the whole manifestation. All the people who were on the roads from Tallinn to Vilnius, they had with them small portable radios because all this event was really managed through radio broadcasting. We started there from the tower, with speeches, and I had a text telling lots of people in the three languages, we say, 'Freedom, Freedom, Freedom'.

It was an unbelievable feeling, an unbelievable day. First when this idea came, I wasn't sure it was possible to organise, but then it became practical and people started to organise it in the different places: the transportation, the roads were divided so that everyone knew which was his or her place, where to go. Sometimes there were tens of kilometres through the forest for example. And everybody came, everybody knew what to do. Everybody knew the reason, the cause, why we are coming, and it was a day of great unity. It was very, very special, the feeling to be in this huge chain and to be visible to the world, because we were visible because CNN sent its operator to film it.

Andrus Öövel

It was our peaceful way to demonstrate to the whole world what we are aiming for and how we would like to achieve it. The Baltic Chain was 660 kilometres long, from the main tower in Tallinn to the main tower in Vilnius. And one element in this chain was to pass a password. We played the children's game of telephone, meaning that Marju Lauristin in Tallinn said one word to the person who stood next to her and this person said it to the next one and next one and next one and next one. And in this way one word went through all participants of the chain from Tallinn to Vilnius. This word was, 'Freedom'. Today it can be very difficult to understand that it is necessary to be brave to pronounce this word, but in this time it was necessary to be brave, to tell the person next to you that you are for independence, that the greatest value of mankind is their freedom.

I still believe that it has been the greatest achievement of my life, and I think that it is a highlight for the whole nation, and maybe even for the world, because it was a peaceful demonstration of the wish and will of three nations. We didn't threaten anybody, but we declared that we would like to be free.

Marju Lauristin

By then there was already a strong feeling, there was no doubt that independence is inevitable. We made a survey approximately at the same time, at the end of 1989, and there was a majority of people who answered the survey [and] said what they want is full independence for Estonia. And the same feeling was in Latvia and Lithuania. What we were fighting for was the denouncement of the Molotov–Ribbentrop Pact, namely because the announcement was the recognition from [the] Soviet Union that the Baltic countries were illegally occupied and this illegal occupation would have to be ended.

Artur Talvik

The local Russians, they had another movement called Interfront. They wanted to keep the Soviet Union. This was a pretty aggressive movement and then one day they wanted to take over the parliament house and the government house, and the head of government called Estonians to come to protect the government. And Estonians really came there and the Russians went away, but no violence happened. That was strange. Everyone was scared that now the big riot starts, with violence, but it didn't start and again it was a clever political move. It's a miracle, it's really a miracle, because they killed people in Latvia and Lithuania, but no one was killed in Estonia. No one was even hurt. Estonians are very calm. Today, I would also say that the leaders were behaving very wisely. They kept this violence away somehow.

*For **Marju Lauristin**, the attempted coup against Gorbachev in August 1991 brought a new opportunity to secure Estonia's freedom.*

In Estonia, Latvia and Lithuania, we had already made our decisions about independence and we were waiting for the moment when the external world would be ready to accept our independence. We saw that the people who were in power in the West were absolutely cautious to make any decisive steps which could in some way harm Gorbachev because they all adored Gorbachev, but we knew that Gorbachev was against our independence because, when I was in Moscow in the Supreme Soviet, I had with him a personal discussion about that. I knew – everyone knew – that he would not agree with independence for the Baltic countries. The same line was very much followed by many leaders in the West. But when this coup happened then we knew that it's the proper moment to say, 'See, the Baltic countries are occupied countries. It's time to recognise that we are free. We have to rejoin the Western community of free states.' And we made on 20 August an Estonian parliament, then already we had free elections in March 1990, so that we had a multiparty parliament – still called the Supreme Council by the way – and we made a resolution appealing to the international community, to the United Nations, to Western countries, to recognise restoration of Estonian independence and reaccept us as a full member of the United Nations and the community of free nations. That was done in the evening of 20 August. I was the person who presented this resolution to parliament, because I was vice speaker of parliament and I was the head of the drafting committee. I was reading this resolution about Estonian independence and it was put to a vote, after 11 o'clock, almost midnight of 20 August 1991, and it was voted with a big majority. When the tanks were at the TV tower it was already the next day.

Artur Talvik
One morning I woke up and turned on my radio and suddenly the news came that a coup happened in Moscow. I was like 'What? What? Oh, hell. Now it's over.' And then things started to happen. We followed all kinds of TVs and radios and everyone was a bit scared. Then next day the news came that Soviet tanks are moving and troops are moving. We had Soviet troops in Estonia, of course, but a special troop from the territory of the Russian Federation moved into Estonia, with tanks. And that was scary news. We really thought that now it's over, and suddenly people started to think how can we act. No one had any guns

because guns were totally forbidden in the Soviet Union for civilians. They brought concrete blocks to block the roads. And then from radio and TV stations, the news anchors started to call people to come and protect radio and TV and the government house. I was alone at home with my two kids and I called to my mother to ask her to drive to my place to take care of my kids. I said to her that I have to go. She was like 'You stupid boy, you're going again where you shouldn't go!' There was a lady in my neighbourhood – she was a really powerful lady, maybe 20 years older than me. She wanted to come as well, so we went into the city and we stayed all night long protecting the radio house.

It was happy and joyful in the beginning. Farmers came and brought milk and other products for the people, to feed them, and some people were singing. It was [a] pretty cheerful situation. But then suddenly we got this information – about four o'clock in the morning or something like that – that tanks had started to move, and they moved towards the radio station. This moment was really scary. We were standing there with nothing, just a human shield in front of the radio station's main entrance, waiting for Soviet tanks. Pretty stupid. But then some hundred metres before the radio station these tanks turned away, towards the TV tower [in a suburban area]. It was a strange night and a strange feeling. So they went to take over the TV tower. They had a plan to stop the transmission of TV programmes, but there were four heroes hiding themselves in the top of the tower, and these four guys were really heroes. Me and people like me, we were just ordinary people, no heroes. We did what we were supposed to do, but those guys there in the TV tower they were really risking their lives. Finally, the Russian soldiers, they didn't occupy the TV tower. Next day, step by step, the coup ended, the tanks went away and finally in the evening independent Estonia was announced. And that was an extremely great feeling. How can I protect the radio house with nothing against trained soldiers with Kalashnikovs and tanks? Well, only with emotion and strong will.

Marju Lauristin
These tanks were there but they didn't have command. Our people were standing and protecting this TV tower and there were three very courageous guys who were policemen who locked themselves in the tower. The tower had this firefighting system, which really was a poisonous gas. They said that if the Soviet soldiers would enter the TV tower then they would activate that system and everybody will be dead in the tower. But that dramatic event was already after Estonia re-announced its independence; it was like the follow-up event. Now we celebrate 20 August as a day of restoration of Estonian independence.

Artur Talvik
I had a discussion with my friend and said that I really like the way things are going in Iceland; I like the Icelandic policy and the people there. And his answer was: 'Don't compare Iceland with Estonia, because Estonia has this Russia as its neighbour.' I said, 'Look, Icelandic people, they have these volcanoes there. The volcanoes can erupt nobody knows when and this is very similar to our life, because Russia is like a volcano that can erupt. Nobody knows when the next eruption comes.' So, this is our life.

'The last nail in the coffin'

The Collapse of the Soviet Union (1991)

On a sleepy, hot Monday morning on 19 August 1991, the people of Moscow woke up to the news that the Soviet President, Mikhail Gorbachev, had been taken ill at his holiday villa by the Black Sea. An emergency committee led by the Vice President was now in charge and had put the country on an emergency footing, suspending political activity and banning all but Communist newspapers. Within hours, columns of tanks rolled into the centre of Moscow and took up positions around key buildings, including the Kremlin. It had all the hallmarks of a classic *coup d'état*. The tensions that had been building up over the last couple of years had exploded into a full-blown crisis.

It had been clear for at least 12 months beforehand that Gorbachev's reforms were in trouble. His introduction of competitive elections and the abolition of the Communist Party's monopoly on power had begun to shift the country towards a democratic system. But he was also facing growing internal pressures. The changes needed to create a functioning market economy had not been brought in. Gorbachev had repeatedly shied away from the essential but risky step of lifting subsidies on prices. As a result, the country was hurtling towards economic catastrophe.

Economic turmoil was further exacerbated by the actions of Soviet republics who began a 'war of laws' with Moscow, rejecting Union-wide laws that conflicted with their local plans, and demanding the right to control their budgets and keep the revenue from taxes. Apart from the three Baltic states, these included the Russian Federation, Ukraine, Belorussia (later Belarus), Moldavia (later Moldova), the three Caucasian republics of Georgia, Armenia and Azerbaijan, plus Kazakhstan and the four Central Asian republics of Uzbekistan, Tadzhikistan (later Tajikistan), Turkmenistan and Kirghizia (later Kyrgyzstan). There was also a growing schism between Gorbachev and the newly elected Russian President, Boris Yeltsin, who used his position to set up a rival Russian power base to challenge Gorbachev's authority as Soviet leader. Unlike the increasingly unpopular Gorbachev, by 1991 Boris Yeltsin had established a massive popular following among many Russians. At the same time, Gorbachev was coming under increasing pressure from the Communist old guard who wanted to thwart his reform agenda and prevent any more power from slipping out of central control.

In an attempt to balance all these opposing forces and to shore up his own weakening grip on central power, Gorbachev brought more old-style hard-line Communists into his government in 1991. He also continued to negotiate with leaders of the republics, led by Boris Yeltsin, to seek a compromise to keep the Soviet Union intact. As he asked the US Ambassador to Moscow, Jack Matlock, to explain to President George H. Bush in early 1991, it was a 'zig and zag' tactic to stop the whole fragile structure from imploding into civil war.

In late July 1991 Gorbachev held final talks with Yeltsin and President Nursultan Nazarbayev of Kazakhstan on a plan for a new Union Treaty to turn the Soviet Union into a looser federation, with a reduced role for central government. Among other things, they discussed the removal of the most hard-line members of the Soviet cabinet: the KGB chief, Vladimir Kryuchkov, and the Interior Minister, Boris Pugo. Then Gorbachev went off to his villa on the Black Sea in Crimea for a few days' rest before the treaty signing, which was scheduled for Tuesday, 20 August.

But Kryuchkov, as KGB head, had got wind of what was being planned – the KGB had taped the conversation. With the backing of other hard-line members of government and the Soviet Vice President, Gennady Yanayev, Kryuchkov resolved that the treaty signing had to be stopped. On Sunday, 18 August, a delegation led by Yanayev was despatched to Crimea to warn Gorbachev that the new treaty would be disastrous. They demanded that he either declare a state of emergency or resign and let them restore order instead.

According to Gorbachev, he refused to cooperate, swore at them and sent them packing. They claimed that he effectively told them to do what they wanted, which they took as a green light. Either way, armed guards were set up around his compound and communications were disabled, essentially leaving him and his family cut off and under house arrest. His wife, Raisa, was so terrified that she had a stroke.

Meanwhile in Moscow on the following day, the coup attempt unfolded, but it did not go according to plan. In the first place, it turned out that not all military commanders were willing to take orders from a self-appointed emergency committee without authorisation from the

Soviet President. Some made clear they would not follow orders to storm buildings or impose control by force. Some tank commanders even demonstrated their defiance by joining the other side.

In the second place, the coup leaders made the fatal mistake of failing to arrest their nemesis, Boris Yeltsin. He slipped through their clutches and made his way to the Russian parliament, or 'White House' as it was known, the symbolic power base of Russian sovereignty at that time. There, Yeltsin's aides hastily drafted a decree in the name of the Russian President, declaring the coup attempt illegal and appealing to Russian citizens and members of armed forces to ignore it. Yeltsin clambered up on to a tank positioned outside the White House to read it out to the crowds of citizens and journalists who were beginning to cluster around what was fast becoming the centre of resistance to the attempted coup. The moment was captured in photographs and on film by the many foreign correspondents present. Soon, along with flyers distributed throughout the city, the word spread in Moscow and beyond that Yeltsin was leading the resistance against the coup.

Abroad, leaders in the West were aghast. They were dismayed at the thought that their ally Gorbachev, whom many of them by now knew personally and liked, was apparently under arrest. They were also worried about what this would mean for international relations. Suddenly, it looked as though all Gorbachev's reforms were about to unravel and the clock would be turned back. The Berlin Wall might have come down and reformist governments might have taken over in Eastern Europe after a spate of mostly peaceful revolutions, but now it looked as though the era of Cold War hostility could come back.

In the United States, President Bush was especially worried. On his visit to Moscow in July, he had signed the largest and most complex arms-control treaty in history, the START agreement to limit offensive nuclear weapons. He now wondered whether the arms control agreements the United States had signed with Gorbachev would survive. And all Western leaders began to register that if there was one person in Moscow who could stop the tide of history reversing, it was probably the Russian President, Boris Yeltsin.

In the end, the coup leaders lacked the nerve and the popular support to see their plan through. More and more Muscovites flocked to the Russian parliament to man makeshift barricades and show their resistance. Within three days, the coup attempt crumbled, the coup plotters were arrested, and Gorbachev and his family were brought back to Moscow.

Gorbachev assumed he was returning to the capital to take up the reins of power again, but in those three days the country had changed. Now, Yeltsin was in charge. In a dramatic televised session of the Russian parliament over which he presided, he moved swiftly to ban the Communist Party and to make clear to a humiliated Gorbachev that he was yesterday's man.

Over the months that followed, Gorbachev struggled to keep the Soviet Union going, but day by day his power and authority dwindled as not only Russia but all the other Soviet republics scrambled to pull free of central control. On 1 December, Ukraine – the second most powerful Soviet republic after the Russian Federation – voted resoundingly in a nationwide referendum for independence. A few days later, on 8 December, Yeltsin secretly met the leaders of Ukraine and Belarus at a hunting lodge in Belarus. There they clinched a deal, known as the

'Belavezha Accords' after the Belavezha Forest, where the meeting took place, to bring the Soviet Union to an end and replace it with a new Commonwealth of Independent States. Then they phoned an astonished and outraged Gorbachev to tell him what they had done.

On 21 December, 11 of the 12 other Soviets (the exception was Georgia) signed up to the new arrangement. Gorbachev called it an unconstitutional coup, yet he had little choice but to accept what had been agreed. On the morning of 25 December he appeared on nationwide television to announce his resignation as Soviet President. He declared that an end had been put to the 'mad militarisation' of the Cold War and that he had no regrets for embarking on democratic reforms in 1985, however risky an undertaking it had turned out to be. He handed over the launching codes of the country's nuclear weapons and all other powers of the head of state to Boris Yeltsin, now President of the newly independent Russian Federation. For the last time, the red Soviet hammer and sickle flag was lowered and the red, blue and white Russian tricolour was raised over the Kremlin. The Soviet Union, once a global power and Communist monolith, had quietly dismantled itself and vanished with barely a murmur.

At midnight on 31 December 1991 the new Russian proprietors of the Kremlin celebrated the transfer of power at the end of a momentous year with a massive firework display on Red Square.

The next day Russians woke up in a new country.

The economist **Sergei Aleksashenko** *graduated from Moscow State University in 1986 and took up a post as a researcher at the Central Economic and Mathematical Institute.*

In the spring of 1986 Gorbachev was visiting one of the industrial enterprises in Leningrad, nowadays St Petersburg, and there was a live TV [broadcast] from there. Suddenly, he asked one of the workers, 'What would you think if a foreign owner would purchase your enterprise?' At that time, to imagine such a question from the General Secretary, it was unbelievable. I was even more surprised by the answer of that worker, who said, 'I don't care. What I care about is my wage. If I'm paid well I don't care who is the owner of this enterprise.' A person asking such a question has some other ideas in his mind and maybe he will be more decisive in the transformation of the country. But I did not believe until mid-1990, I would say, that the country would be transformed in such a radical manner.

For several reasons, the Soviet economy was in a desperate position in the last years. On one hand, oil prices were declining, the economic mechanism was broken, the Soviet Union spent [an] enormous amount of resources in the Cold War at the end of the seventies, beginning of the eighties. By that time, the shortage for ordinary people became evident. I remember by the mid-seventies, when you visited a shop it was possible to purchase, for example, a TV set or a radio. By the beginning of the eighties, it was not possible to find either a TV set or a radio in the shop. By the end of the eighties, shelves in the shops became empty and the government introduced a system of rationing. The whole period of the eighties, it was visible that the system was deteriorating. But despite all that, it was rather stable.

David Remnick *was a 29-year-old reporter when he was offered the post of Moscow correspondent for the* Washington Post *in 1988.*

I was pretty junior. Very few people wanted to go and live in Moscow at that time. I arrived in Moscow with my wife, who's the daughter of someone who had been imprisoned in Stalin's camps and whose grandfather had been lost in the purges, but neither one of us had spent much time in Russia. We lived in a foreigners' compound, which you had to do in those days. In the days of the Cold War, all foreigners either lived on the grounds of an embassy or [in] embassy housing or these housing complexes where they could keep a good watch on you. It was early 1988, Gorbachev had been in since mid-1985, but the economic picture was miserable. There were lines for nearly every consumer good. Grocery stores were empty or close to empty. There were no restaurants. It was not a lively cultural scene, but what was happening – what was most vivid – was politics. Politics was beginning. When I arrived, the first event I covered was the rehabilitation of Nikolai Bukharin, who was one of the old Bolsheviks who'd been arrested and killed by Stalin because he was one of Stalin's rivals. So that was a kind of politics: the opening up of the past. Gorbachev was allowing history to be discussed. He initiated glasnost, and suddenly you could open a literary journal and there were all kinds of things that had been banned for decades and decades. [Poets Anna] Akhmatova and [Osip] Mandelstam and [Aleksandr] Solzhenitsyn eventually, Joseph Brodsky's poems, all kinds of historical chronicles. And you would pick up a newspaper or a magazine which would have [an] article that was quite honest and open about the war in Afghanistan or the economic situation or, if you knew how to read it, conflict within the Communist Party. So that's what there was when I arrived: politics.

Sergei Aleksashenko
At the end of 1989 Gorbachev became more active in economic transformation and a special agency in

the government was established, the Commission for Economic Reform. My boss from the research institute was invited to become head of the department within the commission, and he invited four of his youngsters to join him. He said, 'Sergei, I cannot promise you anything, but if you want to understand how life is organised in this country you would not have any better chance to understand it.' At that time, we were not sure that the Soviet Union would collapse; we were not sure that the economic reform would be realised two years later or three years later. That was beyond our horizons. But he advertised the job as an opportunity to understand the life with a helicopter view. I accepted his invitation.

David Remnick

In a domestic sense, a really important moment that doesn't get as much attention as it should, is when – at a Central Committee plenum – Gorbachev gets up and gives a speech on history. This was on the anniversary of the revolution, a very traditional kind of speech that one gives as the Soviet leader. But instead of celebrating the revolution, Gorbachev got up and analysed it, and he went much further than Khrushchev did in the fifties, analysing the crimes of Stalin. It was the moment at which the past came into play, that it became the requirement of thinking people to study the past in ways that they were never allowed before and come to conclusions about themselves, about the system they lived under, about the politics they lived under and the politics they wanted. This had been, prior to Gorbachev giving that speech, an activity really only given to dissidents, which we must remember, for as much as we admire Andrei Sakharov, Aleksandr Solzhenitsyn, [Andrei] Sinyavsky and [Yuli] Daniel and all the rest, it was a tiny number of people. In the end, as much as there was influence exerted by the dissidents and half-dissidents, in the end an individual mattered in history. In this case, an individual made a decision and in some sense even fooled the people who propelled him to power and set the Soviet Union on a course that was deeply unpredictable. It was a process that went much faster and more out of control than Gorbachev could ever have predicted or wanted, but one man is owed an enormous debt.

Sergei Aleksashenko

There's a big difference between a planned economy and a market economy. The main difference is the equilibrium for the market-based economic system is based on the free movement of prices. So, if there are some imbalances, prices move, production changes and that allows the system to find equilibrium. In the Soviet system, the equilibrium was based on computational models, calculated by Gosplan [the State Planning Committee], Gossnab [the State Supplies Committee], the Committee on Prices, the Committee on Labour. They decided everything: what is going to be produced, who is going to produce it, the price, the wage, who is supplying to whom, where to build a new company. It was a huge computational model. And you cannot move from one system to another in two steps. Sooner or later, you should make a decision that from this particular date the prices should be free, that you're not in control of prices any more. Unfortunately, Mikhail Gorbachev did not make this decision. I don't know why. He never was able to explain it clearly. He talked about resistance in the Politburo and in the presidential administration and in the government.

Gorbachev was active in political transformation because he established the Congress of People's Deputies with electoral competition to a certain extent. It was unbelievable for the Soviet Union to have free elections in 1989 and the People's Congress that was assembled from people with different views that were not supporting official Communist ideology. He made a huge transformation in the organisation of the country, just removing power from the Communist Party and establishing the position of the President. He demolished censorship and allowed free media and freedom of speech. He allowed people of the country to go abroad and to come back. He made a lot of radical changes. But in economics he was constrained by something and to the very end he was never able to accept that he needed to free prices.

In the summer of 1990 there was the 500 Days Plan, which was a joint venture between Gorbachev and Yeltsin and a small group of people, about 15 of us. We drafted an economic plan, a transformation plan that started with the liberalisation of prices. On the other hand, the government, headed by Nikolai Ryzhkov, they drafted their own plan and we had three sessions of debates headed by Gorbachev in the Kremlin. As a result of these debates, Gorbachev said, 'Okay, I have decided to support [the] 500 Days Plan.' And the first step of this plan was to liberalise prices. We were so happy. We went to Washington for a meeting of the IMF to present our plan and, three or four days later, as we arrived in the States, we received information that Gorbachev stopped his decision and decided to establish another plan, decided to come back to controlled prices. That is the problem: in the summer of 1990 Gorbachev lost his chance to transform the economy. As he decided not to go for economic reform, I recognised at this point that this country has no future. The transformation will be much more radical and much more painful because we're losing time. It will be very hard.

By that time, Yeltsin was the head of the Supreme Soviet of the Russian Federation. Before the 500 Days Plan he was in some confrontations with Gorbachev, but they were able to find joint interests and joint efforts in this economic plan. But after that, as Gorbachev refused to support the economic transformation, Yeltsin started to distance himself from Gorbachev and it became evident that there was no political alliance possible between Yeltsin as leader of Russia and Gorbachev as the leader of the Soviet Union. After the events in the Baltic countries, when Gorbachev used the army against people protesting and the Baltic countries proclaimed their independence, it became evident that the breakdown of the Soviet Union as a country [was] inevitable.

David Remnick

In mid-August of 1991, I was preparing to go home. As a kind of farewell present, a leading member of the old Gorbachev team, Aleksandr Yakovlev, really his main liberal adviser for so many years, decided to give me an interview. It was an unusual thing at that time for him to give an interview. He said many things that were incredibly revealing. He said, 'I believe there's going to be a coup, led by the KGB and the military and all the rest.' Now, you have to understand that rumours of coups and apocalyptic talk [were] a staple of Soviet and Russian political conversation, so it wasn't that unusual. But this was Aleksandr Yakovlev saying this to me. So, I dutifully went back to the *Washington Post* bureau and I wrote a long story, and it ran on the front page of the newspaper, and it said, 'Aleksandr Yakovlev predicts a coup'. And then my wife and I got on an airplane on August 18th and, with our almost one-year-old child, we flew back to New York.

Sergei Yevdokimov was a tank commander with Tamanskaya Division, stationed 50 kilometres outside Moscow. He was woken in the early hours of 19 August 1991 and ordered to lead his unit into the city.

We had no idea what was going on. We were given orders without much explanation. When we entered the city, we saw some traffic police and continued to the centre. We saw people going to work. Some of them were waving at us, some had a negative reaction, showing us fists. They knew already what was happening.

The order was: enter Moscow, block the Kalininsky Bridge. We did not fully fulfil that task though. We deployed on the sides of the road which leads to the bridge but didn't block the bridge itself. [We thought] 'People are travelling to work – are we supposed to crash their cars?' While we were there, the barricades came up. There was one barricade constructed in front of our vehicles. They brought a trolley bus there as well. I found myself in the thick of it. We were talking, sharing opinions, discussing what is right or wrong. There were different opinions. Some people quietly supported us, saying it was good we had arrived. The others were asking why [we] were there. We were saying we had orders. We were not sure what orders would follow.

As soon as there was enough information, I made a decision that there should not be any actions performed by me which would result in the loss of life.

David Remnick

At about 11 o'clock at night [in New York], we turned on CNN and there were tanks going by our apartment building [in Moscow]. It was already morning [there], and there were tanks going right down Kutuzovsky Prospekt in the centre of Moscow, which was horrible for the Soviet Union and really horrible for me! It was also a hurricane in

New York and it seemed like it was going to be impossible to get back to Moscow, but somehow the next morning I flew back to Moscow. I fully expected to be met at the airport by guns and tanks and be put on a plane and sent out, but it was no problem. I hitched a ride into town and went on covering the second and third day of the coup and I stayed for weeks thereafter.

Sergei Aleksashenko

My first reaction was: in Russia, we have such a phrase as 'the last nail in the coffin'. It became evident that it is the collapse of the Soviet Union because all formal leaders of the Soviet Union, except the President and Vice President, were all members of this *coup d'état*. Of course, the system could not survive. The first question I asked myself was: 'Okay, these guys want a *coup d'état*, but they do not use force. They cannot win.' I would not say that I was very scared. I was concerned, but it was evident to me that this attempt was toothless.

Sergei Yevdokimov

We saw people gathering around the White House [with] leaflets and heard loudspeakers. I started to get some information, digest it, think what I should do if I get this order, that order. Then we started talking to people. People climbed on to the tanks; we were talking to them. Then we started getting the printouts of Yeltsin's decrees, so we started to realise what was going on.

Sergei Aleksashenko

By that time, Yeltsin was definitely a rising political leader. He was in attack mode, as [were] many other leaders of the Soviet republics, but I would say that Yeltsin was in front of them. He was fighting Gorbachev over power. Yeltsin was very decisive in establishing the authority of the Central Bank of Russia despite the existence of [Soviet central bank] Gosbank, and he dedicated monetary policy and monetary creation to his agency. He prohibited many, many enterprises located in the Russian Federation to pay taxes to the Soviet budget. He was fighting for power and for victory. And it seems to me that Yeltsin was much less concerned about the integrity of the Soviet Union than by his chances to be promoted to the number-one position. He tried to push Gorbachev to remove as much power as possible and this agreement to sign a new Union Treaty next day after the coup, it was the gift of Yeltsin to say let's keep the Soviet Union but with no economic power, no role in the economy. It will be a military union and maybe monetary policy as the central bank, very close to what we see in the European Union at the moment. So, Yeltsin in negotiations, in his policy, was looking for power, and he was looking for his personal political leadership over the Russian territory. For him, those days were the very crucial moment. He could be scared, he could hide, and that means his career's over. But he was a really brave man and he said, 'Okay, I'm ready to fight.'

Sergei Yevdokimov

This guy came. We started talking, discussing the current situation, and he said, 'What if the Commander-in-Chief says you need to *defend* the White House?' 'Well, if an order like that comes – we will think about it.' I was not going to bare my soul; you never know who you are talking to – maybe it is a KGB agent. I told him, 'If you bring some people of authority, we can talk about it. What's the point in talking about it to you?' And then he went to the White House, and then three or four MPs came to me, led by Sergei Yushenkov. And Yushenkov said, 'I am inviting you to talk to Yeltsin.'

We went to the White House. We didn't get to the President, though, just to [Russian Vice President] Aleksandr Rutskoy. So, they also told me what was happening, asked me questions: what my orders were, if we had any ammunition. And they asked: 'Will you help us?' I replied: 'Yes, I will.' I remember one of the last phrases: 'Do you understand that they are criminals?'

So, the decision was made. We figured out where to put the tanks around the White House and that was that. The tanks would now defend the White House. We moved the tanks to the other side of the road and when we moved, people rushed to hug us, flags came out. Coffee, cigarettes, sandwiches. We stayed there for three days.

David Remnick

It was a pathetic coup. It was a coup that was more out of the Marx Brothers than out of Dostoevsky. It was a last-ditch effort in which the old order did not have the gumption or the cruelty to open fire on the people who rose up against it, led by Boris Yeltsin.

All those people in the streets of Moscow, and in St Petersburg as well, who felt an attachment to the new liberties that had been afforded them, who felt that the future was in question and in real doubt, who were willing to stand up against the return of old-style tyranny, congregated around the White House in the most moving and astonishing way. They set up makeshift barricades. They went and climbed all over the tanks and gave these young kids, these young soldiers, some of them gave them a tongue-lashing, some of them gave them flowers. The popular uprising was there. The key is that the bad guys were not willing to fire on the people. Something had clicked, something had changed, so that absolute cruelty of the likes that we had seen so vividly under Soviet rule, they were unwilling to do that. There were leaders in the military that decided, 'I'm not going to follow that order.' At the same time, the leaders of the coup were a wreck: some of them were drunk, some of them could barely get through a press conference without their hands trembling in front of the reporters. They did not have the conviction and the cruelty and the power of their predecessors, and it all collapsed.

Sergei Yevdokimov

Some people say now, if I hadn't moved the tanks, the Union would have survived. I don't think there is any basis for this: it's quite far-fetched. Even though I voted not to keep the Soviet Union as it was, my actions were never against the Soviet Union; they were for the defence of Gorbachev and Yeltsin, because they represented truth. So, how they used the victory they got with my help or without my help, with the help of other military or KGB, with the help of civilians who gathered by the White House, it was up to them. I am not saying either of them is good or bad. They are what they are, they made certain mistakes.

Sergei Aleksashenko

There was no Soviet Union after the coup. The government of the USSR was removed and a special so-called temporary Committee for the Operational Management of the National Economy (COME) was established. There was no parliament of the USSR, because the Supreme Soviet resigned in full in the beginning of September 1991. So, the Soviet Union de facto had disappeared in August 1991. By that time, I was a member [of COME] and I was in the negotiation team who tried to reach some agreements between the Soviet republics on how to rule out economic divorce. So, I saw that from inside. For the bulk of Soviet people, at least for those in Russia, in Moscow, even in Ukraine, they still believed that the Soviet Union existed. The key point for ordinary life after the coup in the autumn and beginning of winter 1991 was an economic disaster and a shortage of everything. By that time, there was no food in the shops of Moscow, and in order to purchase some milk and some bread you needed to stay in line from six in the morning, when the shop opened at eight or nine. The bulk of people were concerned with these day-to-day problems. Inflation started to emerge because the government wasn't able to control prices. There was no government. The only choice to purchase something was on the black market. Economic cooperation between different enterprises was destroyed and the supply chains were not functioning. The country was in a downward spiral and the economy, the government, the nation was collapsing. Even in November of 1991, [when] Boris Yeltsin announced the new Russian government, still many people were not sure that the Soviet Union was going to disappear. It became evident only in December, when leaders of Russia, Ukraine and Belarus signed an agreement to dissolve the Soviet Union. After that it was December 25th when Gorbachev resigned. Life was hard. Life was unpredictable, and it was chaos, catastrophe. People were very depressed by what was going on.

David Remnick
The Cold War in the classic sense – meaning the confrontations between two systems, two superpowers – persists to this day. But the level of concentrated confrontation – of

proxy wars, of both sides being psychologically and politically obsessed with each other – that certainly began to thaw and end in the era of Gorbachev. And I would give Gorbachev more credit than any single person for the end of the Cold War.

Gorbachev's tragedy is that the processes that he unleashed finally overwhelmed him. He could easily have banished Boris Yeltsin to the provinces and never heard from him again. Instead, he kept Yeltsin in the political game, and Yeltsin came to be his opponent from the so-called radical or more progressive side. Those two, Yeltsin and Gorbachev, are often seen as oppositional figures. To me, they're also yin and yang figures; in a historical sense, they are cooperative as well as oppositional. So, he's tragic in the sense that between 1985 and 1991 things begin to spin out of control; he initiates processes that he certainly didn't want to see happen. The notion of a socialist economy, which he still had great store in, began to fade. But he was the great initiator of something important in the end of the Cold War, and humane in introducing far greater liberty than anybody had known in that place for a very, very long time.

Contributor biographies

Sergey Aleksashenko was Russia's Deputy Finance Minister between 1993 and 1995 and former deputy chairman of the Central Bank of Russia and former chairman of Merrill Lynch Russia. He is a Nonresident Senior Fellow at the Brookings Institution.

Vladimir Ashkenazy regularly makes guest appearances with major orchestras around the world. Conducting has formed the larger part of his activities for the past 30 years, but he maintains his devotion to the piano, these days mostly in the recording studio where he continues to build his comprehensive recording catalogue.

Andreas Austilat was 32 when the Berlin Wall fell in 1989 and was writing for the West Berlin daily newspaper *Der Tagesspiegel*. He married the girlfriend he had at the time and they have two children. He still writes for *Der Tagesspiegel* and has published travel guides about the area around Berlin.

Betty Barr went to Wellesley College in the USA after the tumultuous events of Shanghai in 1949, then did teacher training at Jordanhill College in Glasgow. She taught in Glasgow, Hong Kong and Shanghai, experiencing the end of the Cultural Revolution there in the 1970s. After teaching in Fife for nine years, she married George Wang in Shanghai, where she worked as a British council lecturer for ten years. She retired in 2002.

Ingrid Bartel was working as an accountant in West Berlin when the relaxation of travel restrictions allowed her to see her cousin Eva Eberbeck again after a long separation. Until her retirement in 2003, she was an adviser in employment and collective bargaining law. Throughout the years, her relationship with her cousin Eva Eberbeck has remained close and when the Berlin Wall fell, she instinctively knew that her cousin would come the following day with her family. Without hearing a word from her, she prepared everything for their visit, and indeed, that evening they all arrived.

Ciro Bianchi is a prominent Cuban intellectual. He is a journalist and interviewer, and for over 40 years has been one of the main architects of Cuban literary journalism. His work has been published in the magazine *Cuba Internacional*, and he is a regular columnist for the newspaper *Juventud Rebelde*.

Gisela Bilski worked for the East German railway, as a train driver for Berlin's overground trains, as a fire safety inspector, and eventually as deputy manager of building control of operations. She retired in 1989. She never joined the SED Party. Her brother and parents fled to the West, but she remained in East Berlin. Bilski married in 1955, got divorced in 1963 and has four children. Since the early 1990s she has volunteered for the Green Party as an adviser for transport policy and still works in an honorary capacity for the rail union.

Jürgen Blask completed an apprenticeship as an engine fitter and worked in the metal industry until 1963. He then applied to customs and held posts among others at Checkpoint Charlie and Tempelhof Airport. Since his youth he has had a keen interest in photography and he has now turned his hand to painting. He married in 1964 and his daughter was born in the same year. His wife died in 1988 and he remarried in 1995, becoming stepfather to another daughter. He retired in 2003.

Jerzy Borowczak is a politician and trade union activist. A close associate of Lech Wałęsa, he was dismissed from the Lenin Shipyard during the period of Martial Law. He was reinstated in 1989 and became chairman of Solidarity at the shipyard. He is director of the Solidarity Centre Foundation and, since 2010, has represented the Civic Platform party in the Polish parliament.

Bogdan Borusewicz continued his democratic activism after the 1980 strike in Gdansk. He went underground during the period of Martial Law in Poland and was imprisoned in 1986. He has been a long-term member of the Polish parliament and is currently Deputy Marshal of the Senate of the Republic of Poland. He was Acting President of Poland for one day in 2010.

Guy Bower worked as a FedEx Airbus A400 captain after his retirement from the US Air Force. A food and wine enthusiast, he is the host of The Good Life radio show and regularly attends major national wine events and judges at several national and international wine competitions. Bower teaches food and wine pairing classes at Wichita State University and has a

Level 1 Sommelier certificate with the Court of Master Sommeliers. In 1992, he founded the Wichita Chapter of the American Institute of Wine and Food.

Jacques Brassinne de la Buissière is a writer, historian and former diplomat.

Gerhard Bürger worked for the Americans at the Air Base Fire Department at Tempelhof Airport from 1945 to 1951, becoming manager of the German crew during the Airlift. In 1951, he became a customs officer at the border between East Germany and West Berlin, and he remained in the customs department until he retired in 1987. During the Airlift he met his future wife, a dancer, and they married in 1953. Since the 1960s Bürger has volunteered giving talks about the Berlin Airlift to school classes and groups at the Allied Museum.

Scott Camil and seven other members of the Vietnam Veterans Against the War (the 'Gainesville 8') were charged in 1972 with conspiracy to disrupt the Republican National Convention in Miami. They were acquitted on the grounds that they were trying to protect the rights of anti-war protestors. Camil is now president of Veterans For Peace in Gainesville, Florida, and is political chair of the environmental non-profit Suwannee St Johns Group Sierra Club and coordinator of the environmental organization Stand By Our Plan (SBOP). In 2017 he received an award from the League of Women Voters for Citizen Activist of the Year.

John Clarke was wounded in 1946 and returned home for rehabilitation after a military career that had taken him to North Africa, Italy, Greece and

Palestine. He was later awarded an MBE for services to veterans. He is currently campaigning for a Chelsea Hospital-style home for elderly soldiers to be built in Manchester.

Leslie R. Colitt went on to report for *The New York Times* in the mid-1960s, then for *The Observer* (London) and the *Financial Times* as their Berlin-based East Europe correspondent from 1968 until the fall of the Berlin Wall. He witnessed the Soviet-led invasion of Czechoslovakia in 1968, the Polish uprisings of 1970–71 and the 1980s, and wrote extensively on West Germany's Ostpolitik. He married Ingrid in 1962 and they have two children. Ingrid didn't see her parents again until they retired and were able to visit West Berlin. They moved to West Berlin in 1969.

Norman Deptula used the education benefits provided to Korean War veterans to attend Boston University, graduating in 1956 with a degree in liberal arts. He began a career in teaching, did graduate work at Worcester State University and retired in 1990 following a 34-year career. He is a life member of many veterans' organisations. With his wife of over 50 years, he has travelled extensively, including a trip to Korea in 1976, funded by the Revisit Korea programme.

Farhad Diba returned to England after the Iranian Coup. After studying at the Massachusetts Institute of Technology and the University of Oxford, he returned to Iran in 1961 to work for his father's company. He left Iran on a business trip in 1978 and temporarily became a stateless UN refugee due to the Islamic Revolution. He obtained UK citizenship and now spends his time researching the history of the Mosaddegh era.

Jack Devine was awarded the CIA's Meritorious Officer Award for his work as head of the Afghan Task Force. Between 1990 and 1992, he headed the CIA's Counternarcotics Center. He served as both Acting Director and Associate Director of the CIA's operations outside the United States from 1993–1995. He is the recipient of the Agency's Distinguished Intelligence Medal and several meritorious awards. He lives in New York City and is a member of the Council on Foreign Relations.

Eva Eberbeck was 23 in 1966 when she was able to see her cousin Ingrid again for the first time after the Berlin Wall was built. She had just married and given birth to a child. She worked as a stenotypist and secretary until she was made redundant in the mid-1990s. From then on she only worked intermittently, including a period in a care home for the elderly. In 2006 she took early retirement. She is the mother of two sons and still lives with her husband in Falkensee, northwest of Berlin.

Dmitri Fedorov returned to his hometown of Kolomna, near Moscow, after his service in Afghanistan. He spent time in Kosovo with the Special Forces of the Russian Federation and returned to Afghanistan in 2006. He is currently Chairman of the Kolomna section of the Russian veterans organisation, Boevoe Bratstvo.

Hardy Firl spent some time in West Germany after leaving prison, but decided to return to his friends and family in East Berlin. He worked as driver for the Kaufhaus

Zentrum, East Berlin's most prestigious department store, until he retired in 1990. He married in 1958 and has two children. Firl is a member of the Association 17 June 1953, which aims to keep alive the memory of the first people's uprising in Europe against the communist regime after the Second World War. The association awarded him a golden badge of honour for his work for Germany's freedom and unity.

George Flint left the British Army after his National Service and, after working on a pile driving rig, in 1958 he set up his own small tipper haulage business. He became a qualified scuba diving instructor in his spare time and, after the fall of the Berlin Wall, joined the official organization of ex-BRIXMIS members, which meets two or three times a year. He retired at 68, moved to the Isle of Sheppey and bought a motorhome, which he uses to travel the world.

Kenneth Ford finished work on the H-bomb in October 1952 and returned to Princeton to work on his PhD dissertation, which he completed in six months. Although he continued to consult on secret military projects for a few years, his main career was in academia and he held various faculty positions teaching and researching theoretical nuclear physics. In 1968, influenced by his opposition to the Vietnam War, he decided he would no longer work on weapons. He lives in Philadelphia with his wife Joanne. They have seven children and thirteen grandchildren.

René Gatorno stayed in the Special Forces after his return from Angola until 2014, when he retired from the army. Today, he contributes his expertise to those professionally interested in Angola's war.

Alexander Gergel did his best to forget his military experience after returning from Afghanistan. He worked at the State Construction Bureau and studied English at evening classes. After the collapse of the Soviet Union, he became an insurance company manager. He has two sons and is currently a freelancer in the insurance business. He writes novels with an Afghan theme.

Frances Glasspoole is a mother, a photographer and a theatrical costumer. Her professional career was as an orthopaedic nurse, but she has also worked in arts administration, on archaeology sites, with museum collections and even on a steam locomotive crew. Later in life she attended college, majoring in Anthropology and American Indian Studies. It was only then that she realised that her keen interest in other cultures had been shaped by her experiences as a teenager in Cuba.

John Guerrasio went to Catholic seminary and was almost expelled several times for his staunch anti-communist beliefs. He was the only seminarian who belonged to The John Birch Society and wore a Goldwater For President button in 1964. After deciding against the priesthood, he became a professional actor, director and television presenter.

Jacqueline Hayden lectures in politics at Trinity College, Dublin. In August 1980, she travelled all over Poland interviewing dissidents and was the first foreign journalist to interview future Solidarity leader Lech Wałęsa in Gdansk. She was awarded the Knight's Cross of the Order of Merit of the Republic of Poland 'for outstanding services rendered to the promotion of Poland's transition to democracy' in 2013.

Elisabeth Heller worked as a music radio producer at Radio DDR 1 in East Berlin until the GDR's entire broadcasting service was closed after German reunification. As a single parent at the age of 42, she found it difficult to find permanent employment again despite gaining numerous qualifications, and she became severely depressed. She has since recovered and through her interest in music and people, she continues to engage with life while working on a range of multimedia projects.

Katharina Herrmann was 23 and had just started her first job at a teaching hospital in East Berlin when the Wall fell. Two and half years later she was made redundant and, seeing no future for herself in a country where she felt like a second-class citizen, she moved to London in 1992 to complete a Masters in Politics of Human Rights. Having found employment in the city, she stayed and now uses her annual leave to travel the world.

Gisela Hoffmann taught English and Russian at a secondary school in Röbel, a small town in Mecklenburg-Hither Pomerania. After the Berlin Wall fell, she was involved in the transformation of her polytechnical school into a grammar school, which hadn't existed as such in the GDR. During that time, she was headmistress – a post she would not have been able to hold before as she had not joined the SED party. She continued teaching until her retirement in 2014.

Eddy Hsia served as a Commander in the navy before becoming a journalist. He lives in London.

Kathryn Jackson is now a licensed psychologist. Her research interests have centred on the resolution of political trauma. Her experiences as a clinician and supervisor have emphasized the significance of social and political events on individuals and families.

Karel Janovický left Czechoslovakia in 1949 and a year later came to England to study at the Royal College of Music. He joined the BBC in 1964, eventually directing the Czechoslovak Section of the World Service for ten years before retirement. Throughout his career he has continued to compose music and has also built up a reputation for coaching choirs, singers and opera in the Czech vocal repertoire.

John Ketwig went back to his career in the automotive servicing and parts industry after leaving the US Army, first at local stores and then moving up to factory level. He worked with Toyota, Rolls Royce Bentley, Ford Motor Company and Hyundai, in various technical, marketing and consulting roles. He eventually became General Manager of a large New Jersey factory service operation for Prevost high-line buses and motor homes as part of Volvo Bus and Truck.

Sergei Khrushchev is an author, educator and lecturer. Until 1968 he was an engineer for the Soviet missile and space programme. From then until 1991 he served at the Control Computer Institute in Moscow, rising from Section Head to First Deputy Director in charge of research. Beginning in 1967 he helped his father, Nikita Khrushchev, to work on his memoirs. He is the author of many books and articles on engineering, computer science, history, and economy. He lives in Rhode Island in the United States and teaches at Brown University.

Annemarie Knecht fled the GDR as a child in 1953. In 1971, when she was 28 years old, she and her husband moved to Steinstücken, an exclave of West Berlin, where she worked at the local supermarket until the end of 1983.

Lorenz Knecht was born in 1974, three years after his parents moved to Steinstücken in West Berlin. He works as a director of a bank and still lives in Steinstücken.

Hana Laing graduated from the philosophy faculty of Charles University in Prague in 1973. After working in psychiatric clinics and research institutes, troubled by the lack of freedom and resistant to joining the Communist Party, she emigrated to England in 1979. She further trained in neuropsychology at the National Hospital for Neurology and Neurosurgery and later also at the Institute of Psychiatry. She worked as a neuropsychologist until her retirement in 2016.

Otfried Laur grew up in West Berlin. He was 19 when he saw the Berlin Wall being built and 47 when it fell. As manager of a theatregoer club and concert organizer, he has put all his effort into reuniting the two halves of the city, putting on shows in Berlin and the surrounding area. In 2017, his club celebrated its 50th anniversary.

Marju Lauristin is a Member of the European Parliament in the Group of Socialists and Democrats. She has an academic career in social sciences and has been a Professor at Tartu University since 1995. In 1988 she was one of the establishing members of the first large-scale independent political movement in Estonia since the beginning of the Soviet occupation. She has since been Chairman of the Estonian Social Democratic Party, deputy speaker of the Estonian parliament, minister of Social Affairs of Estonia, and member of the Estonian Parliament.

Lee Hoo Ja attended South Korea's top nursing school and worked as a nurse before she starting a family and becoming a homemaker. Her brother stayed in North Korea and she never saw him again.

Osvaldo Leitão was the only survivor of his armoured unit. He continued to fight in the north of Angola until its liberation, and was an officer in the merchant navy of Angola for 12 years. After training in electrical engineering in Cuba and Italy, he worked for 22 years for the Portuguese bank Espirito Santo Group. He is currently administrator of the company Seguros Bonws in Angola.

Pavel Litvinov left the Soviet Union with his family in 1974. They went to Vienna by train and from there to Rome until they moved to United States. He has lived in New York ever since, where he taught physics and mathematics at Hackley School in Tarrytown until his retirement in 2006.

Giorgio Napolitano was born in Naples in 1925. From 1946 to 1948 he was a member of the Secretariat of the Italian Economic Centre for Southern Italy. He also took an active part for over 10 years in the Movement for the Rebirth of Southern Italy. He was elected to the Chamber of Deputies for the first time in 1953, and was a Member of Parliament in Italy until 1996. Giorgio Napolitano was President of Italy from 2006 to 2015.

Gisela Nicolaisen studied at Hamburg University and after graduating she taught natural sciences at a secondary school. After her escape to the West she didn't see her parents again for five years, until she and her husband, whom she'd married a few months before, were allowed to visit them for a few days in 1965. In the early 1980s, after a career break during which she raised three sons, Nicolaisen began teaching reading and writing to adults at a community college. She later led the department for adult literacy until her retirement in 2005.

Georges Nzongola-Ntalaja is a specialist in African politics, development policy and administration, and political theory. He is currently professor of African Studies at the University of North Carolina at Chapel Hill and professor emeritus of African studies at Howard University in Washington, DC. He is the author of several books and numerous articles on African politics, development, and conflict issues.

Matashichi Oishi was hospitalised with radiation sickness in 1954. Afterwards he moved to Tokyo and opened a dry cleaning shop. He didn't talk about his experience aboard the *Lucky Dragon* until 1983, but since then he has used those experiences to call on international societies to commit to a non-nuclear future.

Andrus Öövel has been Director General of the Estonian Border Guard, a member of the Estonian parliament and Estonia's Minister of Defence. Since 2000, he has served in the Geneva Center for the Security, Development and Rule of Law as a chairman of the International Advisory Board on Border Security.

Carla Ottman studied theatre in Leipzig and worked at the Komische Oper in East Berlin. Her father was in West Berlin when the Wall was built, and her mother moved to the West in 1969. In 1974 Ottman married. She was discovered helping her sister flee to the West in 1978 and both were imprisoned. In 1980 Ottman got divorced and a year later she was officially allowed to leave the GDR with her daughter. She was reunited with her parents in West Berlin. Ottman is now chairwoman of Lindenstrasse 54, a memorial to victims of political persecution.

Pavel Palazhchenko was the principal English interpreter for Mikhail Gorbachev and Soviet foreign minister Eduard Shevardnadze. He participated in all US–Soviet ministerial and summit meetings leading up to the end of the Cold War. Since 1992, he has served as head of international and media relations for The Gorbachev Foundation. He also serves as an analyst, spokesperson, interpreter and translator, as well as the president of the Russian Translation Company.

John Palka was born in France, already a refugee from Hitler. Later he was a refugee from Stalin. These early experiences had a profound impact on his life. He was fortunate to find shelter in the United States, a superlative education, and an academic career path filled with opportunities. He has been married for 56 years.

Péter Pallai escaped from Hungary in 1956, eventually making it to the UK. After working on a building site and learning English, he received a scholarship to study economics at LSE, followed by a postgraduate degree in education. He taught history and economics at a London grammar school, then worked for the BBC

Hungarian Service, finishing his career as Bureau Chief in Budapest. He now commutes between London and Budapest, organising jazz concerts.

Terry Pinner was chairman of The Stukeleys Parish Council from 1975 to 2013 and has recently taken up the post again. As well as a long career handling and breaking in horses, he has continued to farm next to RAF Alconbury, and still farms land that was once part of the airbase today.

Lev Ponomarev is a physicist and human rights activist. He was an elected member of the Congress of People's Deputies from 1990 to 1993. In 1997, he founded the Russian human rights organisation For Human Rights, later becoming its executive director.

Peter Pragal was 35 when he moved with his wife and two young children from Munich to East Berlin to take up the newly created post of the GDR correspondent for the newspaper *Süddeutsche Zeitung*. When his assignment ended there, he was able to take up this role again in 1984 while working for the magazine *Der Stern*. This time he divided his time between both parts of the city as his family settled in the West, while he lived in a flat in the East. In 1991 he started writing for the *Berliner Zeitung*, a daily newspaper that originated in East Berlin. He remained with the paper until his retirement in 2004.

Osvaldo Puccio was imprisoned and tortured by the Pinochet regime. He left Chile in 1974 and went into exile in Romania and Germany. He returned to Chile ten years later. He is the former Chilean Ambassador to Austria, Brazil and Spain.

David Remnick's experiences in Moscow formed the basis of his 1993 book *Lenin's Tomb*, which received both the Pulitzer Prize for nonfiction and a George Polk Award for excellence in journalism. He became editor of *The New Yorker* in 1998. He has been a Visiting Fellow at the Council on Foreign Relations and has taught at Princeton, where he received his B.A., in 1981, and at Columbia. He lives in New York City.

Nicholas X. Rizopoulos was born in Athens, Greece, in 1936 and lived there until the age of fourteen, when he moved to the United States. He received his doctorate in history from Yale, where he taught modern European and American history for ten years. He was one of the founders and, for fifteen years, the executive director of the Lehrman Institute, and served for five years as vice president and director of studies at the Council on Foreign Relations. Since 1995, he has served as academic director and lecturer in international politics and diplomacy in the Honors College at Adelphi University.

Sergio Romano is an Italian writer, journalist, historian and former diplomat.

Joachim Rudolph built a tunnel to help others escape the GDR, among them his future wife, whom he married in 1971. In West Berlin he worked as an engineer for several years, then trained as a grammar school teacher. From 1979 to 1987 was a deputy headmaster at a German school in Lagos, Nigeria. Afterwards, until he retired in 1993, he became a director of studies at a grammar school in Berlin. Since 1995 he has also been involved with different foundations and memorial places commemorating German 20th century history.

Mátyás Sárközi studied book illustration at Central St Martin's in London and after graduating he worked for the BBC Hungarian Service and Radio Free Europe. Following the collapse of the Soviet Union he made his first return to Budapest after an absence of 33 years. He is now an author and journalist, has won the Hungarian József Attila Prize and for a while was an elected member of the Executive Committee of the Hungarian Writers' Association. He makes a point of attending the 1956 commemorative celebrations, often in Budapest at the National Museum Gardens or Kossuth Square.

Homa Sarshar was raised in Tehran. Until 1978 she worked as a correspondent, reporter, and columnist for *Zan-e Ruz* weekly magazine and *Kayhan* daily newspaper in Iran. In 1978, Sarshar moved to Los Angeles where she resumed her career as a freelance journalist, radio and television producer, and on-air host. She has received numerous awards for her work.

Sylva Šimsová went into exile with her parents in 1949. In London she worked in public libraries and was Principal Lecturer of librarianship at the Polytechnic of North London. She became a Fellow of the Library Association and obtained an M.Phil degree from the University College London. In her retirement she writes about Czechoslovak exile.

Vladimir Snegirev returned to Moscow after a year in Afghanistan and studied at the Academy of Social Sciences. He continued working as a journalist and editor before and after the fall of communism. At the same time he regularly visited Afghanistan. In 1991 he began to be involved with the issue of the release of prisoners of war in Afghanistan, clarifying the fate of missing soldiers and officers. He has written several books about the Afghan war. He is currently a correspondent for the newspaper *Rossiyskaya Gazeta*.

Sian Snow's family moved from the USA to Switzerland in 1959. They planned to return after a year so her parents could rebuild their careers, but stayed in Europe as the McCarthy witchhunts continued. Sian became fluent in French and went on to work as a translator in Geneva, first for the UN and then for the International Red Cross. Her mother gave up her acting career and wrote several books, while her father continued to work as a journalist. In 1972, shortly before his death, he received a letter from Richard Nixon congratulating him on his 'long and distinguished career'. He ignored the letter.

Sohn Dong Hun arrived in South Korea with a thirst for education and went to university in Seoul. After receiving his doctoral degree in pharmacy, he served as a professor for 36 years.

Jeanne Steinhardt continued to look for ways to practise and to communicate the ideas of non-violence, in particular concentrating on the work of founding and developing a community of support and services for people with learning difficulties and mental health needs.

Paul Sutton worked in private industry for 16 years after leaving the US Marine Corps. He became active in veterans' advocacy in mid-1970 and continues to this day. In 1984, he joined the staff of the New Jersey

Agent Orange Commission. He moved to the New Jersey homeless veterans' programs in 1991, working there until he retired from state government in 2002. Afterwards Sutton worked for several not-for-profit organizations, focusing on homelessness generally and homeless veterans in particular. He finally retired from the working world in mid-2011 and since then has devoted his time to a number of specific veterans' causes.

Minh-Hoa Ta's family settled in Berkeley, California, in 1978. She is now vice president of student services at Ohlone College in Fremont, California.

Artur Talvik is a father of four children, a community activist and head of the voluntary Juminda Sea Rescue Society. He was previously co-owner of two successful production companies in Estonia and has produced and directed a number of documentaries, commercials and feature films. He is currently Chair of the Estonian Free Party and a member of the Estonian Parliament, the Riigikogu.

Julius Tomin was refused an academic position in Czechoslovakia in the 1970s and so worked as a turbine operator and a nightwatchman in a zoo. He was a signatory to Charter 77 and became involved with the Jan Hus Educational Foundation offering philosophy seminars in people's homes. After a period of intense official harassment, he travelled to the UK and his Czech passport was removed in 1981.

Zdena Tomin is a writer and journalist. In the late 1970s she was a spokesperson for Charter 77 and wrote for samizdat publications. She and her husband were declared enemies of the state by the Czech government and their citizenship was revoked in 1981.

Aldo Tortorella is a journalist and former politician. He was a member of the Italian parliament from 1972 to 1992.

Vitaly Tretyakov is a political scientist and journalist. He is Dean of the Television Department at Moscow State University and Editor-in-Chief of the journal Political Class.

Sándor Váci moved to London, where he studied architecture. He became a British subject and worked as an architect before beginning a masters degree at the University of Michigan. In 1967 he returned to London, starting his own architectural practice in 1973. He met his future wife on a visit to Budapest, and they now have two children. Váci has been involved in various projects to foster Anglo–Hungarian cultural connections.

Steven S. Volk is Professor of History Emeritus at Oberlin College in Ohio, where he continues to direct the Center for Teaching Innovation and Excellence. He has published widely on Chile, US–Latin American relations, Mexico, and various issues in pedagogy. In 2011 he was named US Professor of the Year by the Carnegie Foundation for the Advancement of Teaching. In 2001 he was recognised by the Chilean government for his work to help restore democracy in Chile.

Willem van der Waals stayed in the South African army after his participation in the Angolan Civil War and worked in various intelligence roles. From 1990 to

1991 he was the Director of Operations of the South African Defence Force and also completed a doctorate in Political Science at the University of the Orange Free State with Portugal's War in Angola (1961–74) as the subject of his dissertation. After serving as the Director of Foreign Relations of the SADF until 1993 he became the first Executive Director of Community Safety of the capital city of Pretoria, finally retiring in 2006.

George Wang started out working as a messenger boy at the age of 14 and retired as an Associate Professor of English at a Community College in Xuhui District.

Alfred Wegewitz completed his law studies in East Berlin in 1954. At first it was difficult to find work because he had been a prisoner of war in Great Britain and was regarded with suspicion by the communist party, but he worked as a lawyer from 1956 until his retirement in 2002. He married in 1960. His younger brother had been interned by the British after the war and later moved to his mother's family in West Germany where he stayed and supported his relatives in East Germany by sending packages. They were able to visit each other over the years.

Sir John Weston continued in the diplomatic service, in various roles both abroad and in the UK. As Political Director in the Foreign Office (1990–1), he was the UK negotiator for talks on German reunification. He served as the UK's Permanent Representative to NATO (1992–95) and finally as UK Ambassador to the UN and Permanent Representative to the UN Security Council (1995–8). Since his retirement, Weston has been a non-executive director with two FTSE 100 companies and worked in the arts and voluntary sectors.

He has had two collections of his poems published. He keeps bees and has six grandchildren.

Liliane Willens was born of Russian–Jewish parentage in the former French Concession of Shanghai, China. She studied as an undergraduate at Boston University where she also received a PhD in French Language and Literature. She taught these subjects at Boston College and at MIT. Later moving to Washington, DC, she worked for the US Agency for International Development and the Peace Corps. Since retirement Willens has given lectures on history and culture on cruise ships sailing around the world. Presently she speaks at various organisations and book clubs on old and new Shanghai.

Sergey Yevdokimov lives in Moscow. He served in the military office of the Northern District of Moscow until 2000 when he retired from the armed forces.

Zinovy Zinik lost his Soviet citizenship when he emigrated in 1975 to Israel, where he worked as a theatre director for a student theatre group at the Hebrew University of Jerusalem. Since 1976, he has been living and working in Britain, writing in English as well as in his native Russian. He became a British citizen in 1988. The duality of émigré existence, cultural dislocation, estrangement and the evasive nature of memory have become the main topic of Zinik's novels, short stories, essays, lectures and radio broadcasts.

Further Reading: Contributors' Publications

Ciro Bianchi. *Cuba: A Different Story*. Ruth Casa, 2016

Jacques Brassinne de la Buissière *La Sécession du Katanga: Témoignage*. Éditions Scientifiques Internationales, 2016

Jacques Brassinne and Jean Kestergat. *Qui a tué Patrice Lumumba?* Éditions Duculot, 1991

Leslie Colitt *Before the Berlin Wall Came Down: A Foreign Correspondent's Search For Truth Behind the Iron Curtain*. Leslie R. Colitt, 2015

Leslie Colitt. *Spymaster: The Real-life Karla, His Moles, And The East German Secret Police*. Da Capo Press, 1995

Farhad Diba. *Mohammed Mossadegh: A Political Biography*. Routledge, 1986

Jack Devine. *Good Hunting: An American Spymaster's Story*. Picador, 2015

Kenneth W. Ford. *Building the H Bomb: A Personal History*. World Scientific Publishing Company, 2015

Jacqueline Hayden. *The Collapse of Communist Power in Poland*. Routledge, 2011

Jacqueline Hayden. *Poles Apart: Solidarity and the New Poland*. Routledge, 1994

Kathryn Jackson. 'Psychotherapy with College Student Survivors of War and Political Trauma'. The Journal of College Student Psychotherapy, Vol. 23, Issue 1, 2009

Kathryn Jackson. 'Trauma Survivors: Adult Children of McCarthyism and the Smith Act'. Temple University, 1991

Sergei Khrushchev. *Khrushchev on Khrushchev: An Inside Account of the Man and His Era, by His Son*. Edited and translated by William Taubman. Little, Brown, 1990

Sergei Khrushchev. *Nikita Khrushchev and the Creation of a Superpower*. Penn State University Press, 2001

John Ketwig. *… and a hard rain fell: A GI's True Story of the War in Vietnam*. Macmillan, 1985

Marju Lauristin and Peeter Vihalemm. *Return to the Western World*. Tartu University Press, 1997

Pavel Litvinov. *Demonstration in Pushkin Square*. HarperCollins, 1969

Pavel Litvinov. *Trial of the Four*. Viking, 1972

Janet Miller. *Memories of Guantanamo Bay 1960–1962*. Frances Matlock, 2010

Gisela Nicolaisen. *Dann geh jetzt!: Chronik einer Flucht von Deutschland Ost nach Deutschland West 1960*. Pro Business, 2012

Georges Nzongola-Ntalaja. *The Congo from Leopold to Kabila: A People's History*. Zed Books, 2002

Georges Nzongola-Ntalaja. *Patrice Lumumba*. Ohio University Press, 2014

Matashichi Oishi. *The Day the Sun Rose in the West: Bikini, the Lucky Dragon, and I*. University of Hawaii Press, 2011

Pavel Palazhchenko. *My Years with Gorbachev and Shevardnadze: The Memoir of a Soviet Interpreter*. Penn State University Press, 1997

John Palka. *My Slovakia, My Family*. Kirk House, 2012

Peter Pragal. *Der geduldete Klassenfeind: Als West-Korrespondent in der DDR*. Saga Egmont, 2016

David Remnick. *Lenin's Tomb: The Last Days of the Soviet Empire*. Vintage, 2001

Nicholas X. Rizopoulos. *Civil and Uncivil Wars: Memories of a Greek Childhood, 1936–1950*. Tidepool Press, 2014

Homa Sarshar. *Shaban Jafari*. Naab, 2002

Zdena Tomin. *The Coast of Bohemia*. Hutchinson, 1987

Zdena Tomin. *Stalin's Shoe*. Hutchinson, 1986

Willem van der Waals. *Portugal's War in Angola, 1961–1974*. Protea Boekhuis, 2012

George Wang & Betty Barr. *Between Two Worlds: Lessons in Shanghai*. Old China Hand Press, 2004

George Wang & Betty Barr. *Shanghai Boy, Shanghai Girl: Lives in Parallel*. Old China Hand Press, 2002

John Archibald Wheeler, with Kenneth Ford. *Geons, Black Holes, and Quantum Foam: A Life in Physics*. W. W. Norton & Company, 2000

Liliane Willens. *Stateless in Shanghai*. China Economic Review Publishing, 2010

Zinovy Zinik. *History Thieves*. University of Chicago Press, 2011

Further Reading

Mark Philip Bradley. *Vietnam at War*. Oxford University
Press, 2009

Rodric Braithwaite. *Afgantsy: The Russians in Afghanistan,
1979 – 1980*. Profile Books Ltd, 2011

Archie Brown. *The Rise and Fall of Communism*. The
Bodley Head, 2009

Larry Ceplair and Robert Englund. *The Inquisition in
Hollywood: Politics in the Film Community, 1930–1960*.
University of Illinois Press, 2003

John Lewis Gaddis. *The Cold War*. Penguin, 2005

Jeremy Isaacs and Taylor Downing. *Cold War: For Forty-
five Years the World Held its Breath*. Abacus, 2008.

Sheila Miyoshi Jager. *Brothers at War: The Unending
Conflict in Korea*. Profile, 2013

Tony Judt. *Postwar: A History of Europe Since 1945*.
William Heinemann, 2005

Richard Curt Kraus. *The Cultural Revolution: A Very Short
Introduction*. Oxford University Press, 2012

Serhii Plokhy. *The Last Empire: The Final Days of the
Soviet Union*. Oneworld, 2014

Mary Elise Sarotte. *The Struggle to create Post-Cold War
Europe*. Princeton University Press, 2009

Victor Sebestyen. *Twelve Days: Revolution 1956*.
Weidenfeld & Nicolson, 2007

Edgar Snow. *Red Star Over China: The Rise of the Red Army*. Hesperides Press, 2006

(ed.) Kristina Spohr and David Reynolds. *Transcending the Cod War: Summits, Statecraft and the Dissolution of Bipolarity in Europe 1970 – 1990*. Oxford Universtiy Press, 2016

Ann and John Tusa. *The Berlin Airlift*. Atheneum, 1988

Al J. Venter. *Battle for Angola: The End of the Cold War in Africa c. 1975 – 89*. Helion and Company, 2017

Index of Contributors

Index

Picture credits

t: top, b: bottom

All photographs provided by contributors except:

Plate Section 1
1, 2t: PA Images; 2b: Illustrated London News Ltd/Mary Evans; 3t, 3b and 4t: Mary Evans/picture-alliance/dpa; 4b, 5t: Mary Evans/Everett Collection; 5b: PA Images; 6t: Mary Evans/Everett Collection; 6b, 7t: PA Images; 7b: dpa/DPA/PA Images; 8: Mary Evans/Everett Collection

Plate Section 2
1t: Friedrich/Interfoto/Mary Evans; 1b: Mary Evans/Grenville Collins Postcard Collection; 2t: PA images; 2b, 3t, 3b: Mary Evans/Everett Collection; 4t: Personalities/Topham Picturepoint/Press Association Images; 4b: Africa Media Online/Mary Evans; 5t: Viktor Budan/Tass/PA Images; 5b: Keystone Press Agency/Zuma Press/PA Images; 6t: Mathias Brauner/DPA/PA Images; 6b: dpa/DPA/PA Images; 7t: Fotoreport/DPA/PA Images; 7b: ITAR-TASS/Tass/PA Images; 8t, 8b: Tass/PA Images

Maps by Martin Lubikowski, ML Design

Acknowledgements

This book began as two fifteen-episode series for BBC Radio 4, *Cold War: Stories from the Big Freeze*, the first of which was broadcast in July 2016, the second in July 2017. The overall project would have been nothing without the cooperation and kindness of all the contributors, who shared their memories, sometimes very painful ones, with great generosity and insight. It's been a privilege to be able to draw on this rich seam of recollections. Thank you to all of you.

The idea for the radio series came originally from Martin Smith. He and fellow BBC Editor John Goudie helped to shape the project in its early stages. It was commissioned for BBC Radio 4 by Mohit Bakaya, who encouraged us to tell these stories through first-hand testimony alone. Our thanks also to Radio 4 Controller Gwyneth Williams for her support. We hope our thirty stories work together to give some sense of the arc of this strange period, but individually do something to dispel generalised clichés of the Cold War in favour of the specifics as experienced on the ground. Cambridge historian David Reynolds played an invaluable role as Series Advisor in helping us to select them.

Holly Weldon's expert research work was central to casting what has become the first half of the book. The German chapters relied heavily on the specialist knowledge and tireless hard work of Sabine Schereck, who was instrumental in finding, interviewing, transcribing and translating those interviews, and to whom much thanks is due. Michael Rossi, along with Natacha De Bivar Palhares and Susana Rios Moore, played a similar role for the Angolan Civil War chapter. In Moscow, Alexander Ratnikov and Svetlana Ivanova were invaluable, as was Christiana Chiranagnostaki in Athens, Agata Jujeczka in Poland and Yoko Ishitani in Tokyo. And Debbie Waddell, Sian Grace, Eleri Selwood and Michelle Woodham helped make sure everything actually happened.

Many people helped us to find contributors – in particular Nanci Adler, Oliver Bast, Darioush Bayandor, Protea Boekhuis, Chris Bowlby, Rodric Braithwaite, Malcolm Byrne, Stephen Cohen, Hugo Rojas Corral, Stephanie Danyi, Frank Dikotter, Adam Easton, Steve Fullerton, Sally Garwood, Mark Gasiorowski, Luong Hoang Giap, Will Grant, Robin Milner-Gulland, Gaspard Ibumbu, General Miguel Júnior, Kevin Kim, David Kimbangi, Stephen Kinzer, Dmitry Kokorin, Sergey Kozlovsky, Dima Litvinov, historian Robert McNamara, Jamie Miller, Kaeten Mistry, Baqer Moin, Pavel Podvig, Silvio Pons, Mary Raine, Martin Sherwin, Ludmila Stane, Helena Svojsikova, William Taubman, Marek Tomin, Vietnam Veterans of America, Vietnam Veterans Against the War, Youqin Wang, Alex Wellerstein and Vladislav Zubok.

Additional thanks to Rob Cameron, Carlo Catalogna, Victor Chan, Ariel Dorfman, David Goren, Sara Halfpenny, Paulus Van Horne, Alexander Kan, Stephen Langlie, translator Cao Li, Vladlen Loginov, Gideon Long, Todd Melby, Charlène Pelé, William Rakip, Nadja Saborova, Renata Tairbekova, Anastasia Uspenskaya, Will Vernon and Danny Vincent.

In the radio series, Luigi Bonomi at LBA Books and Albert DePetrillo at Penguin Random House heard a BBC

ACKNOWLEDGEMENTS

Book in the making; editor Bethany Wright oversaw the project with grace under pressure; and Steve Tribe played a key role in helping us transform radio scripts and transcripts into book form.

For their expert reviews of particular chapters, thanks are due to Michael Axworthy, Rodric Braithwaite, Ken Ford, Robin Milner-Gulland, Rana Mitter, and Nick Witham. Any errors, needless to say, remain ours alone.

Finally thanks most of all to our families, for Bridget to Amanda, for Phil to Polly, Amy and Sam, and for Martin to Roscoe, Emmett and Catherine.

Author biographies

Bridget Kendall was the BBC's foreign correspondent in Moscow during the collapse of the Soviet Union, then Washington correspondent and diplomatic correspondent. She is now the first female master of Peterhouse, Cambridge University's oldest college.

Phil Tinline and **Martin Williams** are the producers of the landmark BBC Radio 4 series *Cold War: Stories from the Big Freeze*.